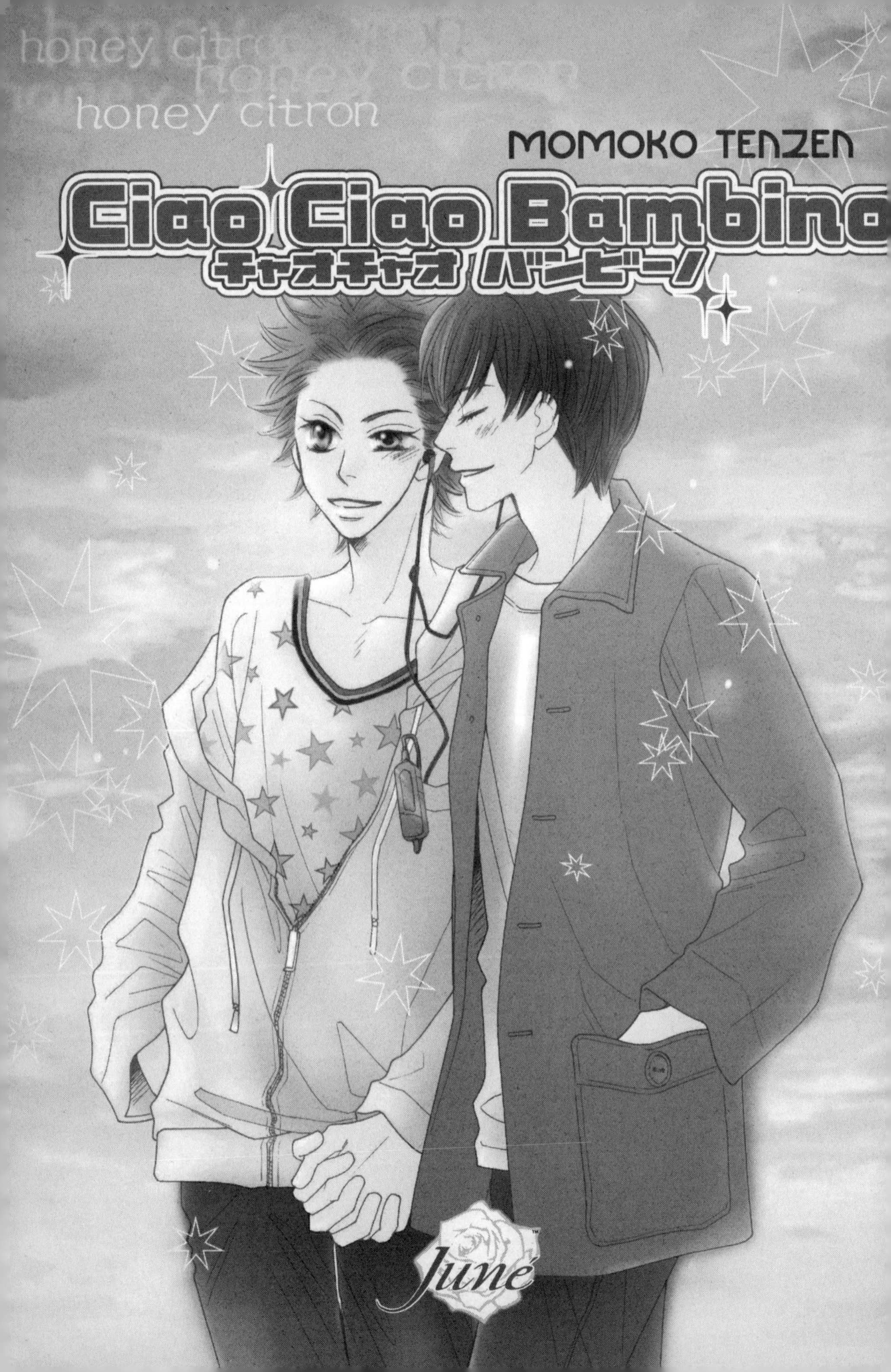
honey citron
MOMOKO TENZEN
Ciao Ciao Bambino
チャオチャオ バンビーノ
June

Ciao Ciao Bambino
チャオチャオ バンビーノ

CONTENTS

Translation — Melanie Schoen
Lettering — Replibooks
Graphic Design — Michelle Mauk
Editing — Stephanie Donnelly
Editor in Chief — Fred Lui
Publisher — Hikaru Sasahara

English Edition Published by
DIGITAL MANGA PUBLISHING
A division of DIGITAL MANGA, Inc.
1487 W 178th Street, Suite 300
Gardena, CA 90248

www.dmpbooks.com

First Edition: October 2009
ISBN-10: 1-56970-077-X
ISBN-13: 978-1-56970-077-8

1 3 5 7 9 10 8 6 4 2

Printed in Canada

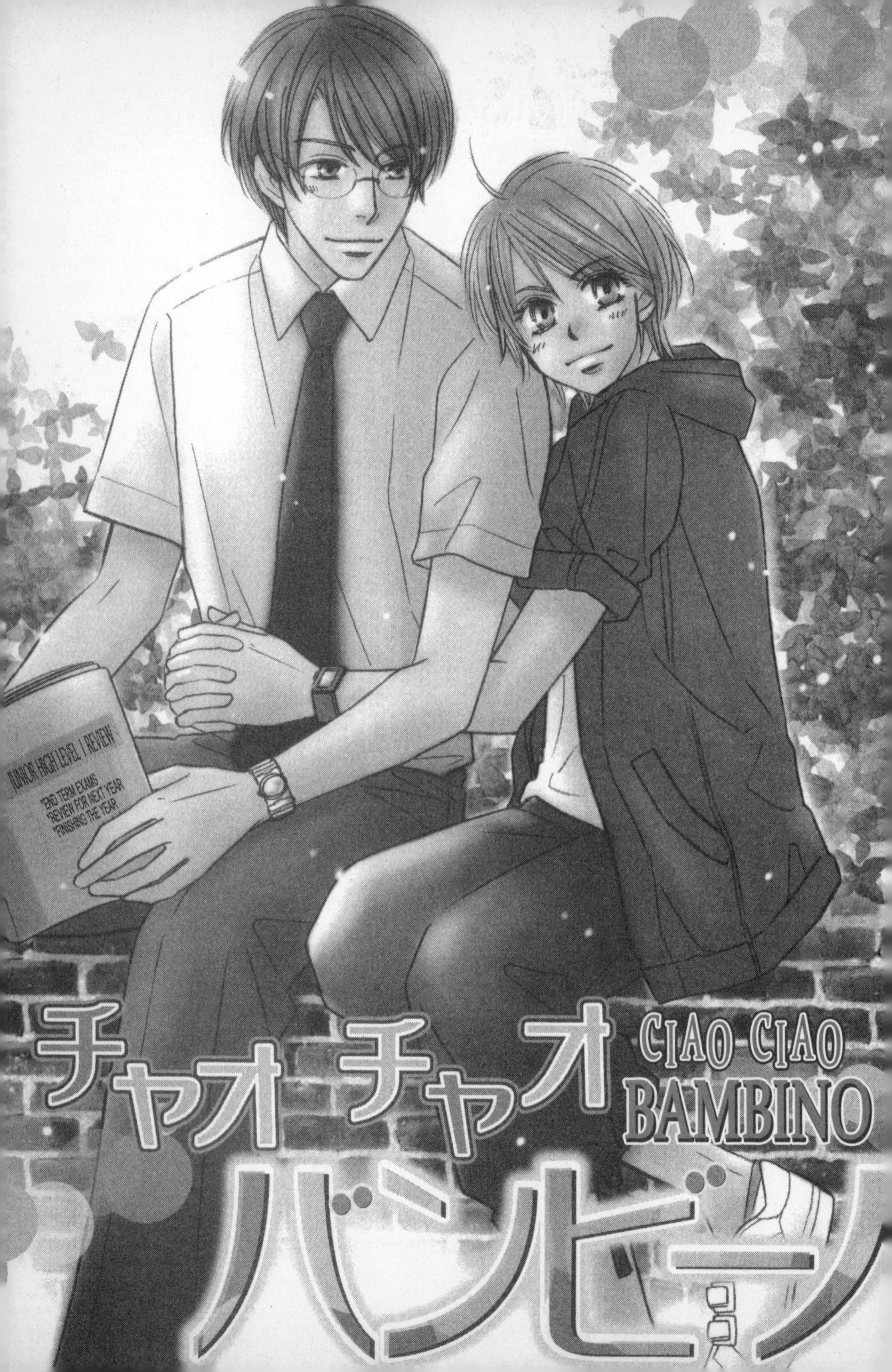
JUNIOR HIGH LEVEL 1 REVIEW
*END TERM EXAMS
*REVIEW FOR NEXT YEAR
*FINISHING THE YEAR
チャオ チャオ
CIAO CIAO
BAMBINO
バンビーノ

Ciao
Ciao
Bambino

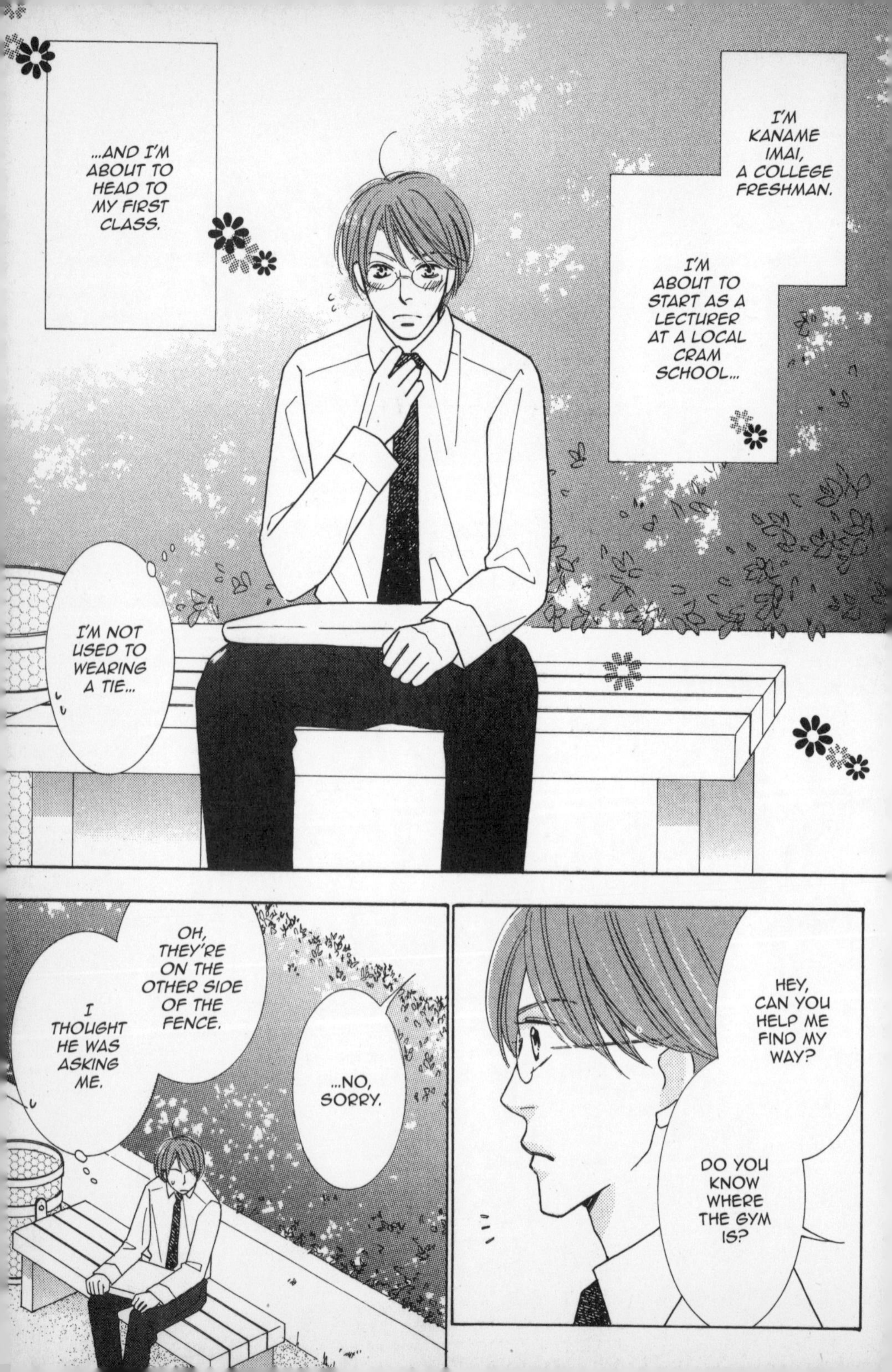
I'M KANAME IMAI, A COLLEGE FRESHMAN.
I'M ABOUT TO START AS A LECTURER AT A LOCAL CRAM SCHOOL...
...AND I'M ABOUT TO HEAD TO MY FIRST CLASS.
I'M NOT USED TO WEARING A TIE...
HEY, CAN YOU HELP ME FIND MY WAY?
DO YOU KNOW WHERE THE GYM IS?
...NO, SORRY.
OH, THEY'RE ON THE OTHER SIDE OF THE FENCE.
I THOUGHT HE WAS ASKING ME.

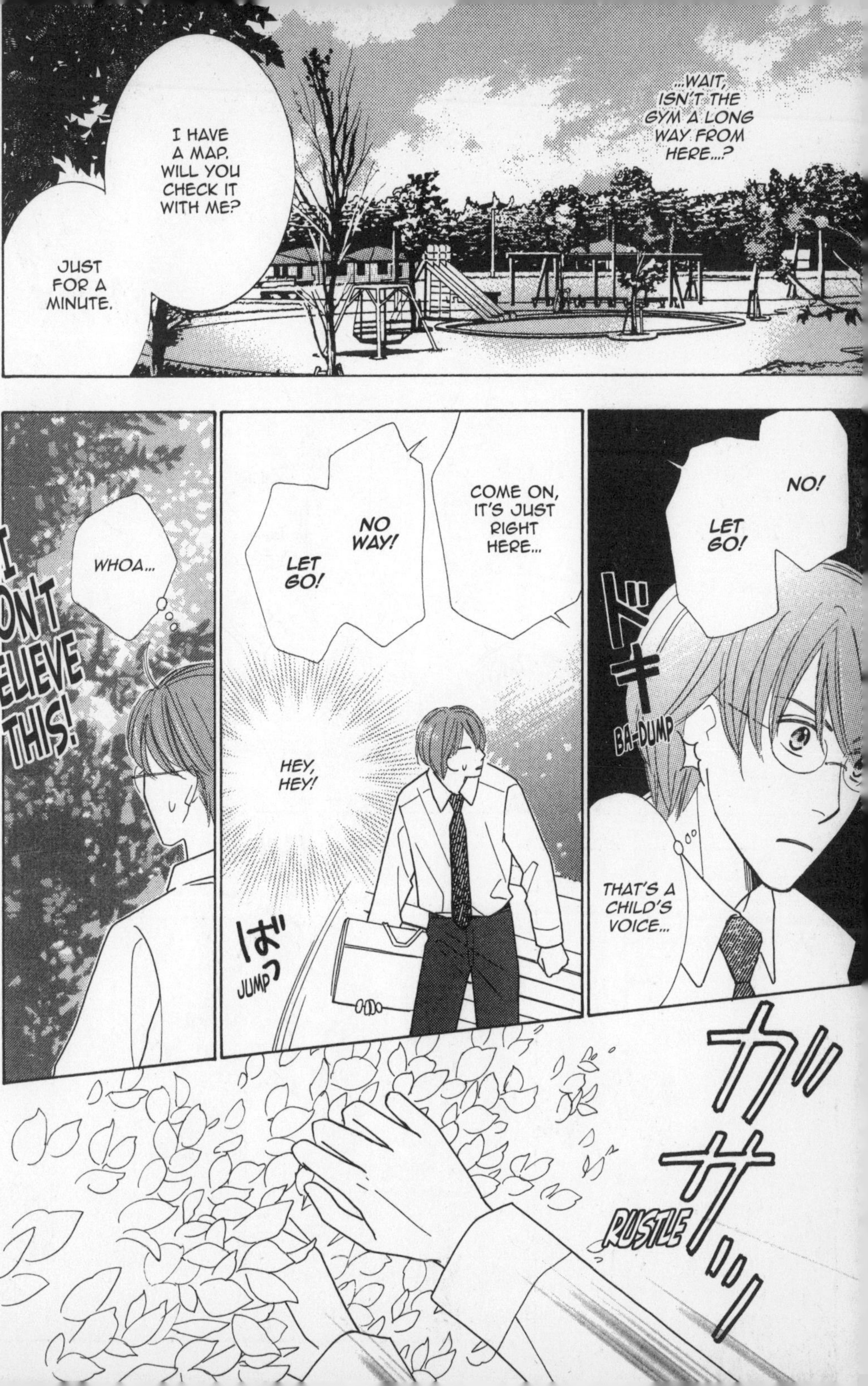
...WAIT, ISN'T THE GYM A LONG WAY FROM HERE...?
I HAVE A MAP. WILL YOU CHECK IT WITH ME?
JUST FOR A MINUTE.
NO!
LET GO!
ドキ
BA-DUMP
THAT'S A CHILD'S VOICE...
COME ON, IT'S JUST RIGHT HERE...
NO WAY!
LET GO!
HEY, HEY!
ばっ
JUMP
WHOA...
I DON'T BELIEVE THIS!
ガサッ
RUSTLE

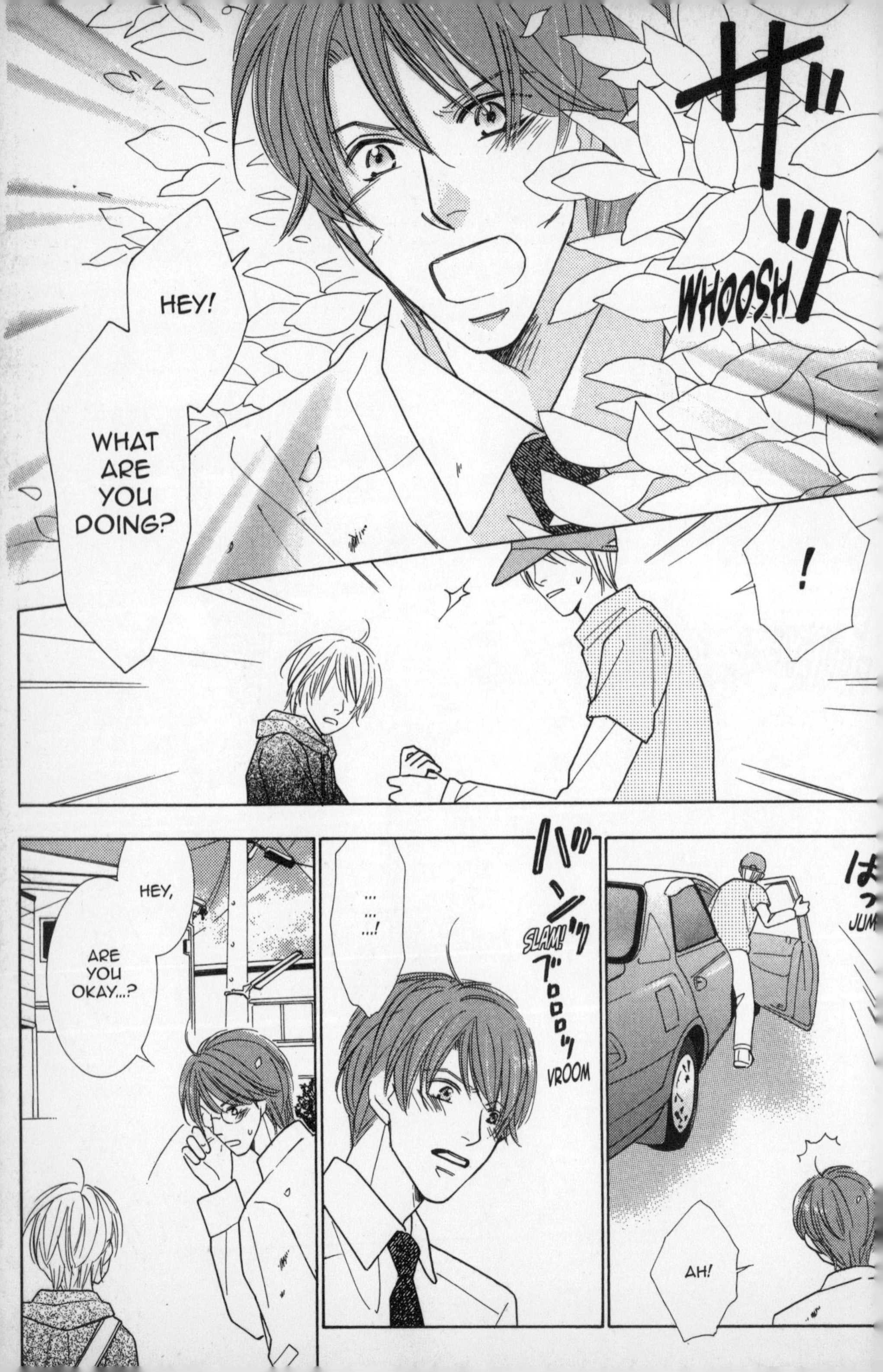

ザッ
WHOOSH
HEY!
WHAT ARE YOU DOING?
!
はっ
JUM
AH!
バンッ
SLAM!
ブロロロッ
VROOM
... ...!
HEY,
ARE YOU OKAY...?

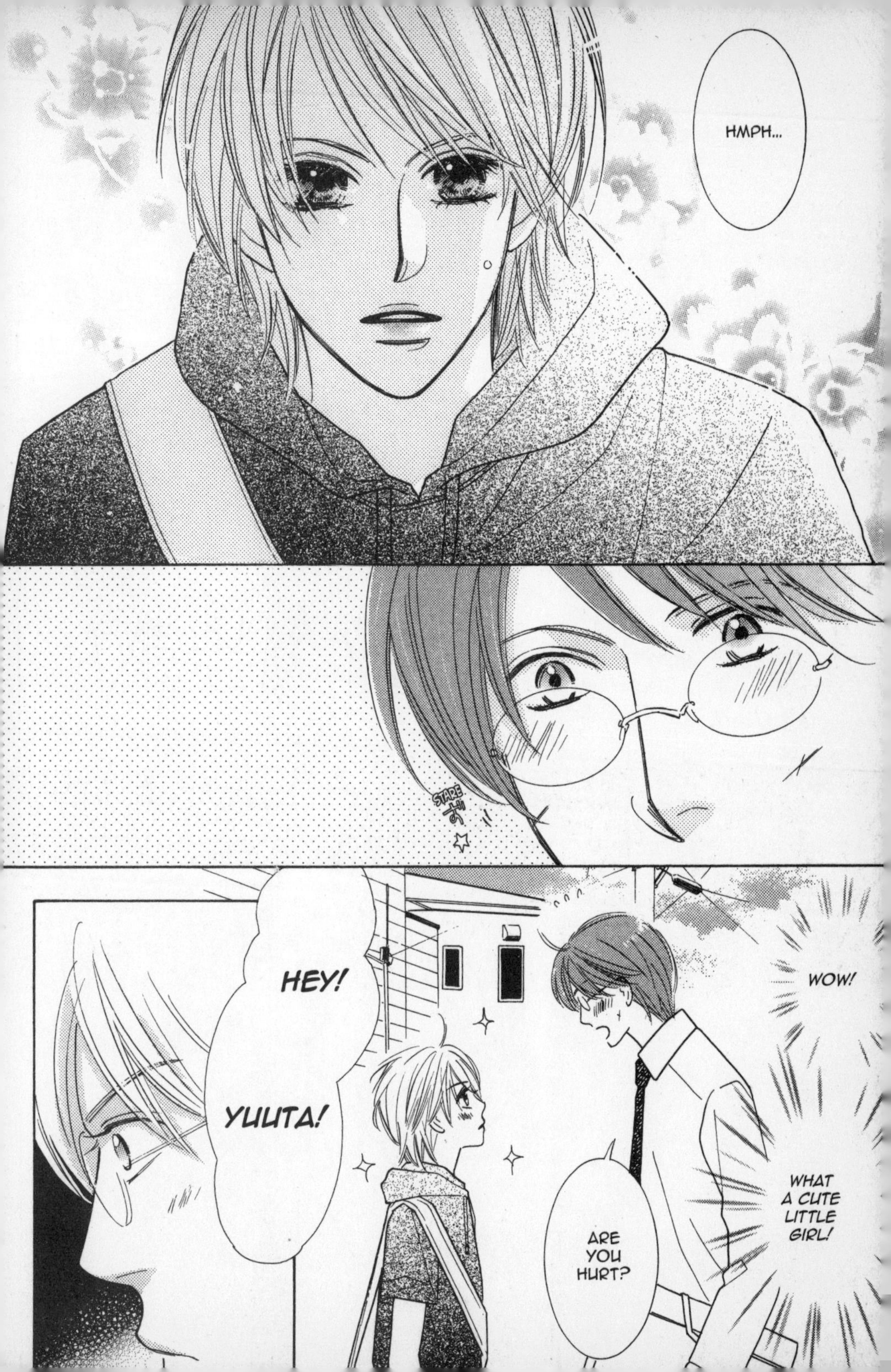
HMPH...
STARE
WOW!
WHAT A CUTE LITTLE GIRL!
ARE YOU HURT?
HEY!
YUUTA!

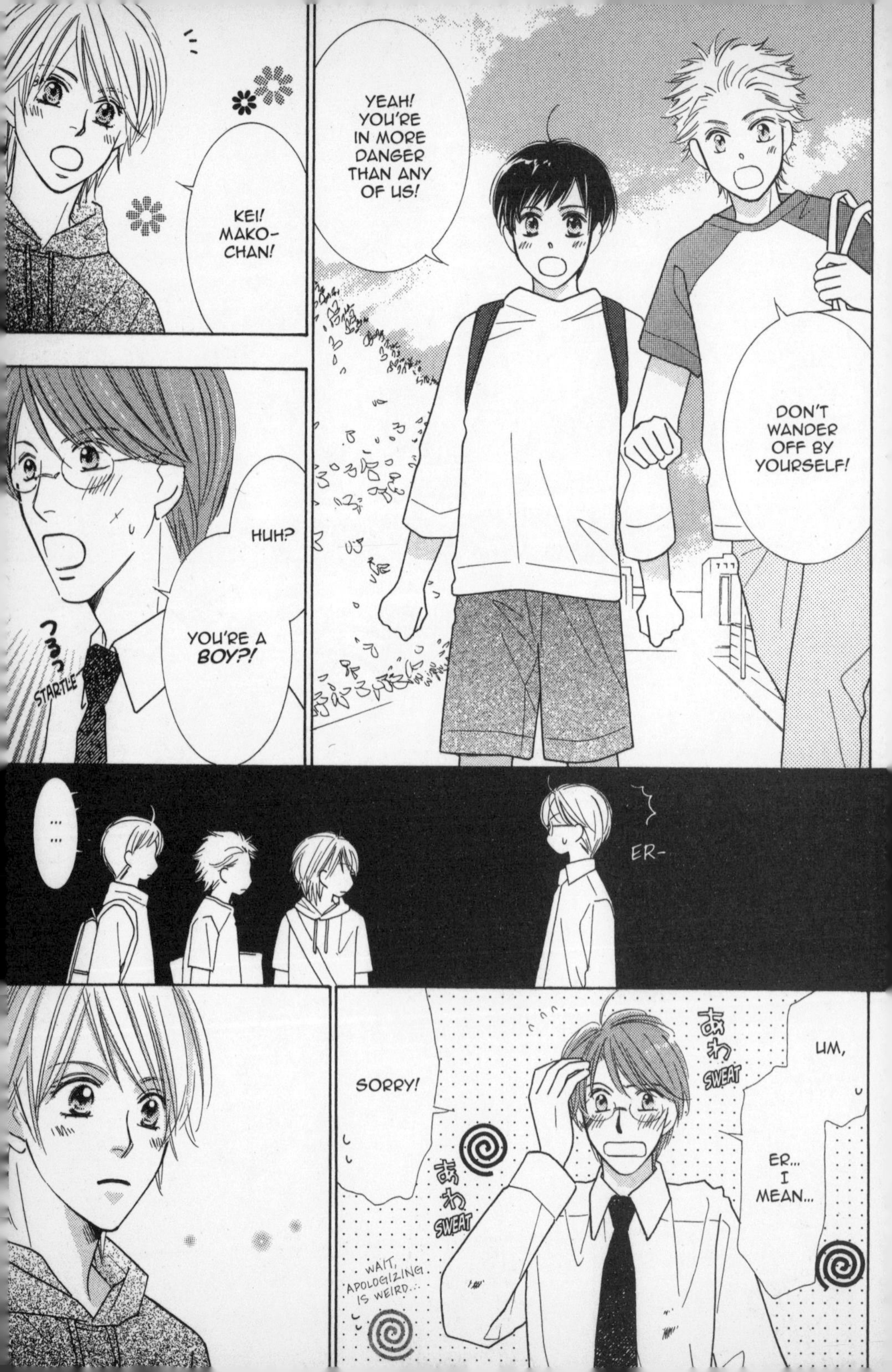
DON'T WANDER OFF BY YOURSELF!
YEAH! YOU'RE IN MORE DANGER THAN ANY OF US!
KEI! MAKO-CHAN!
HUH?
YOU'RE A BOY?!
STARTLE
ER-
... ...
UM,
あわ SWEAT
ER... I MEAN...
SORRY!
あわ SWEAT
WAIT, APOLOGIZING IS WEIRD...

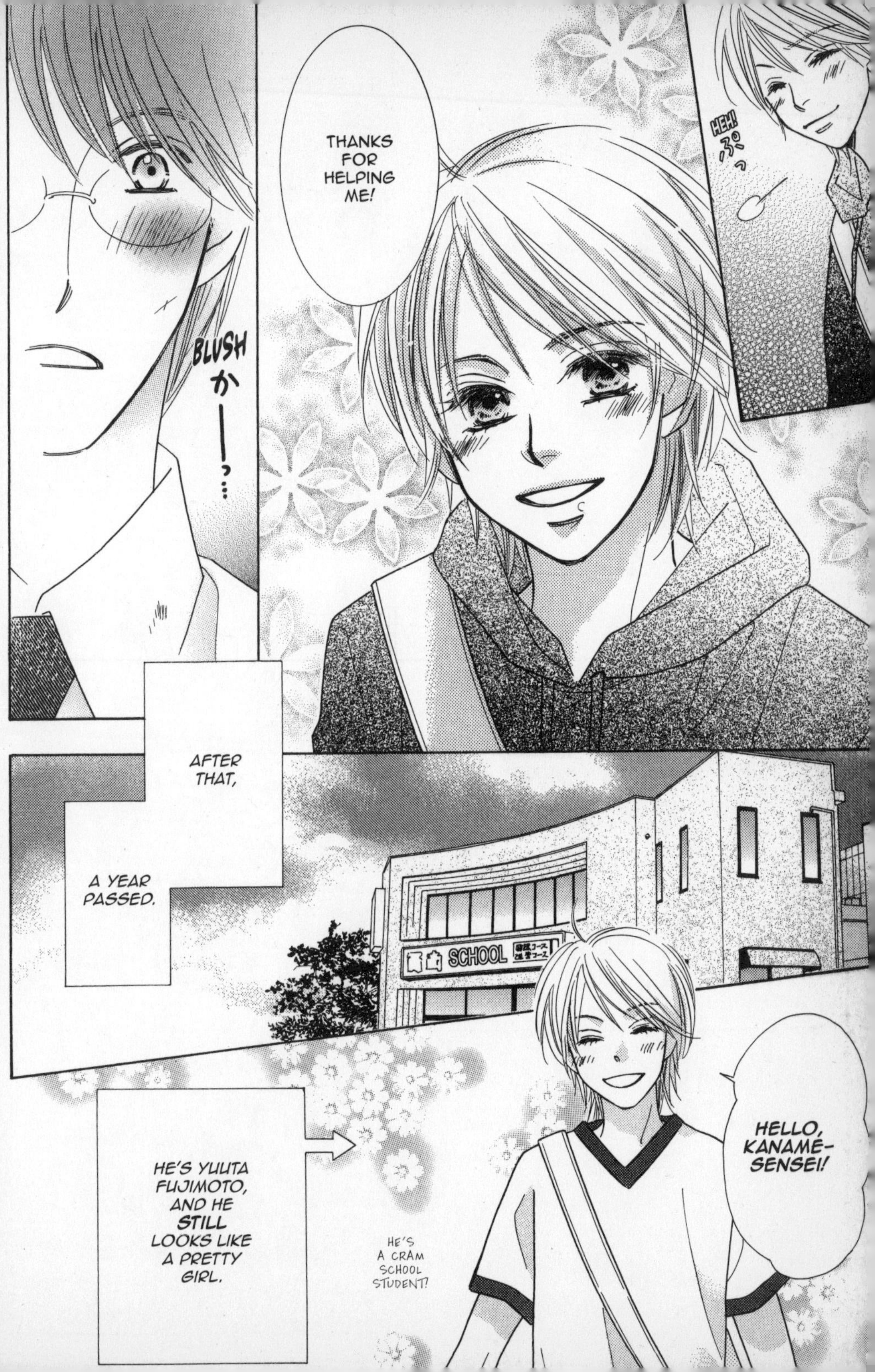
HEH!
ぷっ
THANKS FOR HELPING ME!
BLUSH
かーーっ…
AFTER THAT,
A YEAR PASSED.
SCHOOL
HELLO, KANAME-SENSEI!
HE'S YUUTA FUJIMOTO, AND HE STILL LOOKS LIKE A PRETTY GIRL.
HE'S A CRAM SCHOOL STUDENT!?

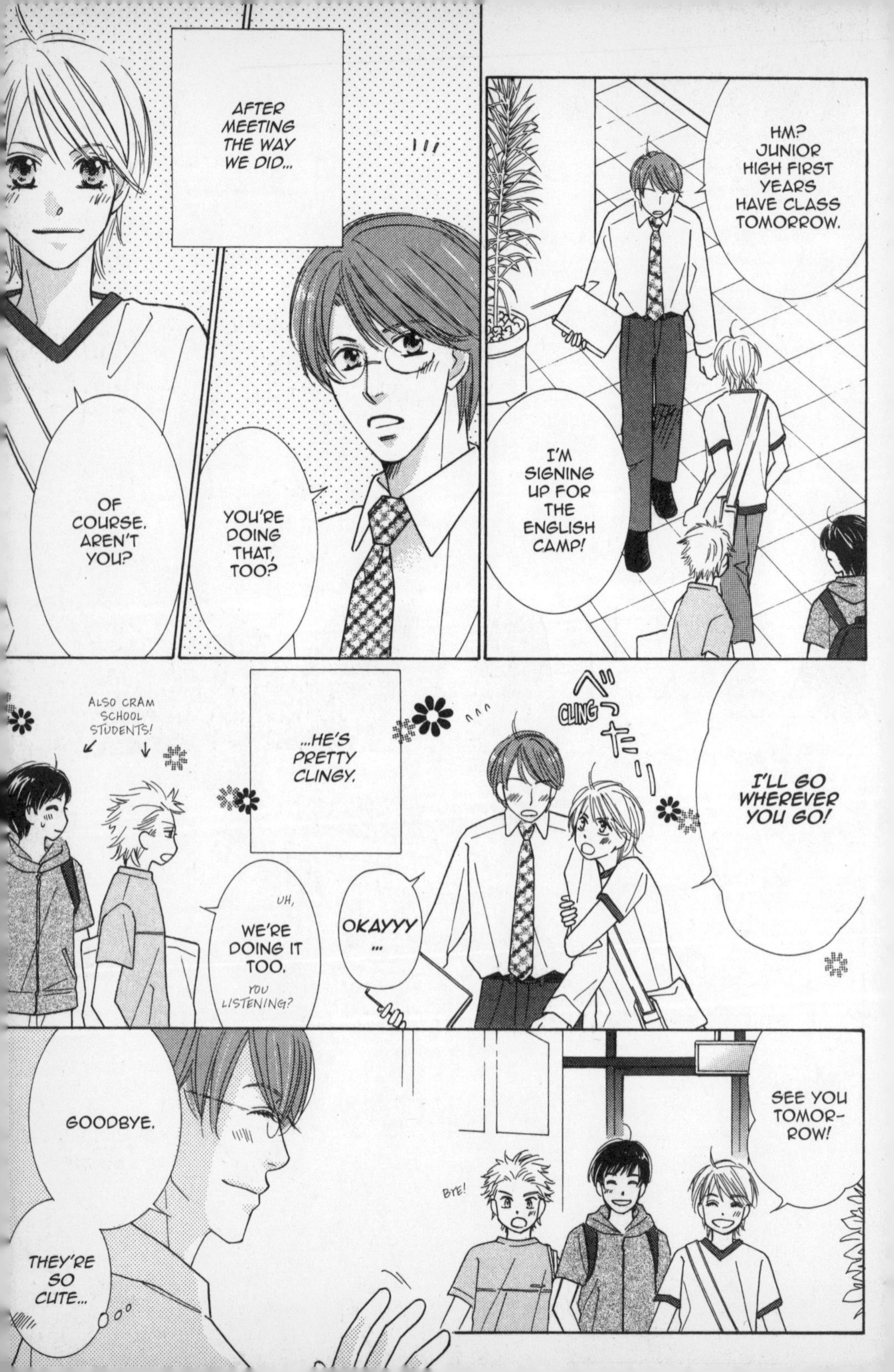
HM? JUNIOR HIGH FIRST YEARS HAVE CLASS TOMORROW.
I'M SIGNING UP FOR THE ENGLISH CAMP!
AFTER MEETING THE WAY WE DID...
YOU'RE DOING THAT, TOO?
OF COURSE. AREN'T YOU?
I'LL GO WHEREVER YOU GO!
CLING
...HE'S PRETTY CLINGY.
OKAYYY ...
UH,
WE'RE DOING IT TOO.
YOU LISTENING?
ALSO CRAM SCHOOL STUDENTS!
SEE YOU TOMORROW!
BYE!
GOODBYE.
THEY'RE SO CUTE...

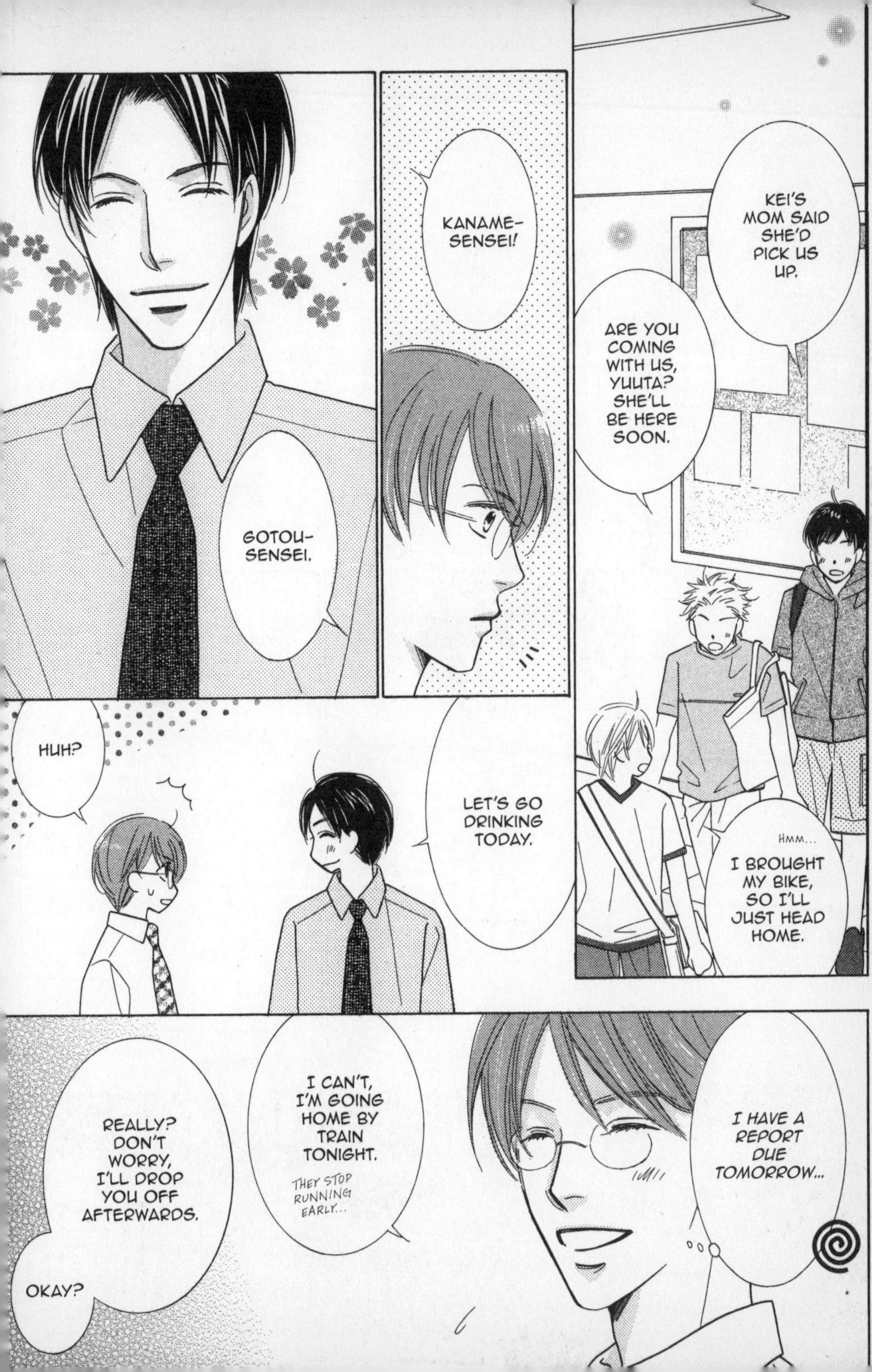
KEI'S MOM SAID SHE'D PICK US UP.
ARE YOU COMING WITH US, YUUTA? SHE'LL BE HERE SOON.
HMM...
I BROUGHT MY BIKE, SO I'LL JUST HEAD HOME.
KANAME-SENSEI!
GOTOU-SENSEI.
LET'S GO DRINKING TODAY.
HUH?
I HAVE A REPORT DUE TOMORROW...
I CAN'T, I'M GOING HOME BY TRAIN TONIGHT.
THEY STOP RUNNING EARLY...
REALLY? DON'T WORRY, I'LL DROP YOU OFF AFTERWARDS.
OKAY?

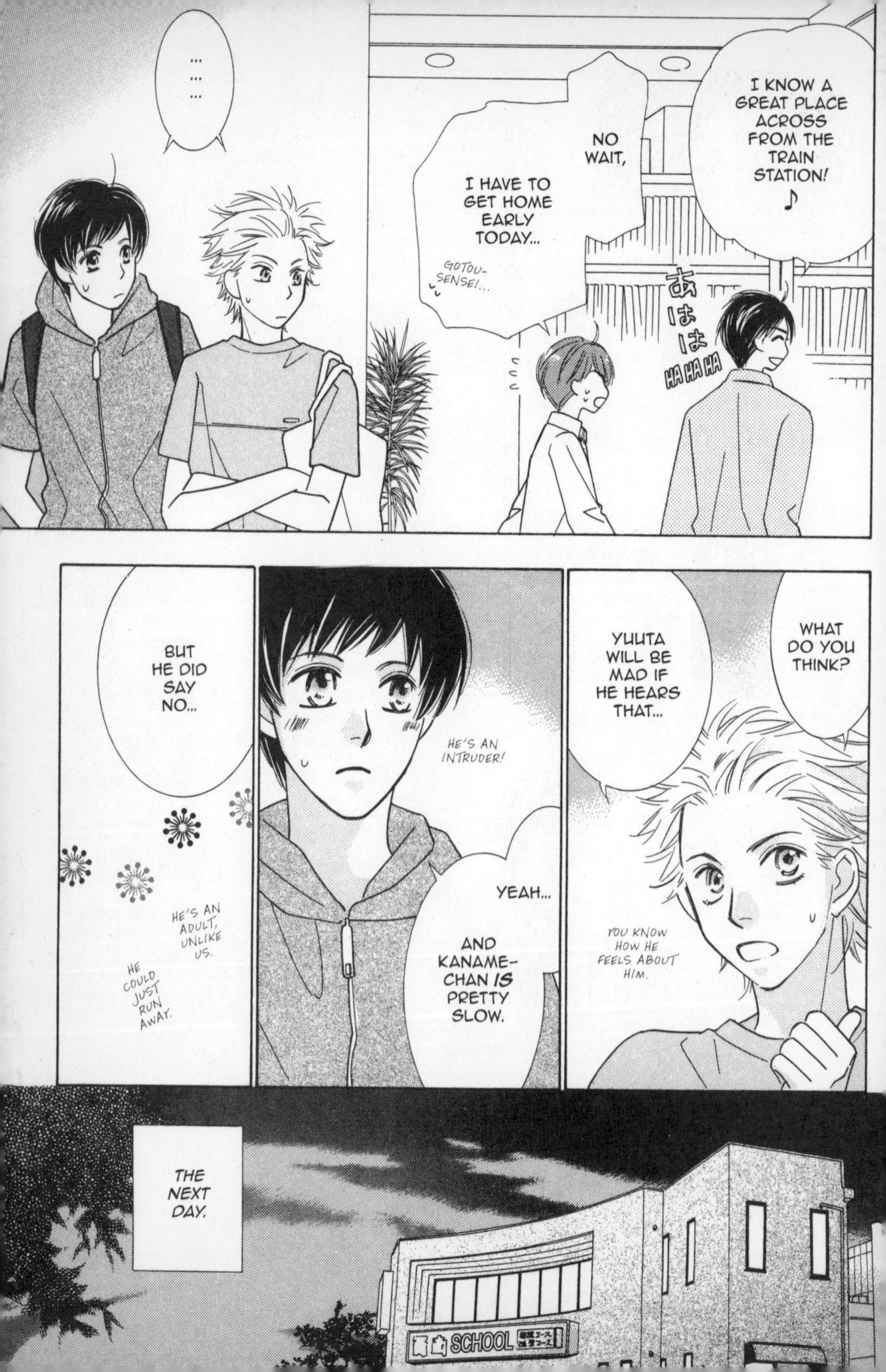
I KNOW A GREAT PLACE ACROSS FROM THE TRAIN STATION! ♪
あはは
HA HA HA
NO WAIT,
I HAVE TO GET HOME EARLY TODAY...
GOTOU-SENSEI...
...
...
...
WHAT DO YOU THINK?
YUUTA WILL BE MAD IF HE HEARS THAT...
YOU KNOW HOW HE FEELS ABOUT HIM.
YEAH...
AND KANAME-CHAN *IS* PRETTY SLOW.
HE'S AN INTRUDER!
BUT HE DID SAY NO...
HE'S AN ADULT, UNLIKE US.
HE COULD JUST RUN AWAY.
THE NEXT DAY.
SCHOOL

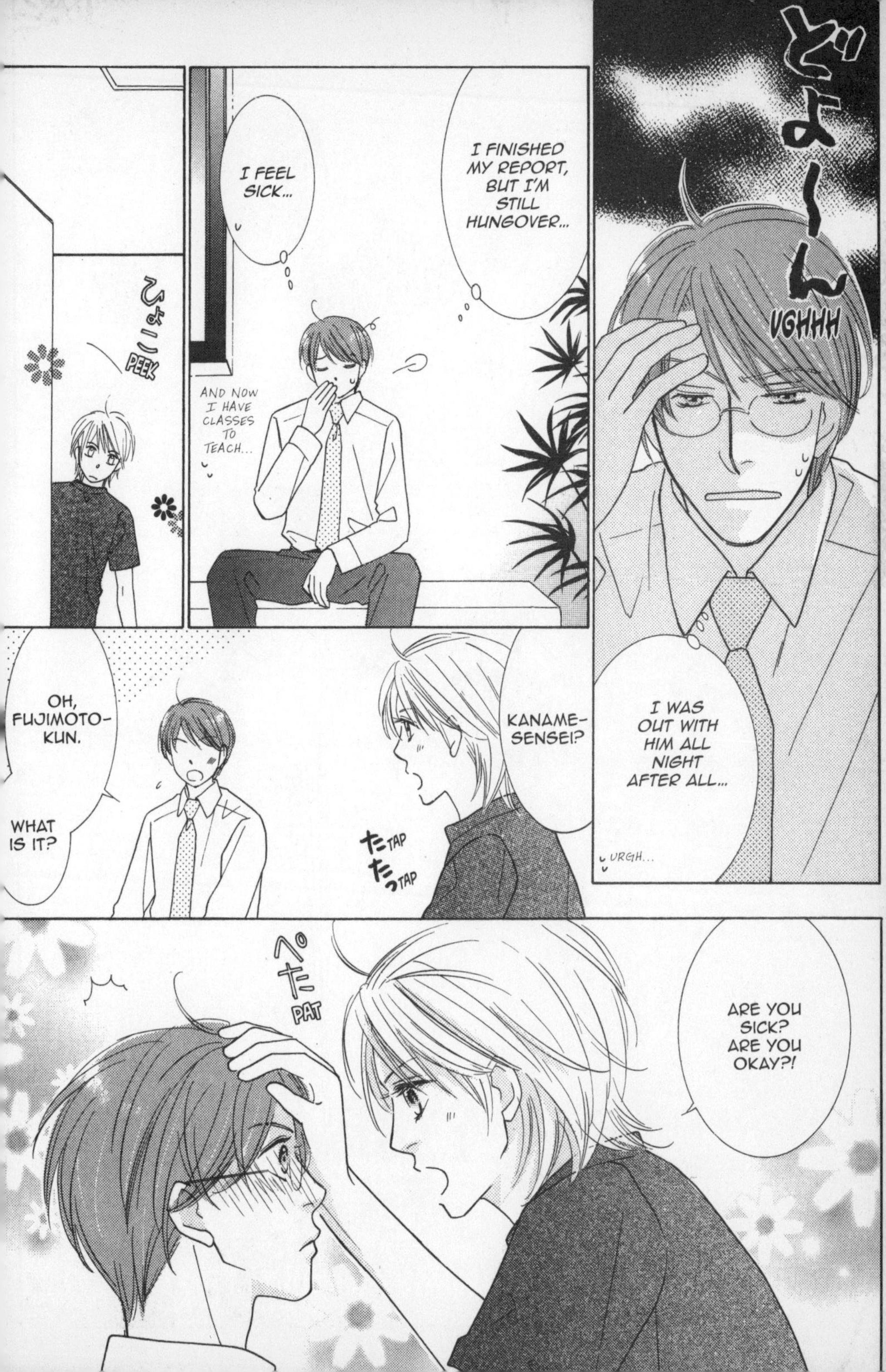
どよ～ん
UGHHH
I WAS OUT WITH HIM ALL NIGHT AFTER ALL...
URGH...
I FINISHED MY REPORT, BUT I'M STILL HUNGOVER...
I FEEL SICK...
AND NOW I HAVE CLASSES TO TEACH...
ひょこ
PEEK
KANAME-SENSEI?
たTAP
たっTAP
OH, FUJIMOTO-KUN.
WHAT IS IT?
ARE YOU SICK? ARE YOU OKAY?!
ぺた
PAT

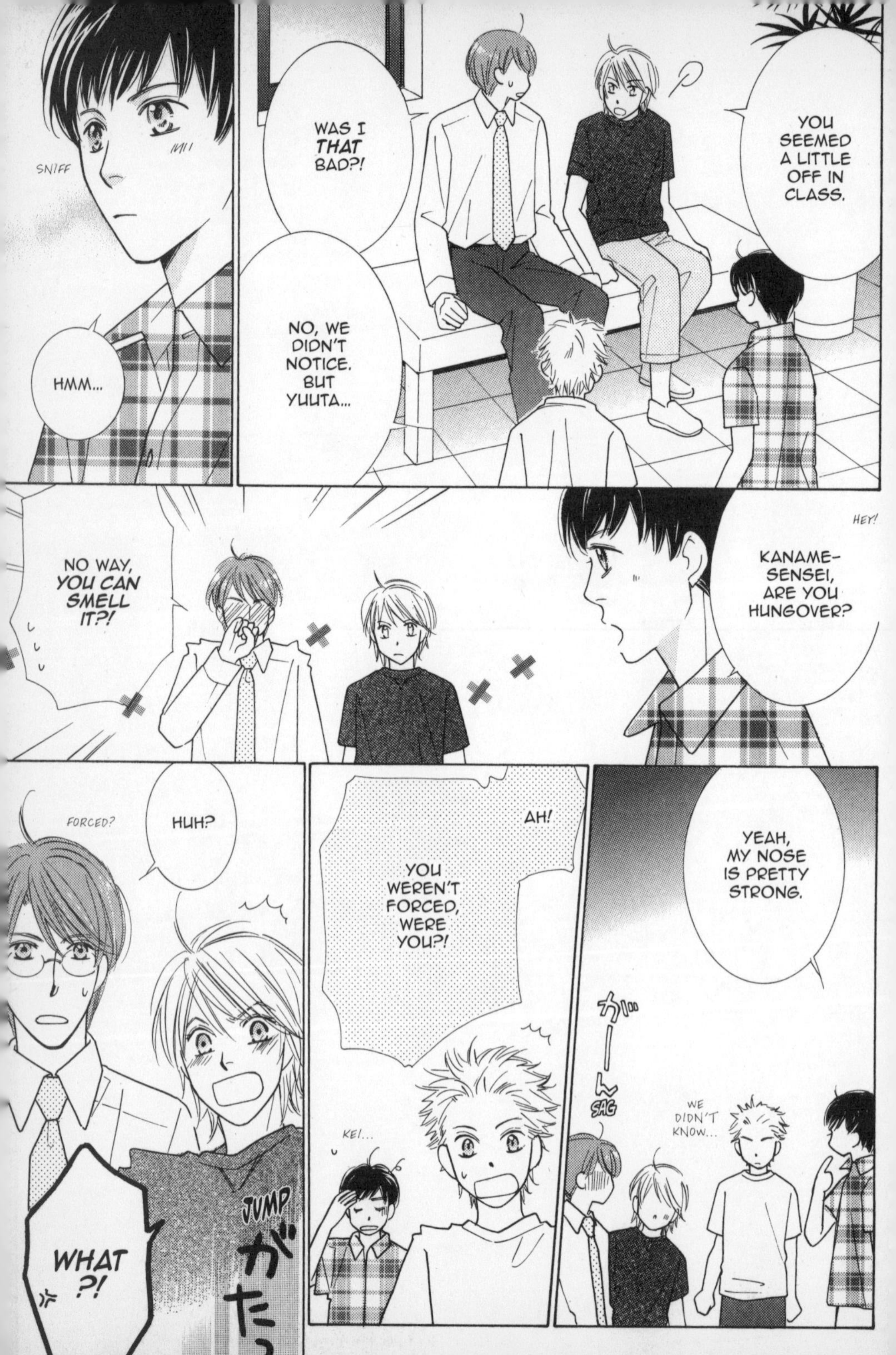
YOU SEEMED A LITTLE OFF IN CLASS.
WAS I *THAT* BAD?!
NO, WE DIDN'T NOTICE. BUT YUUTA...
SNIFF
HMM...
HEY!
KANAME-SENSEI, ARE YOU HUNGOVER?
NO WAY, *YOU CAN SMELL IT?!*
YEAH, MY NOSE IS PRETTY STRONG.
SAG
WE DIDN'T KNOW...
AH!
YOU WEREN'T FORCED, WERE YOU?!
KEI...
FORCED?
HUH?
JUMP
がたっ
WHAT?!

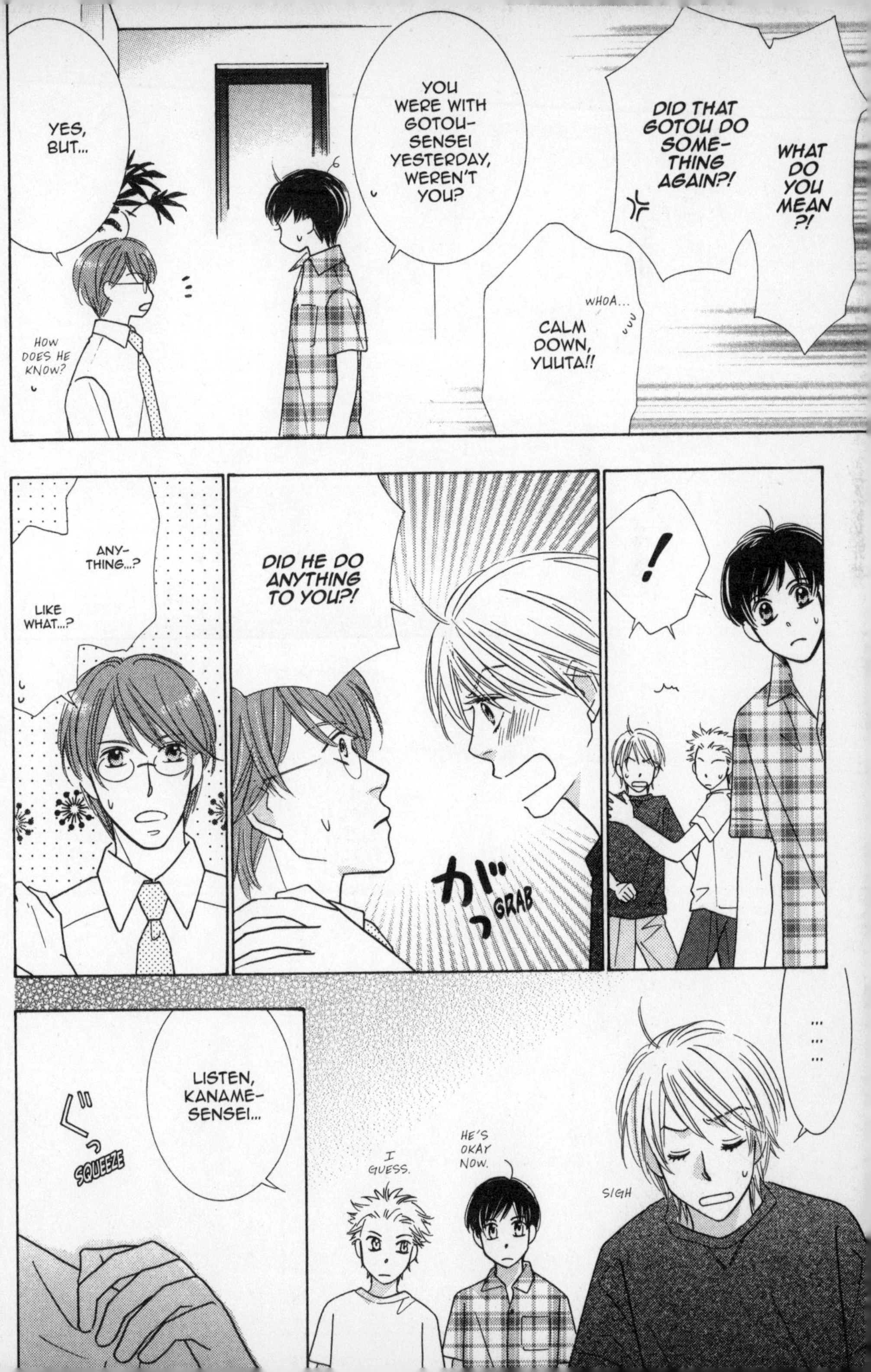
WHAT DO YOU MEAN?!
DID THAT GOTOU DO SOME-THING AGAIN?!
WHOA...
CALM DOWN, YUUTA!!
YOU WERE WITH GOTOU-SENSEI YESTERDAY, WEREN'T YOU?
YES, BUT...
HOW DOES HE KNOW?
!
DID HE DO ANYTHING TO YOU?!
GRAB
ANY-THING...?
LIKE WHAT...?
... ...
SIGH
HE'S OKAY NOW.
I GUESS.
LISTEN, KANAME-SENSEI...
SQUEEZE

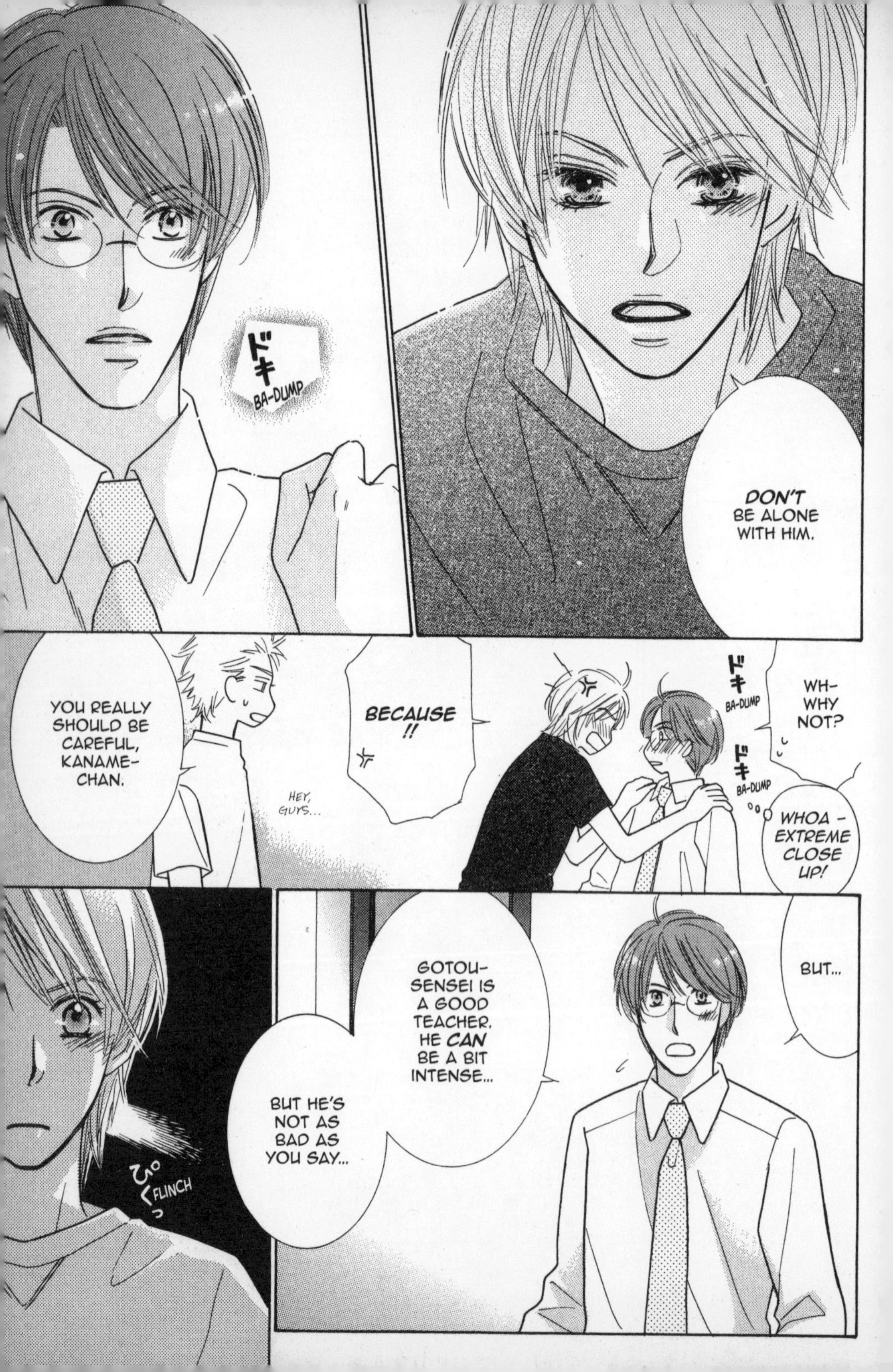
DON'T BE ALONE WITH HIM.
ドキ BA-DUMP
WH- WHY NOT?
ドキ BA-DUMP
ドキ BA-DUMP
WHOA - EXTREME CLOSE UP!
BECAUSE !!
HEY, GUYS...
YOU REALLY SHOULD BE CAREFUL, KANAME-CHAN.
BUT...
GOTOU-SENSEI IS A GOOD TEACHER. HE CAN BE A BIT INTENSE...
BUT HE'S NOT AS BAD AS YOU SAY...
ぴくっ FLINCH

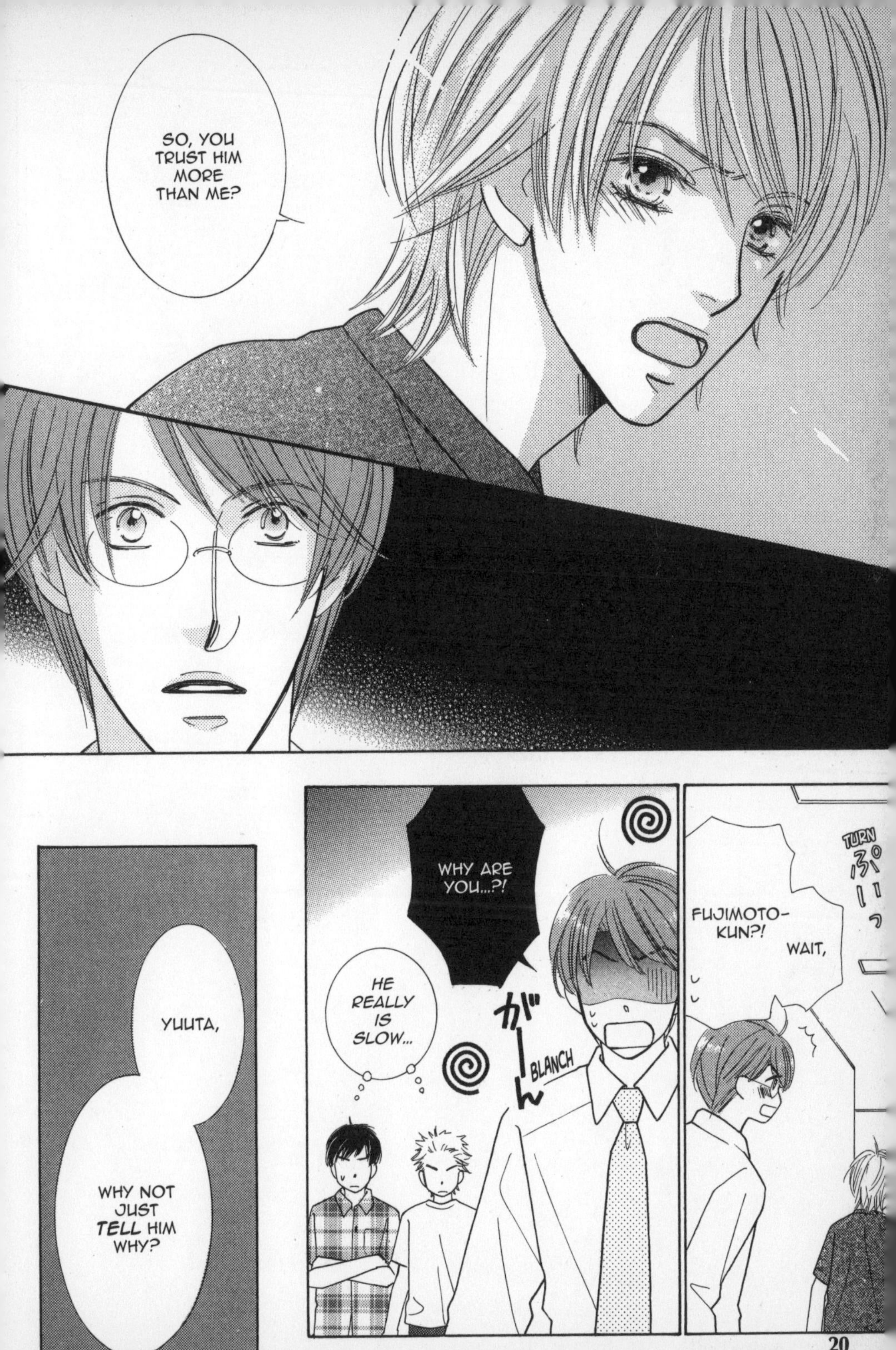
SO, YOU TRUST HIM MORE THAN ME?
TURN
ぷいっ
FUJIMOTO-KUN?!
WAIT,
WHY ARE YOU...?!
がーん
BLANCH
HE REALLY IS SLOW...
YUUTA,
WHY NOT JUST **TELL** HIM WHY?

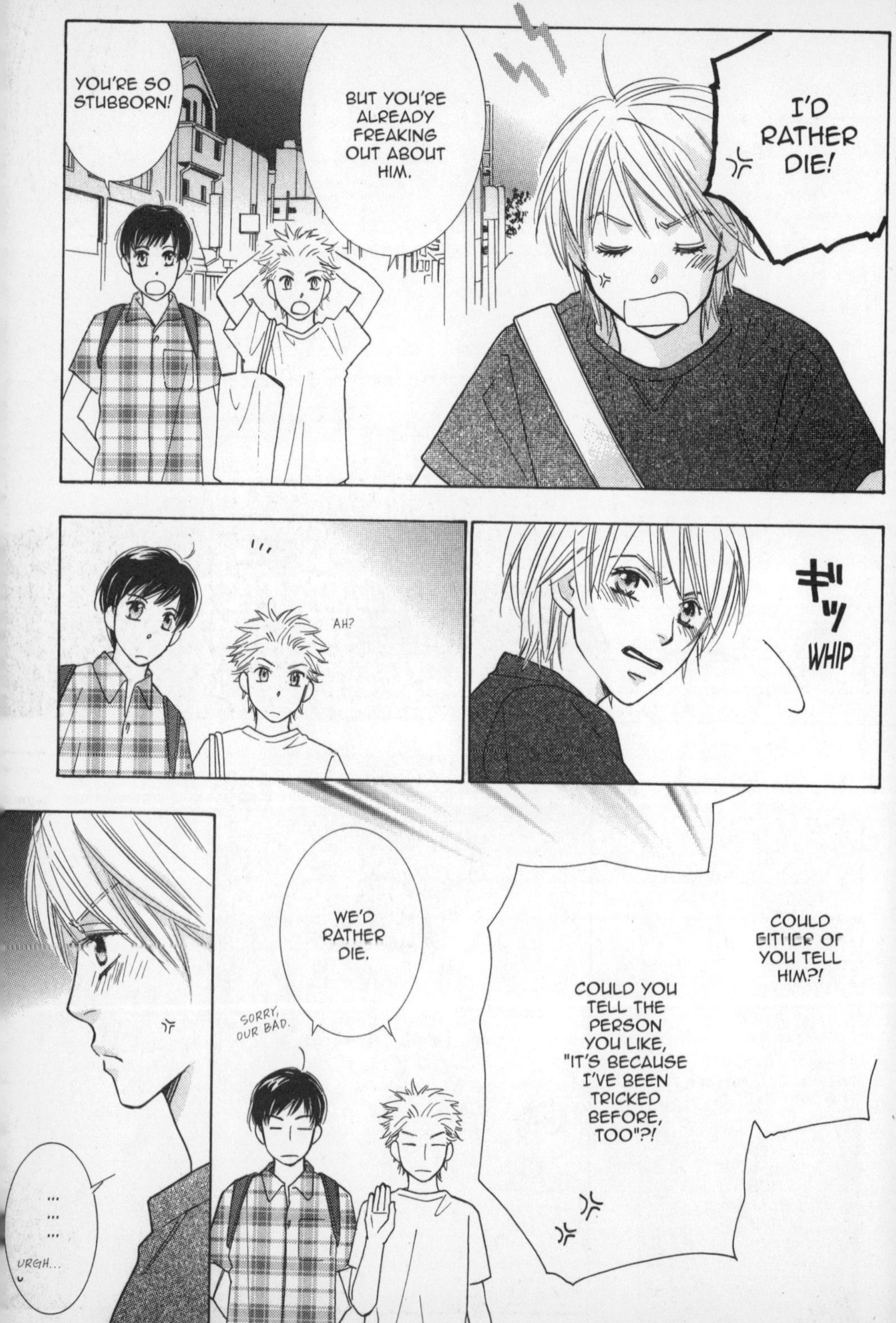
I'D RATHER DIE!
BUT YOU'RE ALREADY FREAKING OUT ABOUT HIM.
YOU'RE SO STUBBORN!
ギッ
WHIP
AH?
COULD EITHER OF YOU TELL HIM?!
COULD YOU TELL THE PERSON YOU LIKE, "IT'S BECAUSE I'VE BEEN TRICKED BEFORE, TOO"?!
WE'D RATHER DIE.
SORRY, OUR BAD.
... ... URGH...

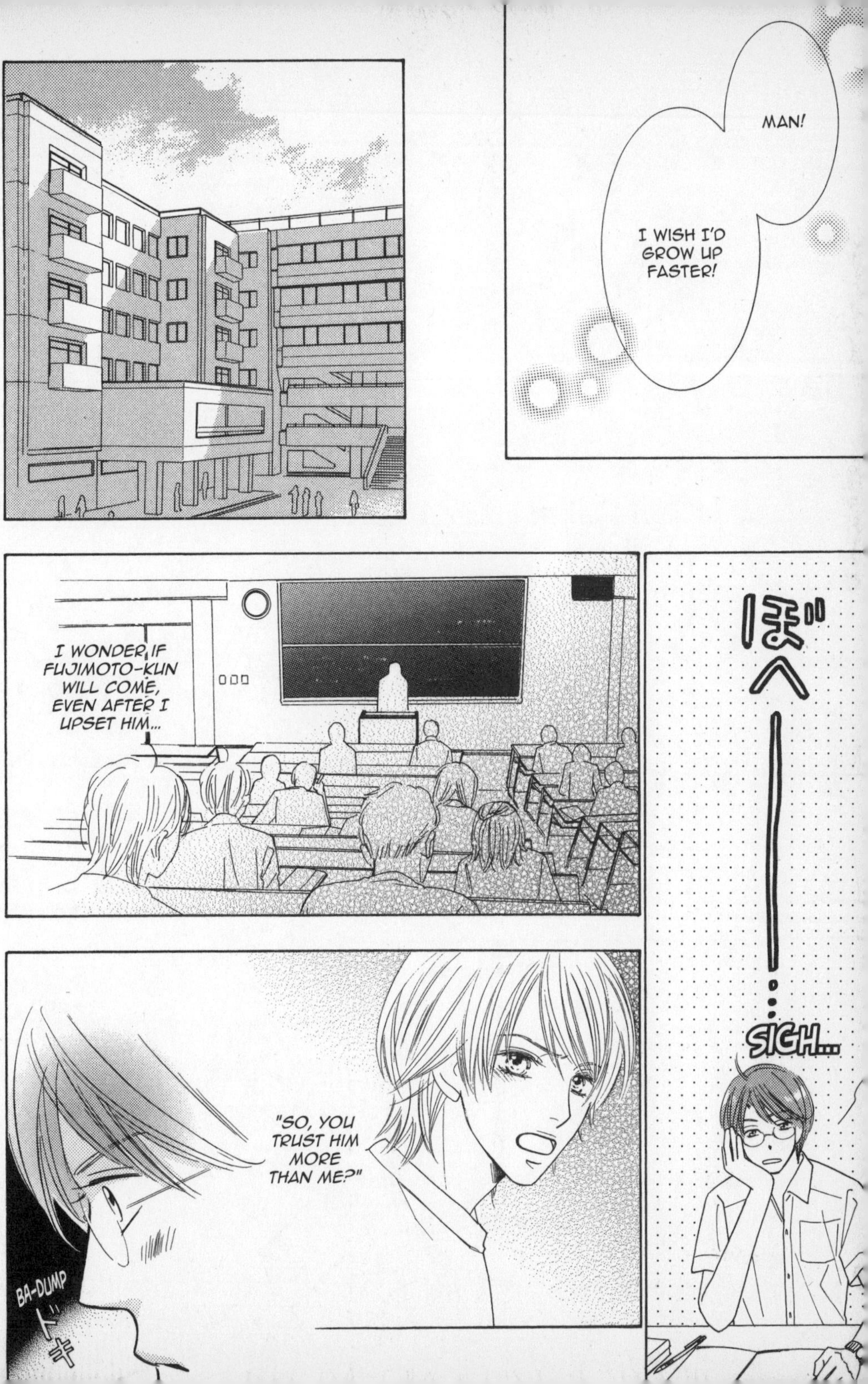
MAN!
I WISH I'D GROW UP FASTER!
ぼへー…
SIGH...
I WONDER IF FUJIMOTO-KUN WILL COME, EVEN AFTER I UPSET HIM...
"SO, YOU TRUST HIM MORE THAN ME?"
BA-DUMP
ドキ

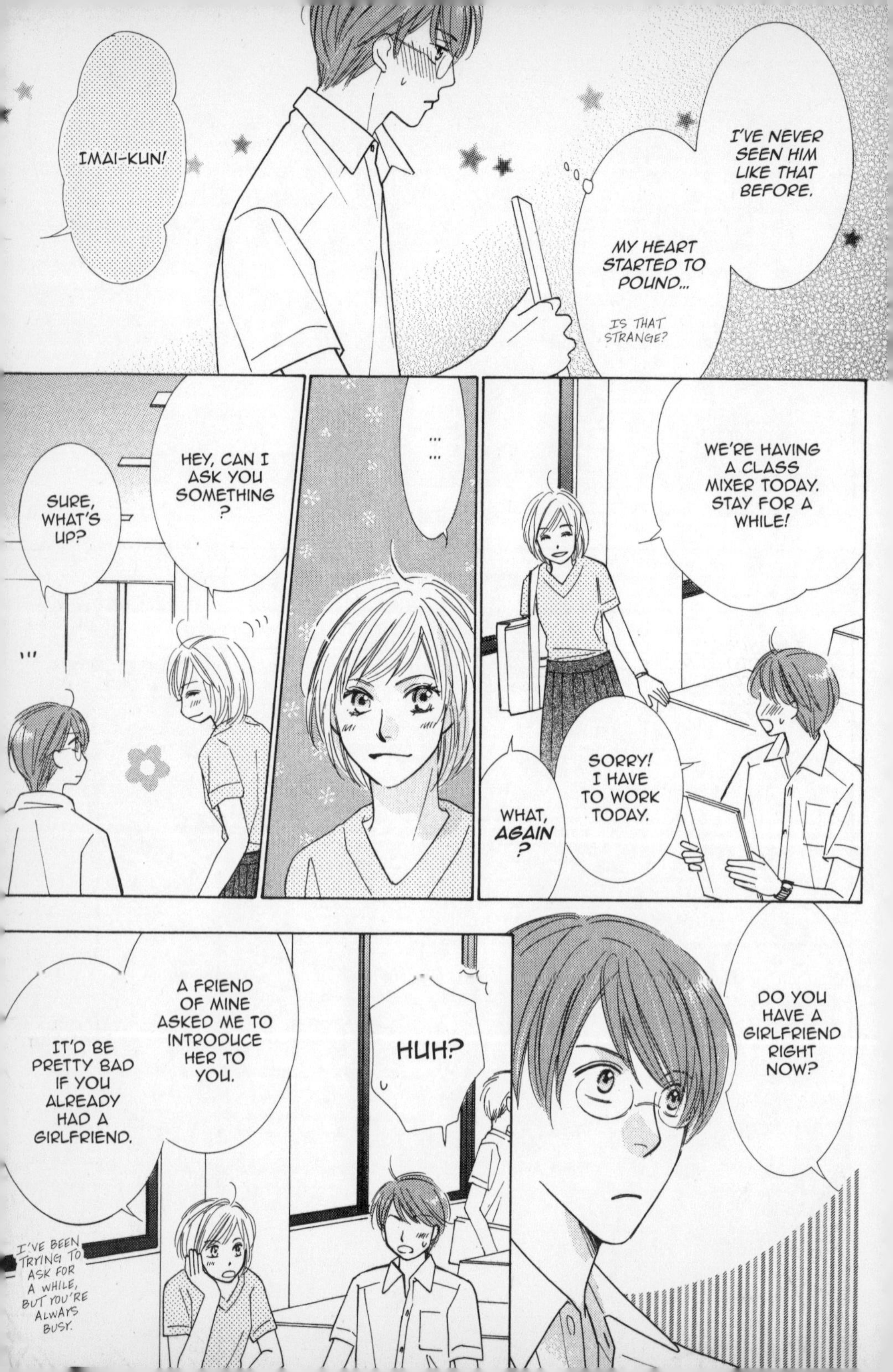
I'VE NEVER SEEN HIM LIKE THAT BEFORE.
MY HEART STARTED TO POUND...
IS THAT STRANGE?
IMAI-KUN!
WE'RE HAVING A CLASS MIXER TODAY. STAY FOR A WHILE!
SORRY! I HAVE TO WORK TODAY.
WHAT, AGAIN?
... ...
HEY, CAN I ASK YOU SOMETHING?
SURE, WHAT'S UP?
...
DO YOU HAVE A GIRLFRIEND RIGHT NOW?
HUH?
A FRIEND OF MINE ASKED ME TO INTRODUCE HER TO YOU.
IT'D BE PRETTY BAD IF YOU ALREADY HAD A GIRLFRIEND.
I'VE BEEN TRYING TO ASK FOR A WHILE, BUT YOU'RE ALWAYS BUSY.

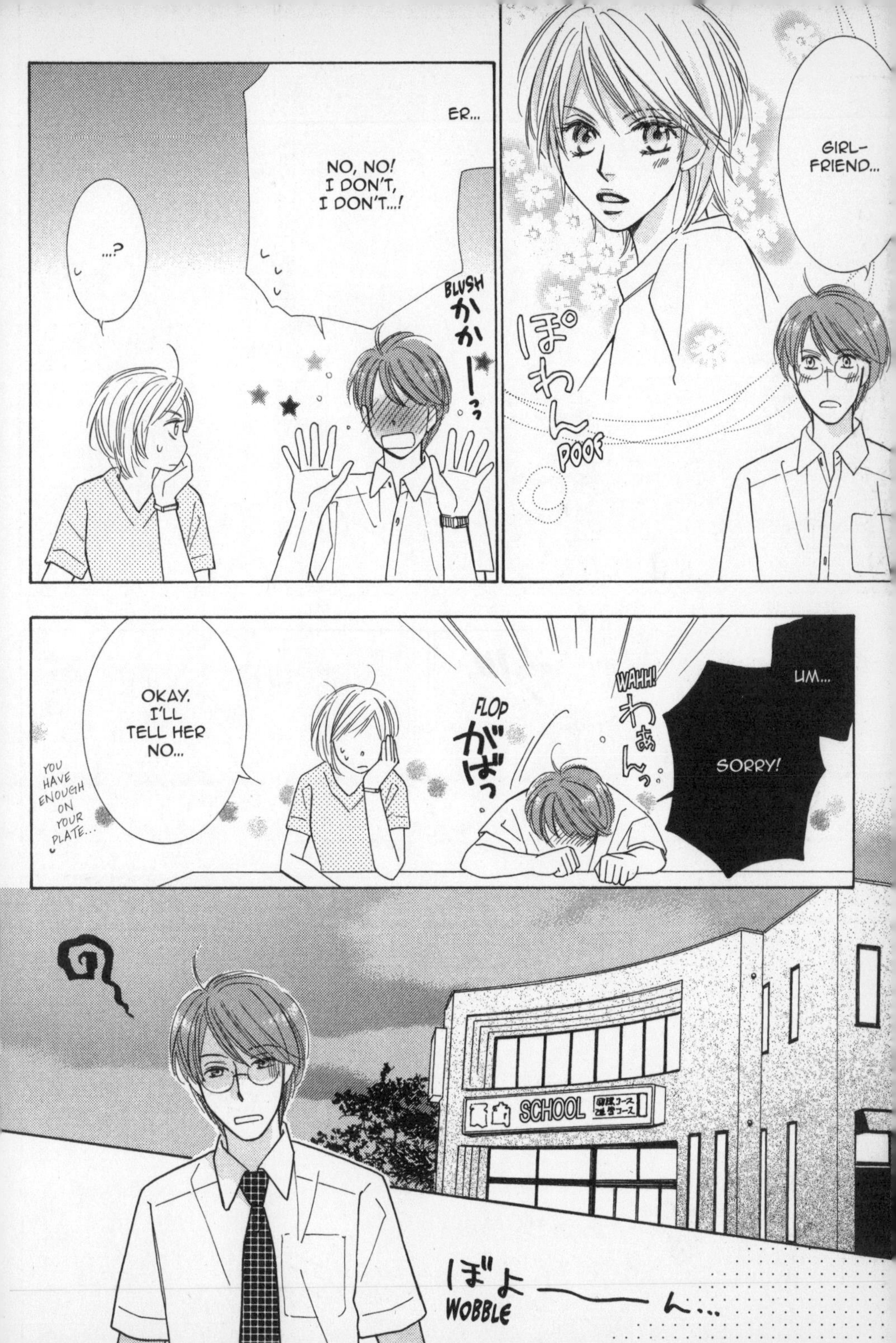
GIRL-FRIEND...
ぽわん~
POOF
ER...
NO, NO! I DON'T, I DON'T...!
BLUSH
かかーっ
...?
UM...
SORRY!
WAHH!
わぁんっ
FLOP
がばっ
OKAY. I'LL TELL HER NO...
YOU HAVE ENOUGH ON YOUR PLATE...
SCHOOL
ぼよーーん…
WOBBLE

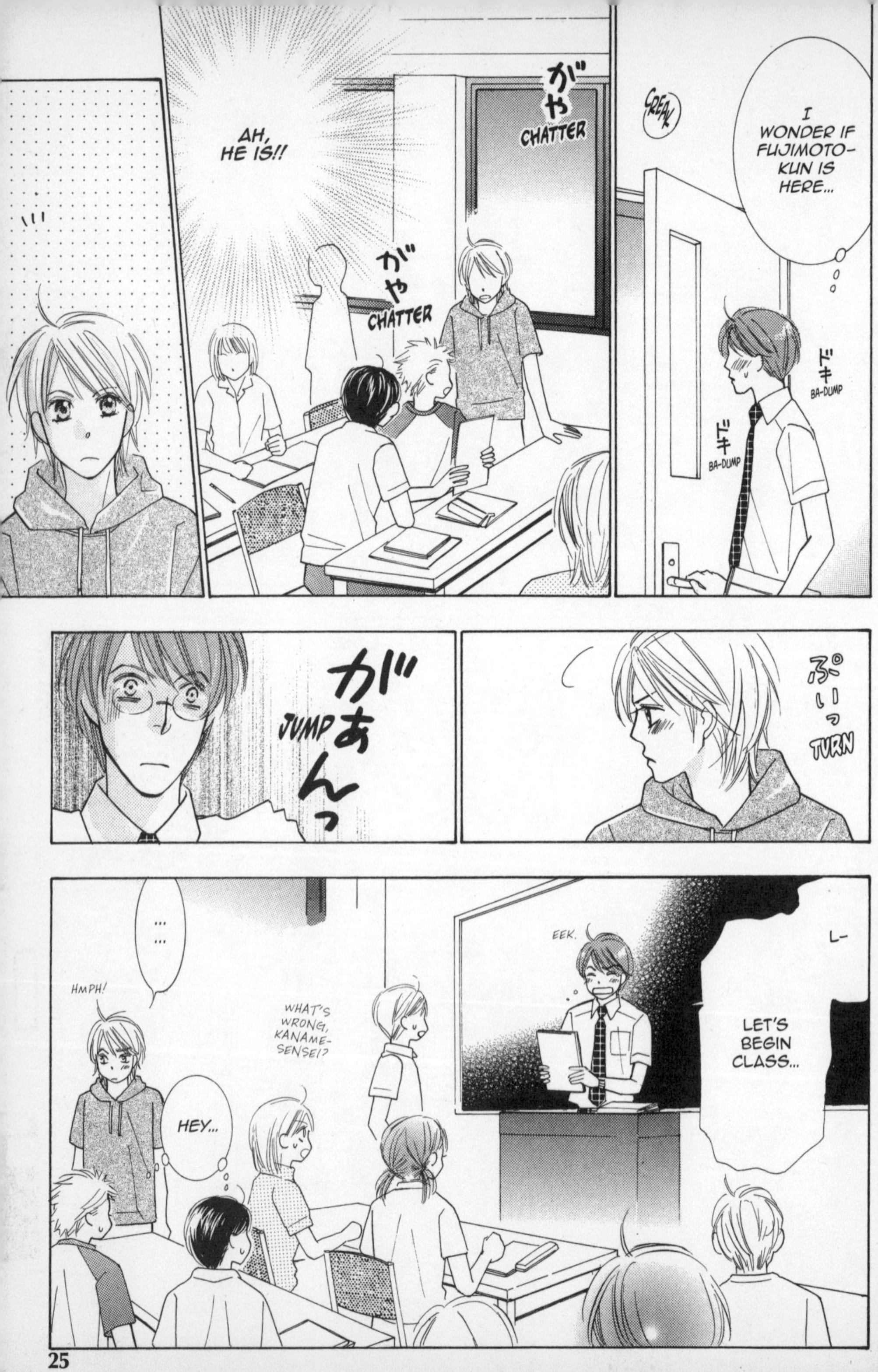
I WONDER IF FUJIMOTO-KUN IS HERE...
CREAK
ドキ
BA-DUMP
ドキ
BA-DUMP
がや
CHATTER
AH, HE IS!!
がや
CHATTER
ぷいっ
TURN
があんっ
JUMP
LET'S BEGIN CLASS...
レー
EEK.
WHAT'S WRONG, KANAME-SENSEI!?
...
...
HMPH!
HEY...

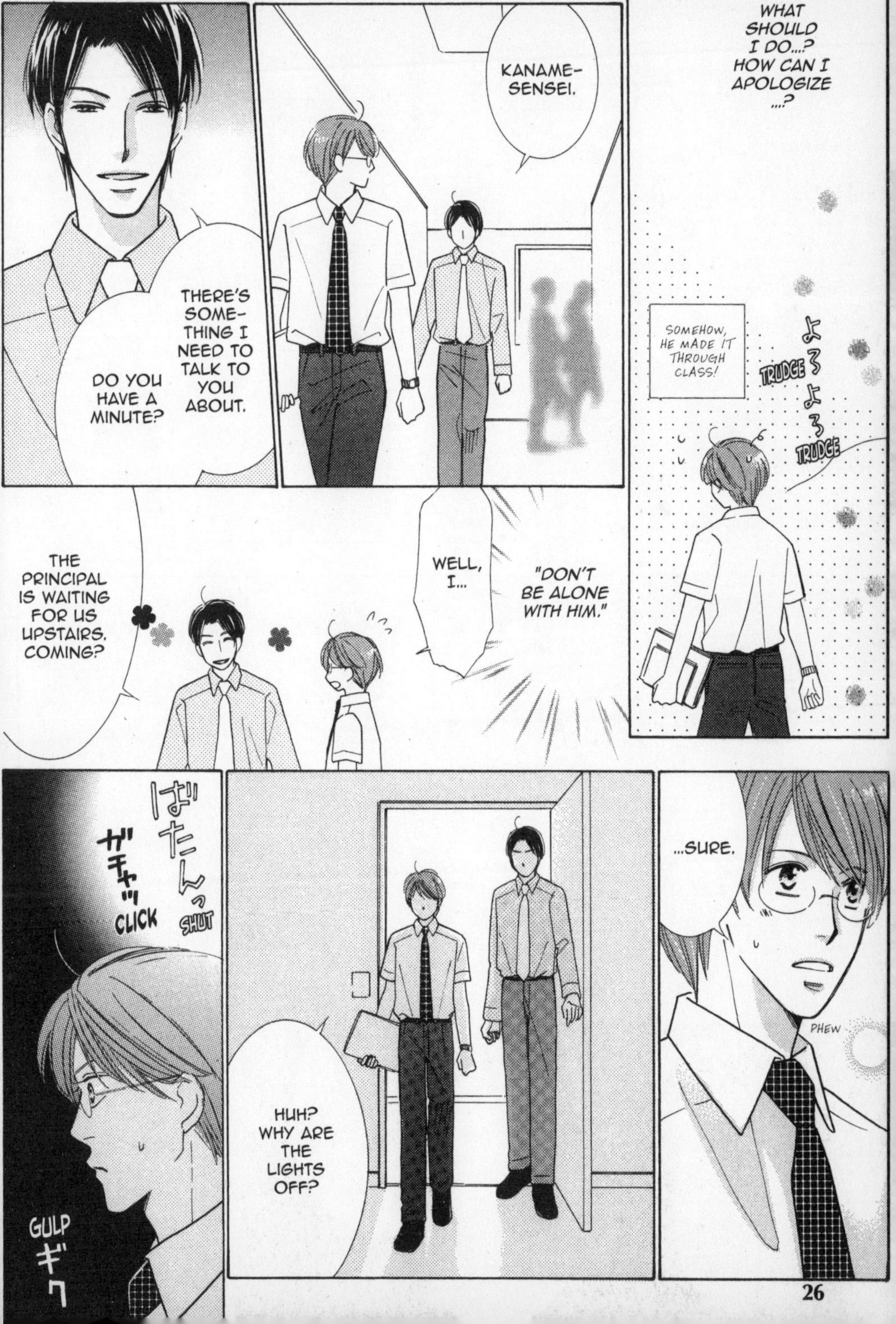

WHAT SHOULD I DO...? HOW CAN I APOLOGIZE ...?
SOMEHOW, HE MADE IT THROUGH CLASS!
よろよろ
TRUDGE
TRUDGE
KANAME-SENSEI.
THERE'S SOMETHING I NEED TO TALK TO YOU ABOUT.
DO YOU HAVE A MINUTE?
"DON'T BE ALONE WITH HIM."
WELL, I...
THE PRINCIPAL IS WAITING FOR US UPSTAIRS. COMING?
...SURE.
PHEW
HUH? WHY ARE THE LIGHTS OFF?
ばたんっ
SHUT
ガチャッ
CLICK
GULP
ギク

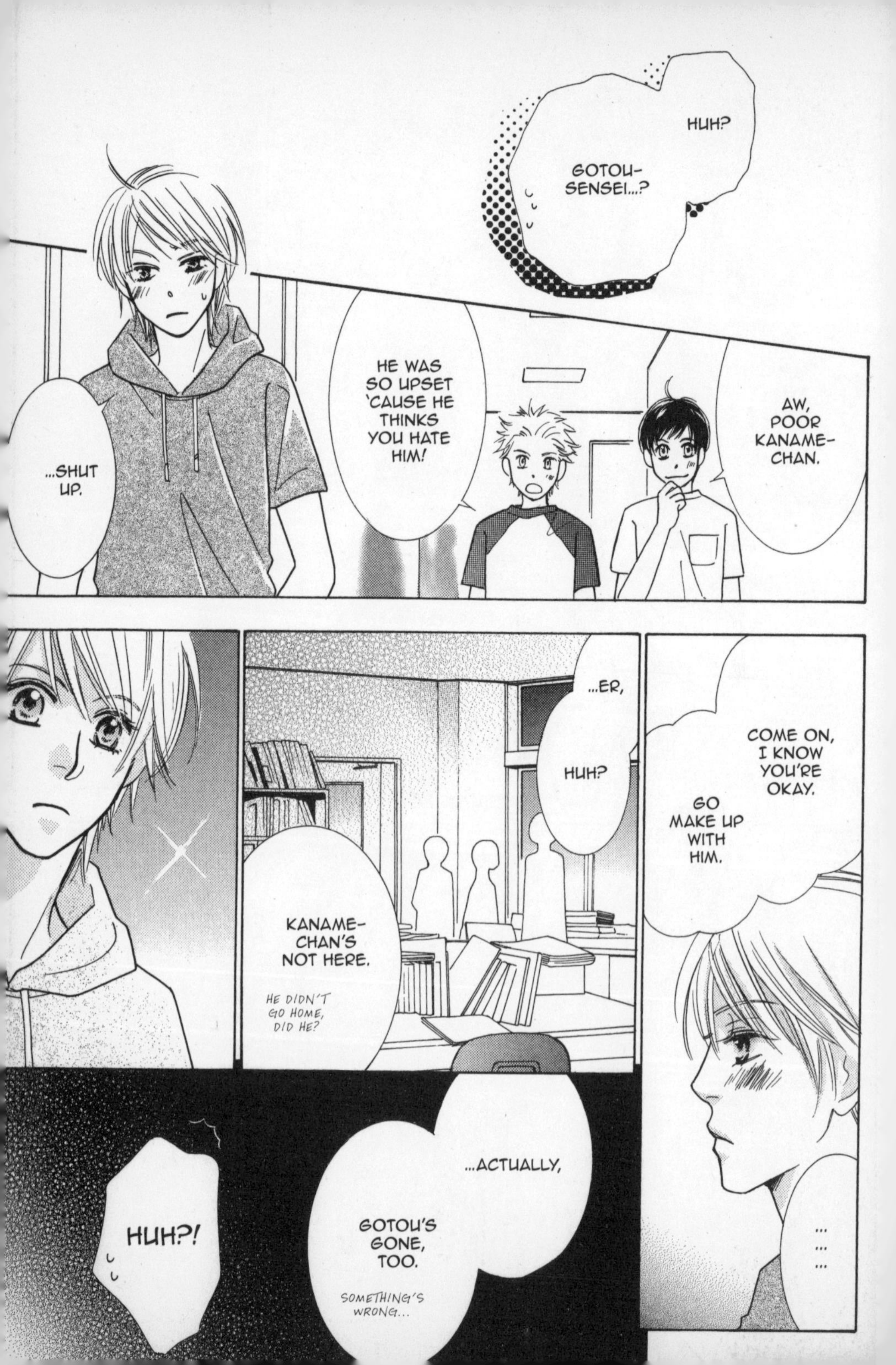
HUH?
GOTOU-SENSEI...?
AW, POOR KANAME-CHAN.
HE WAS SO UPSET 'CAUSE HE THINKS YOU HATE HIM!
...SHUT UP.
COME ON, I KNOW YOU'RE OKAY.
GO MAKE UP WITH HIM.
...
...
...
...ER,
HUH?
KANAME-CHAN'S NOT HERE.
HE DIDN'T GO HOME, DID HE?
...ACTUALLY,
GOTOU'S GONE, TOO.
SOMETHING'S WRONG...
HUH?!

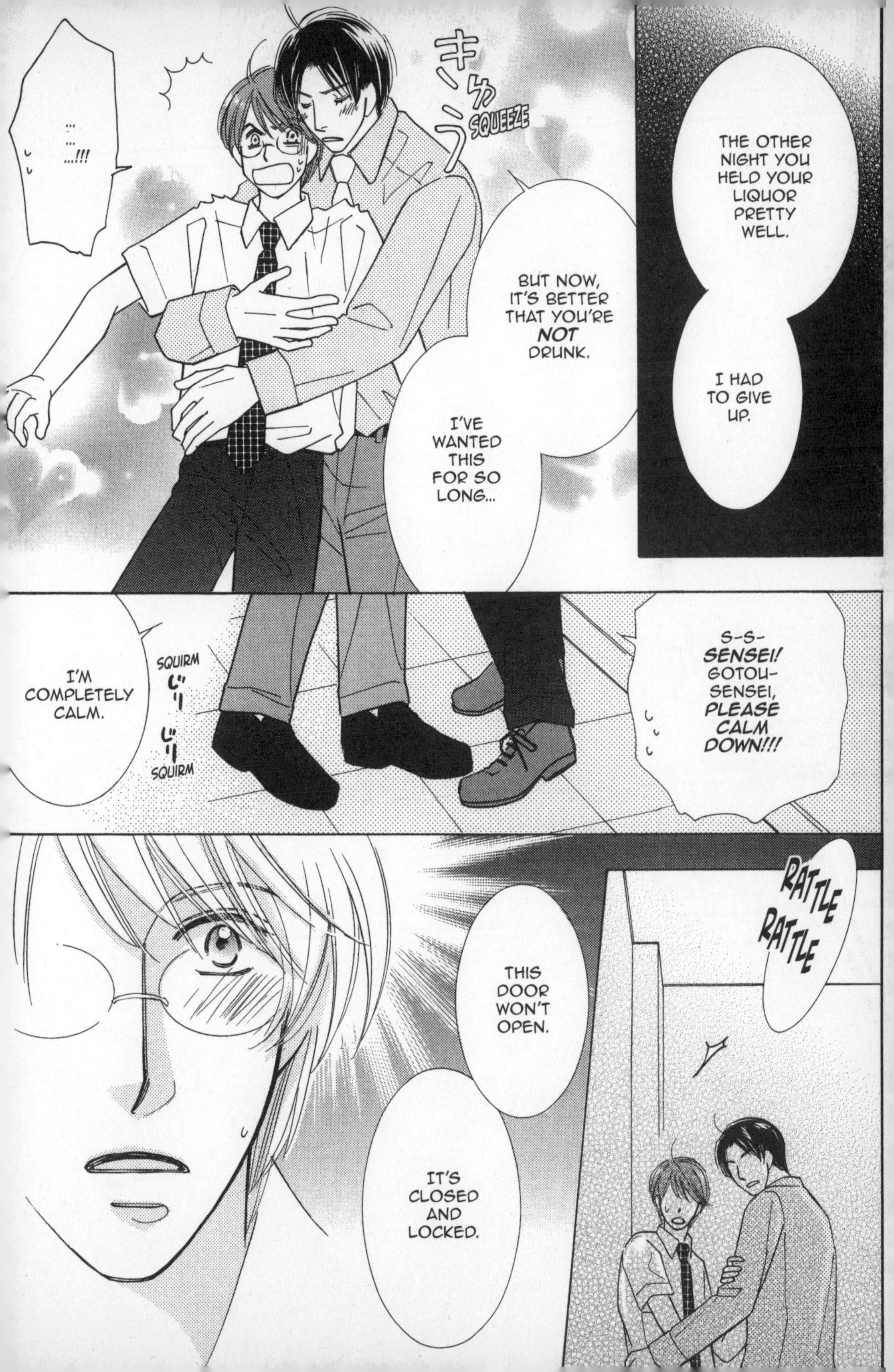
THE OTHER NIGHT YOU HELD YOUR LIQUOR PRETTY WELL.
I HAD TO GIVE UP.
きゅう SQUEEZE
BUT NOW, IT'S BETTER THAT YOU'RE *NOT* DRUNK.
I'VE WANTED THIS FOR SO LONG...
...
...
...!!!
S-S-*SENSEI!* GOTOU-SENSEI, *PLEASE CALM DOWN!!!*
I'M COMPLETELY CALM.
SQUIRM ジリ
ジリ SQUIRM
RATTLE RATTLE
THIS DOOR WON'T OPEN.
IT'S CLOSED AND LOCKED.

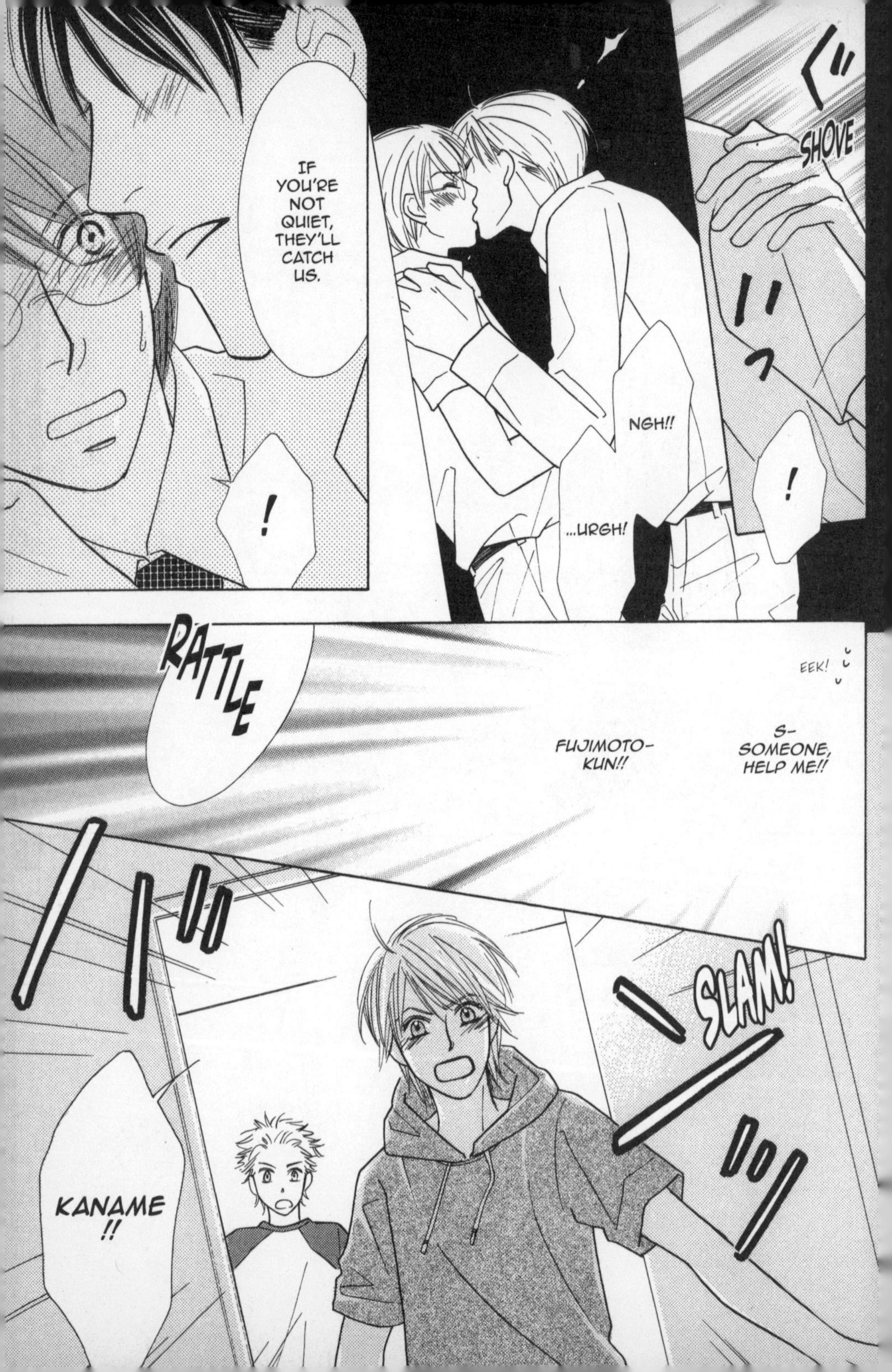
SHOVE
!
NGH!!
...URGH!
IF YOU'RE NOT QUIET, THEY'LL CATCH US.
!
EEK!
S-SOMEONE, HELP ME!!
FUJIMOTO-KUN!!
RATTLE
SLAM!
KANAME!!

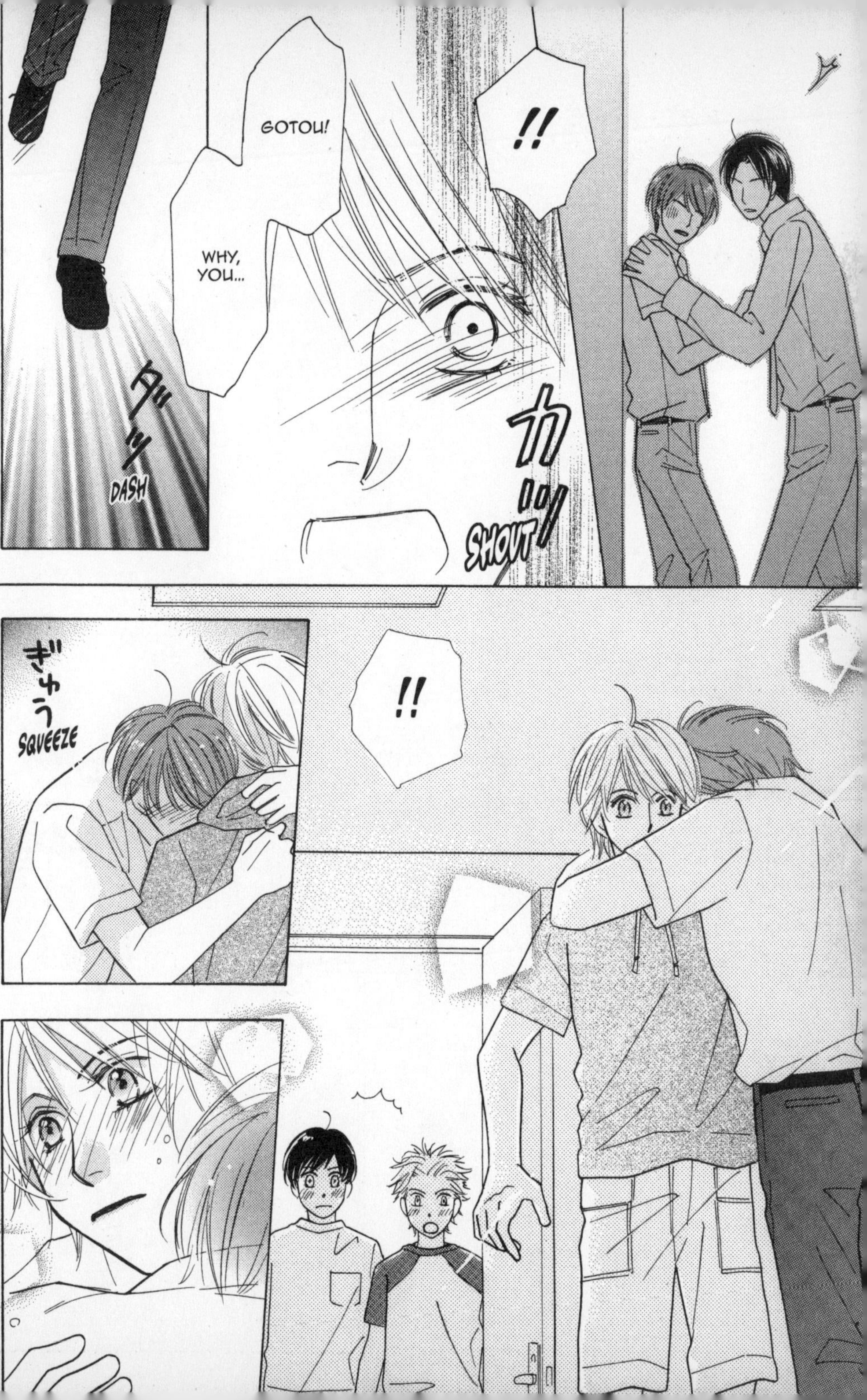
!!
GOTOU!
WHY, YOU...
カッ
SHOUT
ダッ
DASH
!!
ぎゅう
SQUEEZE

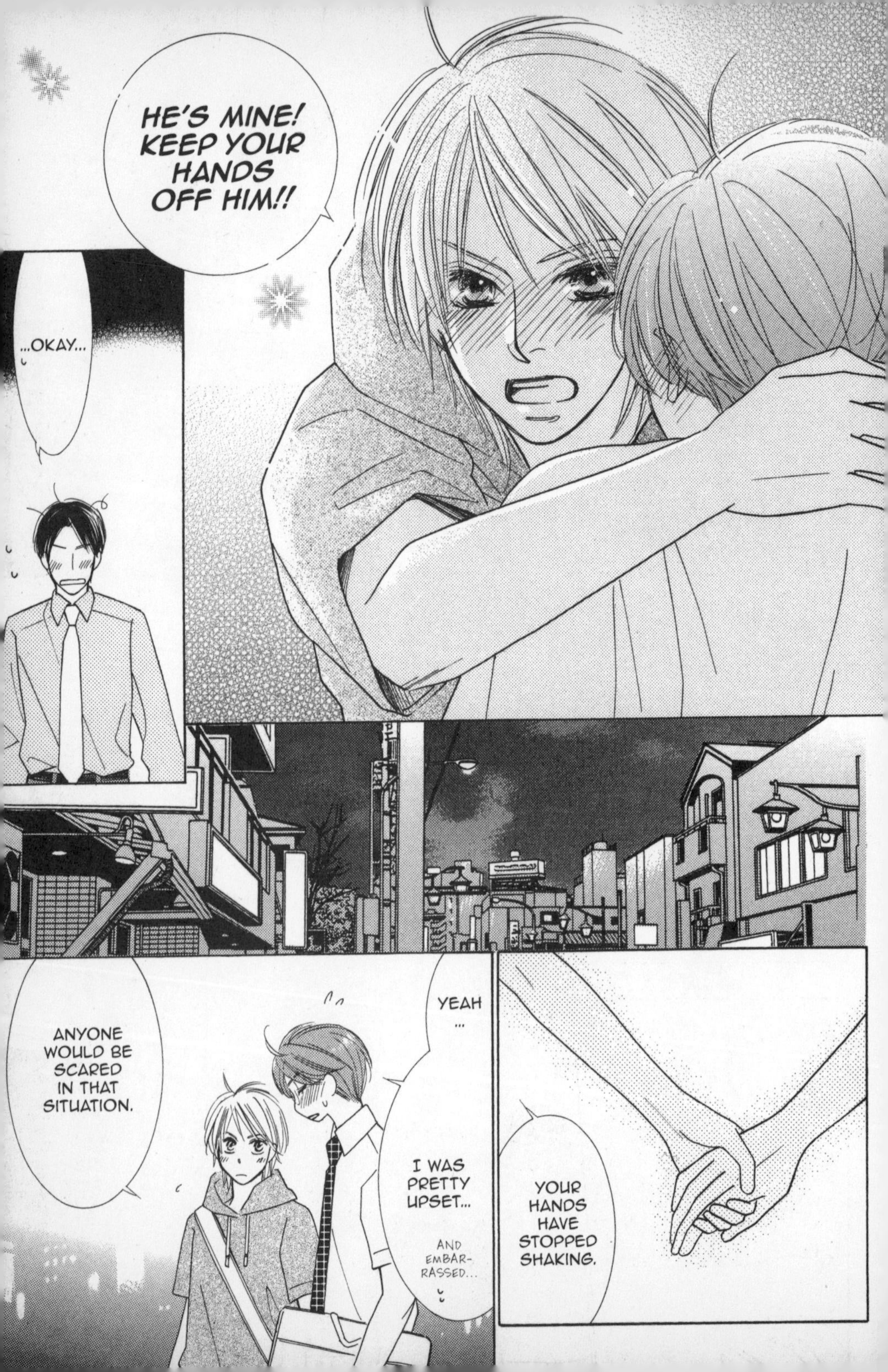
HE'S MINE! KEEP YOUR HANDS OFF HIM!!
...OKAY...
YOUR HANDS HAVE STOPPED SHAKING.
YEAH ...
I WAS PRETTY UPSET...
AND EMBARRASSED...
ANYONE WOULD BE SCARED IN THAT SITUATION.

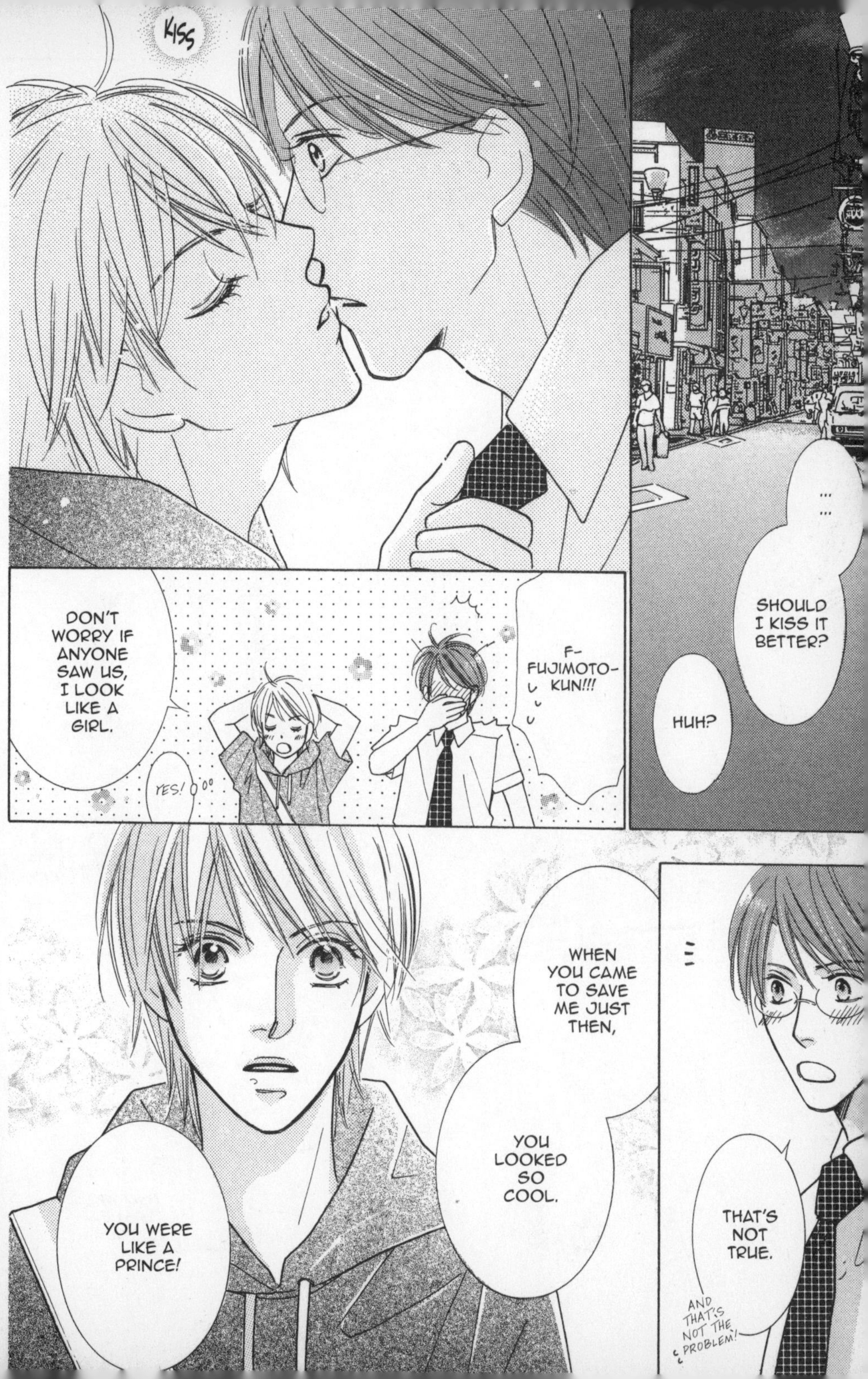
... ...
SHOULD I KISS IT BETTER?
HUH?
KISS
F-FUJIMOTO-KUN!!!
DON'T WORRY IF ANYONE SAW US, I LOOK LIKE A GIRL.
YES!
THAT'S NOT TRUE.
AND THAT'S NOT THE PROBLEM!
WHEN YOU CAME TO SAVE ME JUST THEN,
YOU LOOKED SO COOL.
YOU WERE LIKE A PRINCE!

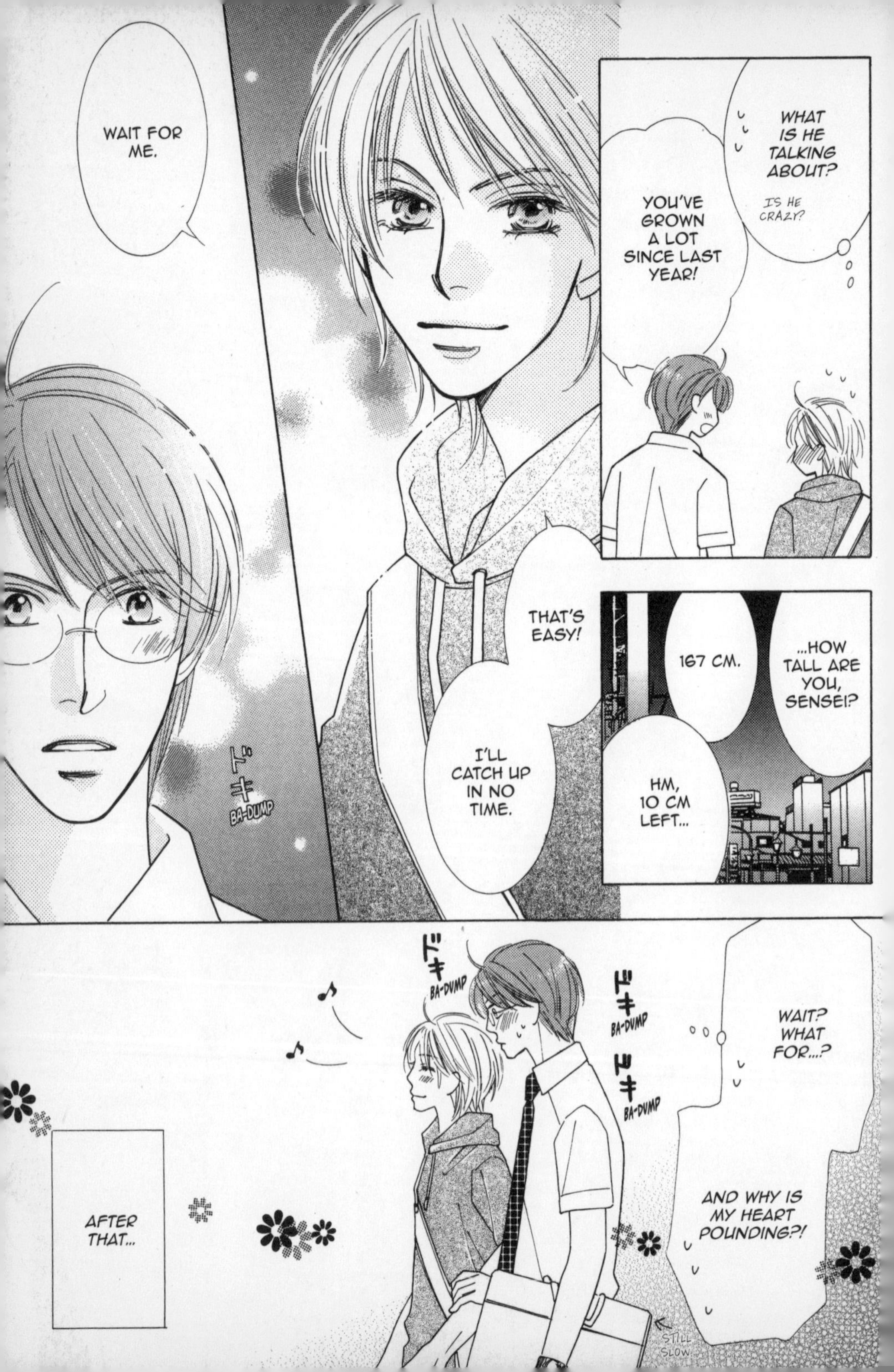
WHAT IS HE TALKING ABOUT?
IS HE CRAZY?
YOU'VE GROWN A LOT SINCE LAST YEAR!
...HOW TALL ARE YOU, SENSEI?
167 CM.
HM, 10 CM LEFT...
THAT'S EASY!
I'LL CATCH UP IN NO TIME.
WAIT FOR ME.
ドキ
BA-DUMP
WAIT? WHAT FOR...?
AND WHY IS MY HEART POUNDING?!
ドキ
BA-DUMP
ドキ
BA-DUMP
ドキ
BA-DUMP
STILL SLOW
AFTER THAT...

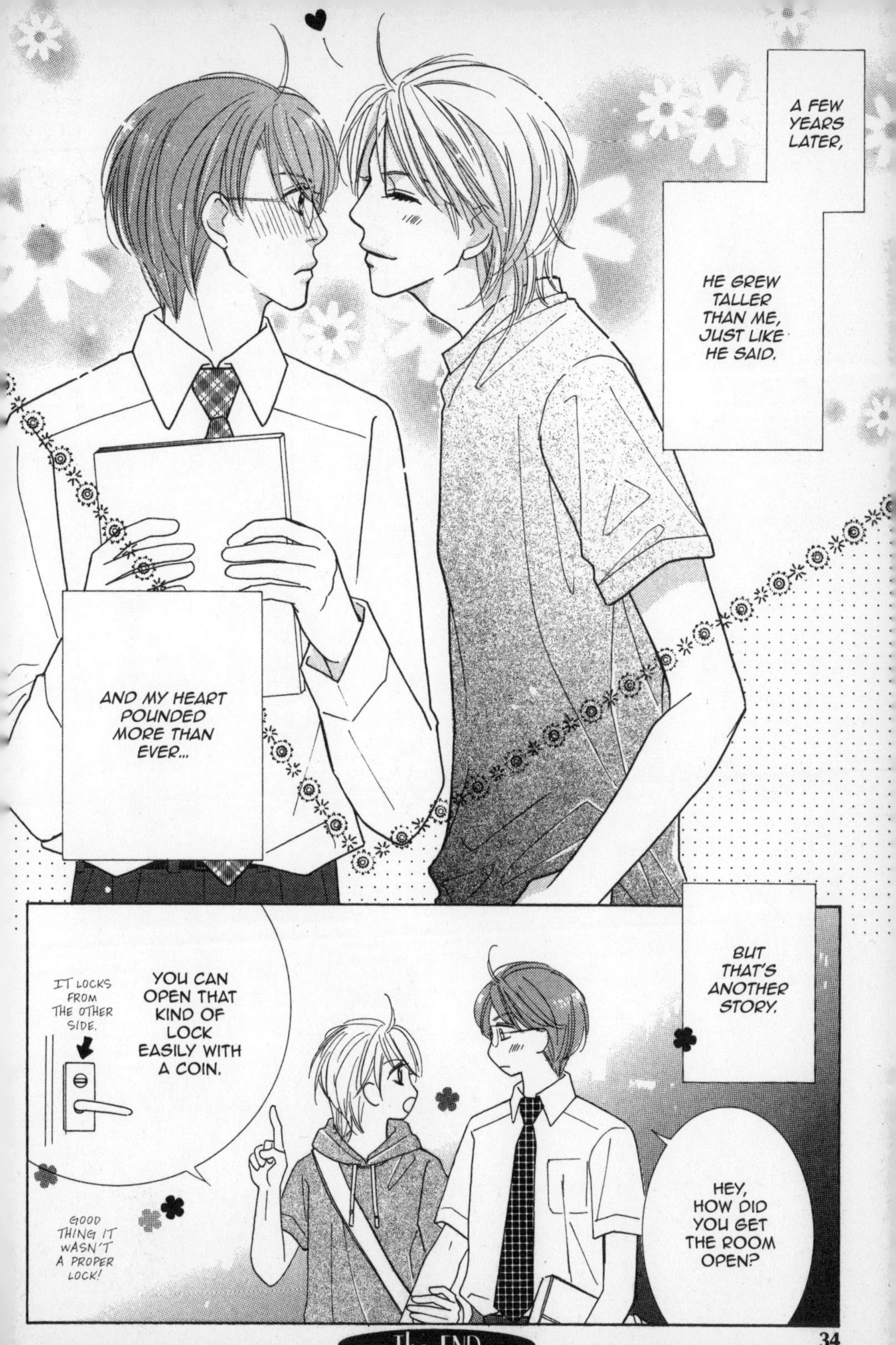
A FEW YEARS LATER,
HE GREW TALLER THAN ME, JUST LIKE HE SAID.
AND MY HEART POUNDED MORE THAN EVER...
BUT THAT'S ANOTHER STORY.
HEY, HOW DID YOU GET THE ROOM OPEN?
YOU CAN OPEN THAT KIND OF LOCK EASILY WITH A COIN.
IT LOCKS FROM THE OTHER SIDE.
GOOD THING IT WASN'T A PROPER LOCK!

The END

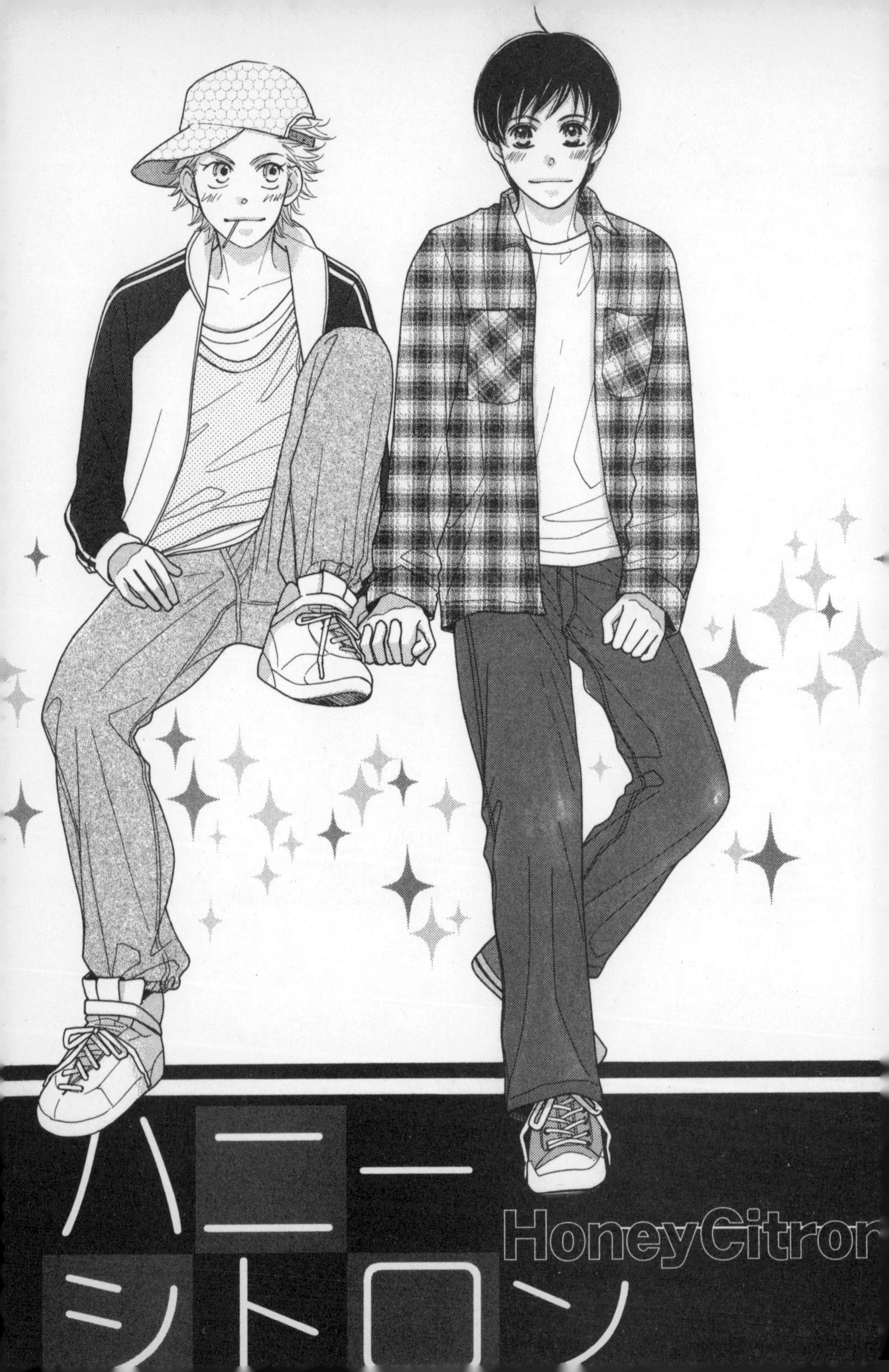
ハニーシトロン
HoneyCitron

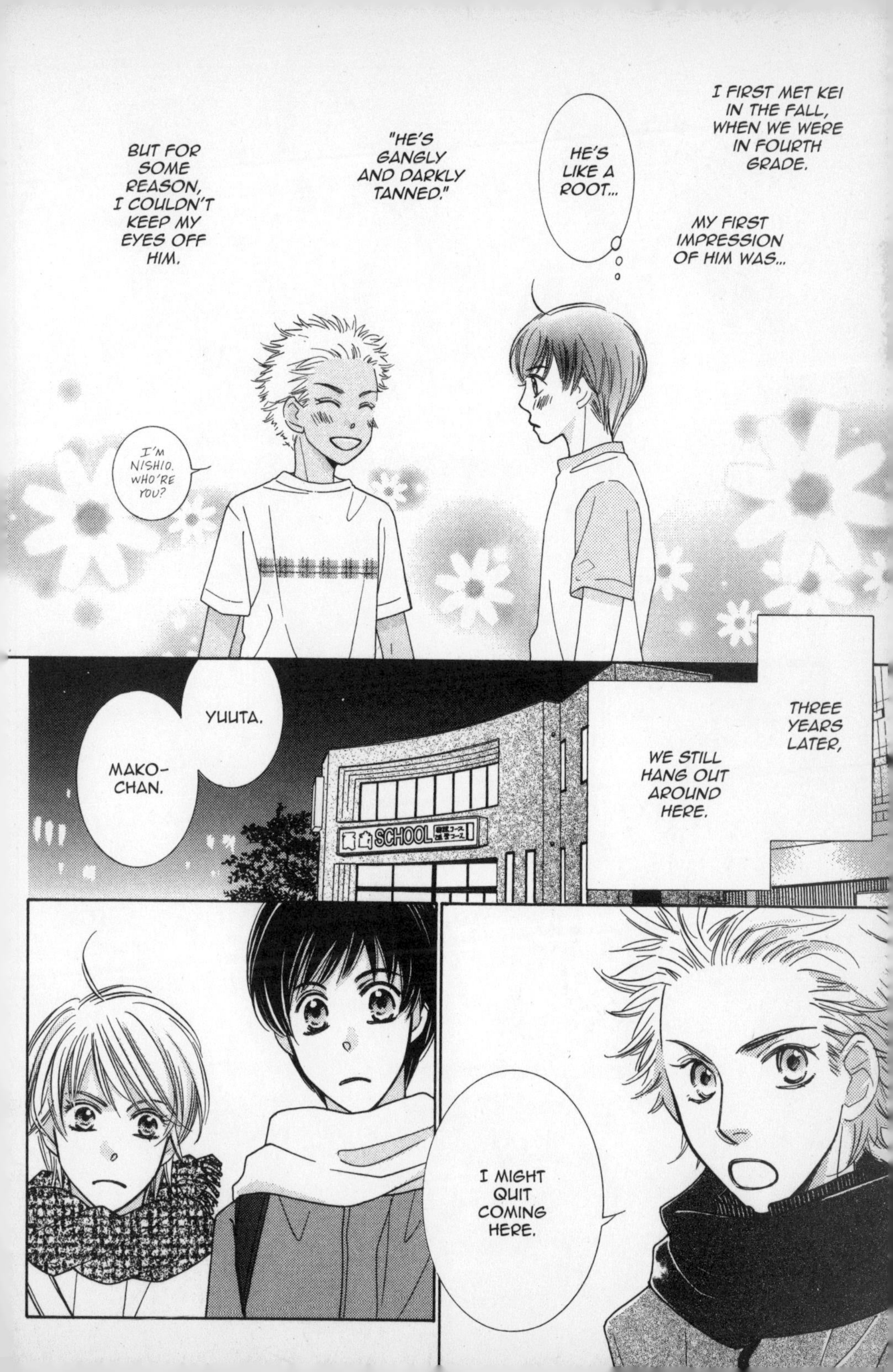
I FIRST MET KEI IN THE FALL, WHEN WE WERE IN FOURTH GRADE.
MY FIRST IMPRESSION OF HIM WAS...
HE'S LIKE A ROOT...
"HE'S GANGLY AND DARKLY TANNED."
BUT FOR SOME REASON, I COULDN'T KEEP MY EYES OFF HIM.
I'M NISHIO. WHO'RE YOU?
THREE YEARS LATER,
WE STILL HANG OUT AROUND HERE.
SCHOOL
YUUTA.
MAKO-CHAN.
I MIGHT QUIT COMING HERE.

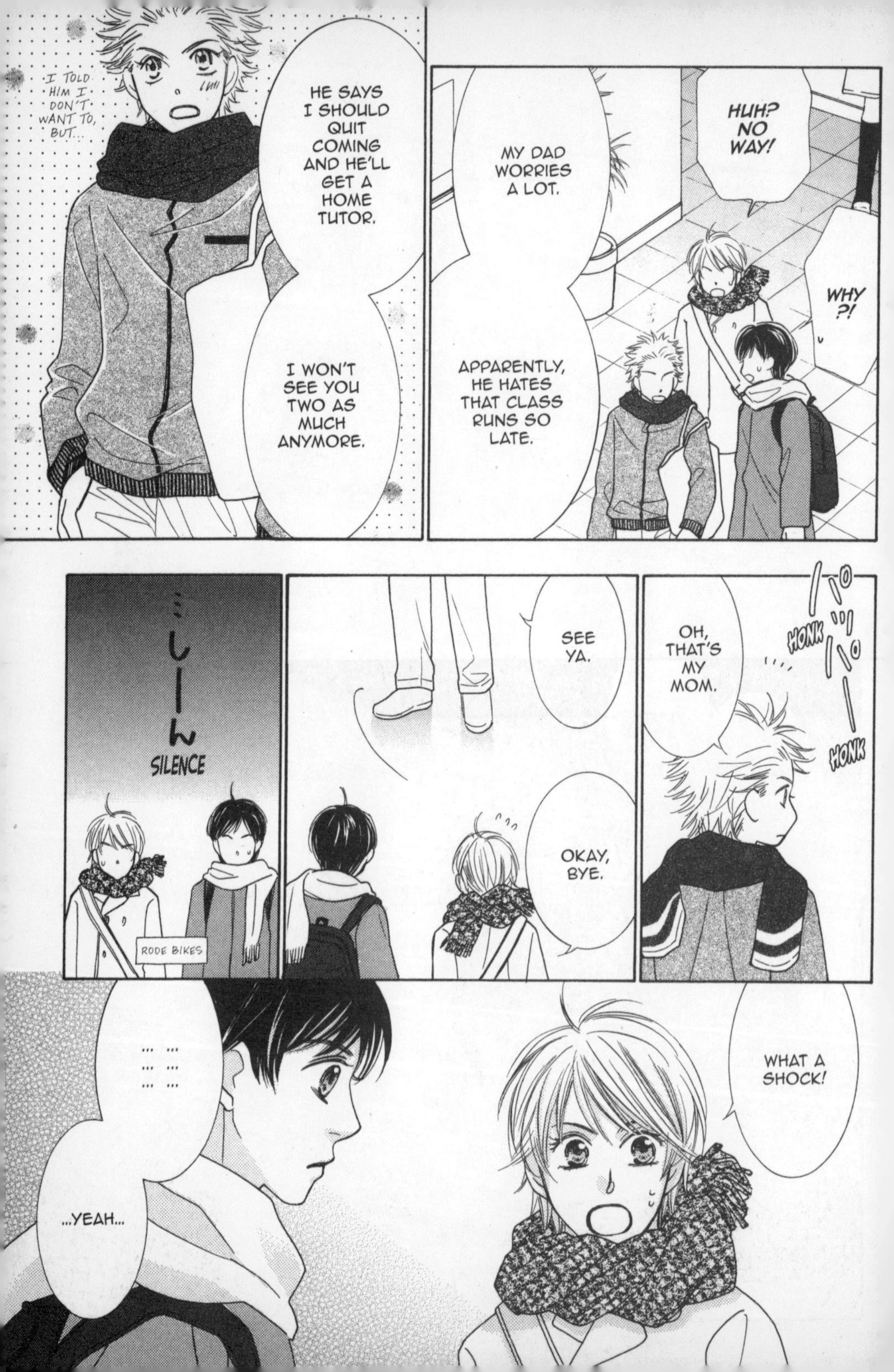

HUH? NO WAY!
WHY?!
MY DAD WORRIES A LOT.
APPARENTLY, HE HATES THAT CLASS RUNS SO LATE.
HE SAYS I SHOULD QUIT COMING AND HE'LL GET A HOME TUTOR.
I WON'T SEE YOU TWO AS MUCH ANYMORE.
I TOLD HIM I DON'T WANT TO, BUT...
HONK
HONK
OH, THAT'S MY MOM.
SEE YA.
OKAY, BYE.
SILENCE
RODE BIKES
WHAT A SHOCK!
......
...YEAH...

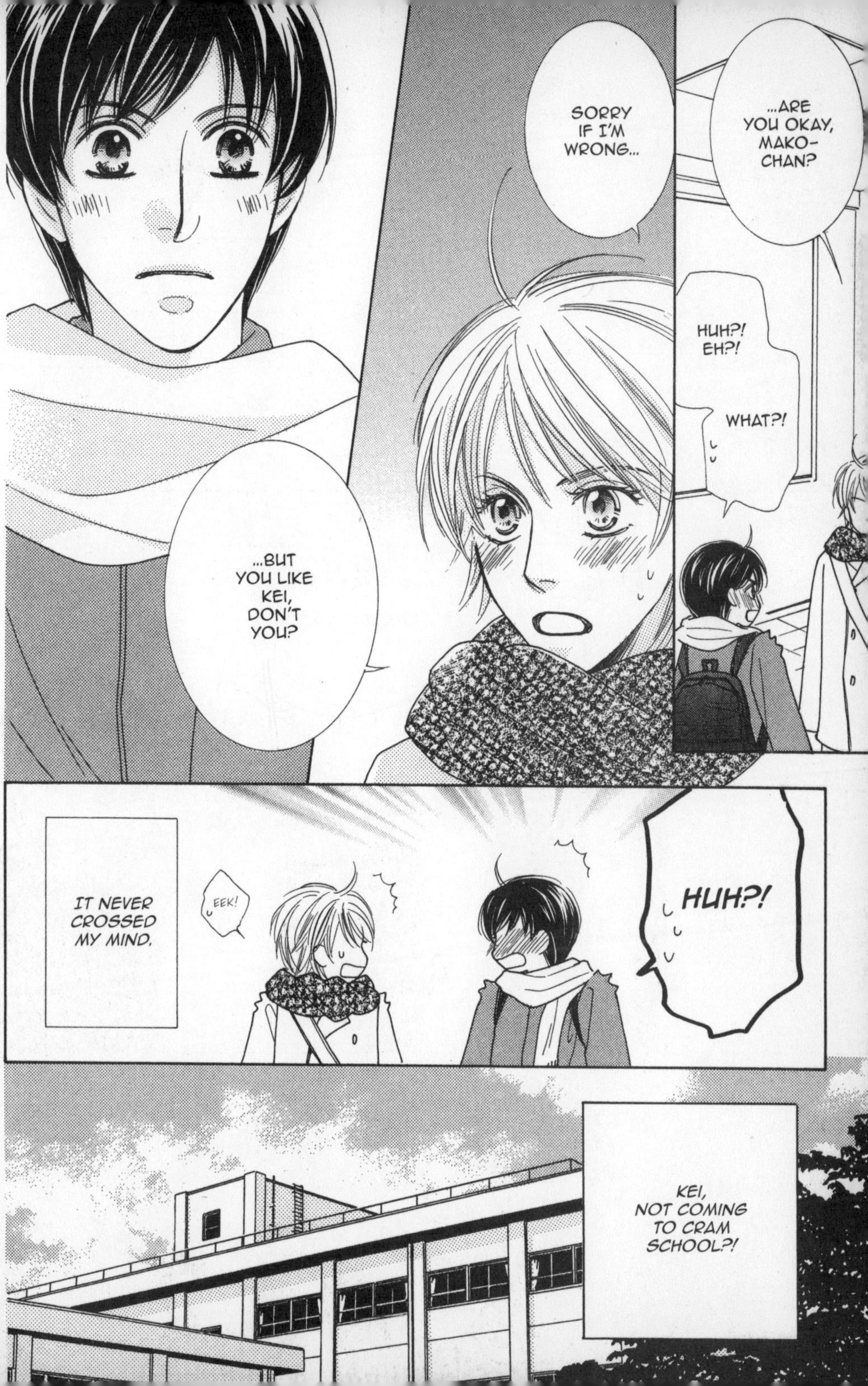
...ARE YOU OKAY, MAKO-CHAN?
HUH?! EH?!
WHAT?!
SORRY IF I'M WRONG...
...BUT YOU LIKE KEI, DON'T YOU?
HUH?!
EEK!
IT NEVER CROSSED MY MIND.
KEI, NOT COMING TO CRAM SCHOOL?!

ひょこ PEEK

WE HARDLY SEE EACH OTHER AT SCHOOL...

BUT WE'RE IN DIFFERENT CLASSES AND DO DIFFERENT THINGS.

THE THREE OF US GO TO THE SAME JUNIOR HIGH.

TRACK

3F	1-4	1-5		

2F	1-1	1-2	1-3		

SOCCER

BASKETBALL

YOSHIZAWA, ARE YOU HERE?

LUNCH BREAK

...HUH? WHAT?

UM,

YOU KNOW...

ザワ CHATTER

ザワ CHATTER

THAT'S FUJIMOTO-KUN! ♡

HM? WHAT?

ばっ BOW

STARTLE ぎょっ

SORRY FOR BEING WEIRD YESTERDAY!!

...USUALLY, ANYWAY.

HUH?

YUUTA!

WHAT'S UP?

FULL NAME: MAKOTO YOSHIZAWA

...

LET'S GO SOMEWHERE ELSE.

OKAY.

WHAT'S HE SORRY FOR?

MAKO'S FRIENDS WITH FUJIMOTO?

I WONDER WHAT'S GOING ON.

わい CHATTER

わい CHATTER

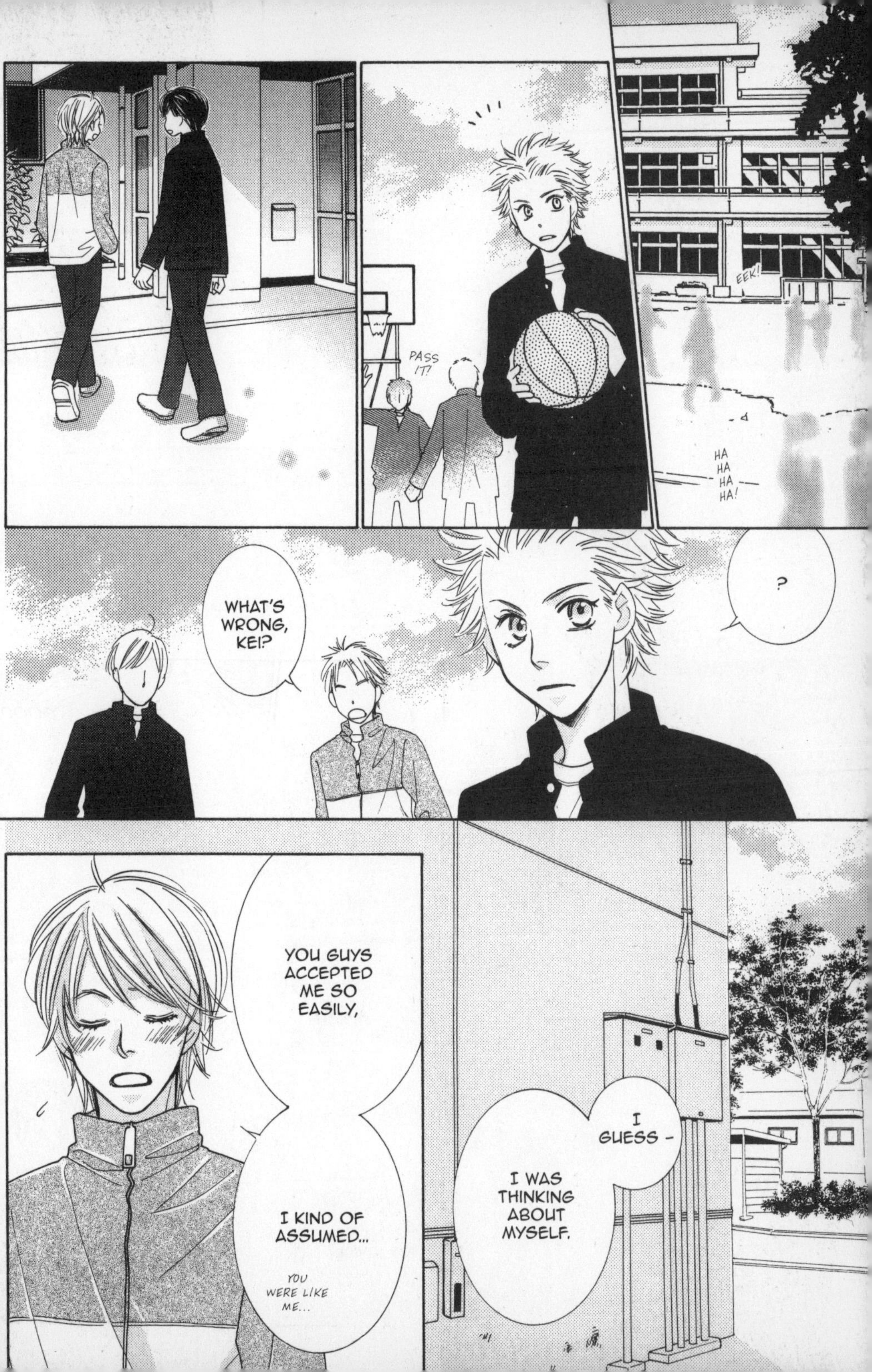
EEK!
HA HA HA HA!
PASS IT!
?
WHAT'S WRONG, KEI?
I GUESS -
I WAS THINKING ABOUT MYSELF.
YOU GUYS ACCEPTED ME SO EASILY,
I KIND OF ASSUMED...
YOU WERE LIKE ME...

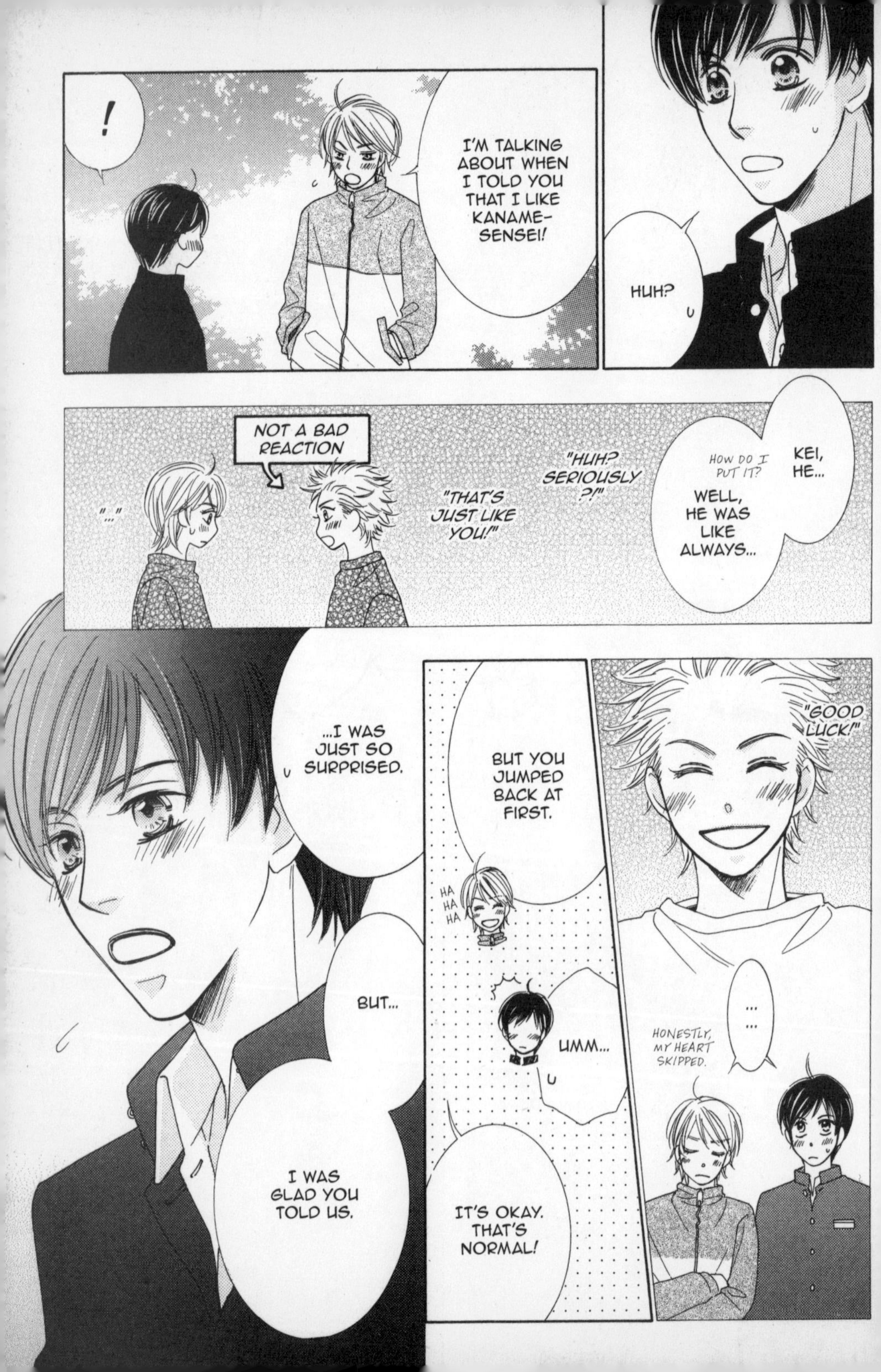
HUH?
I'M TALKING ABOUT WHEN I TOLD YOU THAT I LIKE KANAME-SENSEI!
!
KEI, HE...
HOW DO I PUT IT?
WELL, HE WAS LIKE ALWAYS...
"HUH? SERIOUSLY?!"
"THAT'S JUST LIKE YOU!"
NOT A BAD REACTION
"..."
"GOOD LUCK!"
... ...
HONESTLY, MY HEART SKIPPED.
BUT YOU JUMPED BACK AT FIRST.
HA HA HA
UMM...
IT'S OKAY. THAT'S NORMAL!
...I WAS JUST SO SURPRISED.
BUT...
I WAS GLAD YOU TOLD US.

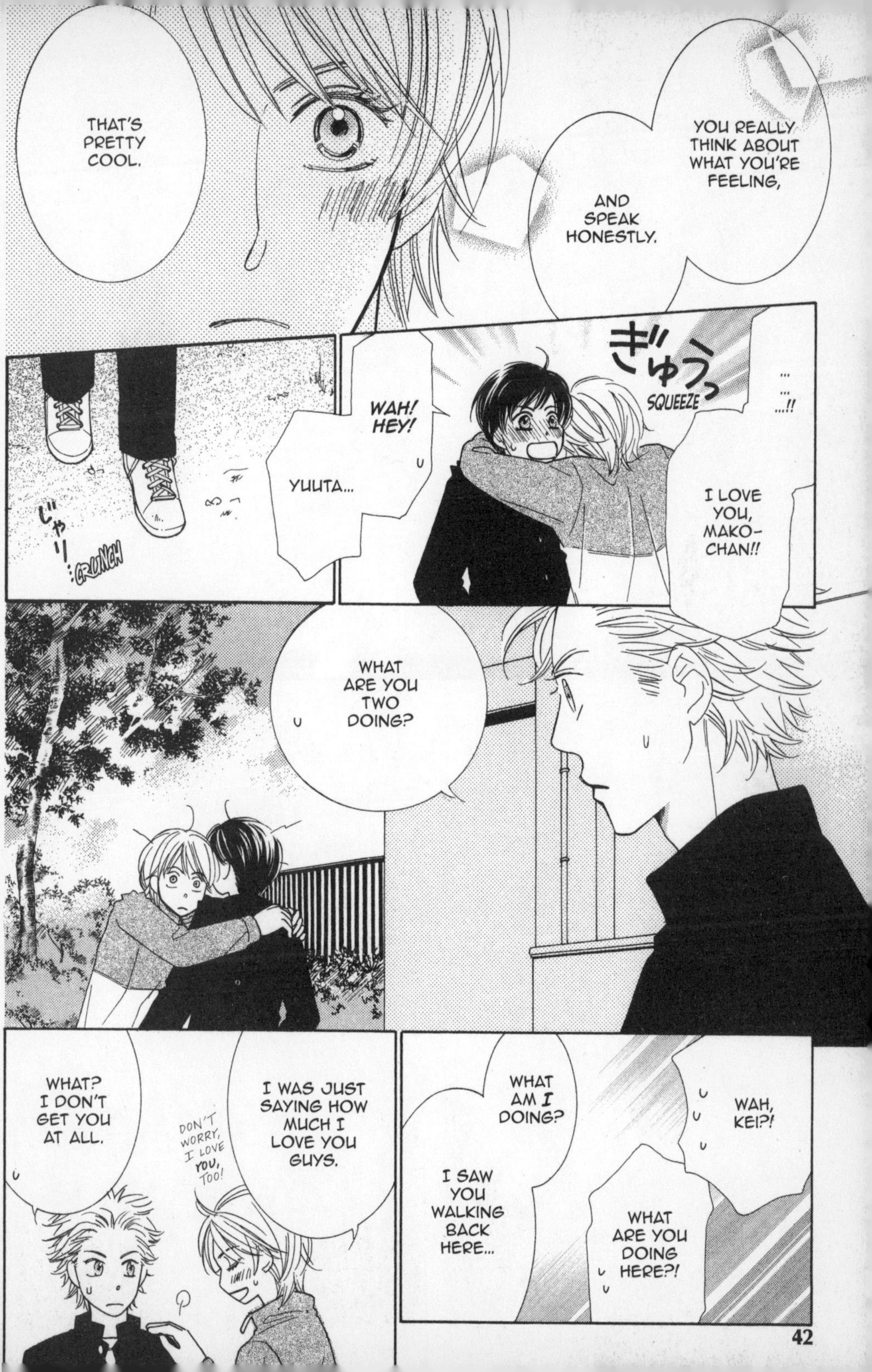
YOU REALLY THINK ABOUT WHAT YOU'RE FEELING,
AND SPEAK HONESTLY.
THAT'S PRETTY COOL.
ぎゅうっ
SQUEEZE
... ...!!
I LOVE YOU, MAKO-CHAN!!
WAH! HEY!
じゃり
CRUNCH
YUUTA...
WHAT ARE YOU TWO DOING?
WAH, KEI?!
WHAT ARE YOU DOING HERE?!
WHAT AM I DOING?
I SAW YOU WALKING BACK HERE...
I WAS JUST SAYING HOW MUCH I LOVE YOU GUYS.
DON'T WORRY, I LOVE YOU, TOO!
WHAT? I DON'T GET YOU AT ALL.

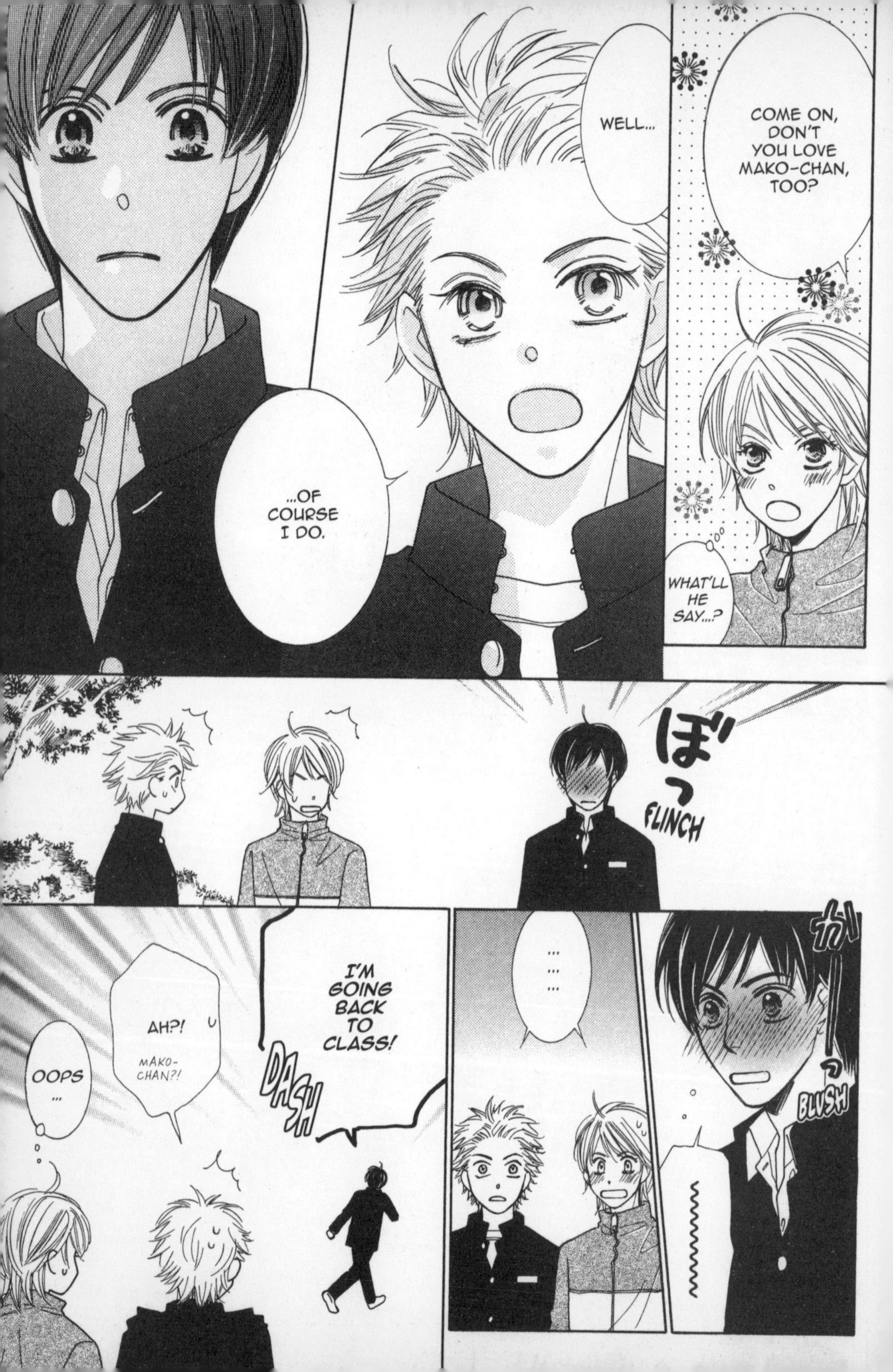
COME ON, DON'T YOU LOVE MAKO-CHAN, TOO?
WHAT'LL HE SAY...?
WELL...
...OF COURSE I DO.
ぼっ
FLINCH
かーっ
BLUSH
... ...
I'M GOING BACK TO CLASS!
DASH
AH?!
MAKO-CHAN?!
OOPS ...

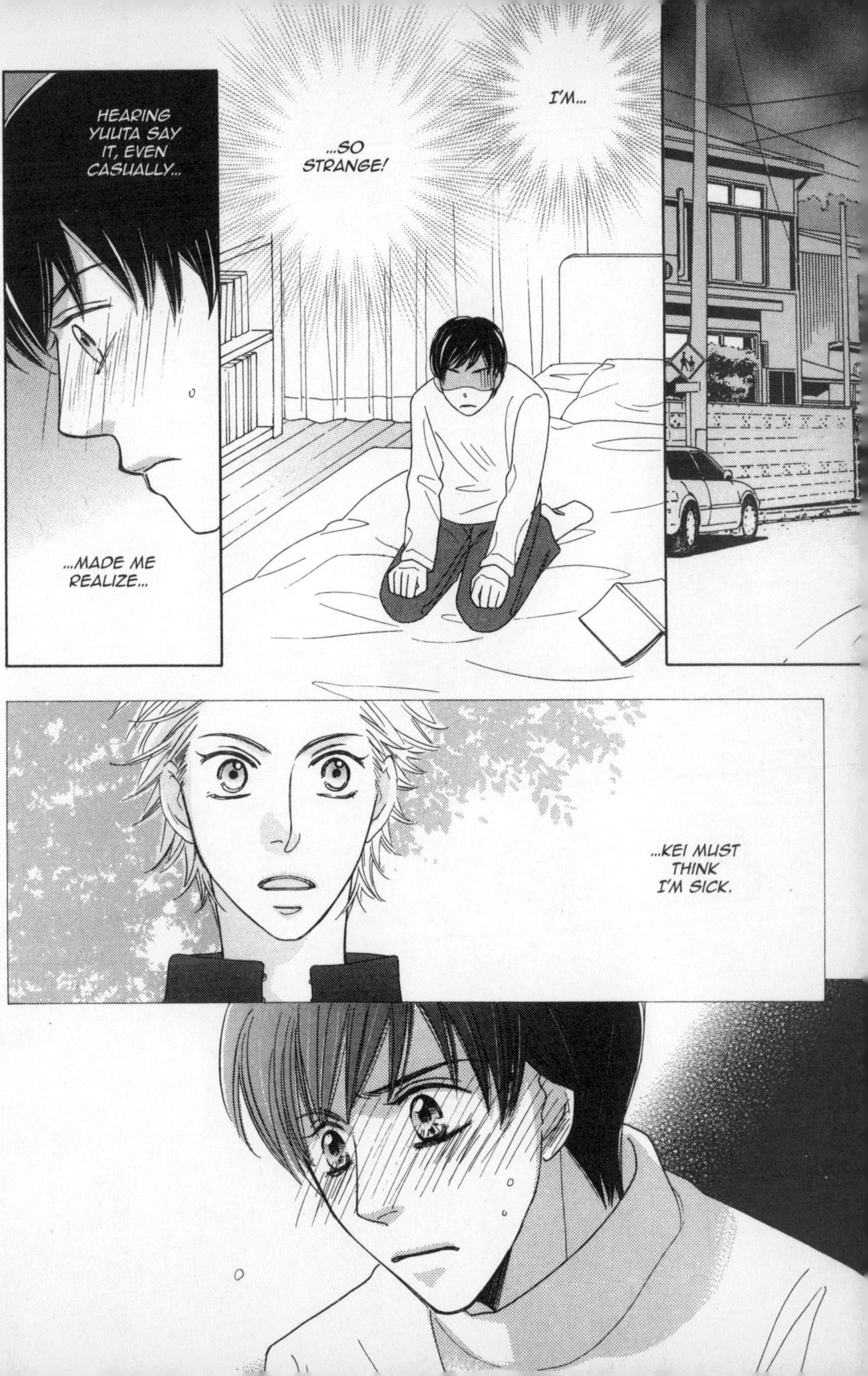
I'M...
...SO STRANGE!
HEARING YUUTA SAY IT, EVEN CASUALLY...
...MADE ME REALIZE...
...KEI MUST THINK I'M SICK.

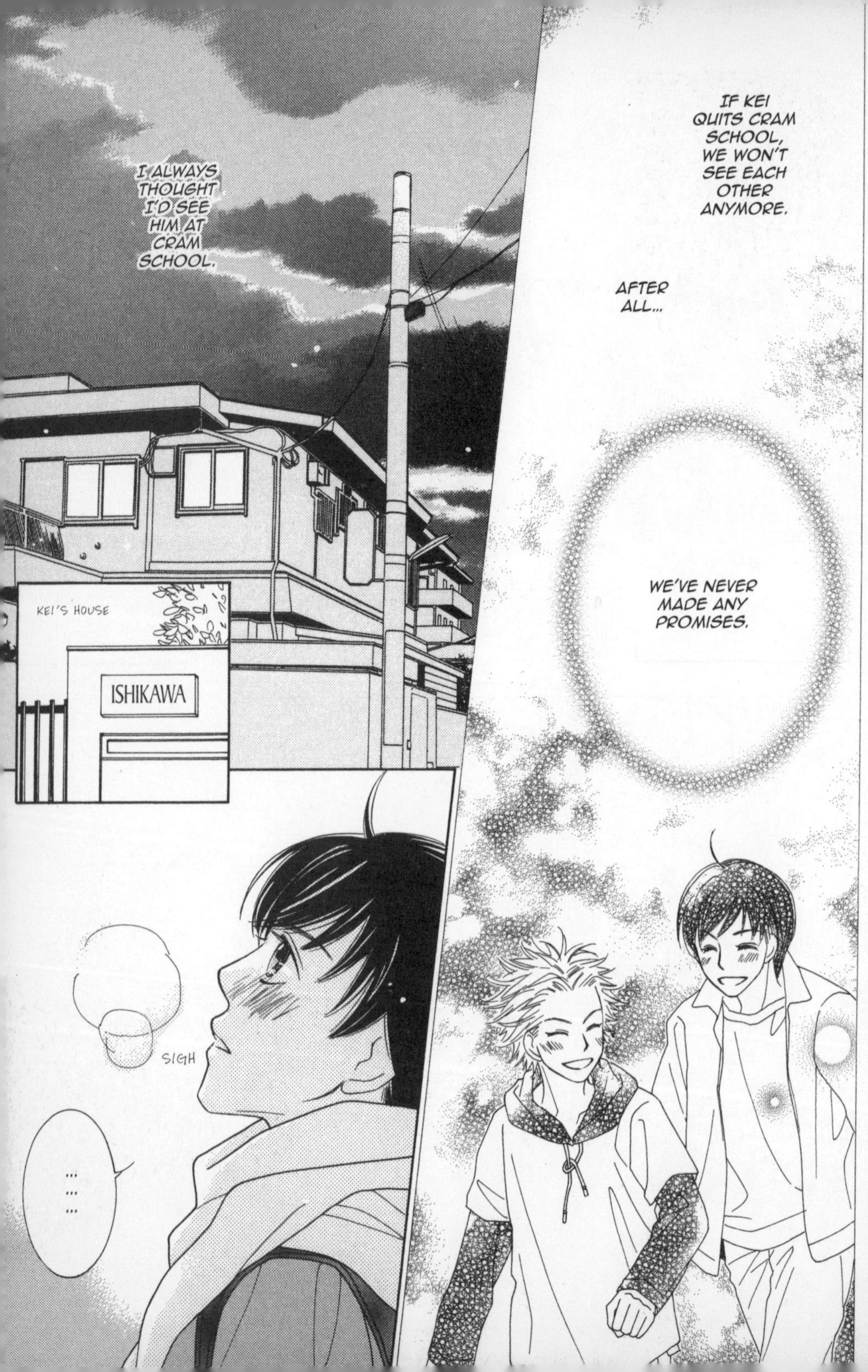
IF KEI QUITS CRAM SCHOOL, WE WON'T SEE EACH OTHER ANYMORE.
AFTER ALL...
WE'VE NEVER MADE ANY PROMISES.
I ALWAYS THOUGHT I'D SEE HIM AT CRAM SCHOOL.
KEI'S HOUSE
ISHIKAWA
SIGH
... ...

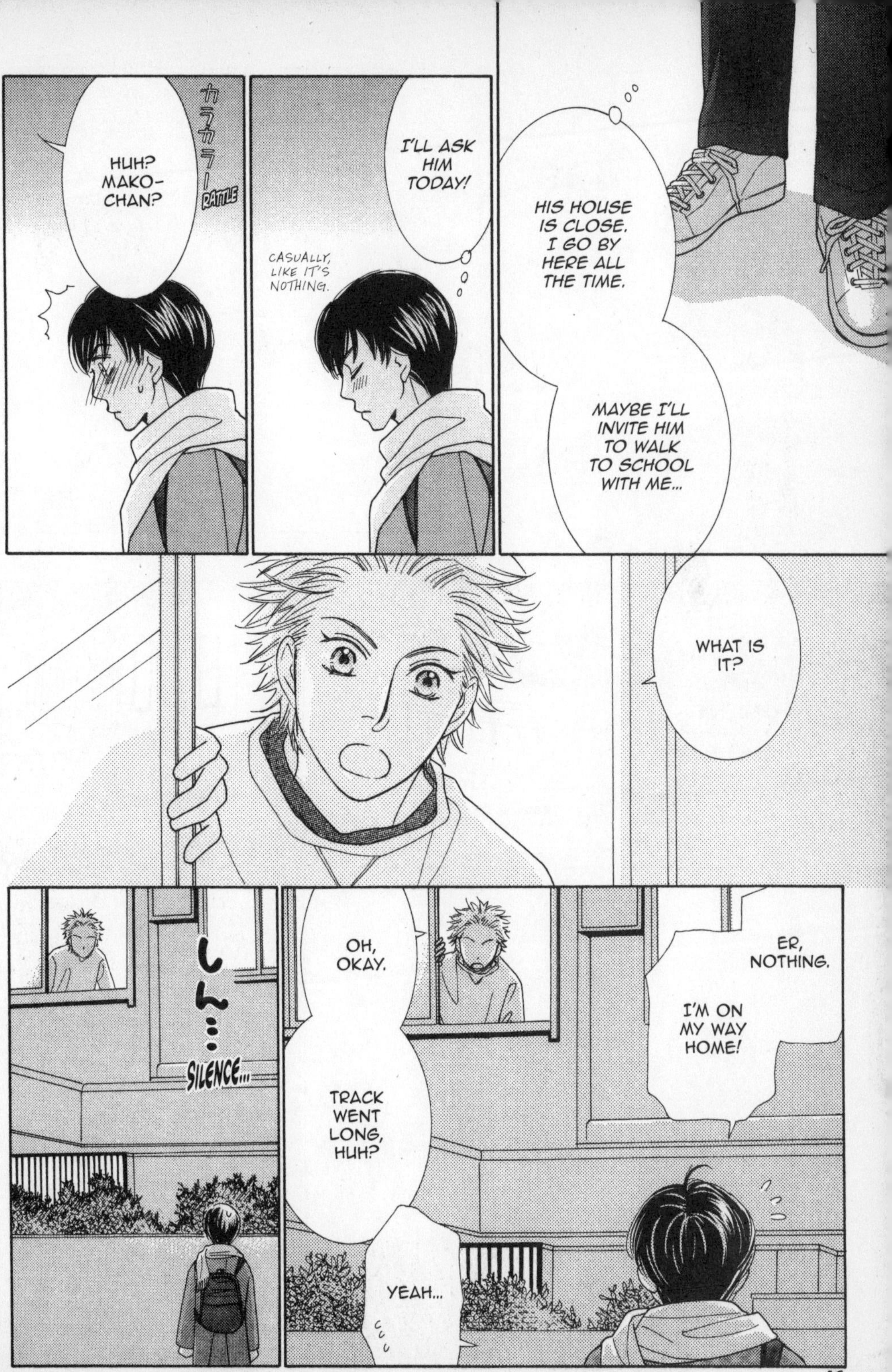
HIS HOUSE IS CLOSE. I GO BY HERE ALL THE TIME.
MAYBE I'LL INVITE HIM TO WALK TO SCHOOL WITH ME...
I'LL ASK HIM TODAY!
CASUALLY, LIKE IT'S NOTHING.
HUH? MAKO-CHAN?
カラカラ
RATTLE
WHAT IS IT?
ER, NOTHING.
I'M ON MY WAY HOME!
OH, OKAY.
TRACK WENT LONG, HUH?
YEAH...
しん…
SILENCE...

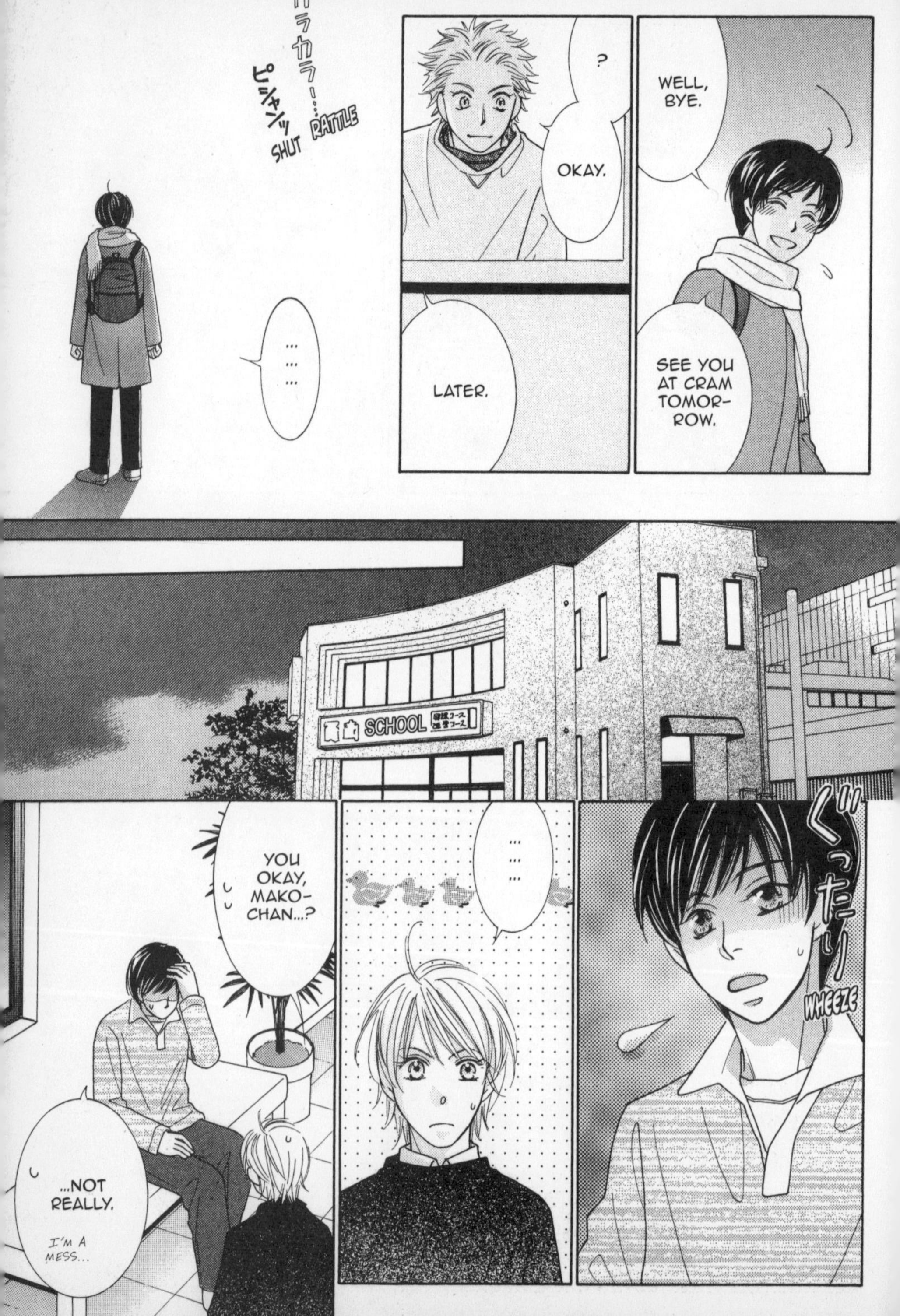
WELL, BYE.
SEE YOU AT CRAM TOMOR-ROW.
?
OKAY.
LATER.
カラカラ…
RATTLE
ピシャンッ
SHUT
……
SCHOOL
ぐったり
WHEEZE
……
YOU OKAY, MAKO-CHAN...?
...NOT REALLY.
I'M A MESS...

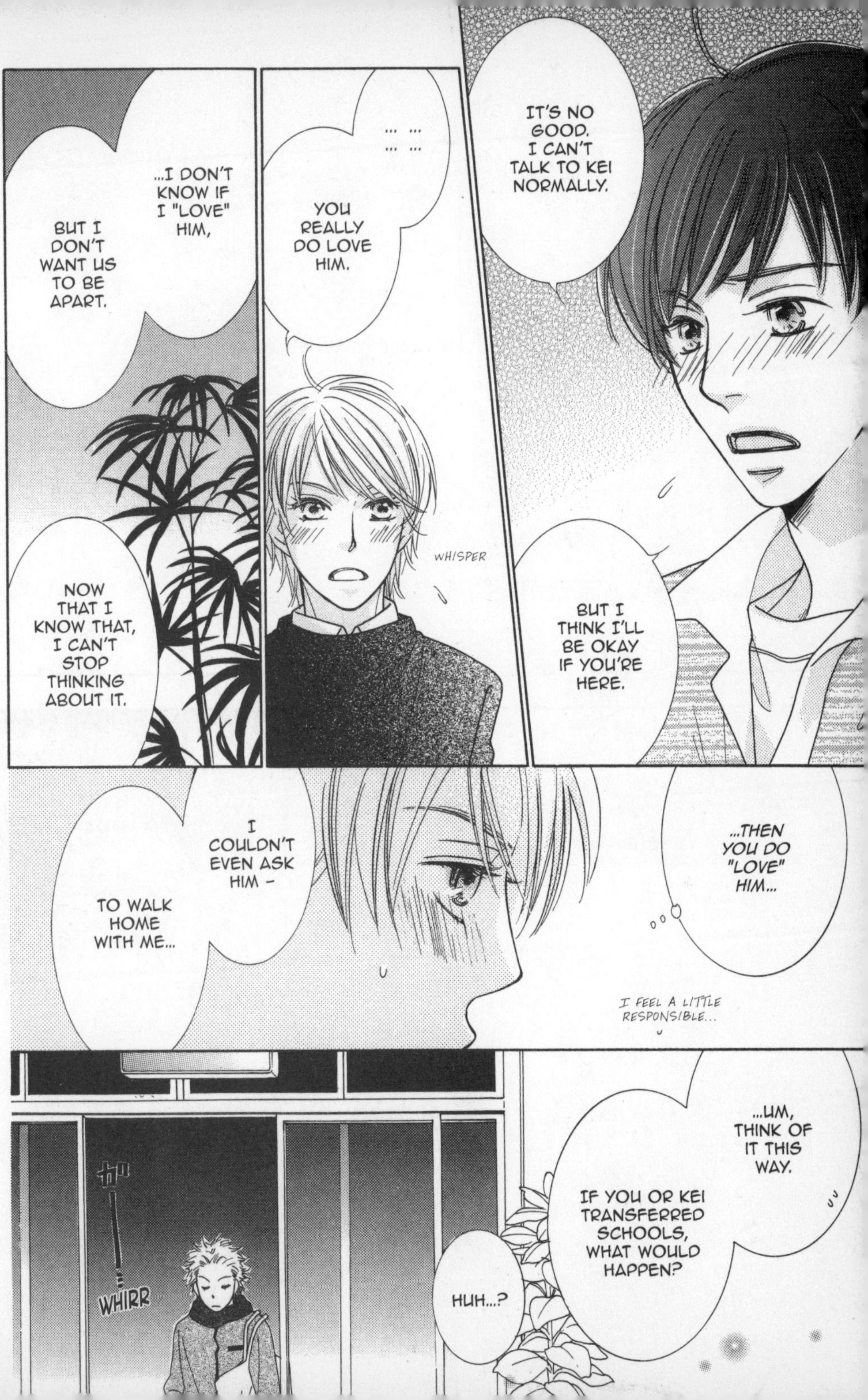
IT'S NO GOOD. I CAN'T TALK TO KEI NORMALLY.
BUT I THINK I'LL BE OKAY IF YOU'RE HERE.
... ...
... ...
YOU REALLY DO LOVE HIM.
WHISPER
...I DON'T KNOW IF I "LOVE" HIM,
BUT I DON'T WANT US TO BE APART.
NOW THAT I KNOW THAT, I CAN'T STOP THINKING ABOUT IT.
...THEN YOU DO "LOVE" HIM...
I FEEL A LITTLE RESPONSIBLE...
I COULDN'T EVEN ASK HIM -
TO WALK HOME WITH ME...
...UM, THINK OF IT THIS WAY.
IF YOU OR KEI TRANSFERRED SCHOOLS, WHAT WOULD HAPPEN?
HUH...?
WHIRR

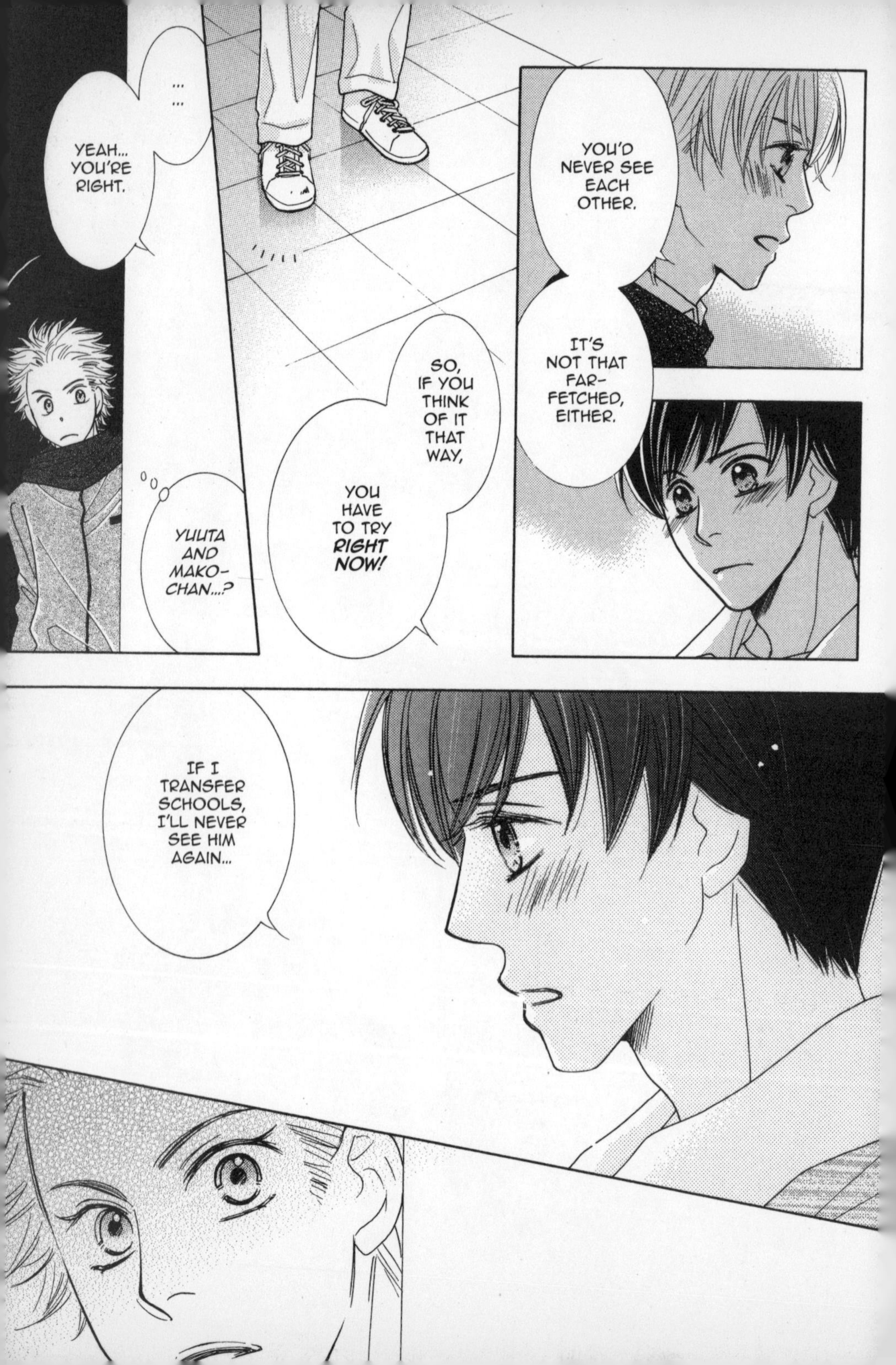
YOU'D NEVER SEE EACH OTHER.
IT'S NOT THAT FAR-FETCHED, EITHER.
SO, IF YOU THINK OF IT THAT WAY,
YOU HAVE TO TRY *RIGHT NOW!*
YUUTA AND MAKO-CHAN...?
... ...
YEAH... YOU'RE RIGHT.
IF I TRANSFER SCHOOLS, I'LL NEVER SEE HIM AGAIN...

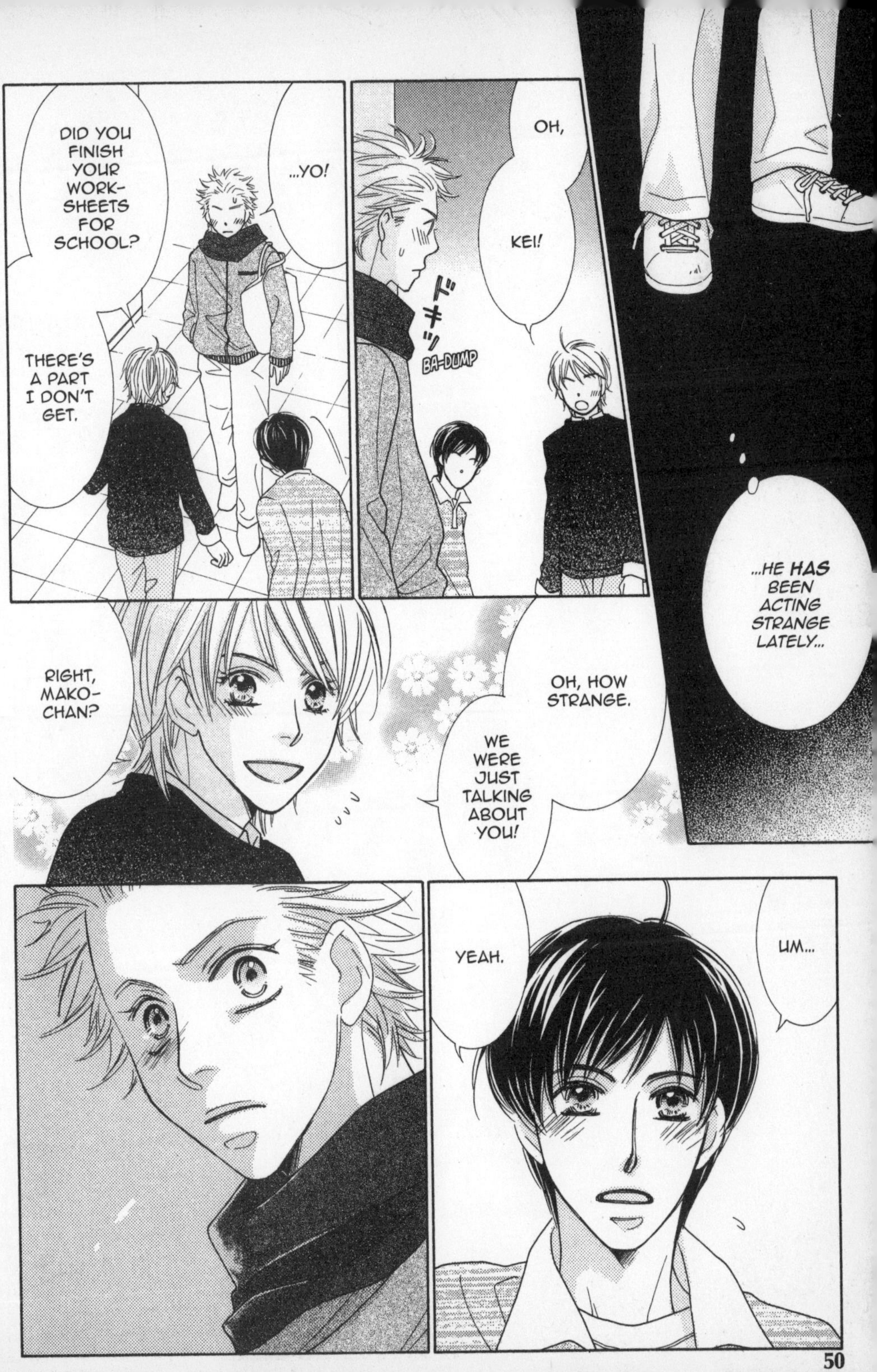
...HE HAS BEEN ACTING STRANGE LATELY...
OH,
KEI!
ドキッ
BA-DUMP
...YO!
DID YOU FINISH YOUR WORK-SHEETS FOR SCHOOL?
THERE'S A PART I DON'T GET.
OH, HOW STRANGE.
WE WERE JUST TALKING ABOUT YOU!
RIGHT, MAKO-CHAN?
UM...
YEAH.

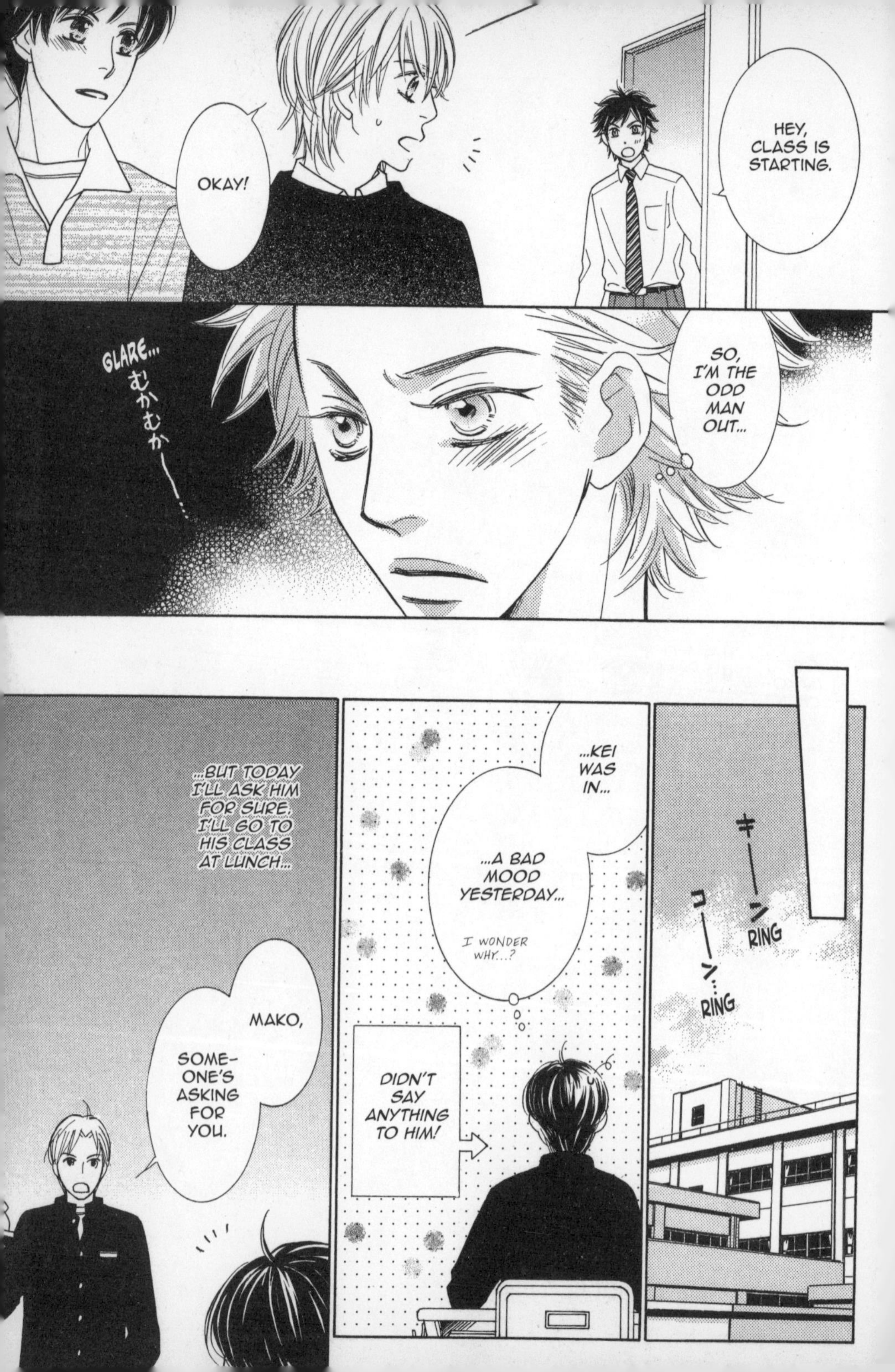
HEY, CLASS IS STARTING.
OKAY!
SO, I'M THE ODD MAN OUT...
GLARE...
むかむかー…
!
キーン
RING
コーン…
RING
...KEI WAS IN...
...A BAD MOOD YESTERDAY...
I WONDER WHY...?
DIDN'T SAY ANYTHING TO HIM!
...BUT TODAY I'LL ASK HIM FOR SURE. I'LL GO TO HIS CLASS AT LUNCH...
MAKO, SOME-ONE'S ASKING FOR YOU.

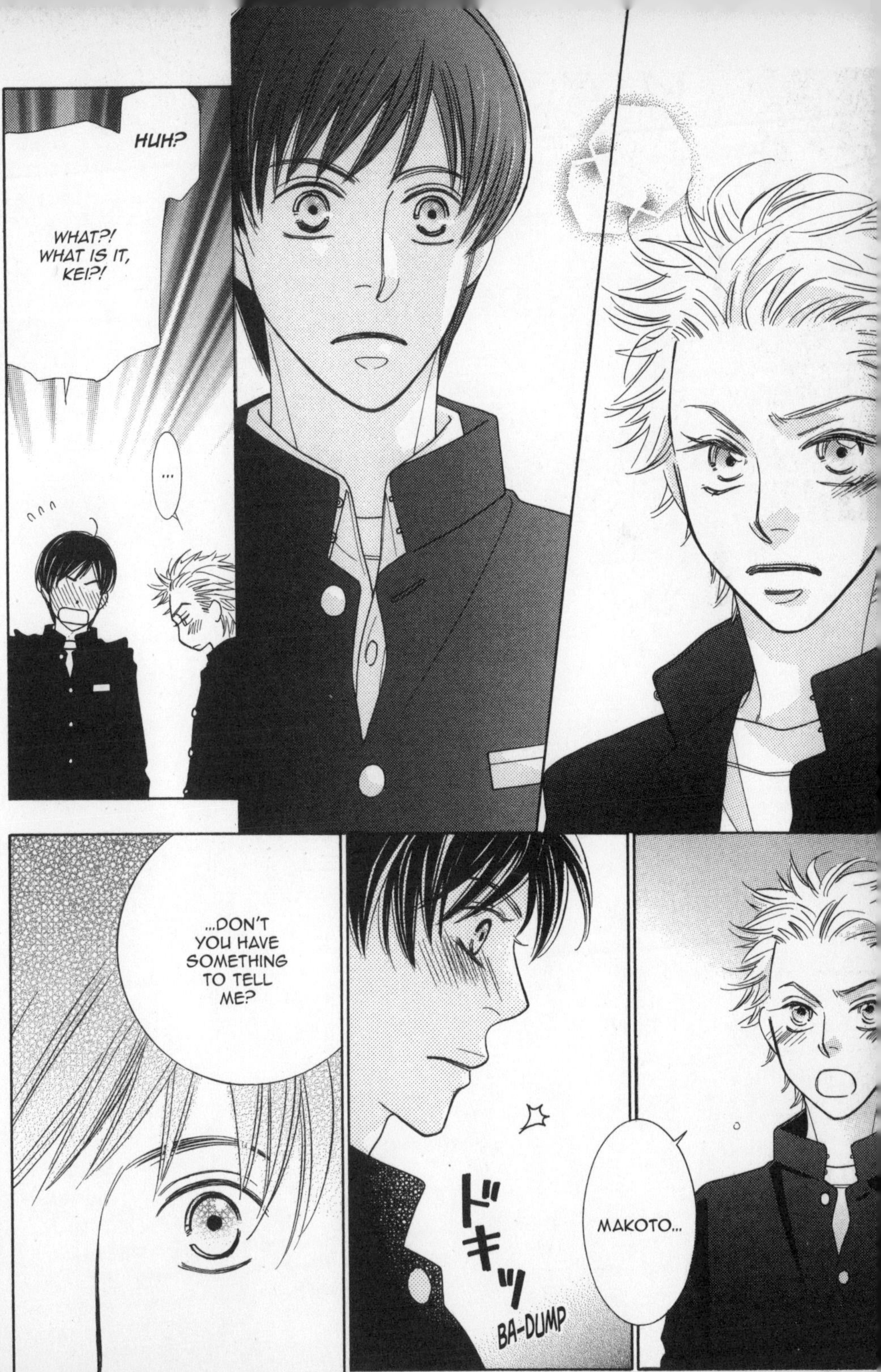
HUH?
WHAT?! WHAT IS IT, KEI?!
...
MAKOTO...
ドキッ
BA-DUMP
...DON'T YOU HAVE SOMETHING TO TELL ME?

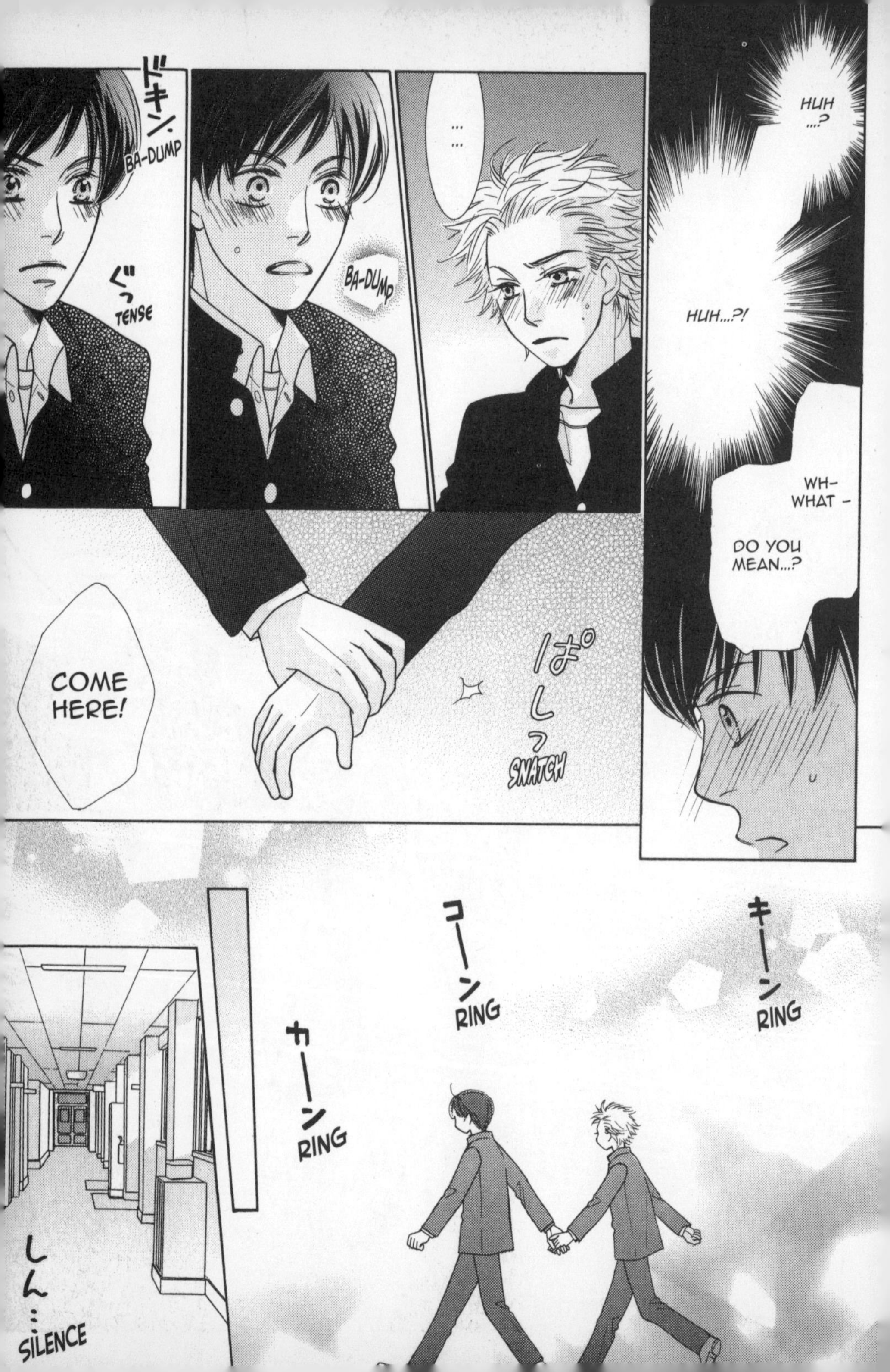
HUH ...?
HUH...?!
WH- WHAT -
DO YOU MEAN...?
... ...
BA-DUMP
ドキン
BA-DUMP
ぐっ
TENSE
ぱしっ
SNATCH
COME HERE!
キーン
RING
コーン
RING
カーン
RING
しん…
SILENCE

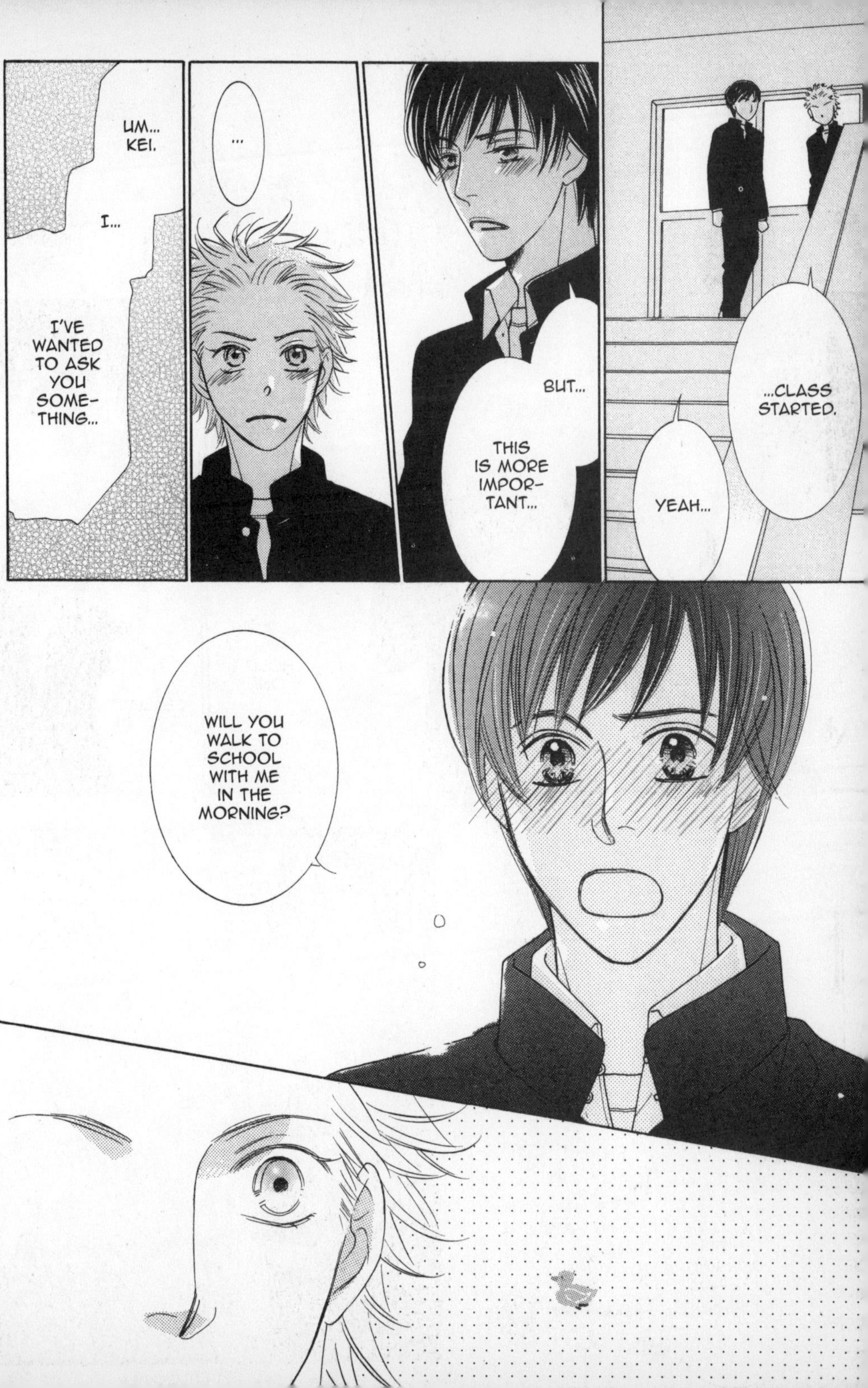
...CLASS STARTED.
YEAH...
BUT...
THIS IS MORE IMPORTANT...
...
UM... KEI.
I...
I'VE WANTED TO ASK YOU SOMETHING...
WILL YOU WALK TO SCHOOL WITH ME IN THE MORNING?

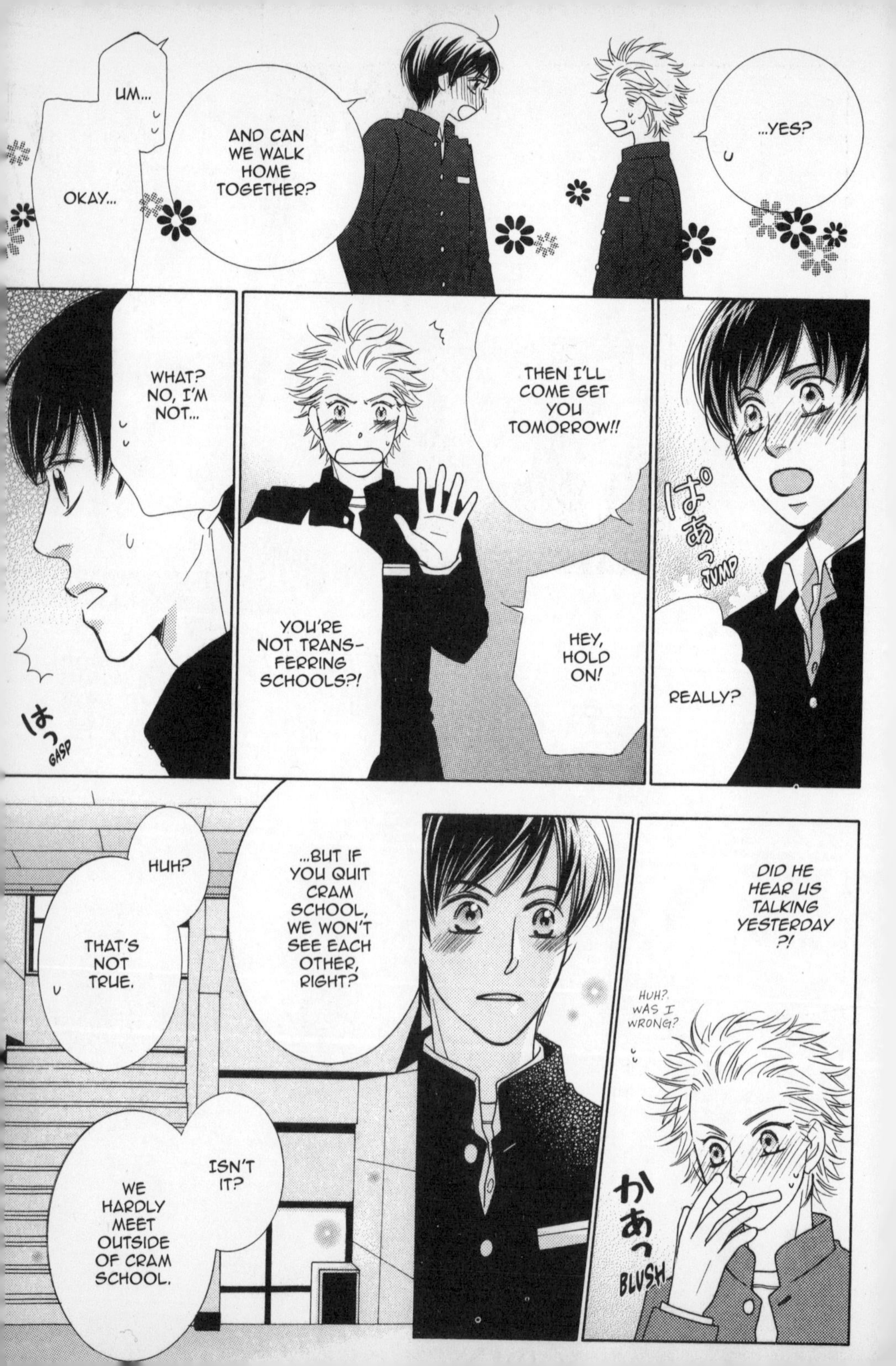
...YES?
AND CAN WE WALK HOME TOGETHER?
UM...
OKAY...
ぱあっ
JUMP
REALLY?
THEN I'LL COME GET YOU TOMORROW!!
HEY, HOLD ON!
YOU'RE NOT TRANS-FERRING SCHOOLS?!
WHAT? NO, I'M NOT...
はっ
GASP
DID HE HEAR US TALKING YESTERDAY ?!
HUH?. WAS I WRONG?
かあっ
BLUSH
...BUT IF YOU QUIT CRAM SCHOOL, WE WON'T SEE EACH OTHER, RIGHT?
HUH?
THAT'S NOT TRUE.
ISN'T IT?
WE HARDLY MEET OUTSIDE OF CRAM SCHOOL.

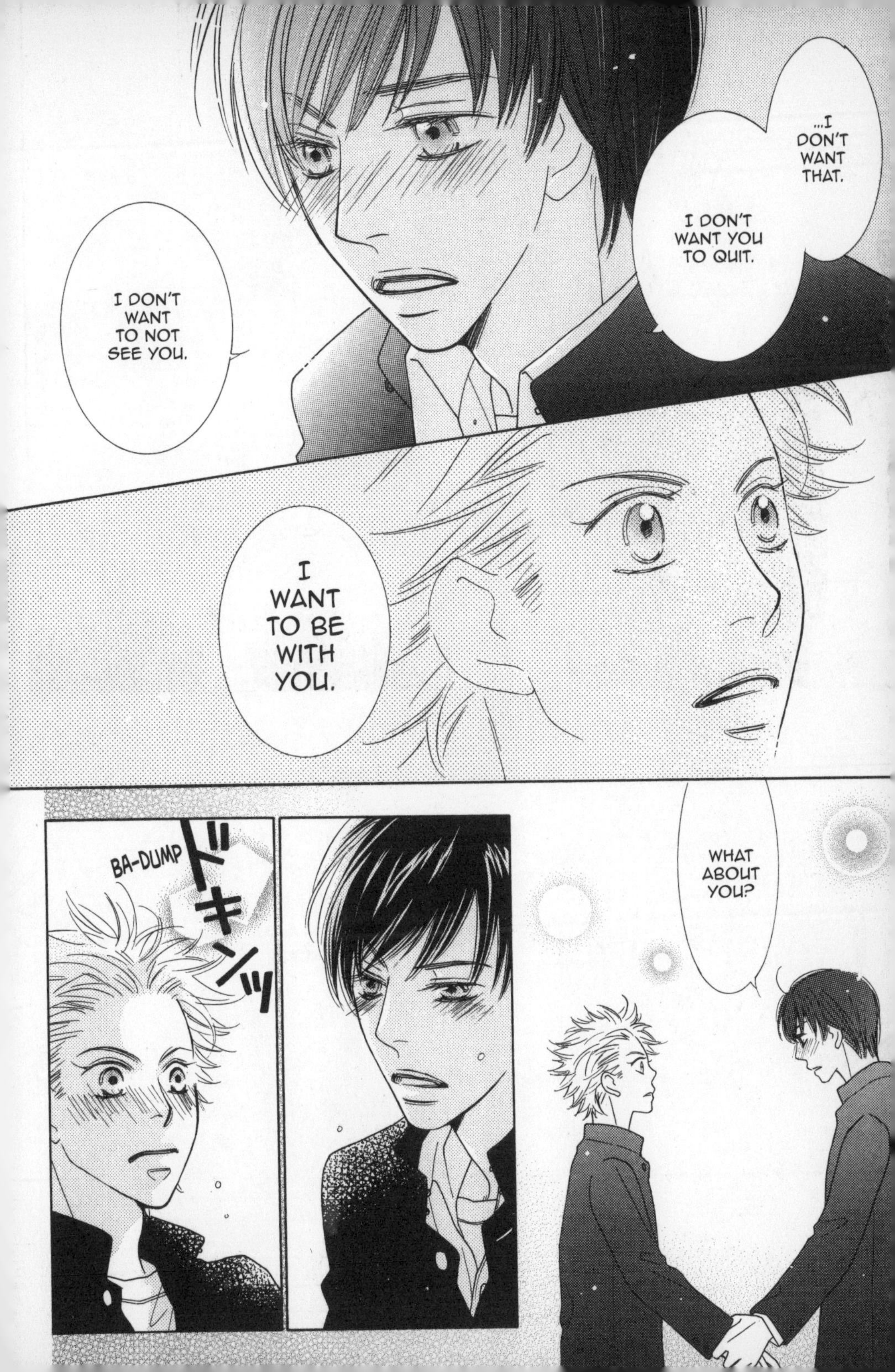
...I DON'T WANT THAT.
I DON'T WANT YOU TO QUIT.
I DON'T WANT TO NOT SEE YOU.
I WANT TO BE WITH YOU.
WHAT ABOUT YOU?
ドキンッ
BA-DUMP

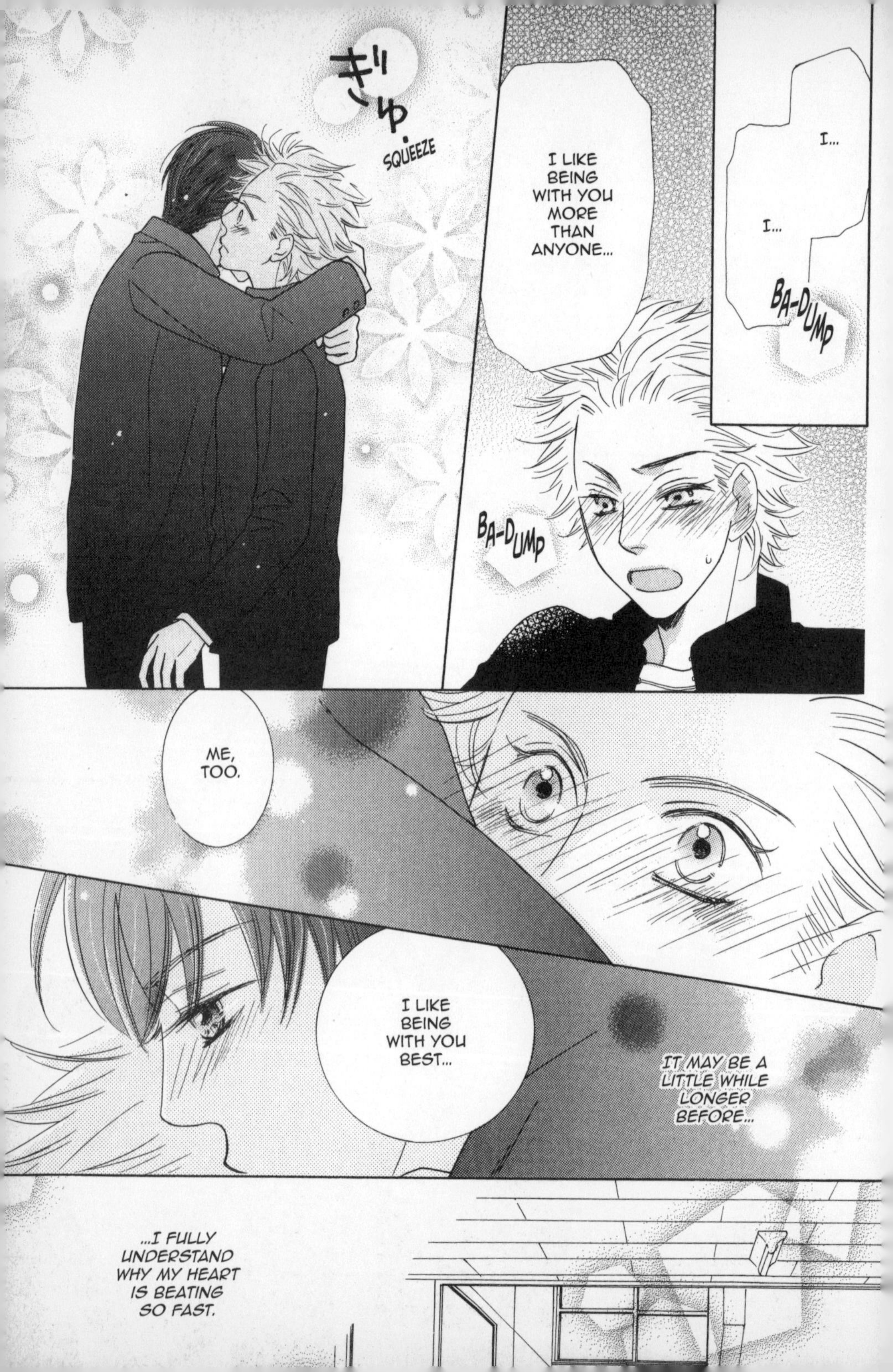
I...
I...
BA-DUMP
I LIKE BEING WITH YOU MORE THAN ANYONE...
BA-DUMP
ぎゅ
SQUEEZE
ME, TOO.
I LIKE BEING WITH YOU BEST...
IT MAY BE A LITTLE WHILE LONGER BEFORE...
...I FULLY UNDERSTAND WHY MY HEART IS BEATING SO FAST.

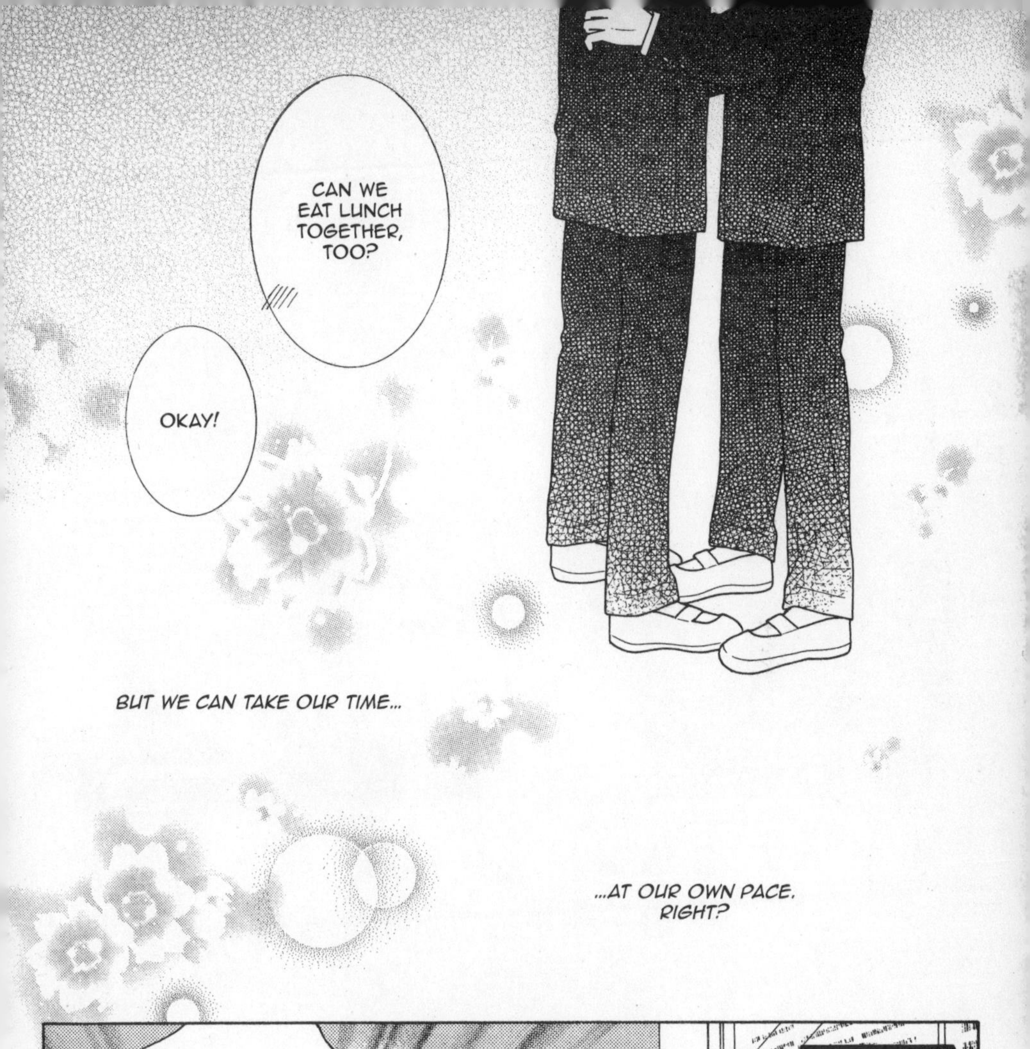
CAN WE EAT LUNCH TOGETHER, TOO?
OKAY!
BUT WE CAN TAKE OUR TIME...
...AT OUR OWN PACE. RIGHT?
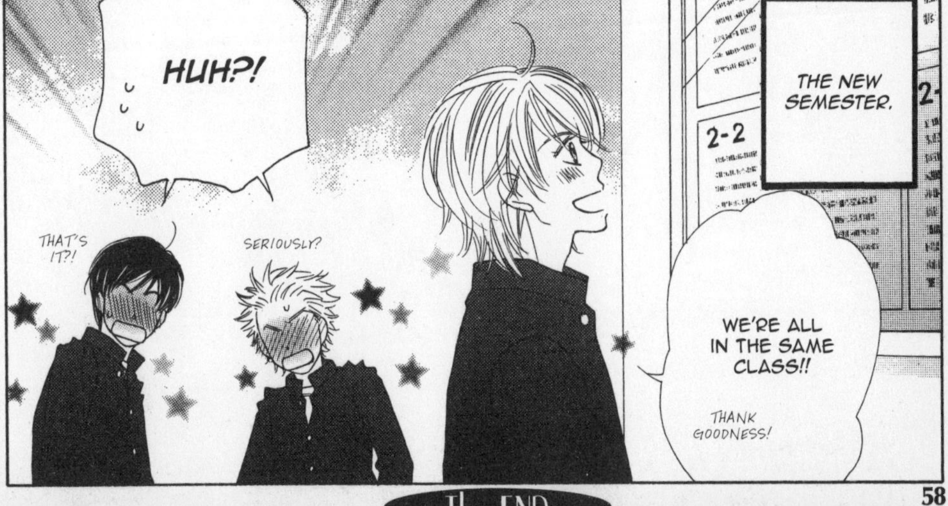
THE NEW SEMESTER.
2-2
WE'RE ALL IN THE SAME CLASS!!
THANK GOODNESS!
HUH?!
SERIOUSLY?
THAT'S IT?!

The END

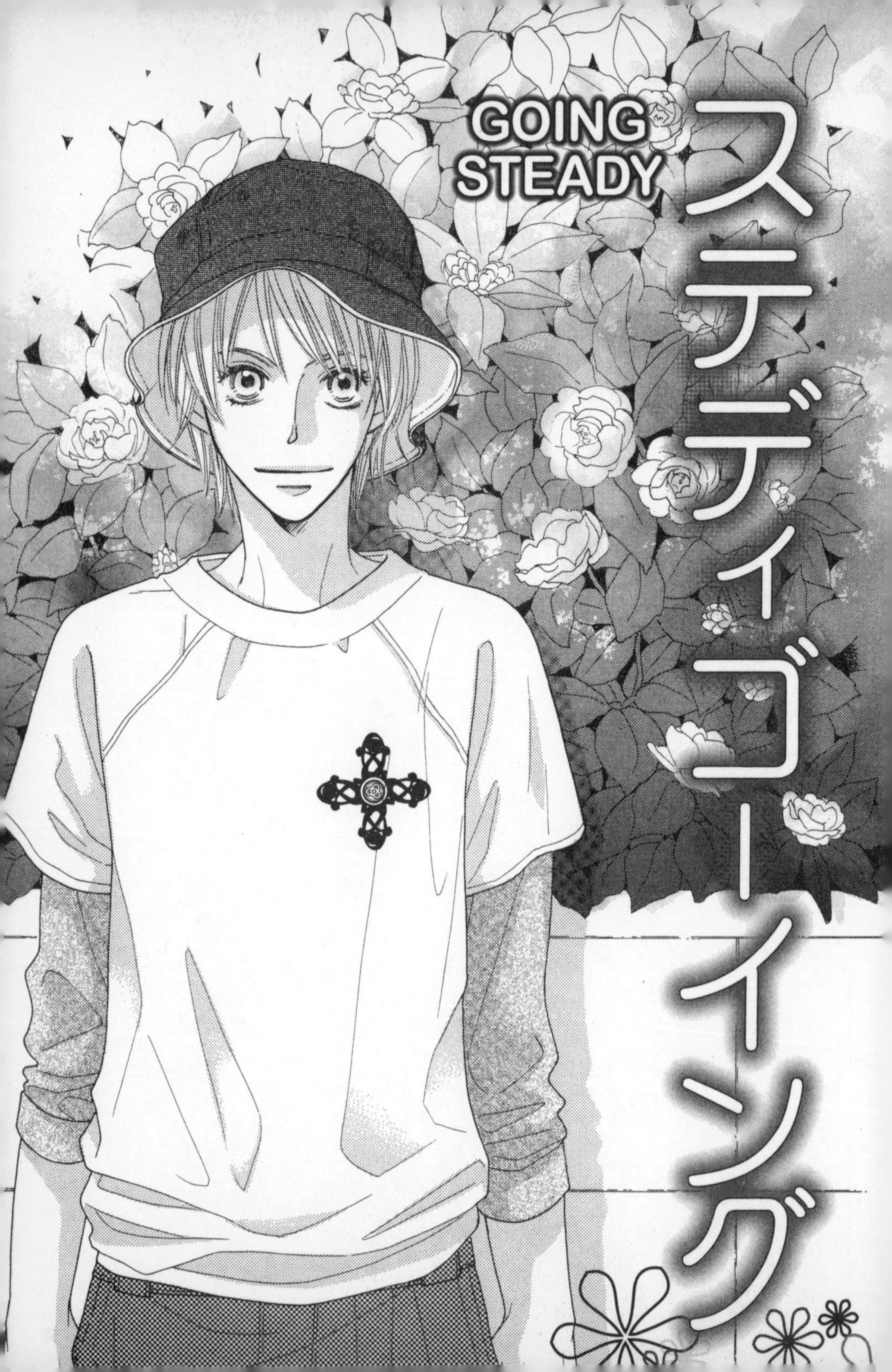
GOING STEADY
ステディゴーイング

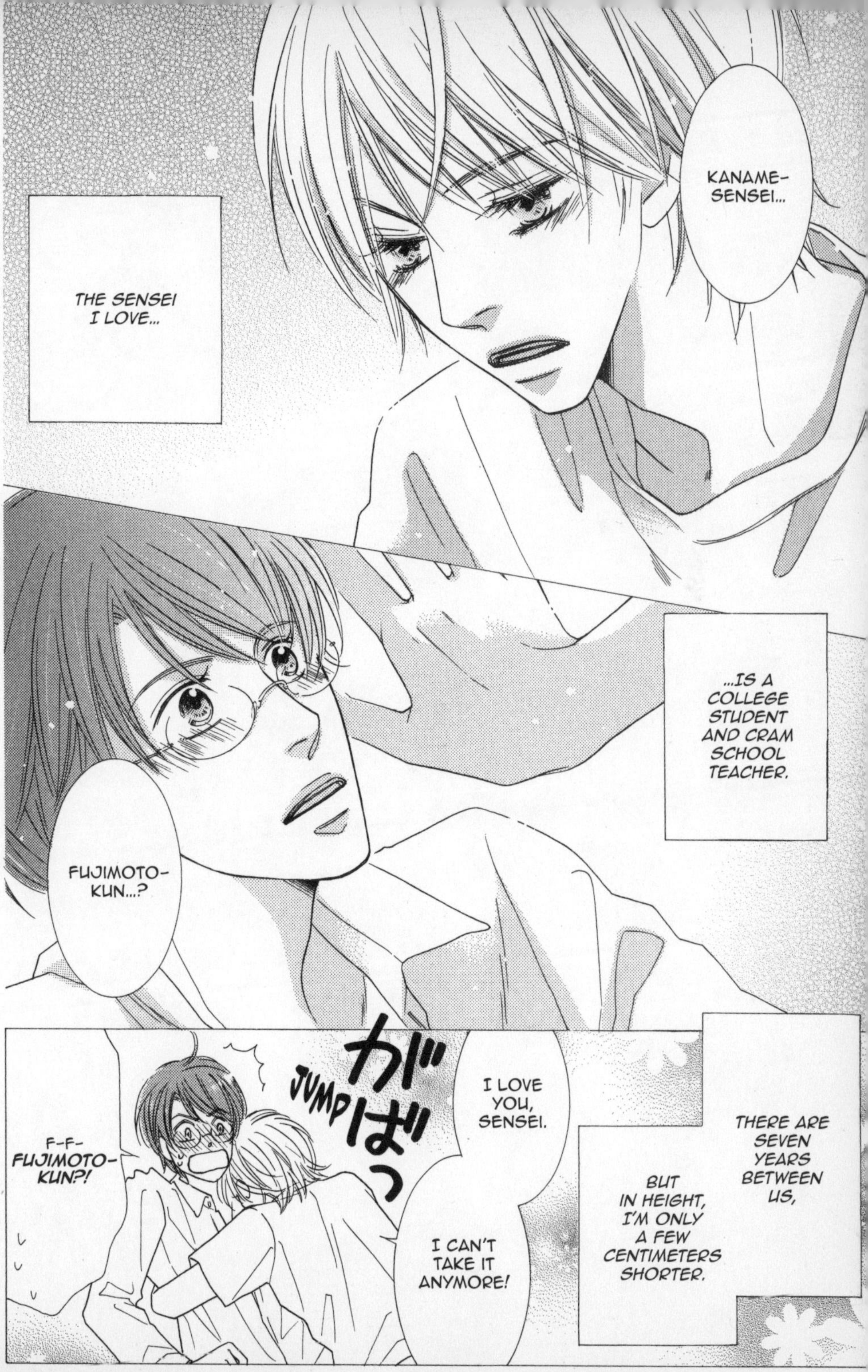
KANAME-SENSEI...
THE SENSEI I LOVE...
...IS A COLLEGE STUDENT AND CRAM SCHOOL TEACHER.
FUJIMOTO-KUN...?
THERE ARE SEVEN YEARS BETWEEN US,
BUT IN HEIGHT, I'M ONLY A FEW CENTIMETERS SHORTER.
I LOVE YOU, SENSEI.
I CAN'T TAKE IT ANYMORE!
がばっ
JUMP
F-F-FUJIMOTO-KUN?!

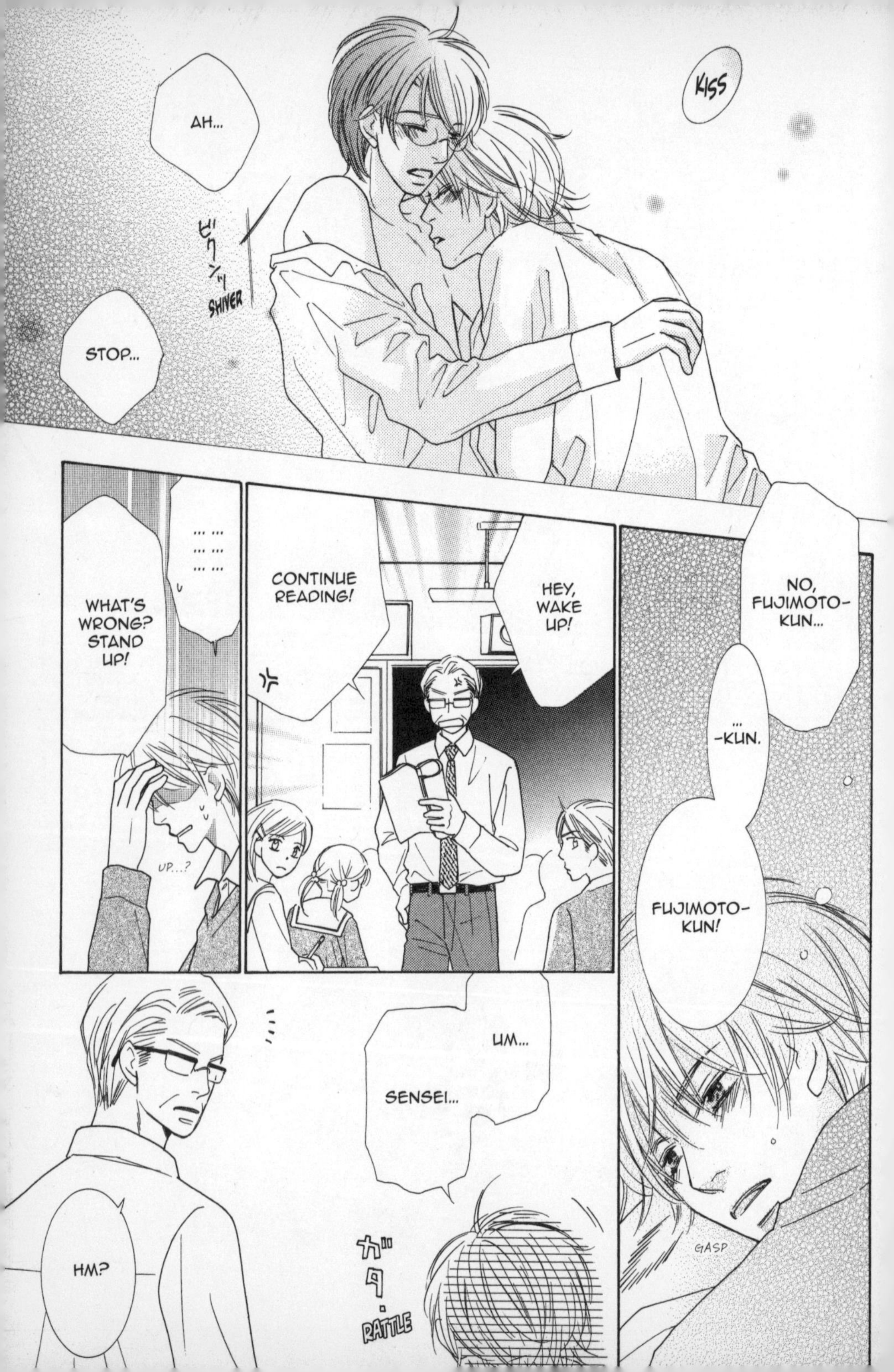
KISS
AH...
ビクンッ
SHIVER
STOP...
NO, FUJIMOTO-KUN...
... -KUN.
FUJIMOTO-KUN!
GASP
HEY, WAKE UP!
CONTINUE READING!
... ...
... ...
... ...
WHAT'S WRONG? STAND UP!
UP...?
UM...
SENSEI...
ガタ
RATTLE
HM?

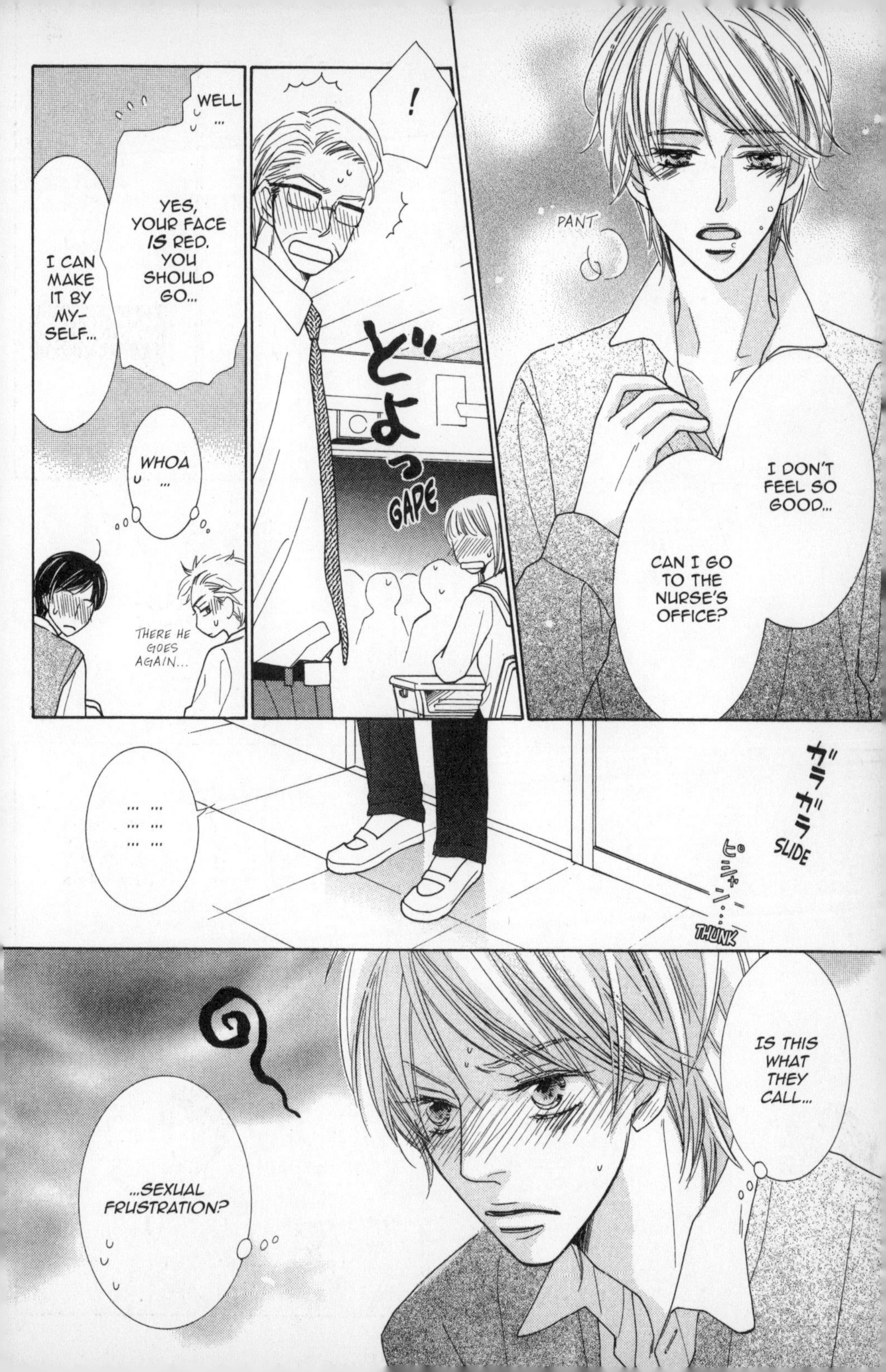
PANT
I DON'T FEEL SO GOOD...
CAN I GO TO THE NURSE'S OFFICE?
!
どよっ
GAPE
WELL ...
YES, YOUR FACE IS RED. YOU SHOULD GO...
I CAN MAKE IT BY MY-SELF...
WHOA ...
THERE HE GOES AGAIN...
ガラガラ
SLIDE
ピシャン...
THUNK
... ...
IS THIS WHAT THEY CALL...
...SEXUAL FRUSTRATION?

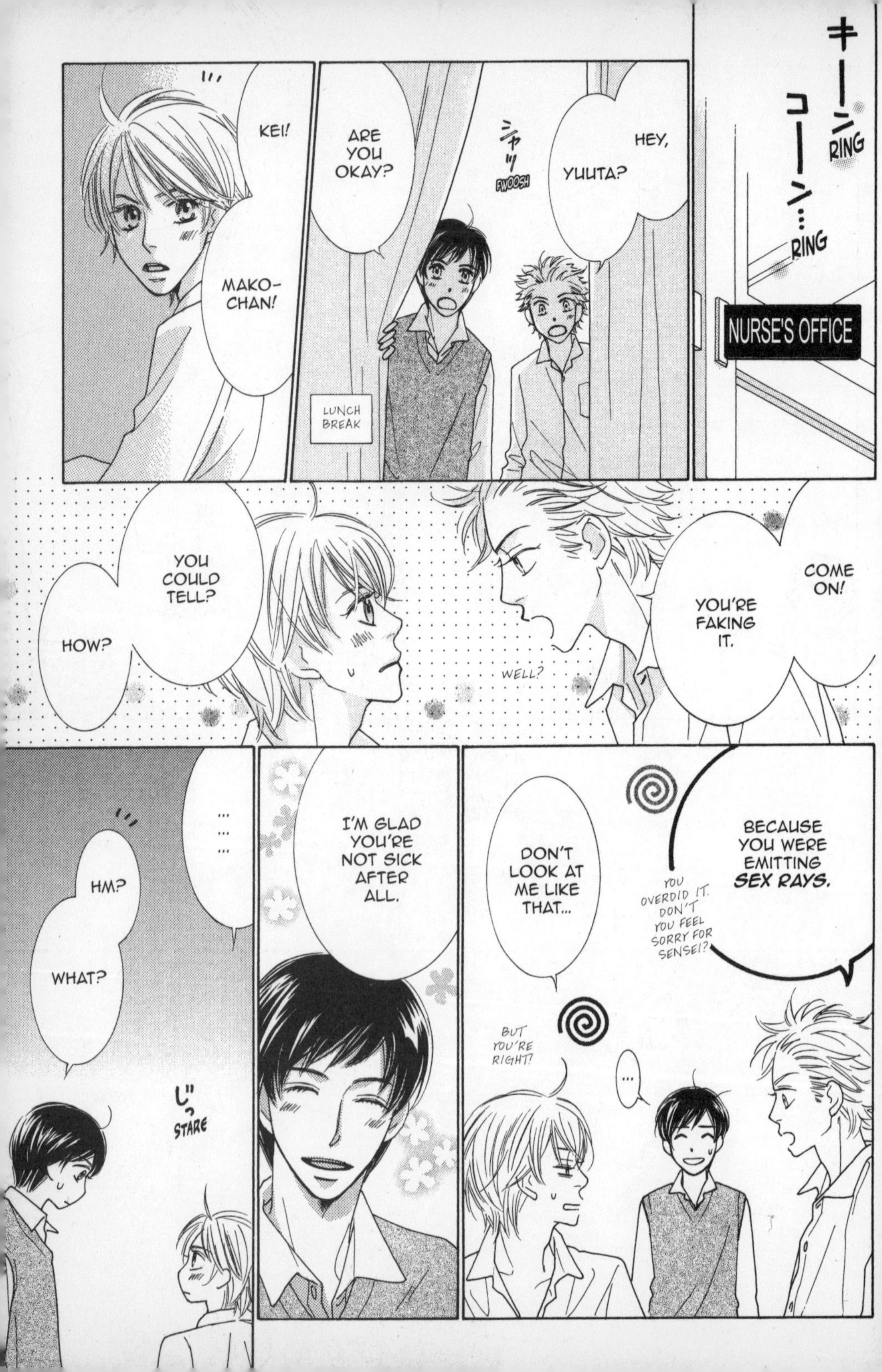
キーン
RING
コーン…
RING
NURSE'S OFFICE
HEY,
YUUTA?
シャッ
FWOOSH
ARE YOU OKAY?
LUNCH BREAK
KEI!
MAKO-CHAN!
COME ON!
YOU'RE FAKING IT.
WELL?
YOU COULD TELL?
HOW?
BECAUSE YOU WERE EMITTING **SEX RAYS.**
YOU OVERDID IT. DON'T YOU FEEL SORRY FOR SENSEI?
DON'T LOOK AT ME LIKE THAT...
BUT YOU'RE RIGHT!
...
I'M GLAD YOU'RE NOT SICK AFTER ALL.
... ...
HM?
WHAT?
じっ
STARE

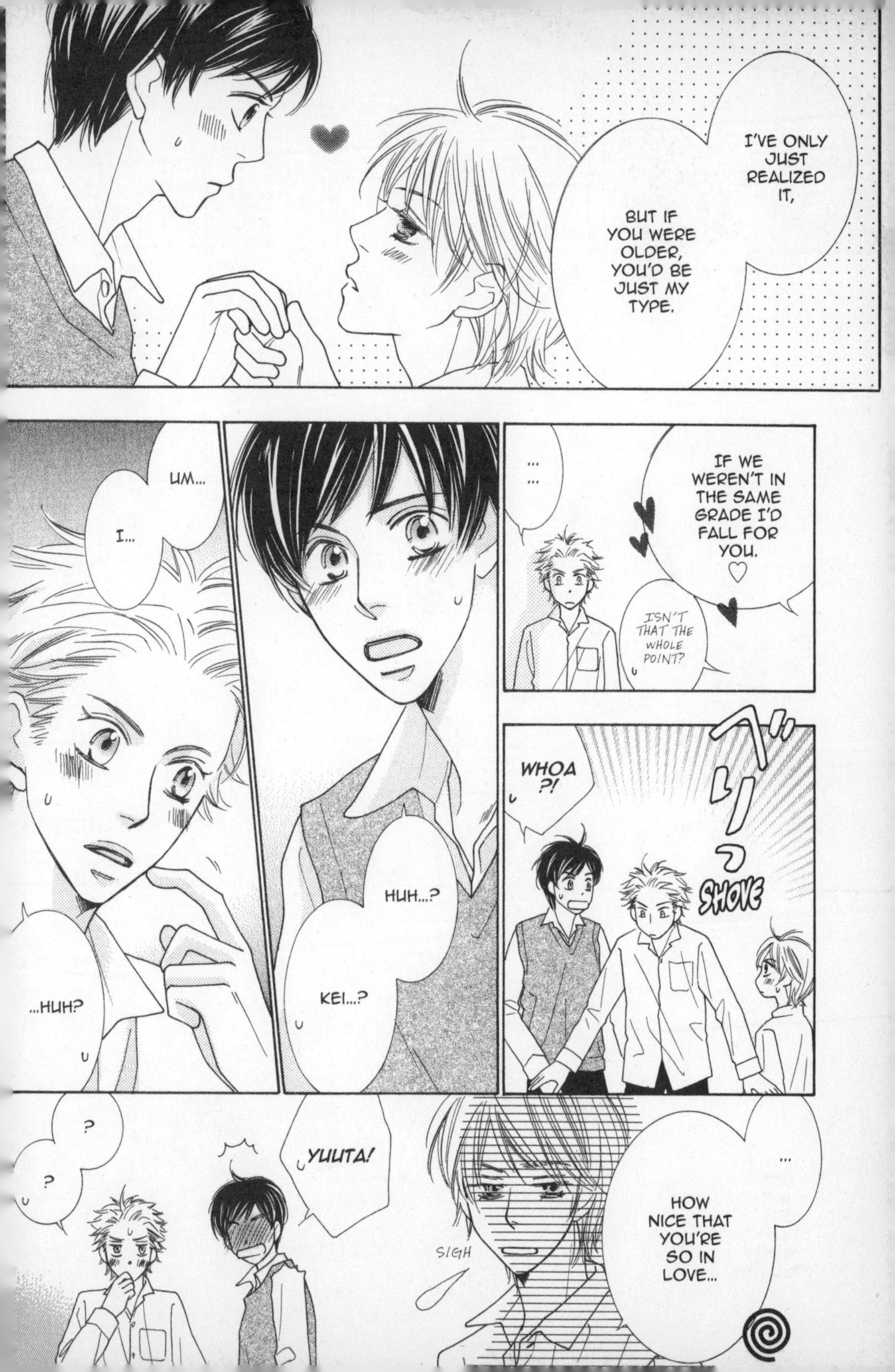
I'VE ONLY JUST REALIZED IT,
BUT IF YOU WERE OLDER, YOU'D BE JUST MY TYPE.
IF WE WEREN'T IN THE SAME GRADE I'D FALL FOR YOU. ♡
ISN'T THAT THE WHOLE POINT?
... ...
WHOA ?!
SHOVE
HUH...?
KEI...?
UM...
I...
...HUH?
...
HOW NICE THAT YOU'RE SO IN LOVE...
SIGH
YUUTA!
?
?

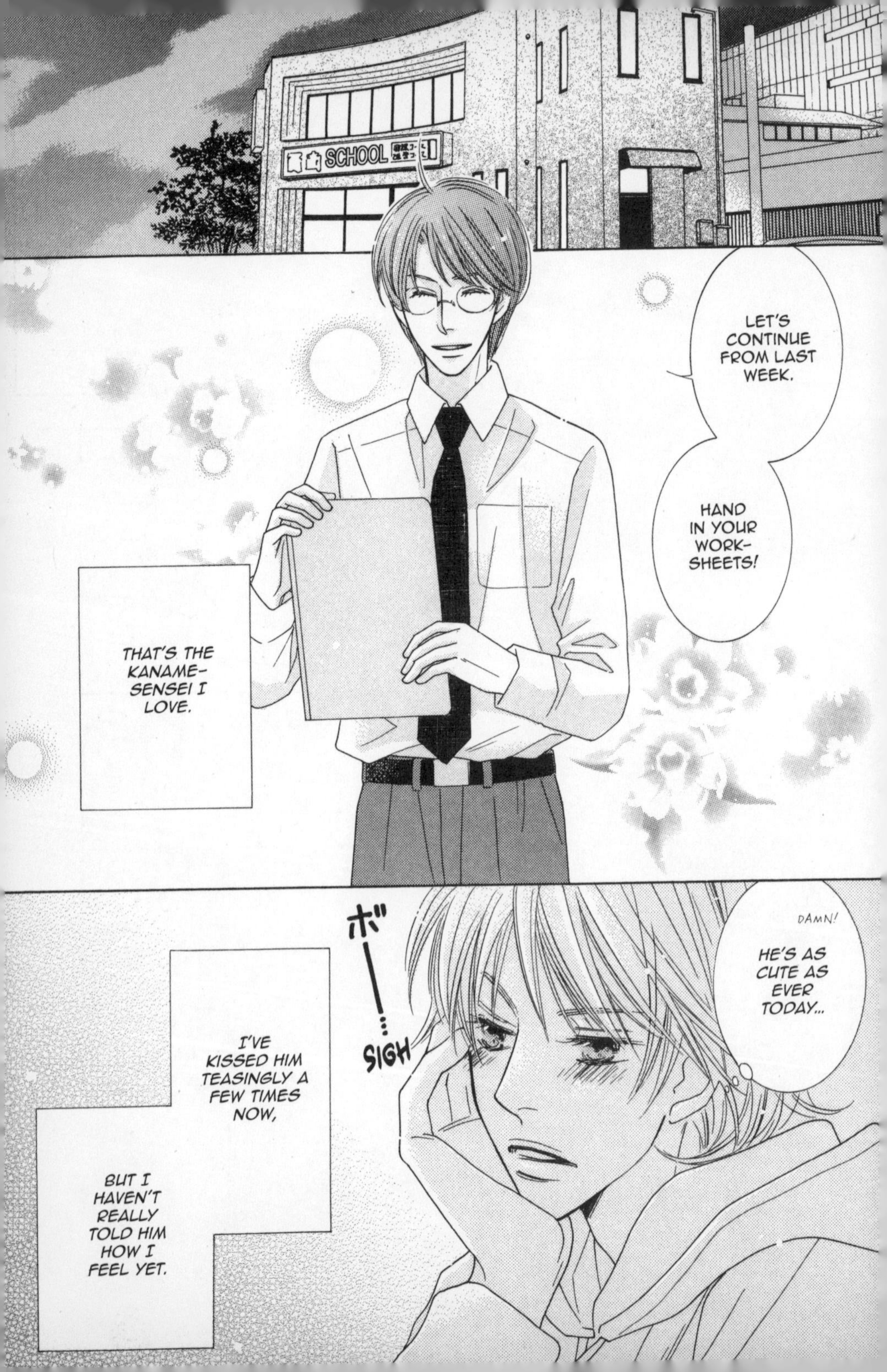
SCHOOL
LET'S CONTINUE FROM LAST WEEK.
HAND IN YOUR WORK-SHEETS!
THAT'S THE KANAME-SENSEI I LOVE.
DAMN!
HE'S AS CUTE AS EVER TODAY...
ボー…
SIGH
I'VE KISSED HIM TEASINGLY A FEW TIMES NOW,
BUT I HAVEN'T REALLY TOLD HIM HOW I FEEL YET.

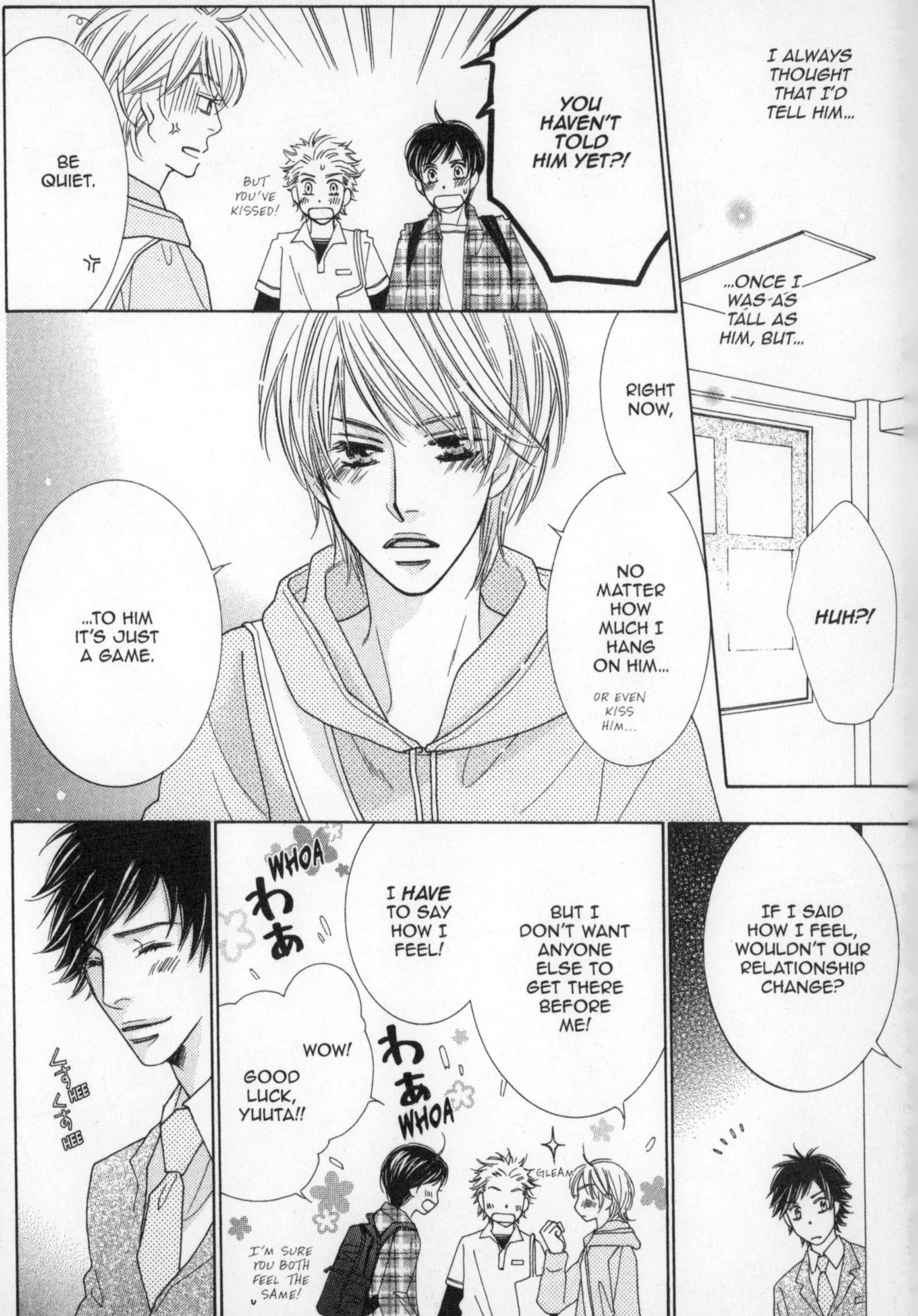

I ALWAYS THOUGHT THAT I'D TELL HIM...
...ONCE I WAS AS TALL AS HIM, BUT...
HUH?!
YOU HAVEN'T TOLD HIM YET?!
BUT YOU'VE KISSED!
BE QUIET.
RIGHT NOW,
NO MATTER HOW MUCH I HANG ON HIM...
OR EVEN KISS HIM...
...TO HIM IT'S JUST A GAME.
IF I SAID HOW I FEEL, WOULDN'T OUR RELATIONSHIP CHANGE?
I HAVE TO SAY HOW I FEEL!
BUT I DON'T WANT ANYONE ELSE TO GET THERE BEFORE ME!
わあ WHOA
WOW!
GOOD LUCK, YUUTA!!
わあ WHOA
GLEAM
I'M SURE YOU BOTH FEEL THE SAME!
くすくす HEE HEE

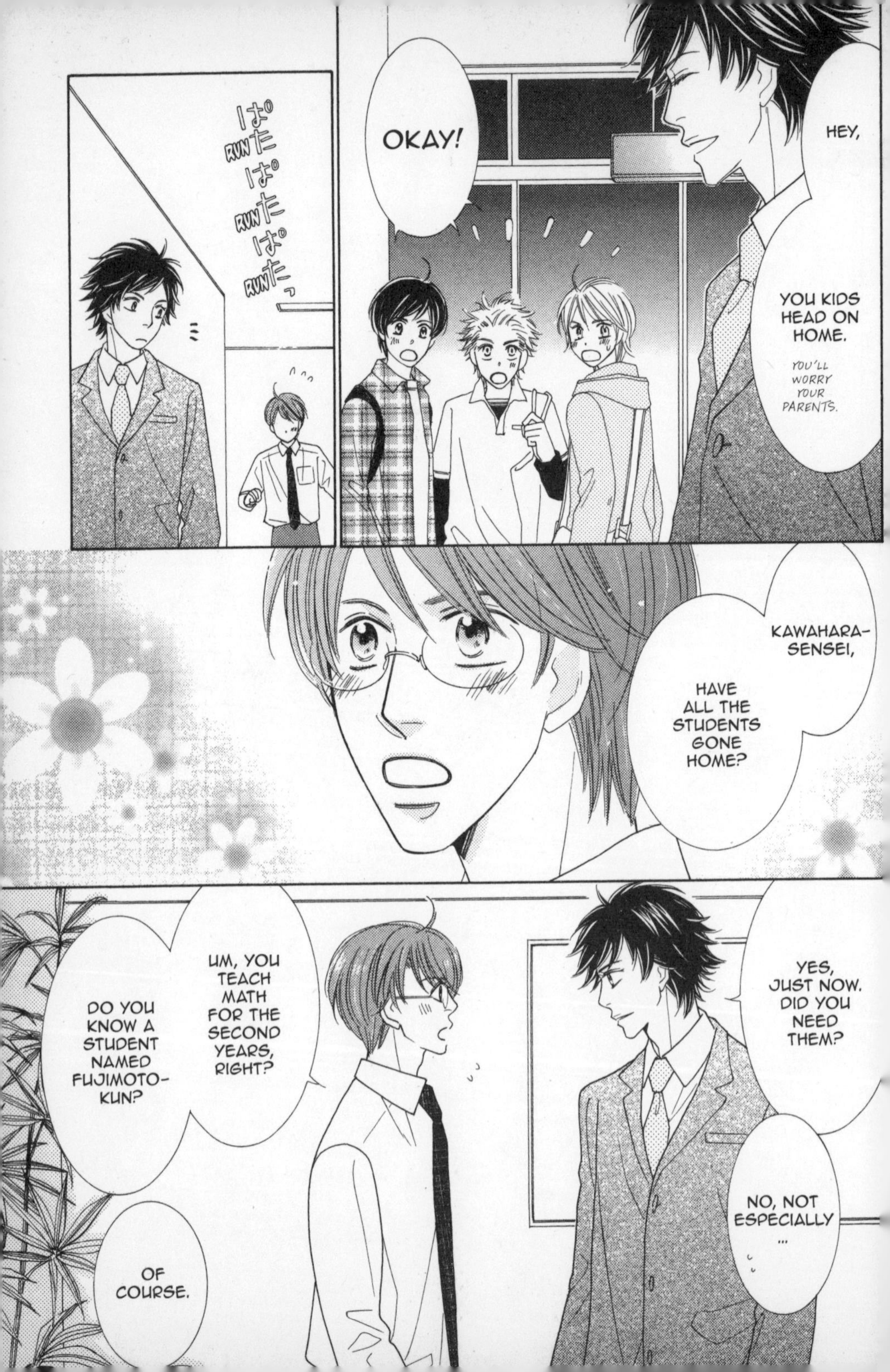

HEY,
YOU KIDS HEAD ON HOME.
YOU'LL WORRY YOUR PARENTS.
OKAY!
ぱたぱたぱた
RUN RUN RUN
KAWAHARA-SENSEI,
HAVE ALL THE STUDENTS GONE HOME?
YES, JUST NOW. DID YOU NEED THEM?
UM, YOU TEACH MATH FOR THE SECOND YEARS, RIGHT?
DO YOU KNOW A STUDENT NAMED FUJIMOTO-KUN?
NO, NOT ESPECIALLY ...
OF COURSE.

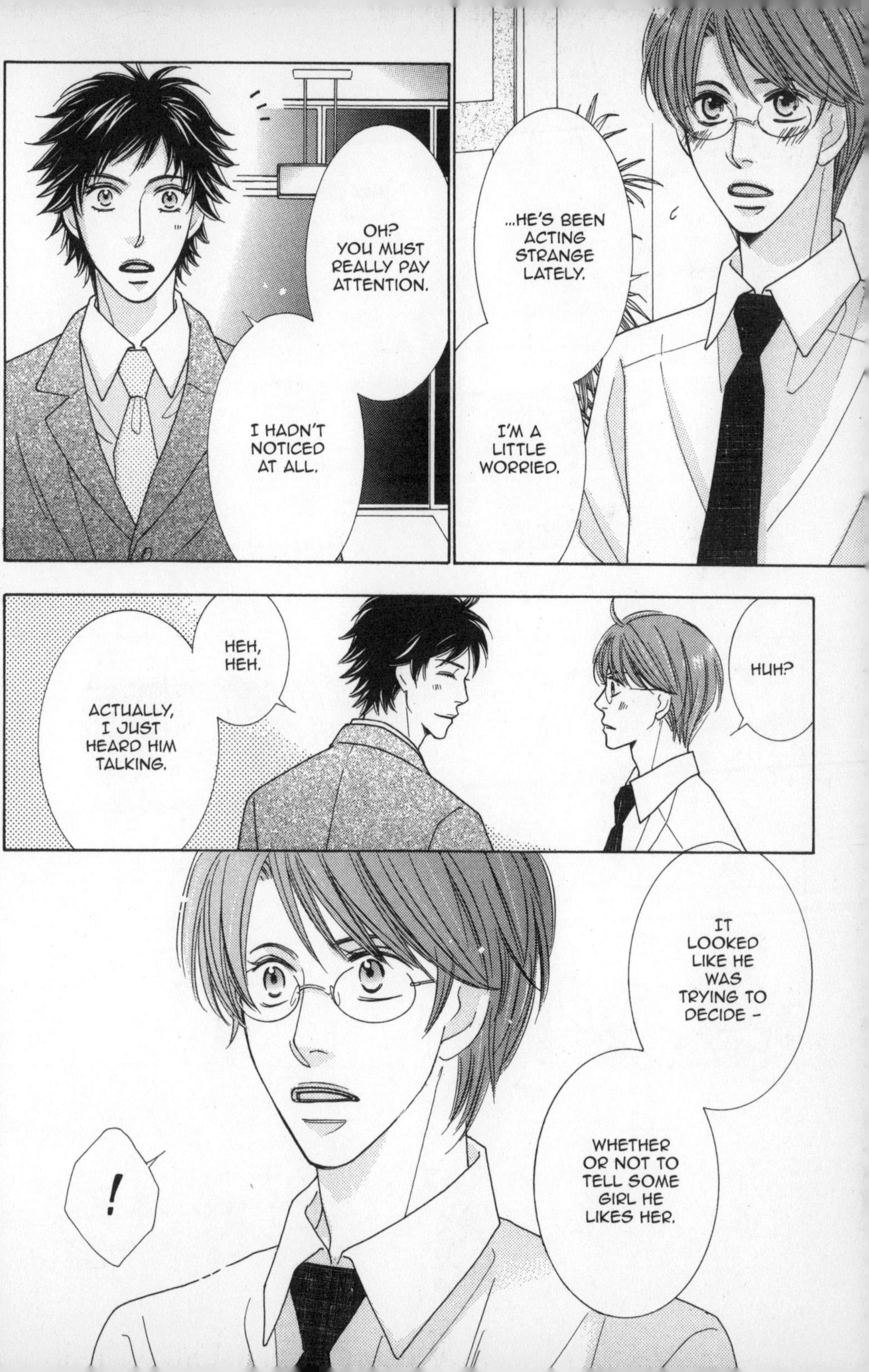
...HE'S BEEN ACTING STRANGE LATELY.
I'M A LITTLE WORRIED.
OH? YOU MUST REALLY PAY ATTENTION.
I HADN'T NOTICED AT ALL.
HUH?
HEH, HEH.
ACTUALLY, I JUST HEARD HIM TALKING.
IT LOOKED LIKE HE WAS TRYING TO DECIDE –
WHETHER OR NOT TO TELL SOME GIRL HE LIKES HER.
!

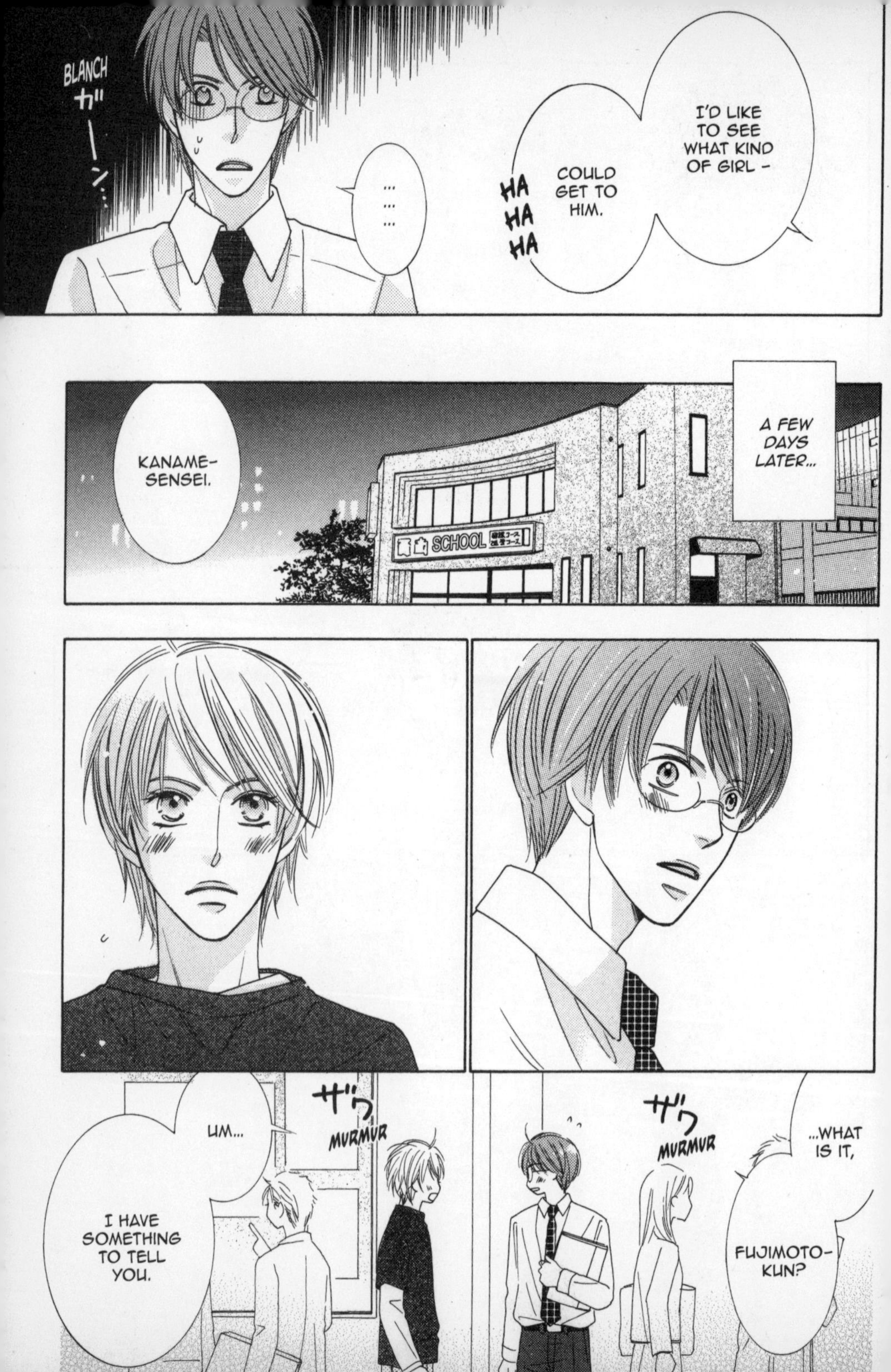
I'D LIKE TO SEE WHAT KIND OF GIRL -
COULD GET TO HIM.
HA HA HA
... ...
BLANCH
ガーン...
A FEW DAYS LATER...
SCHOOL
KANAME-SENSEI.
...WHAT IS IT, FUJIMOTO-KUN?
ザワ
MURMUR
ザワ
MURMUR
UM...
I HAVE SOMETHING TO TELL YOU.

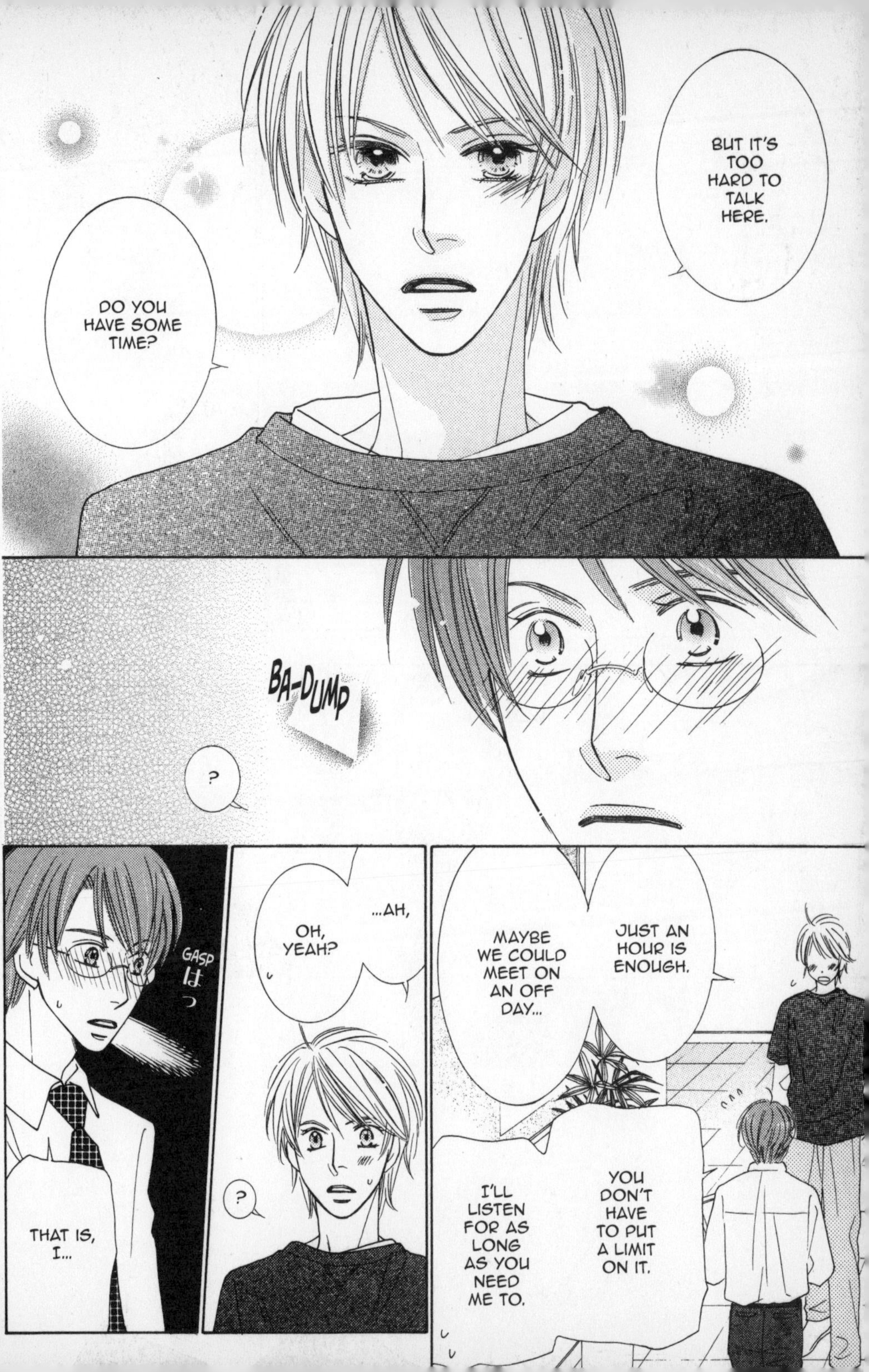
BUT IT'S TOO HARD TO TALK HERE.
DO YOU HAVE SOME TIME?
BA-DUMP
?
JUST AN HOUR IS ENOUGH.
MAYBE WE COULD MEET ON AN OFF DAY...
YOU DON'T HAVE TO PUT A LIMIT ON IT.
I'LL LISTEN FOR AS LONG AS YOU NEED ME TO.
...AH,
OH, YEAH?
?
GASP
はっ
THAT IS, I...

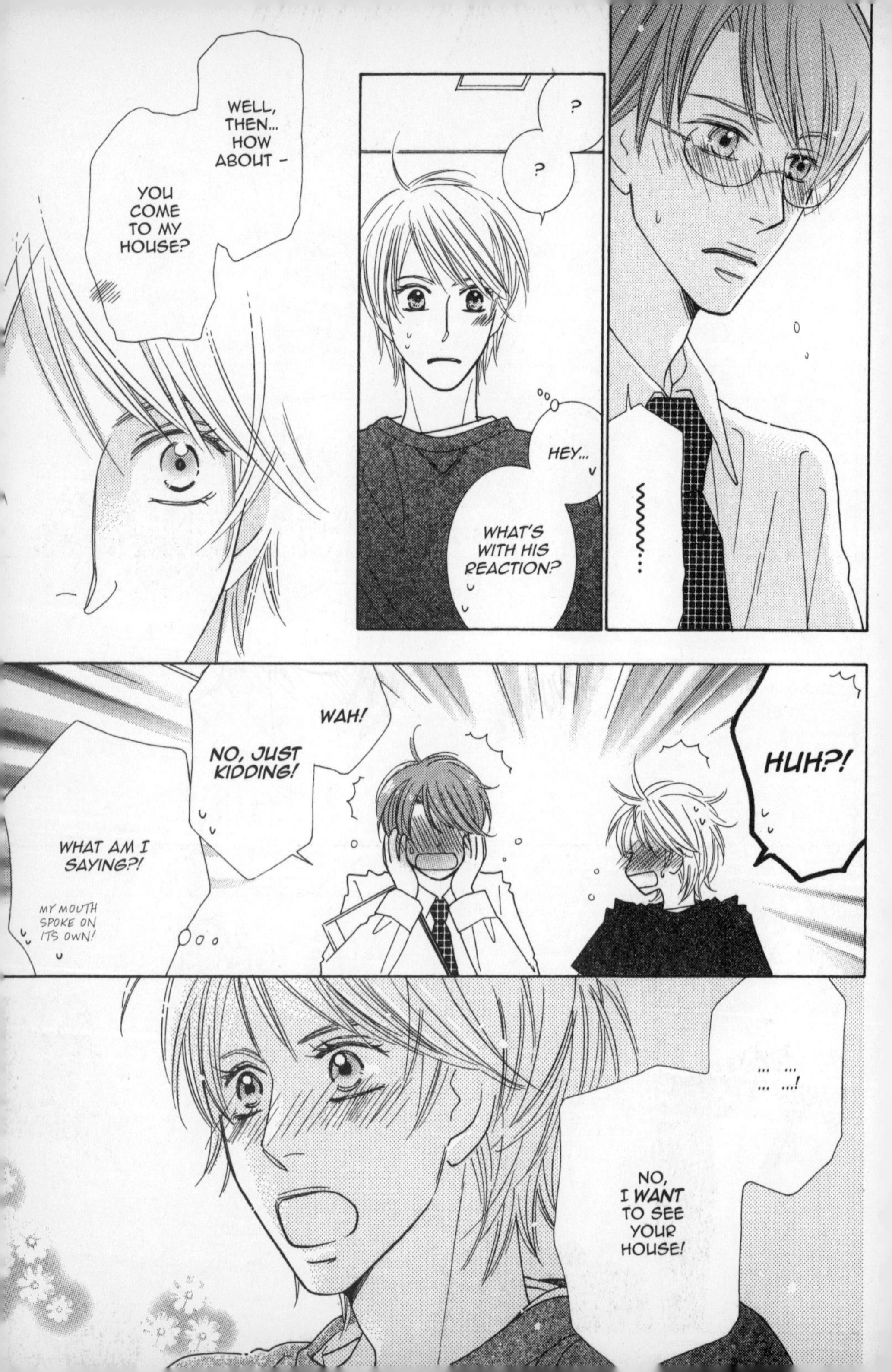
?
?
HEY...
WHAT'S WITH HIS REACTION?
WELL, THEN... HOW ABOUT –
YOU COME TO MY HOUSE?
HUH?!
WAH!
NO, JUST KIDDING!
WHAT AM I SAYING?!
MY MOUTH SPOKE ON ITS OWN!
... ...
... ...!
NO, I WANT TO SEE YOUR HOUSE!

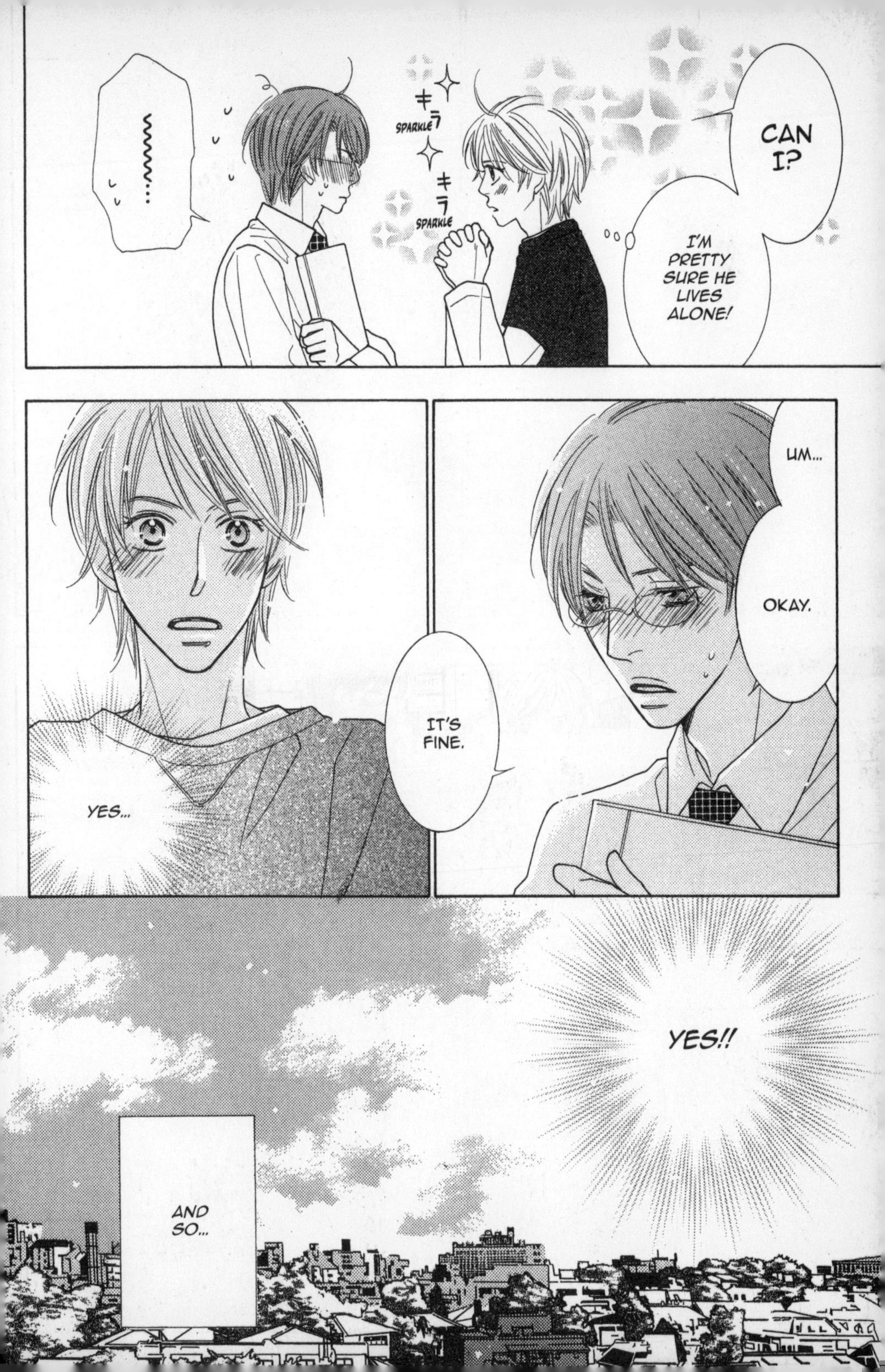
CAN I?
I'M PRETTY SURE HE LIVES ALONE!
キラ SPARKLE
キラ SPARKLE
......
UM...
OKAY.
IT'S FINE.
YES...
YES!!
AND SO...

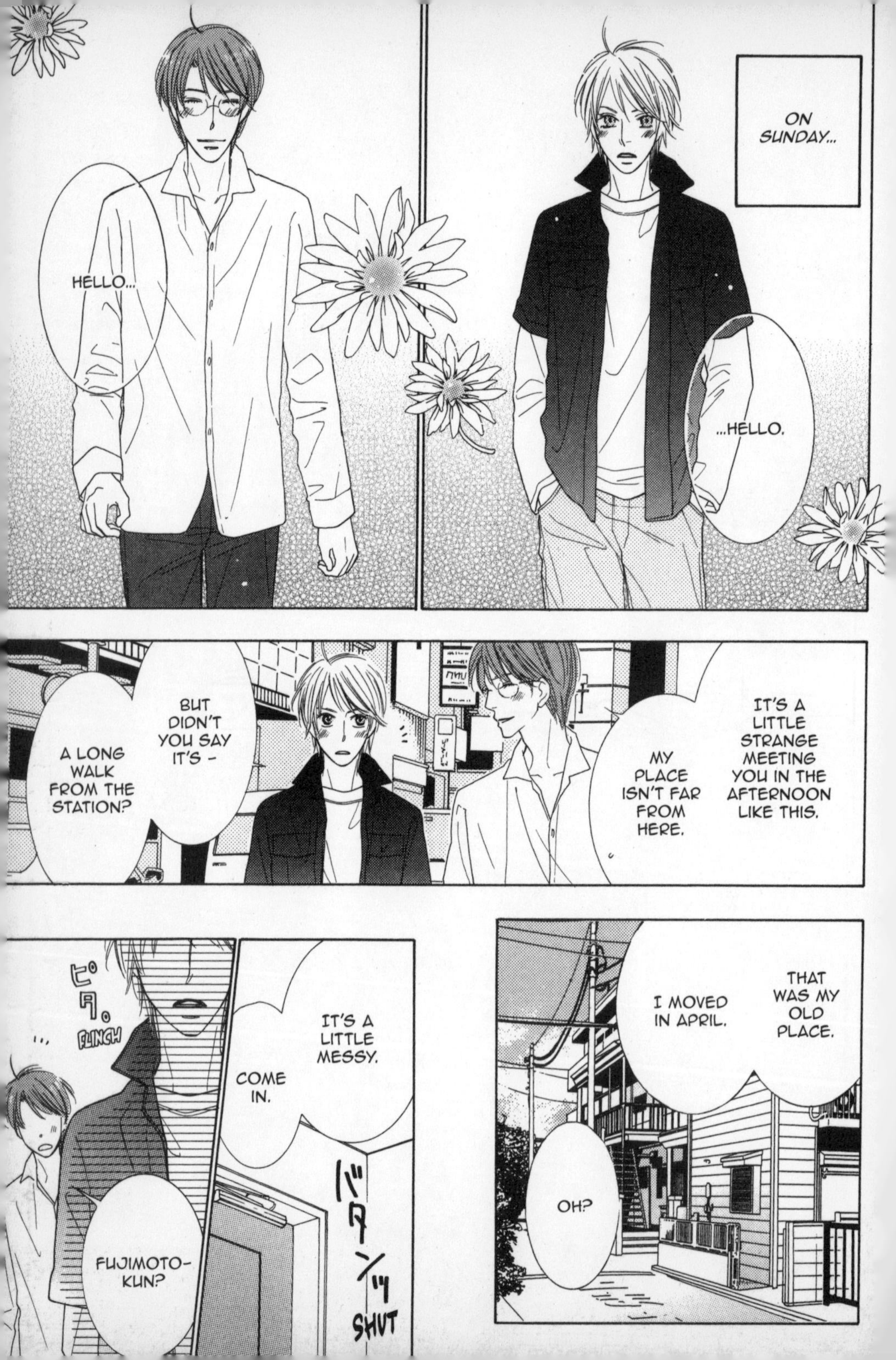
ON SUNDAY...
...HELLO.
HELLO...
IT'S A LITTLE STRANGE MEETING YOU IN THE AFTERNOON LIKE THIS.
MY PLACE ISN'T FAR FROM HERE.
BUT DIDN'T YOU SAY IT'S –
A LONG WALK FROM THE STATION?
THAT WAS MY OLD PLACE.
I MOVED IN APRIL.
OH?
IT'S A LITTLE MESSY.
COME IN.
バタンッ
SHUT
FUJIMOTO-KUN?
ピタ。
FLINCH
...

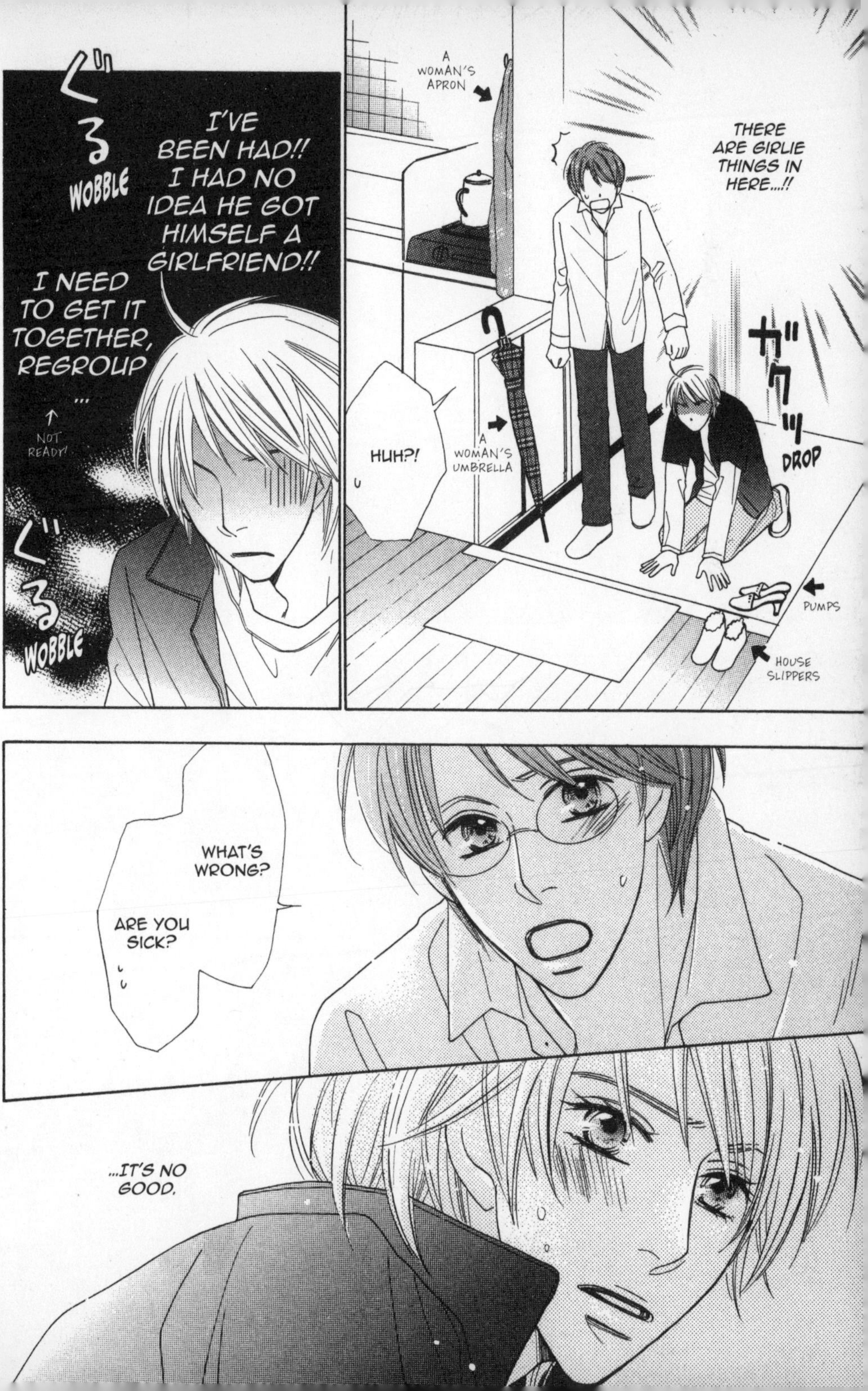
THERE ARE GIRLIE THINGS IN HERE...!!
A WOMAN'S APRON
ガクッ
DROP
A WOMAN'S UMBRELLA
HUH?!
PUMPS
HOUSE SLIPPERS
ぐる
WOBBLE
I'VE BEEN HAD!! I HAD NO IDEA HE GOT HIMSELF A GIRLFRIEND!!
I NEED TO GET IT TOGETHER, REGROUP...
NOT READY!
ぐる
WOBBLE
WHAT'S WRONG?
ARE YOU SICK?
...IT'S NO GOOD.

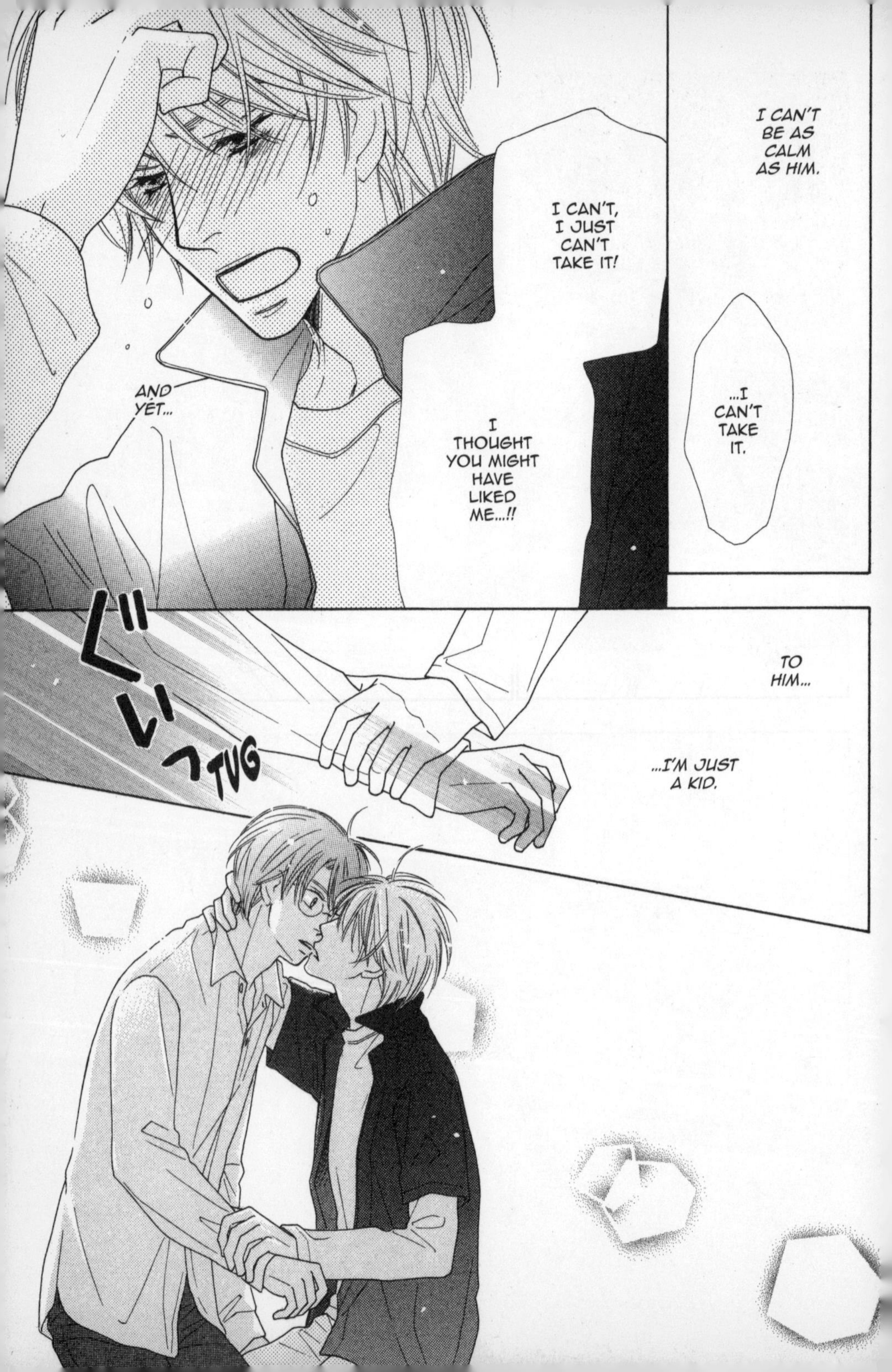
I CAN'T BE AS CALM AS HIM.
...I CAN'T TAKE IT.
I CAN'T, I JUST CAN'T TAKE IT!
I THOUGHT YOU MIGHT HAVE LIKED ME...!!
AND YET...
TO HIM...
...I'M JUST A KID.
TUG

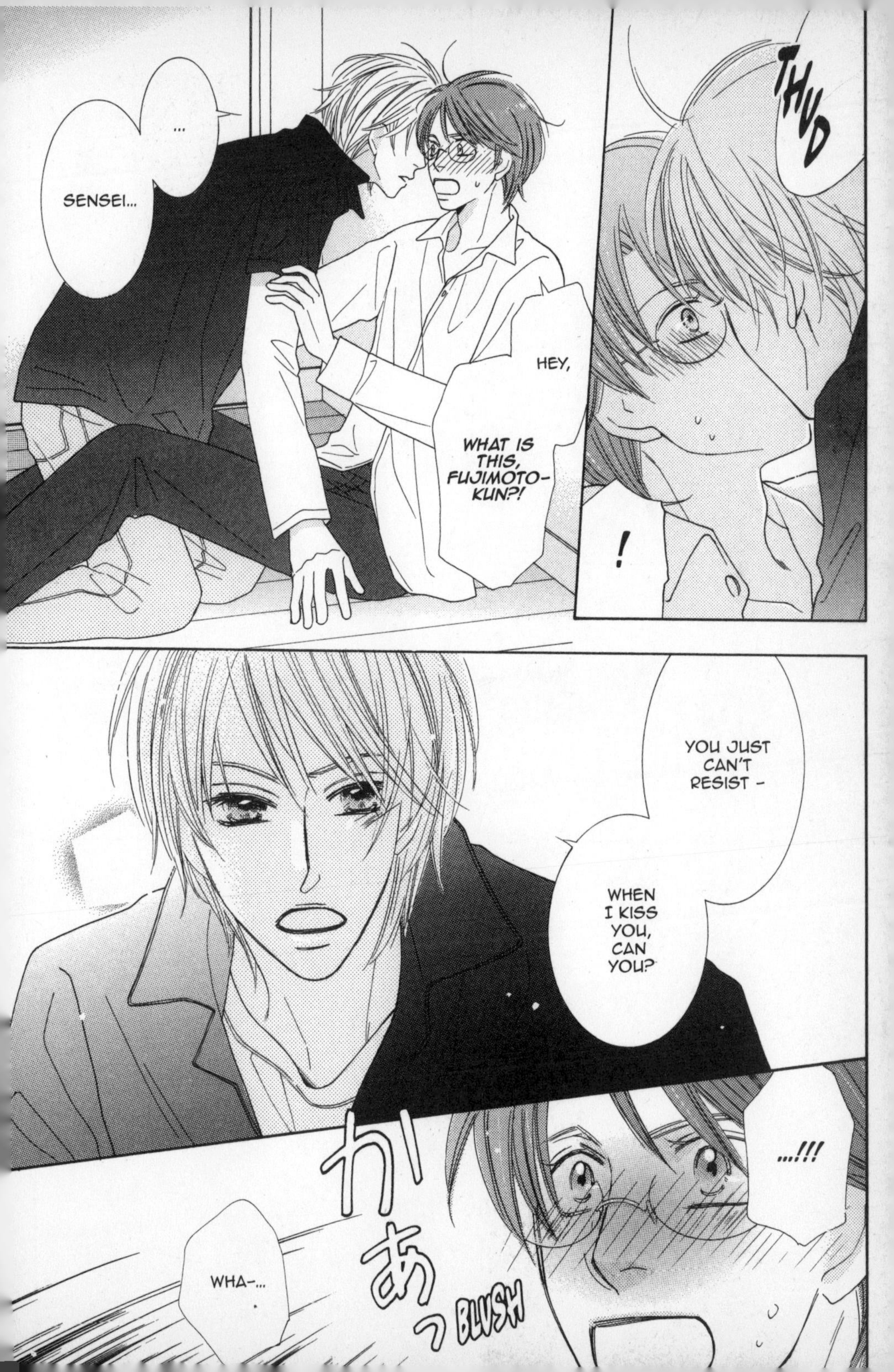
THUD
!
...
SENSEI...
HEY,
WHAT IS THIS, FUJIMOTO-KUN?!
YOU JUST CAN'T RESIST -
WHEN I KISS YOU, CAN YOU?
...!!!
わぁっ BLUSH
WHA-...

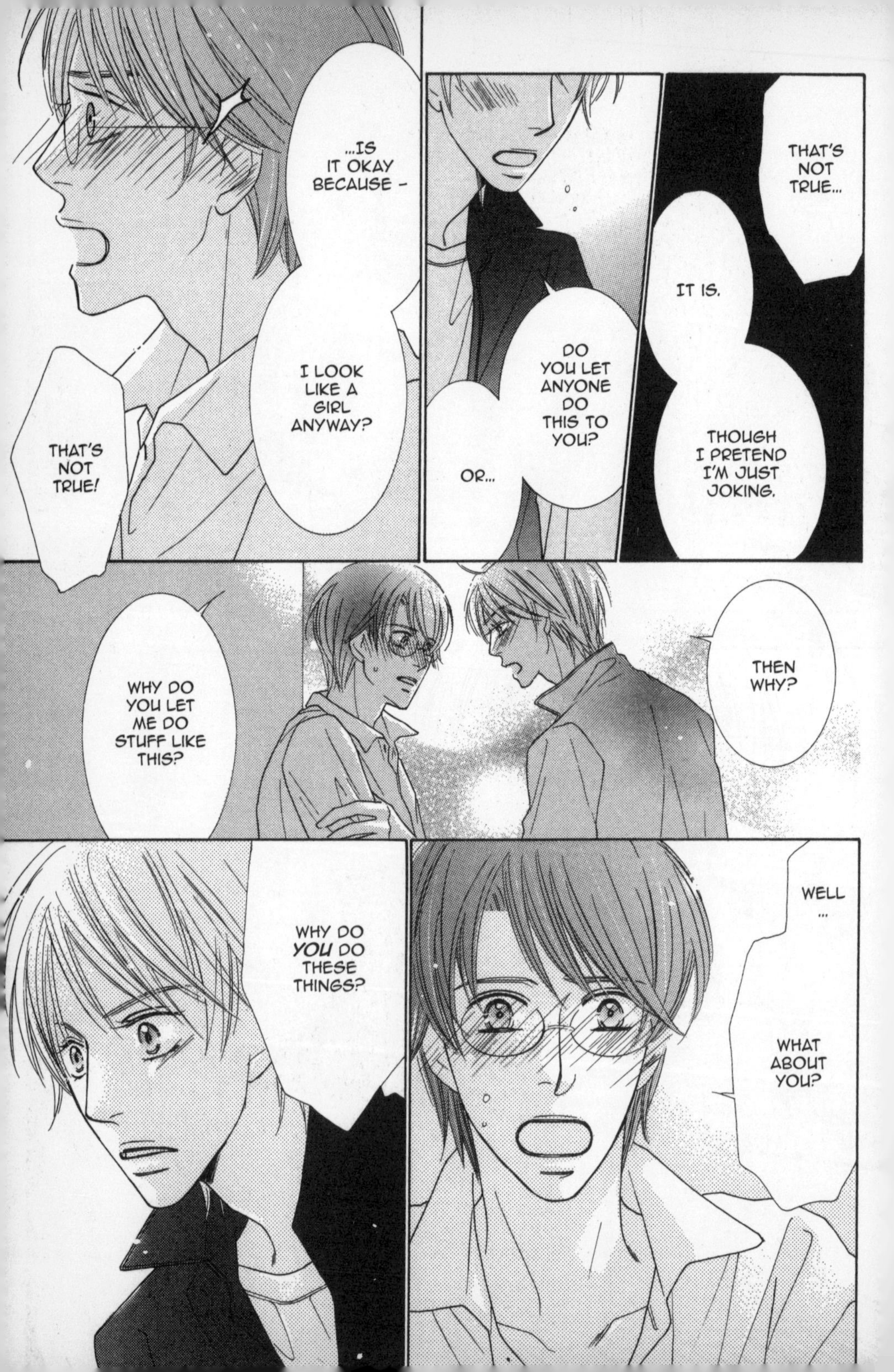
THAT'S NOT TRUE...
IT IS.
THOUGH I PRETEND I'M JUST JOKING.
DO YOU LET ANYONE DO THIS TO YOU?
OR...
...IS IT OKAY BECAUSE -
I LOOK LIKE A GIRL ANYWAY?
THAT'S NOT TRUE!
THEN WHY?
WHY DO YOU LET ME DO STUFF LIKE THIS?
WELL ...
WHAT ABOUT YOU?
WHY DO *YOU* DO THESE THINGS?

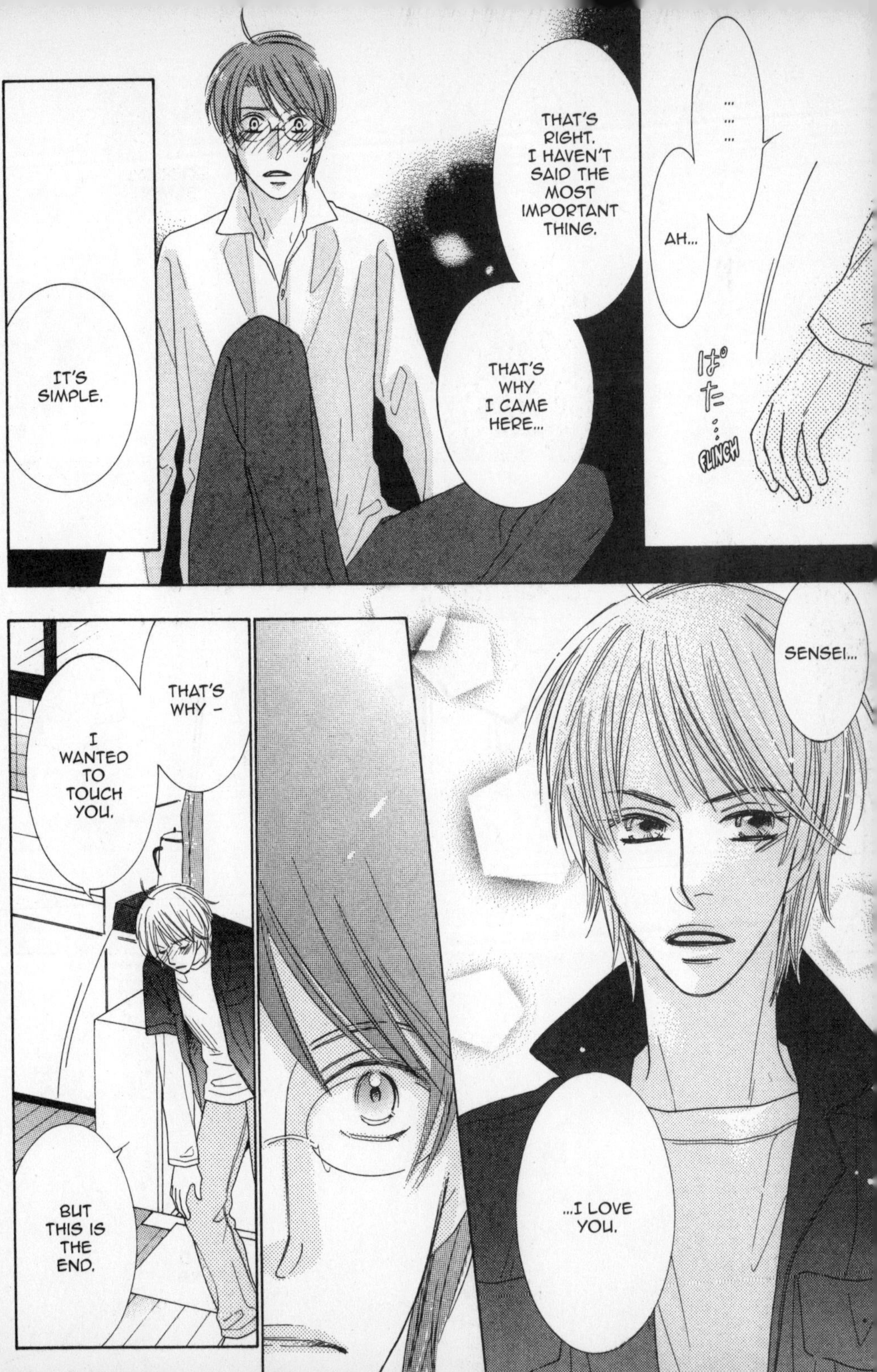

...
...
...
AH...
ぱた…
FLINCH
THAT'S RIGHT. I HAVEN'T SAID THE MOST IMPORTANT THING.
THAT'S WHY I CAME HERE...
IT'S SIMPLE.
SENSEI...
...I LOVE YOU.
THAT'S WHY -
I WANTED TO TOUCH YOU.
BUT THIS IS THE END.

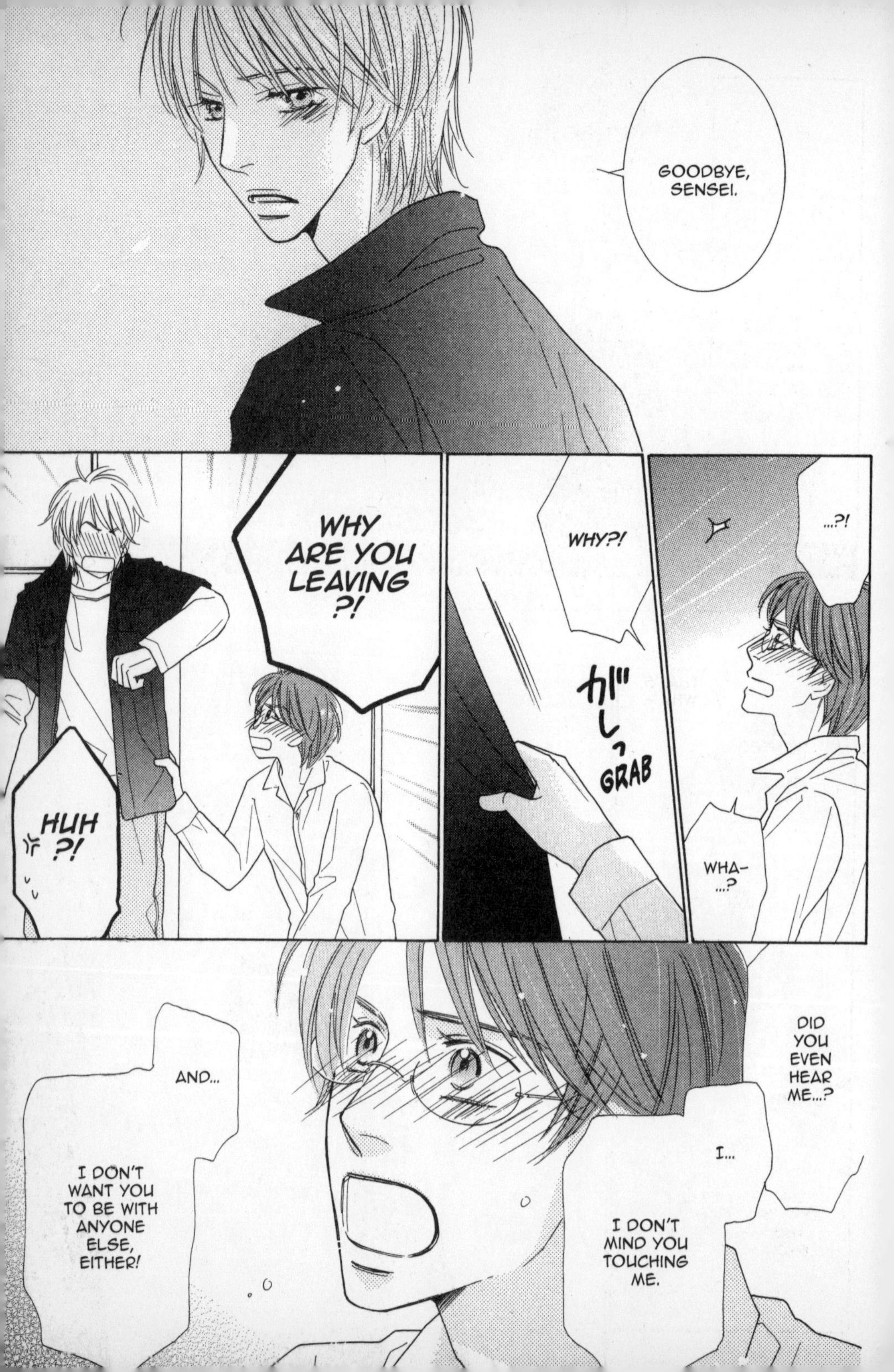
GOODBYE, SENSEI.
...?!
WHA- ...?
WHY?!
がしっ
GRAB
WHY ARE YOU LEAVING ?!
HUH ?!
DID YOU EVEN HEAR ME...?
I...
I DON'T MIND YOU TOUCHING ME.
AND...
I DON'T WANT YOU TO BE WITH ANYONE ELSE, EITHER!

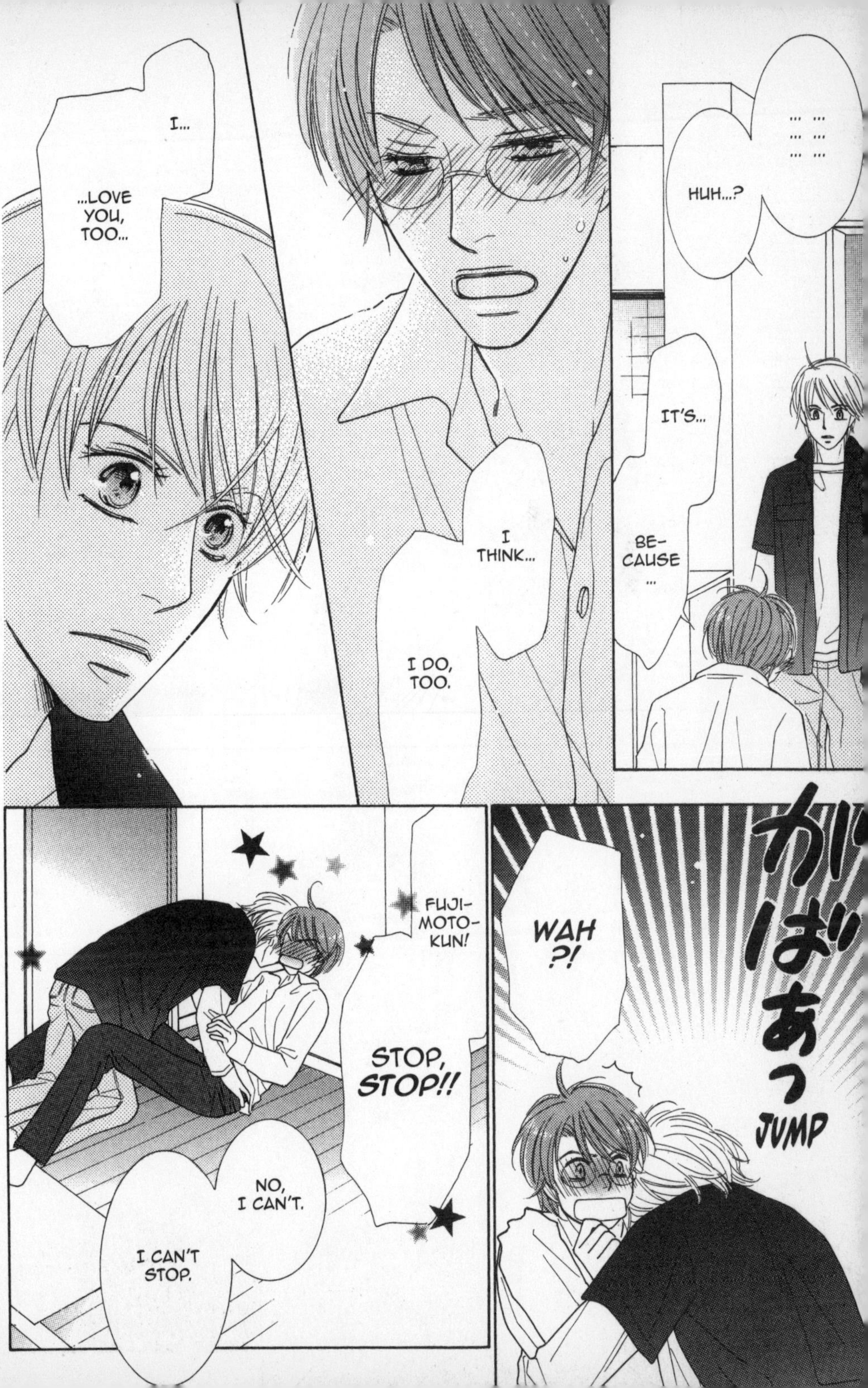
......
......
HUH...?
IT'S...
BE-CAUSE ...
I THINK...
I DO, TOO.
I...
...LOVE YOU, TOO...
がばあっ
JUMP
WAH?!
FUJI-MOTO-KUN!
STOP, STOP!!
NO, I CAN'T.
I CAN'T STOP.

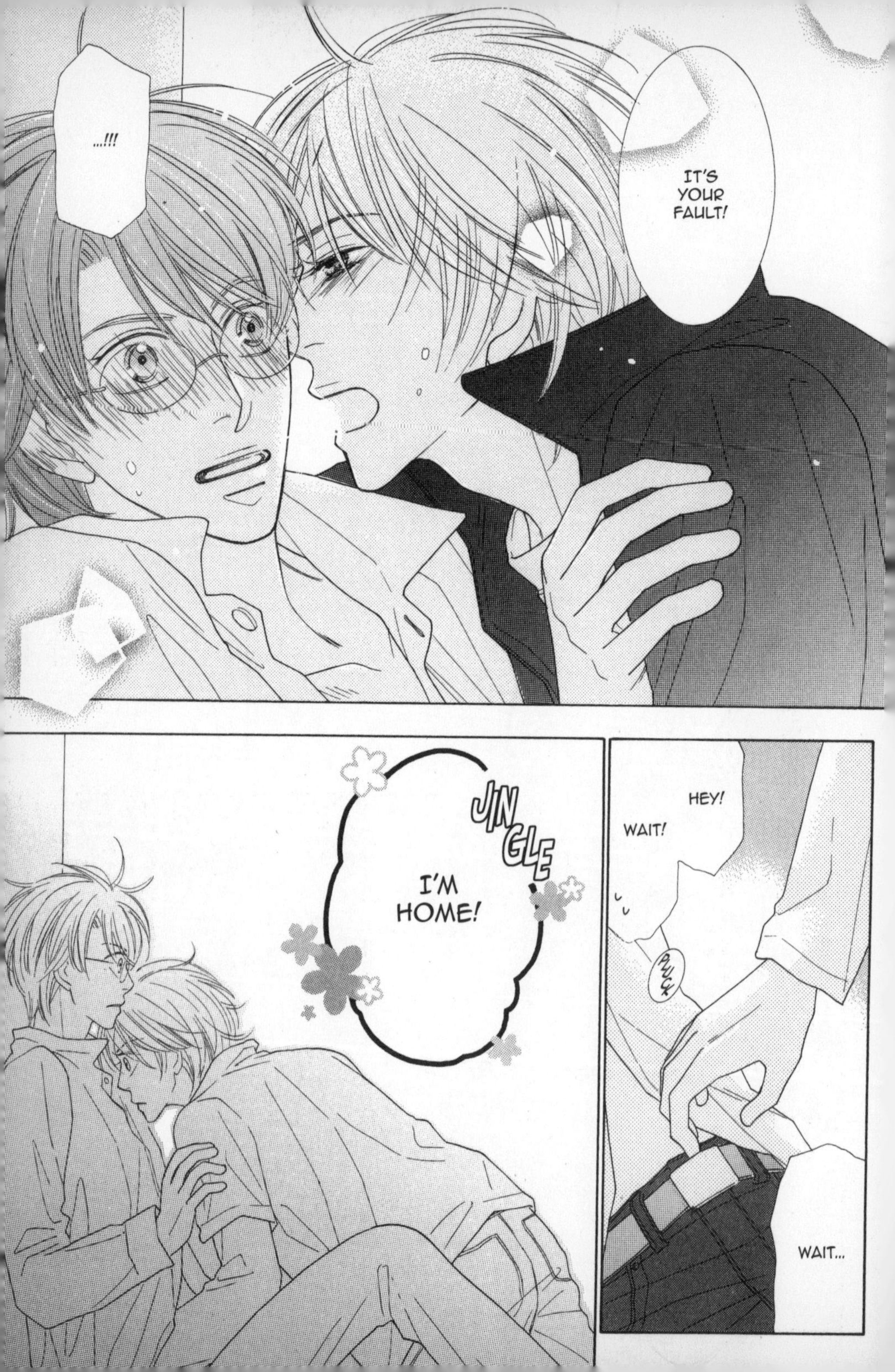
IT'S YOUR FAULT!
...!!!
HEY!
WAIT!
PLUCK
WAIT...
JINGLE
I'M HOME!

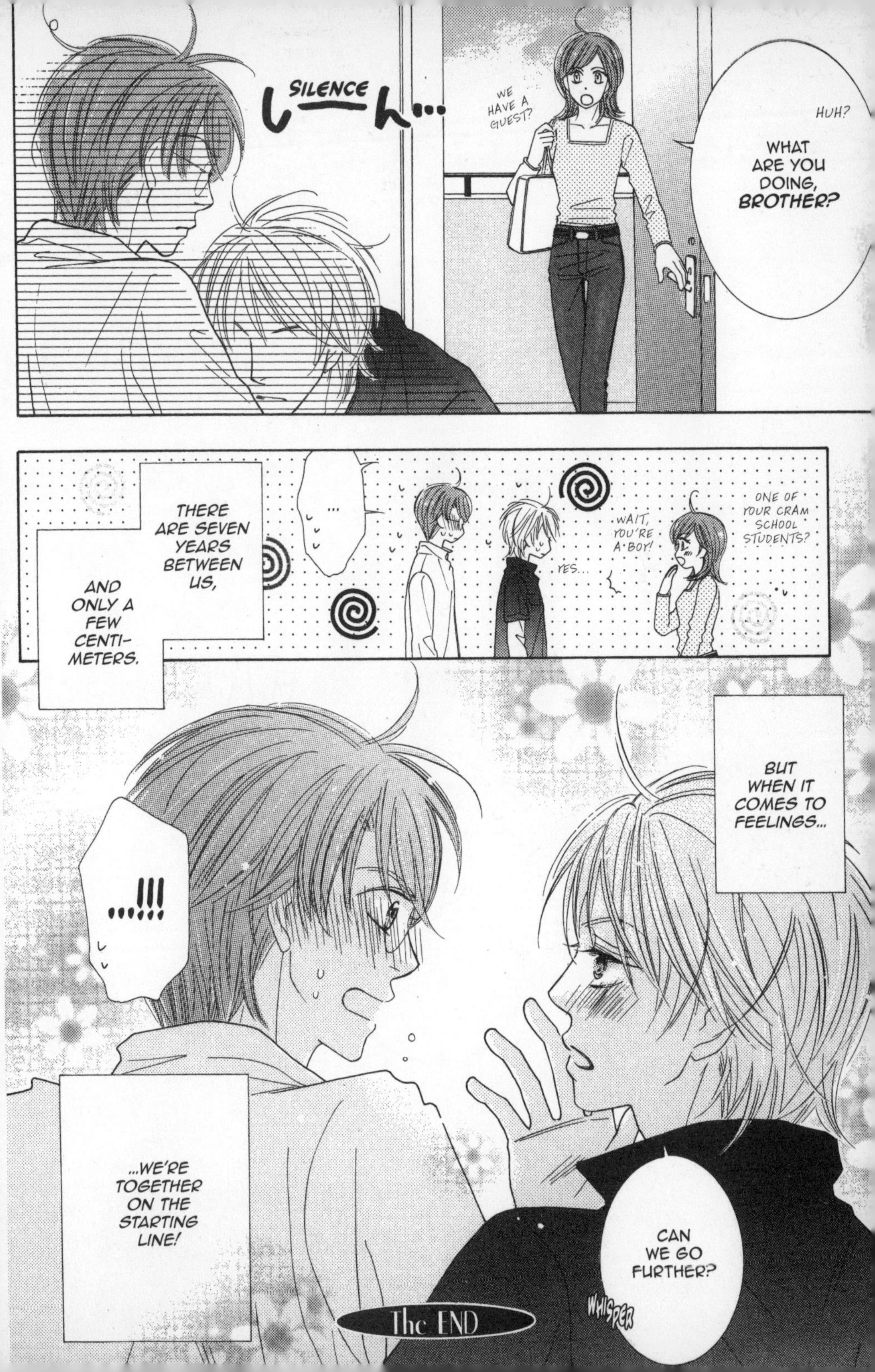

HUH?
WHAT ARE YOU DOING, BROTHER?
WE HAVE A GUEST?
SILENCE
ONE OF YOUR CRAM SCHOOL STUDENTS?
WAIT, YOU'RE A BOY!
YES...
...
THERE ARE SEVEN YEARS BETWEEN US,
AND ONLY A FEW CENTI-METERS.
BUT WHEN IT COMES TO FEELINGS...
...!!!
CAN WE GO FURTHER?
WHISPER
...WE'RE TOGETHER ON THE STARTING LINE!
The END

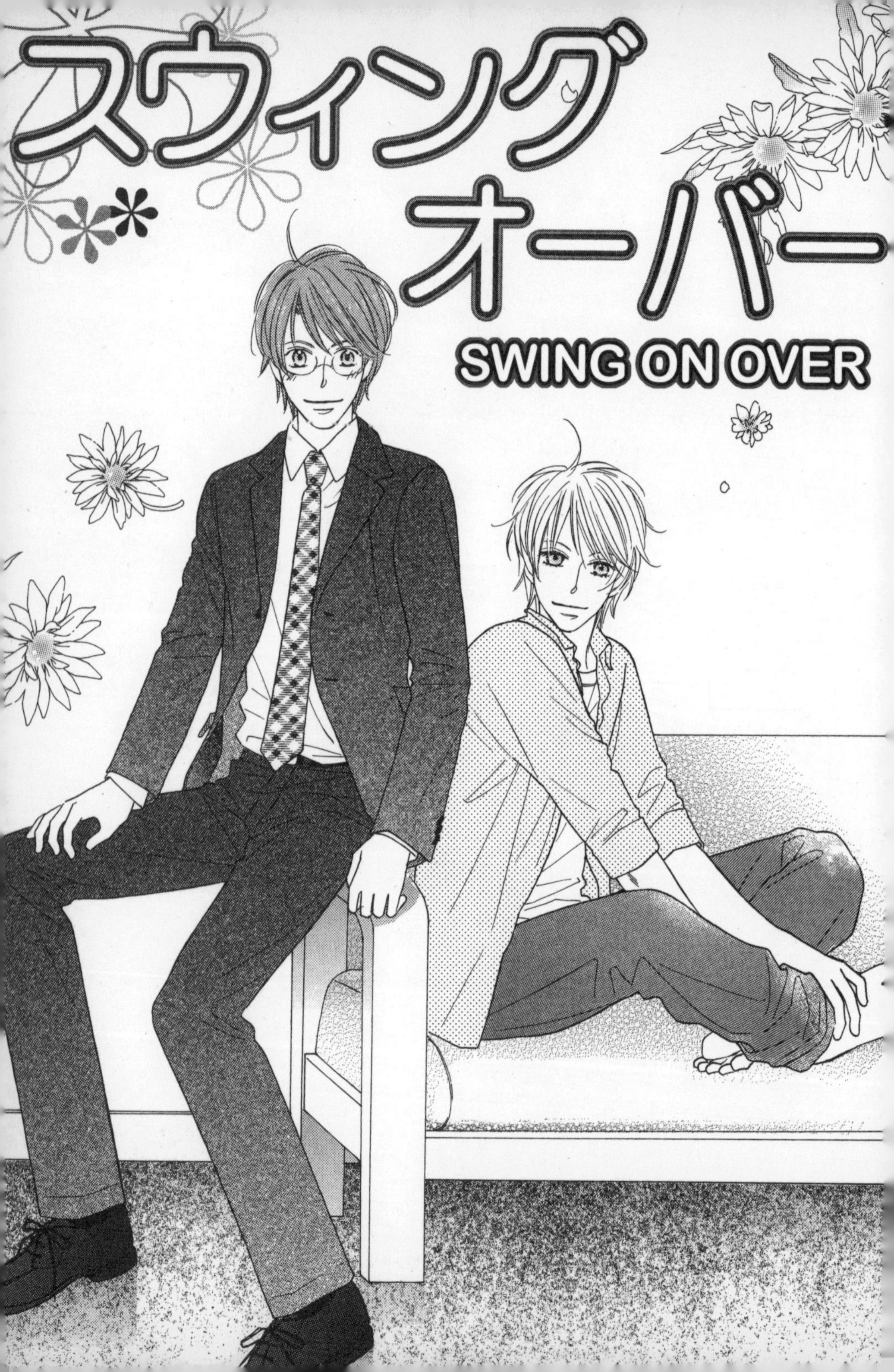
スウィングオーバー
SWING ON OVER

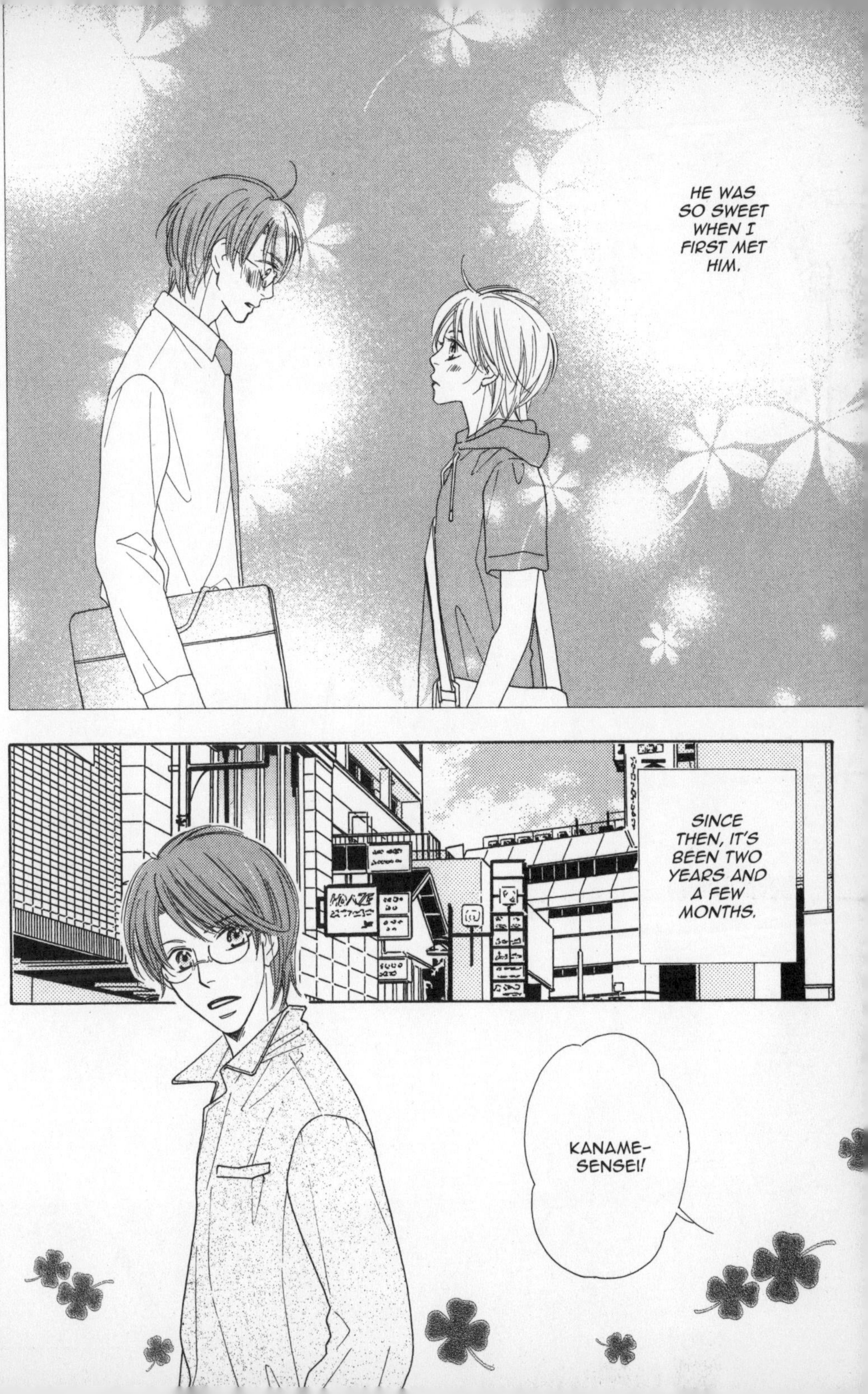
HE WAS SO SWEET WHEN I FIRST MET HIM.
SINCE THEN, IT'S BEEN TWO YEARS AND A FEW MONTHS.
KANAME-SENSEI!

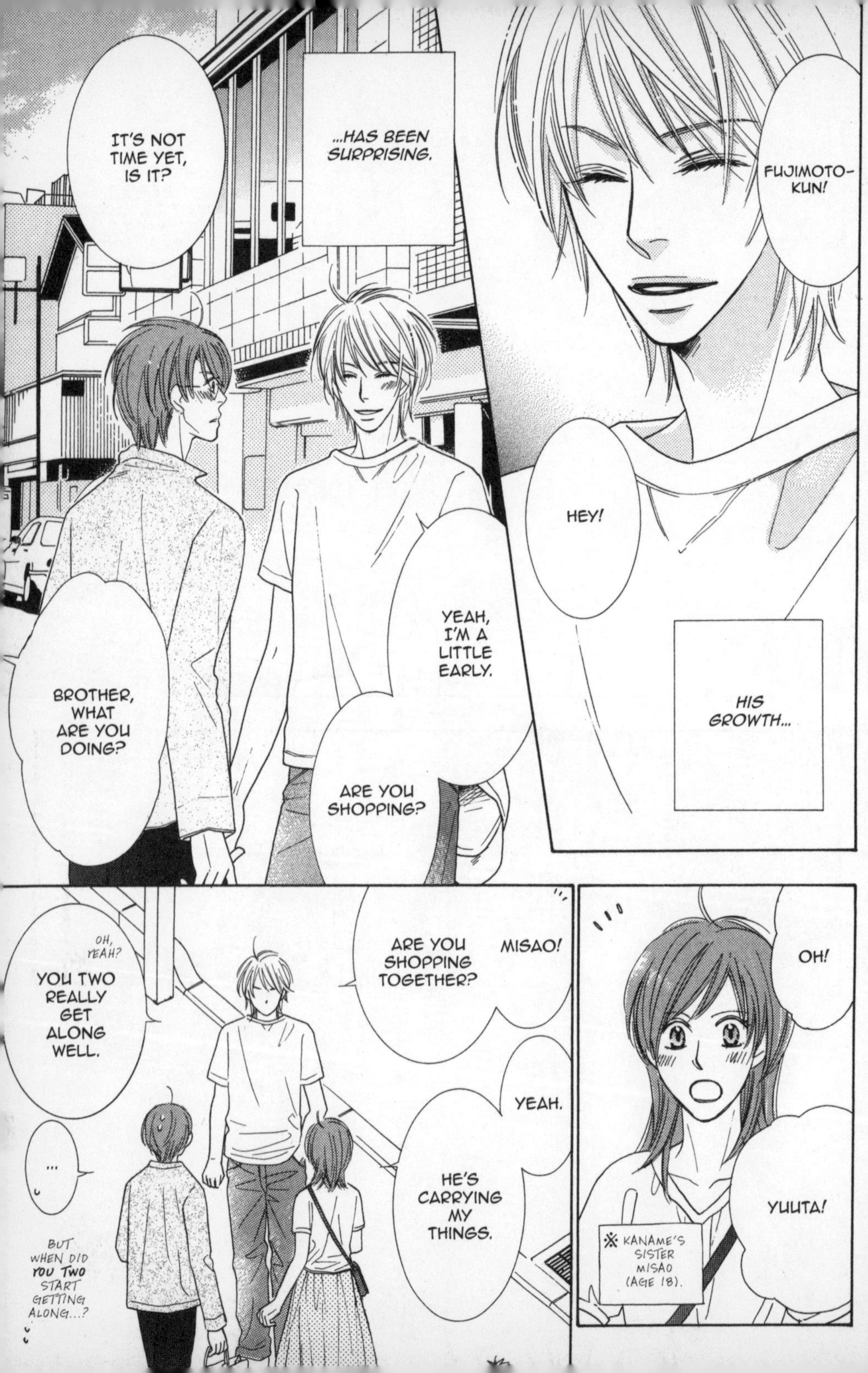
FUJIMOTO-KUN!
HEY!
HIS GROWTH...
...HAS BEEN SURPRISING.
IT'S NOT TIME YET, IS IT?
YEAH, I'M A LITTLE EARLY.
ARE YOU SHOPPING?
BROTHER, WHAT ARE YOU DOING?
OH!
YUUTA!
※ KANAME'S SISTER MISAO (AGE 18).
MISAO!
ARE YOU SHOPPING TOGETHER?
YEAH.
HE'S CARRYING MY THINGS.
OH, YEAH?
YOU TWO REALLY GET ALONG WELL.
...
BUT WHEN DID YOU TWO START GETTING ALONG...?

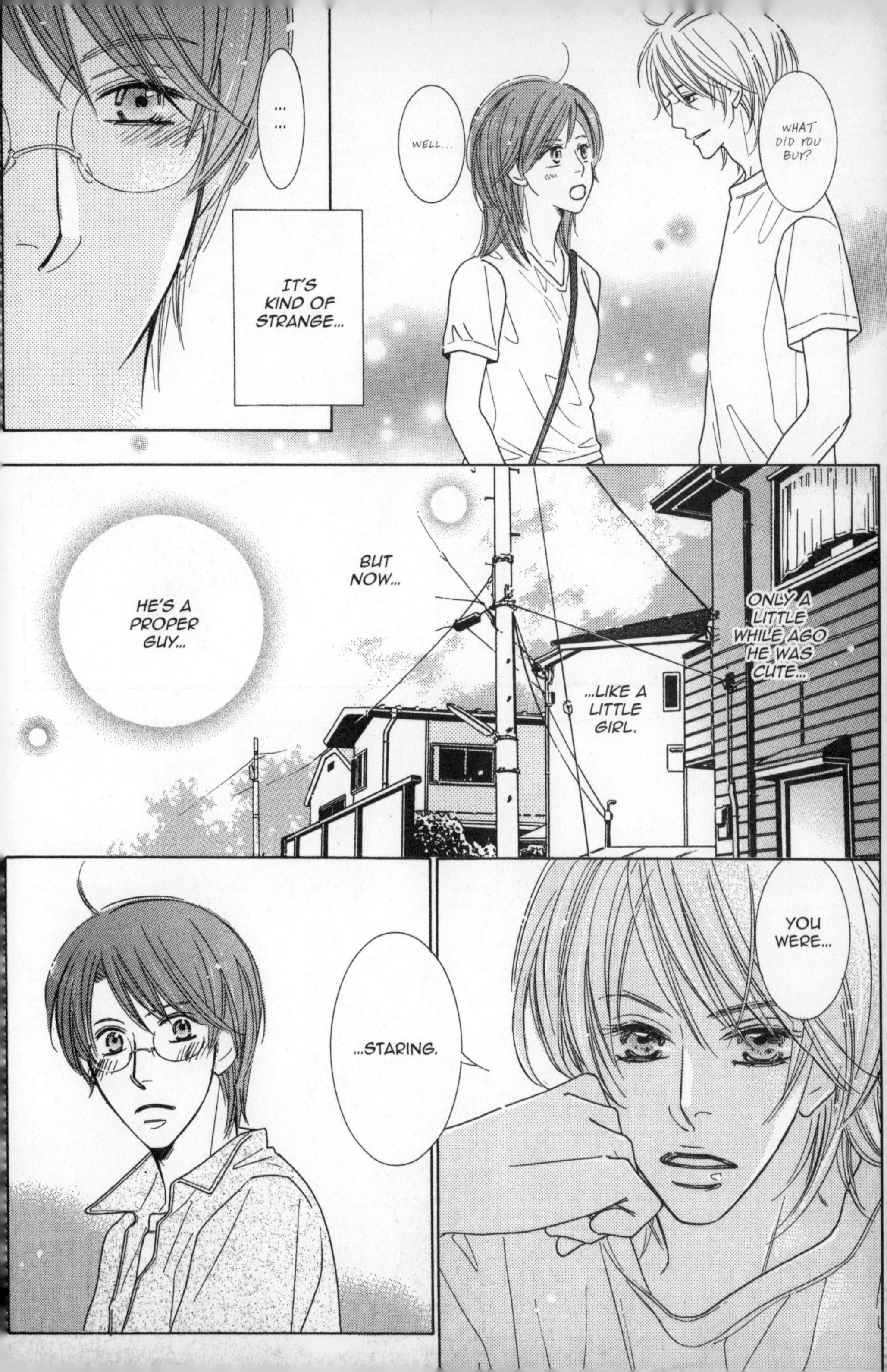
WHAT DID YOU BUY?
WELL...
... ...
IT'S KIND OF STRANGE...
ONLY A LITTLE WHILE AGO HE WAS CUTE...
...LIKE A LITTLE GIRL.
BUT NOW...
HE'S A PROPER GUY...
YOU WERE...
...STARING.

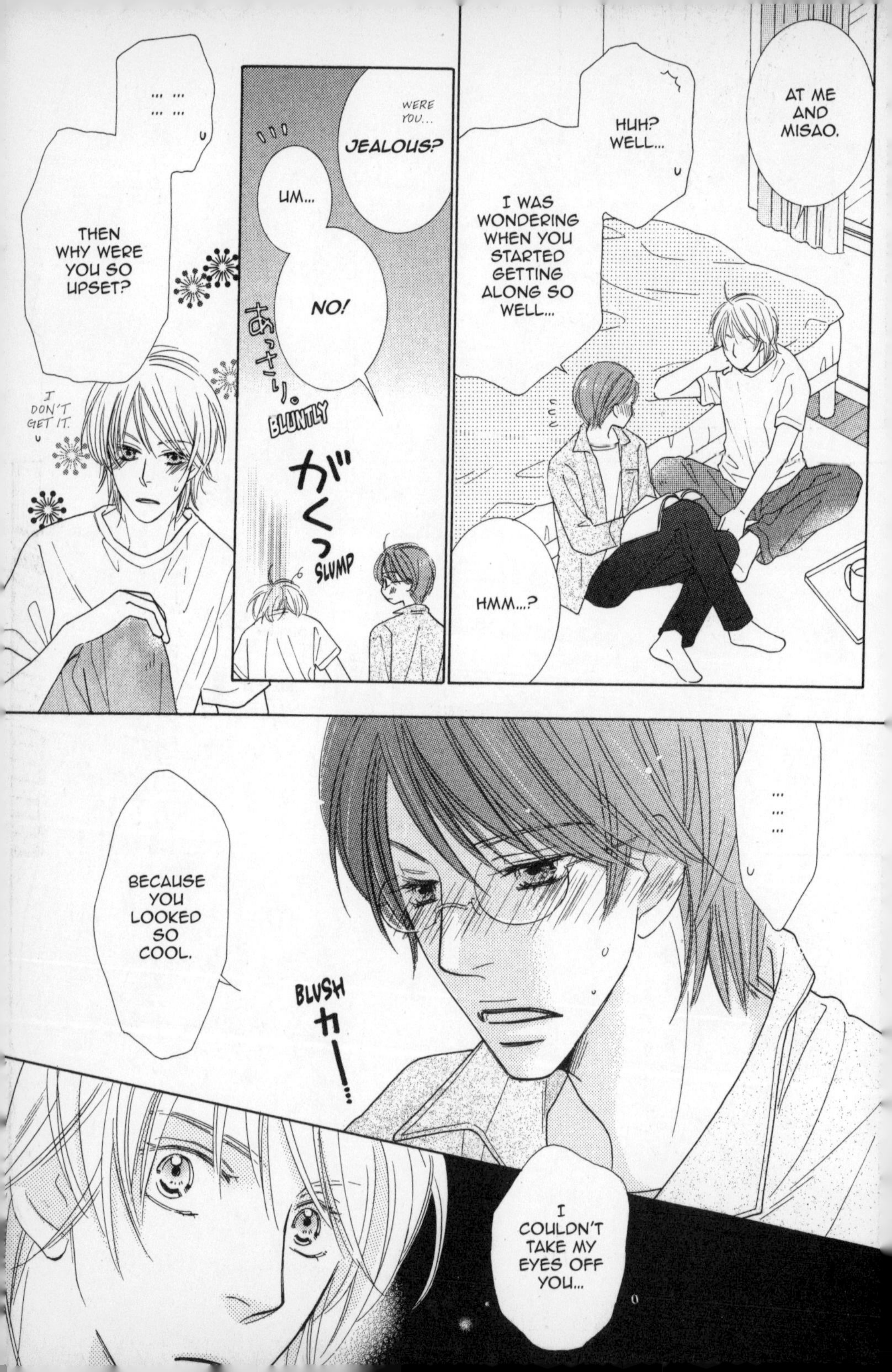
AT ME AND MISAO.
HUH? WELL...
I WAS WONDERING WHEN YOU STARTED GETTING ALONG SO WELL...
HMM...?
WERE YOU... JEALOUS?
UM...
NO!
あっさり。
BLUNTLY
がくっ
SLUMP
... ...
THEN WHY WERE YOU SO UPSET?
I DON'T GET IT.
... ...
BECAUSE YOU LOOKED SO COOL.
BLUSH
カー…!
I COULDN'T TAKE MY EYES OFF YOU...

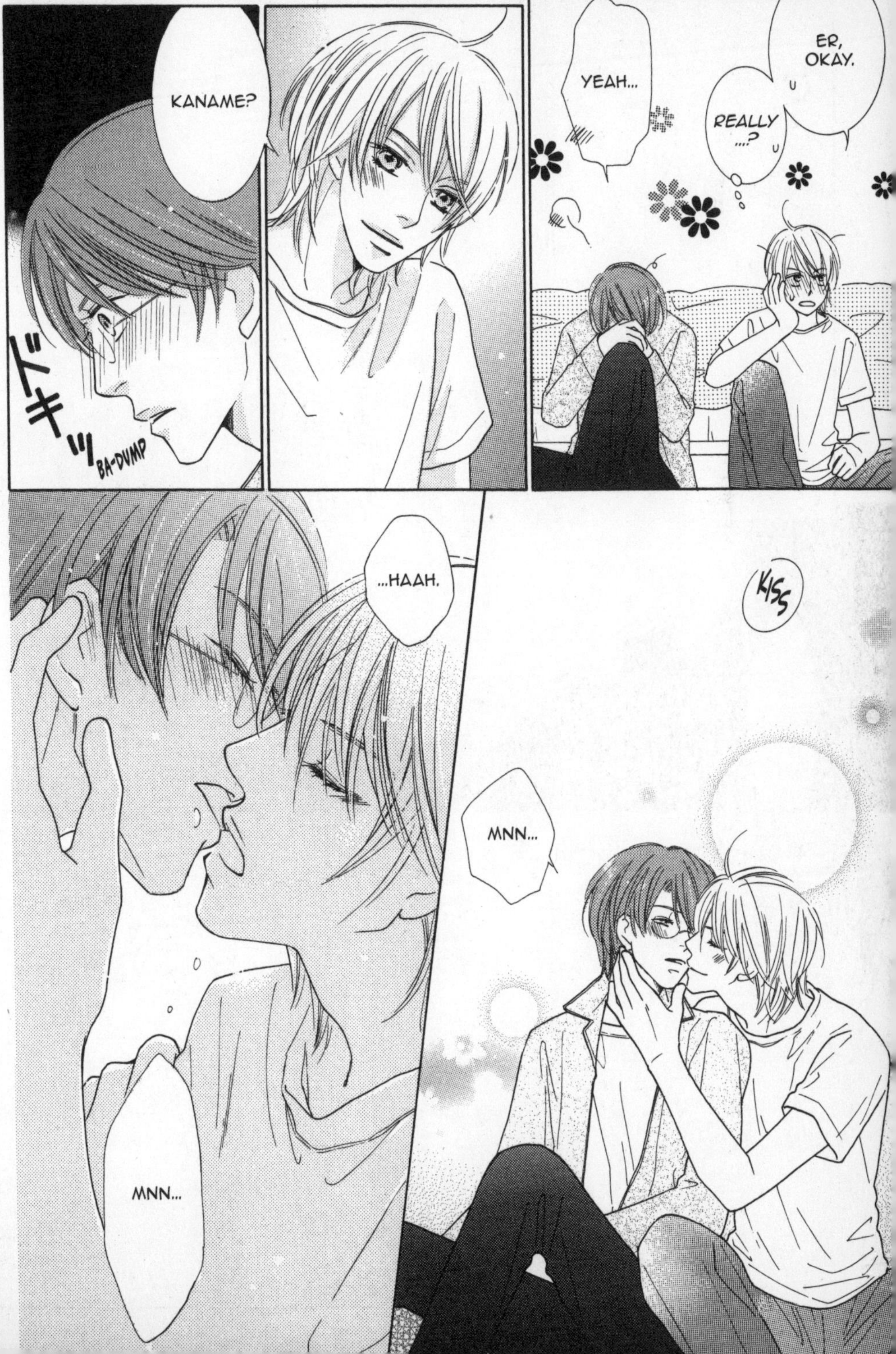
ER, OKAY.
REALLY ...?
YEAH...
KANAME?
ドキッ
BA-DUMP
KISS
MNN...
...HAAH.
MNN...

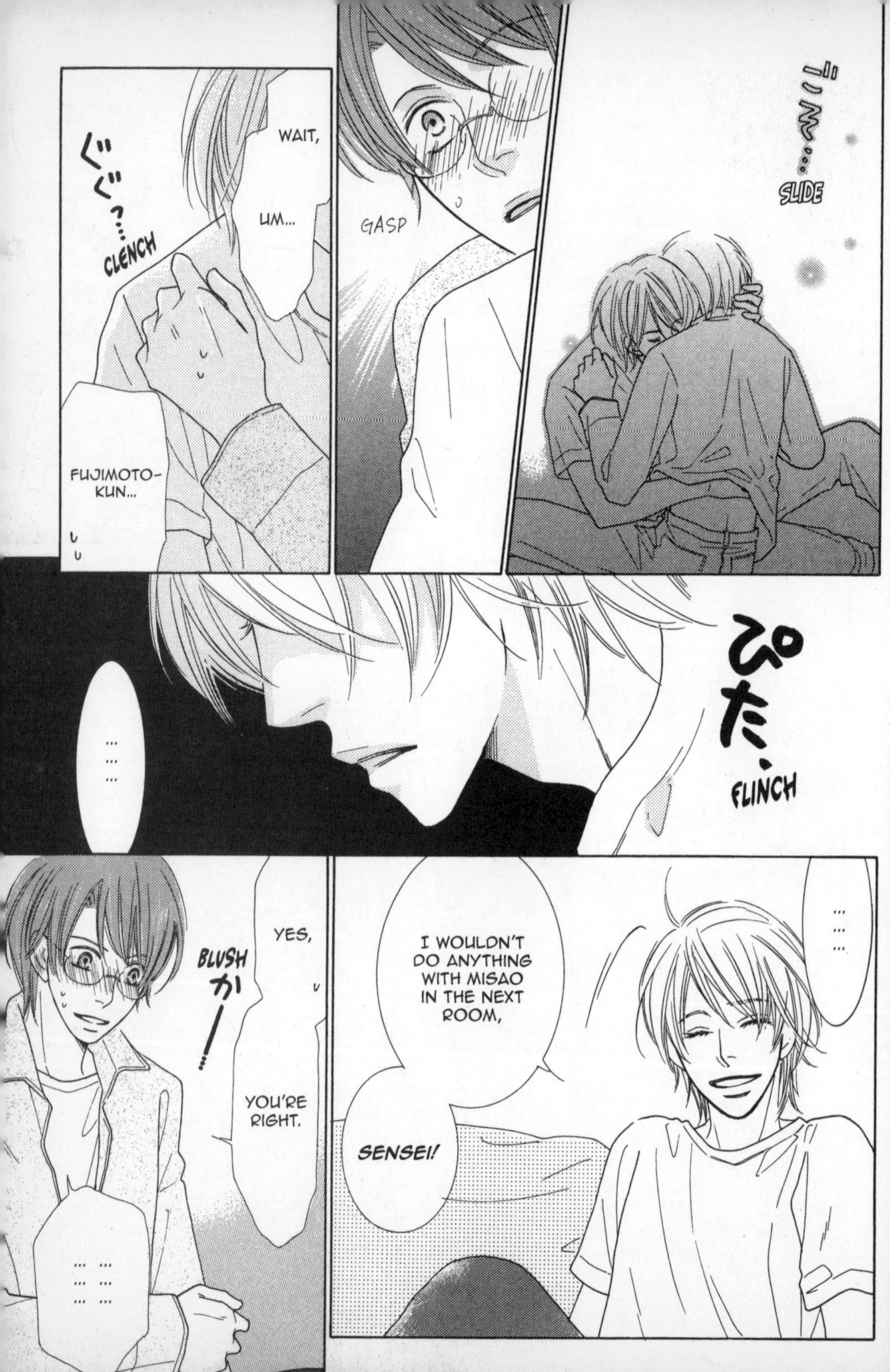

ごそ…
SLIDE
GASP
WAIT,
UM...
ぐぐっ…
CLENCH
FUJIMOTO-KUN...
ぴた。
FLINCH
......
......
I WOULDN'T DO ANYTHING WITH MISAO IN THE NEXT ROOM,
SENSEI!
YES,
YOU'RE RIGHT.
BLUSH
かーっ!!
......

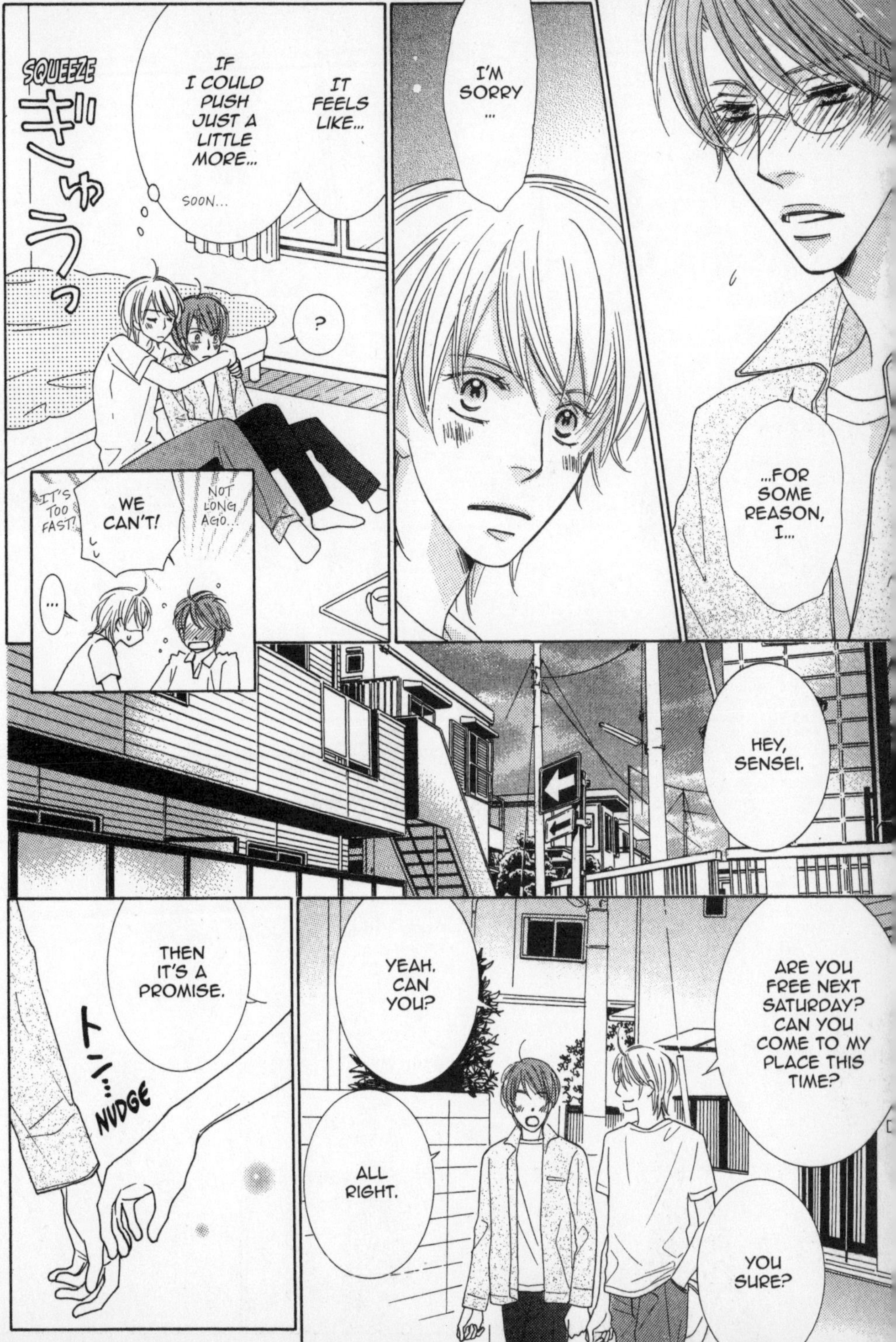
...FOR SOME REASON, I...
I'M SORRY ...
IT FEELS LIKE...
IF I COULD PUSH JUST A LITTLE MORE...
SOON...
SQUEEZE
?
NOT LONG AGO...
WE CAN'T!
IT'S TOO FAST!
...
HEY, SENSEI.
ARE YOU FREE NEXT SATURDAY? CAN YOU COME TO MY PLACE THIS TIME?
YOU SURE?
YEAH. CAN YOU?
ALL RIGHT.
THEN IT'S A PROMISE.
NUDGE

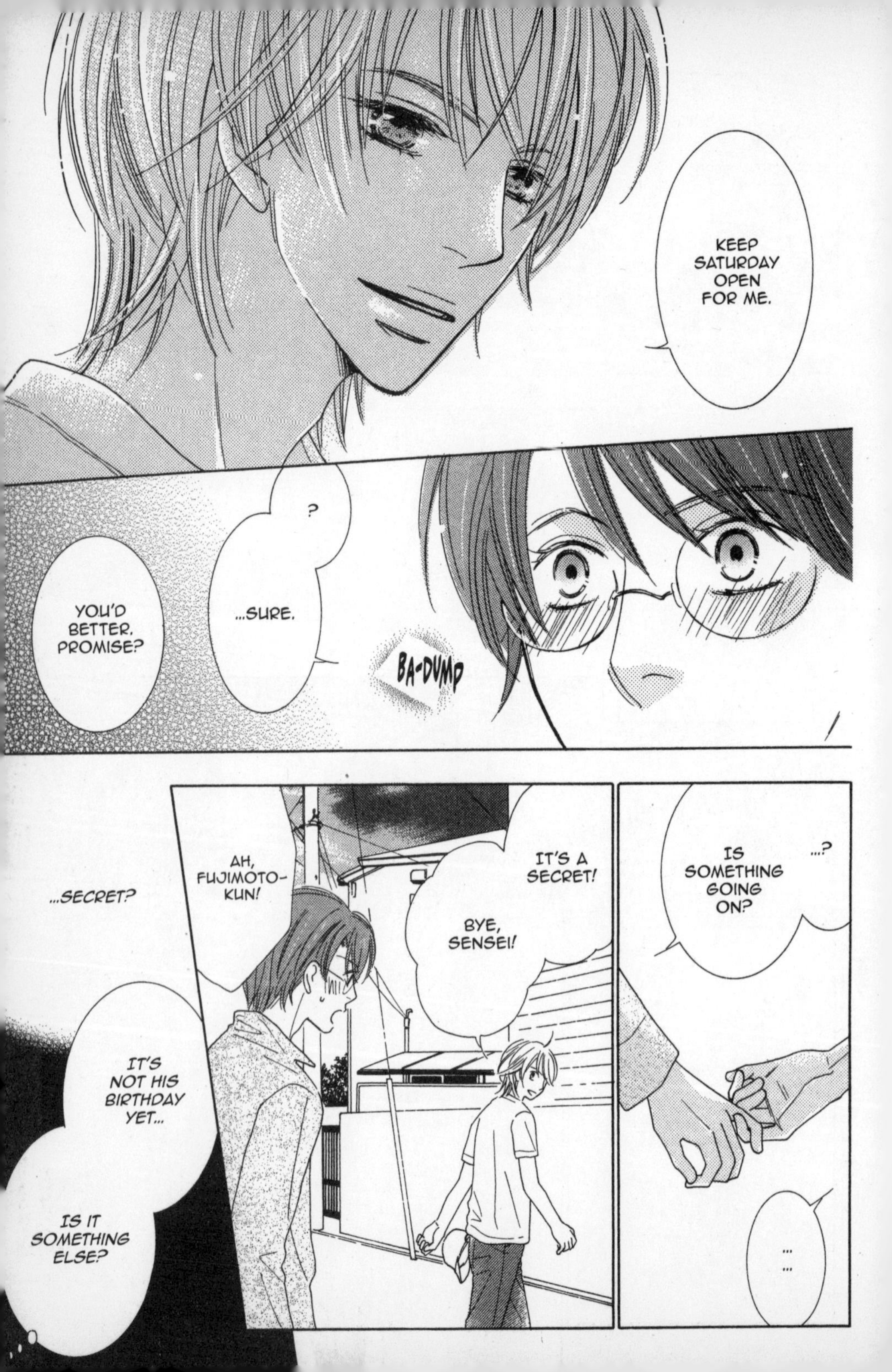
KEEP SATURDAY OPEN FOR ME.
BA-DUMP
? ...SURE.
YOU'D BETTER. PROMISE?
...?
IS SOMETHING GOING ON?
... ...
IT'S A SECRET!
BYE, SENSEI!
AH, FUJIMOTO-KUN!
...SECRET?
IT'S NOT HIS BIRTHDAY YET...
IS IT SOMETHING ELSE?

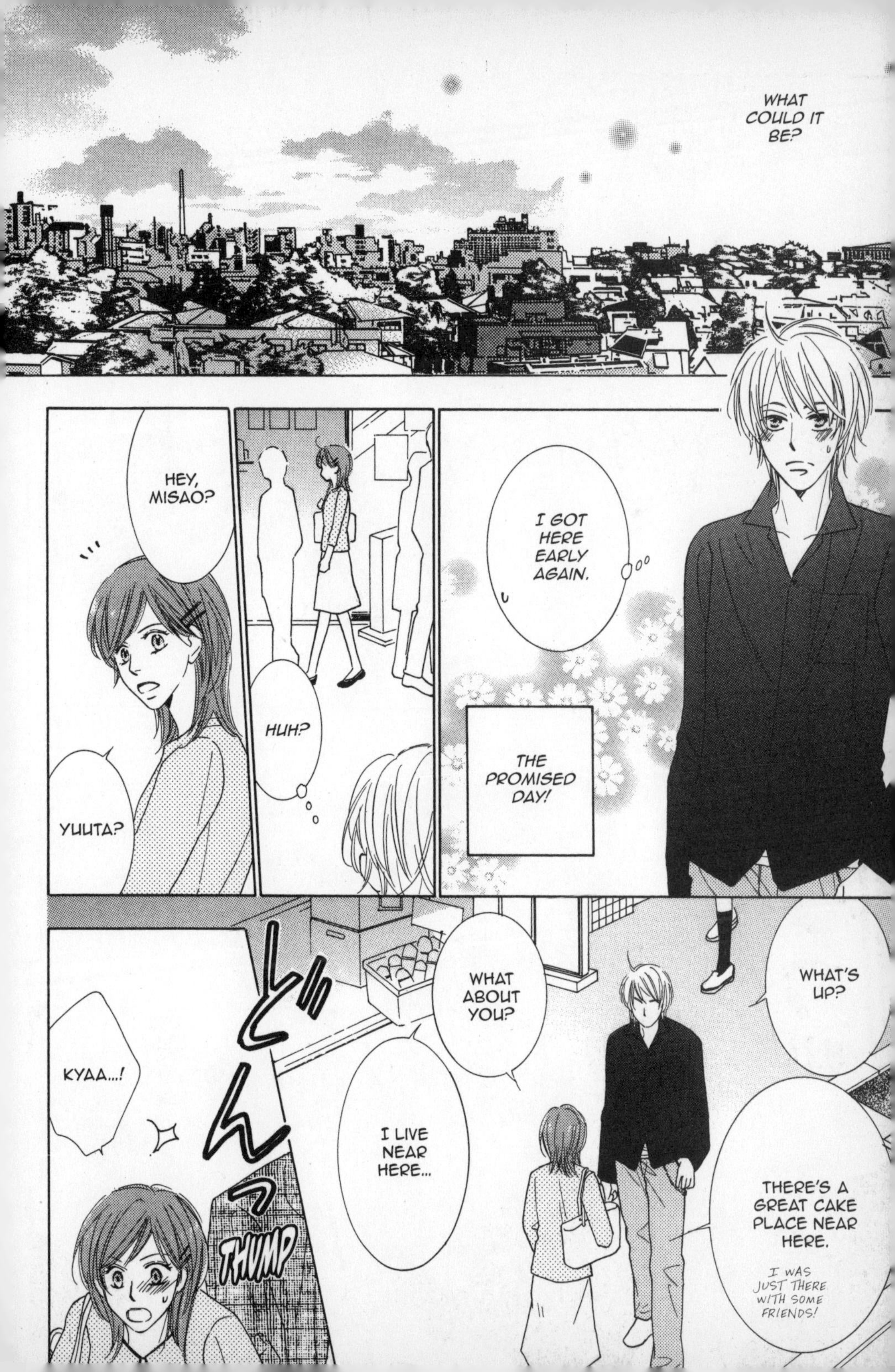
WHAT COULD IT BE?
I GOT HERE EARLY AGAIN.
THE PROMISED DAY!
HUH?
HEY, MISAO?
YUUTA?
WHAT'S UP?
THERE'S A GREAT CAKE PLACE NEAR HERE.
I WAS JUST THERE WITH SOME FRIENDS!
WHAT ABOUT YOU?
I LIVE NEAR HERE...
どんっ
THUMP
KYAA...!

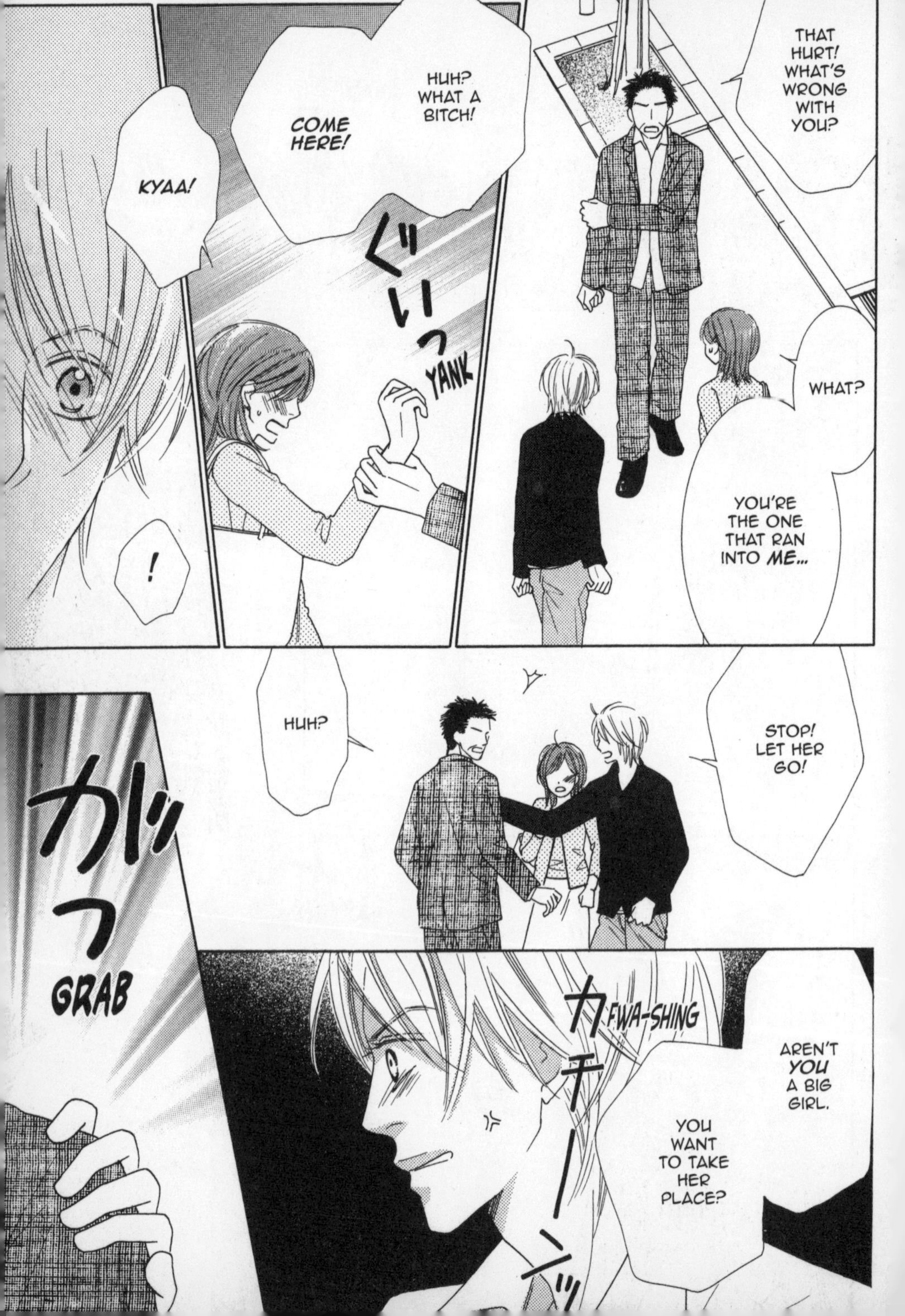
THAT HURT! WHAT'S WRONG WITH YOU?
WHAT?
YOU'RE THE ONE THAT RAN INTO *ME*...
HUH? WHAT A BITCH!
COME HERE!
ぐいっ
YANK
KYAA!
!
STOP! LET HER GO!
HUH?
AREN'T *YOU* A BIG GIRL.
YOU WANT TO TAKE HER PLACE?
カチーンッ
FWA-SHING
がっ
GRAB

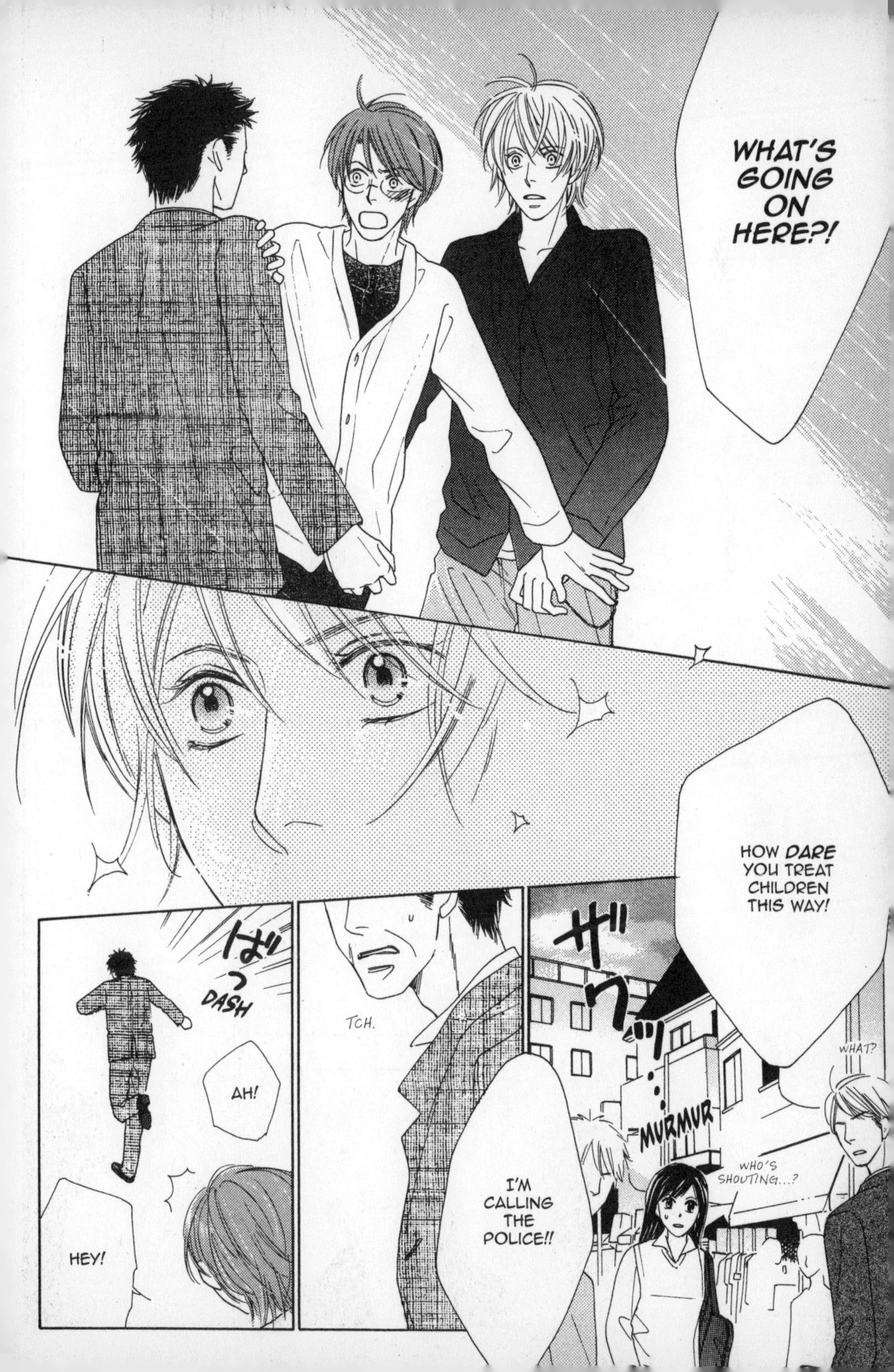
WHAT'S GOING ON HERE?!
HOW DARE YOU TREAT CHILDREN THIS WAY!
ザワッ
MURMUR
WHAT?
WHO'S SHOUTING...?
I'M CALLING THE POLICE!!
TCH.
ばっ
DASH
AH!
HEY!

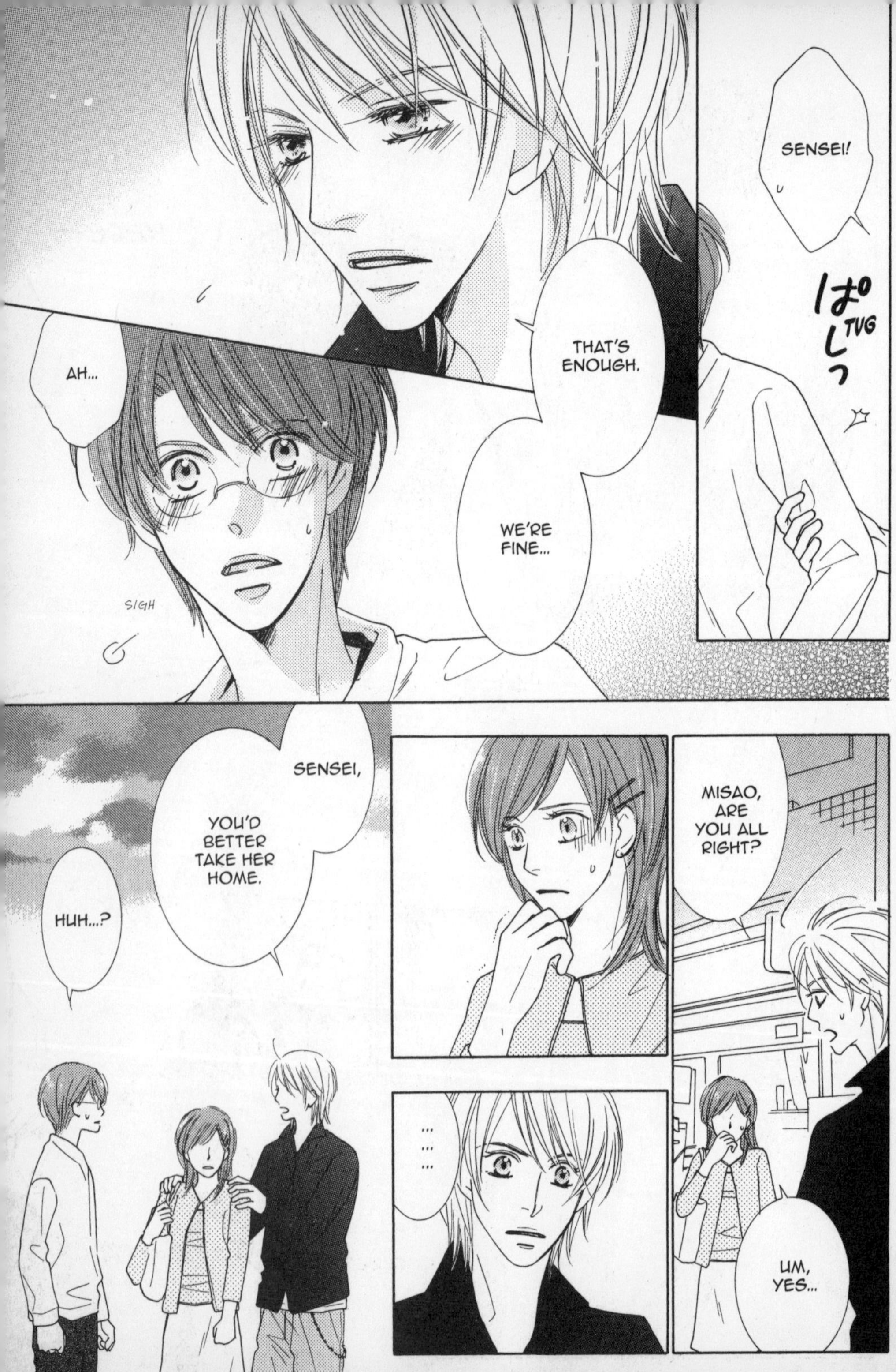
SENSEI!
ぱしっ
TVG
THAT'S ENOUGH.
WE'RE FINE...
AH...
SIGH
MISAO, ARE YOU ALL RIGHT?
UM, YES...
...
...
...
SENSEI,
YOU'D BETTER TAKE HER HOME.
HUH...?

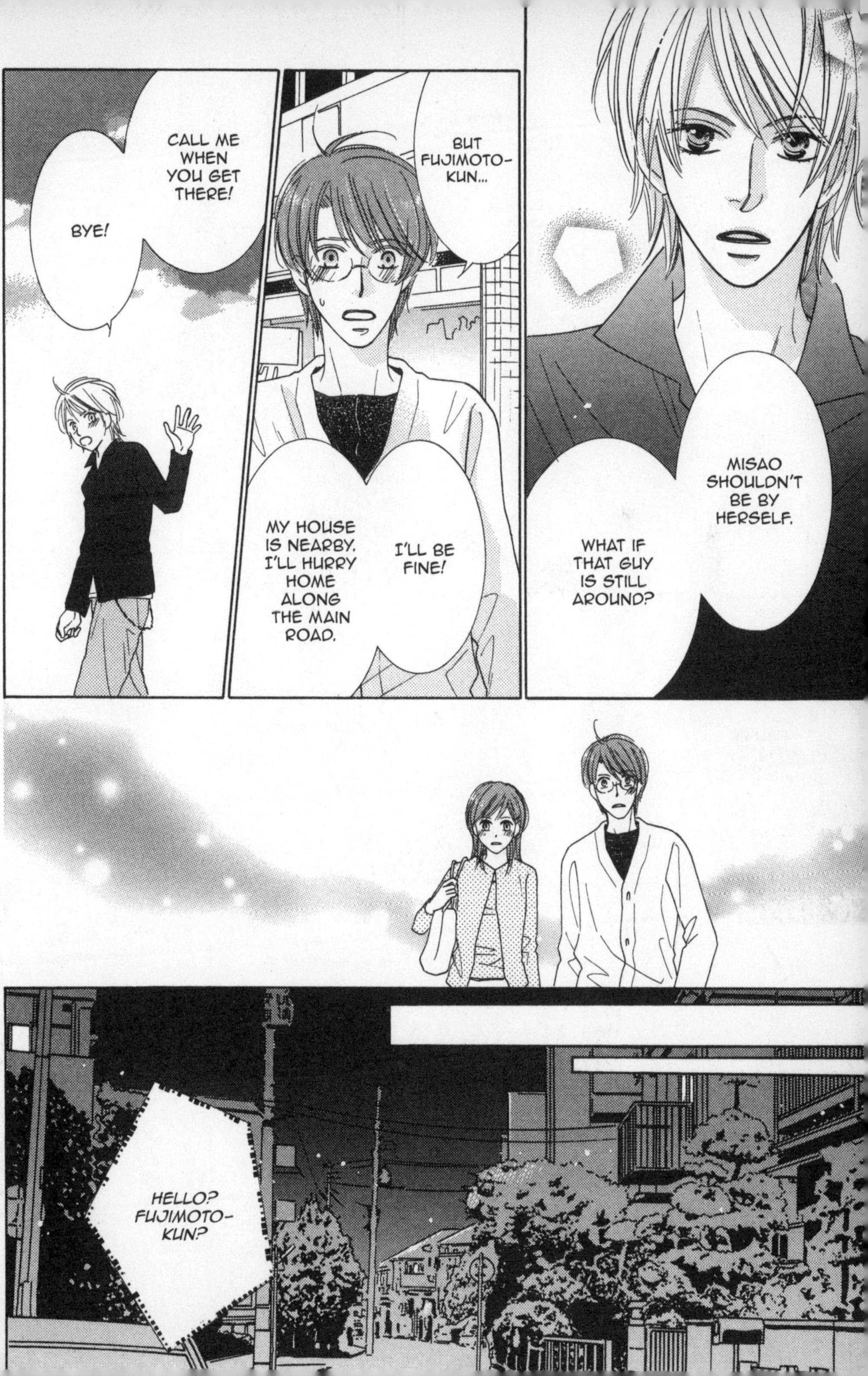
MISAO SHOULDN'T BE BY HERSELF.
WHAT IF THAT GUY IS STILL AROUND?
BUT FUJIMOTO-KUN...
I'LL BE FINE!
MY HOUSE IS NEARBY. I'LL HURRY HOME ALONG THE MAIN ROAD.
CALL ME WHEN YOU GET THERE!
BYE!
HELLO? FUJIMOTO-KUN?

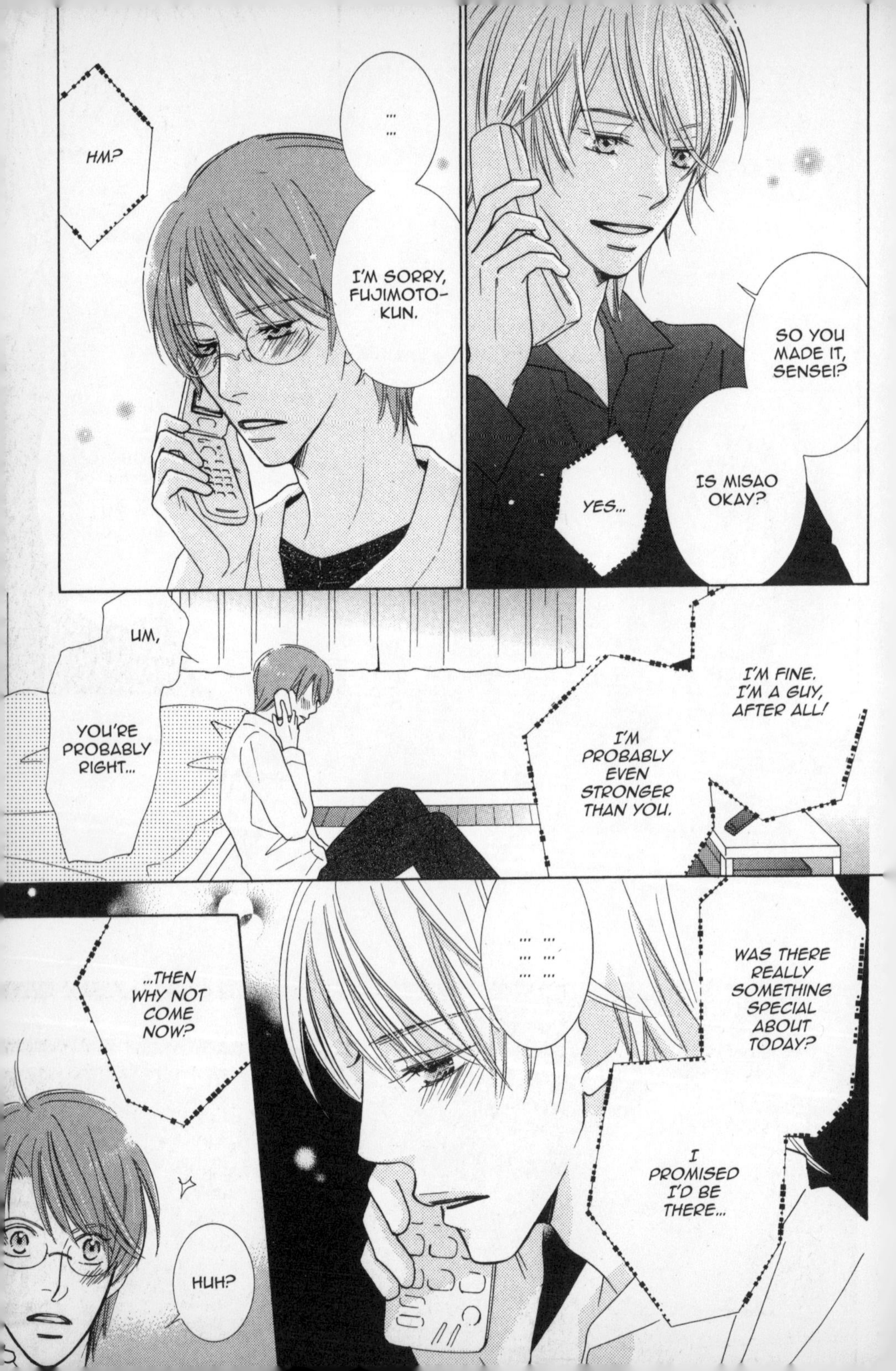
SO YOU MADE IT, SENSEI?
IS MISAO OKAY?
YES...
...
...
I'M SORRY, FUJIMOTO-KUN.
HM?
I'M FINE. I'M A GUY, AFTER ALL!
I'M PROBABLY EVEN STRONGER THAN YOU.
UM,
YOU'RE PROBABLY RIGHT...
WAS THERE REALLY SOMETHING SPECIAL ABOUT TODAY?
I PROMISED I'D BE THERE...
... ...
...THEN WHY NOT COME NOW?
HUH?

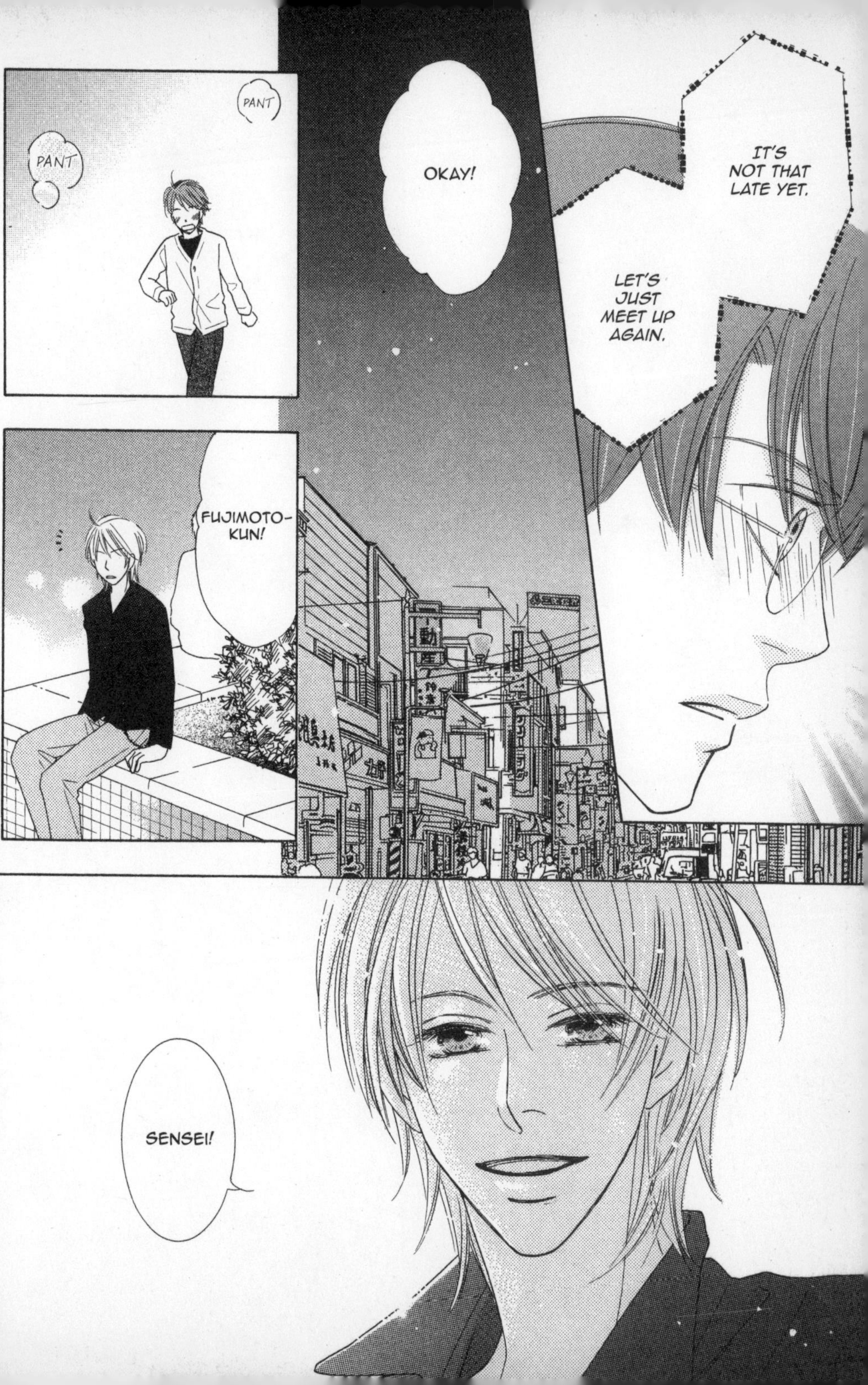
IT'S NOT THAT LATE YET.
LET'S JUST MEET UP AGAIN.
OKAY!
PANT
PANT
FUJIMOTO-KUN!
SENSEI!

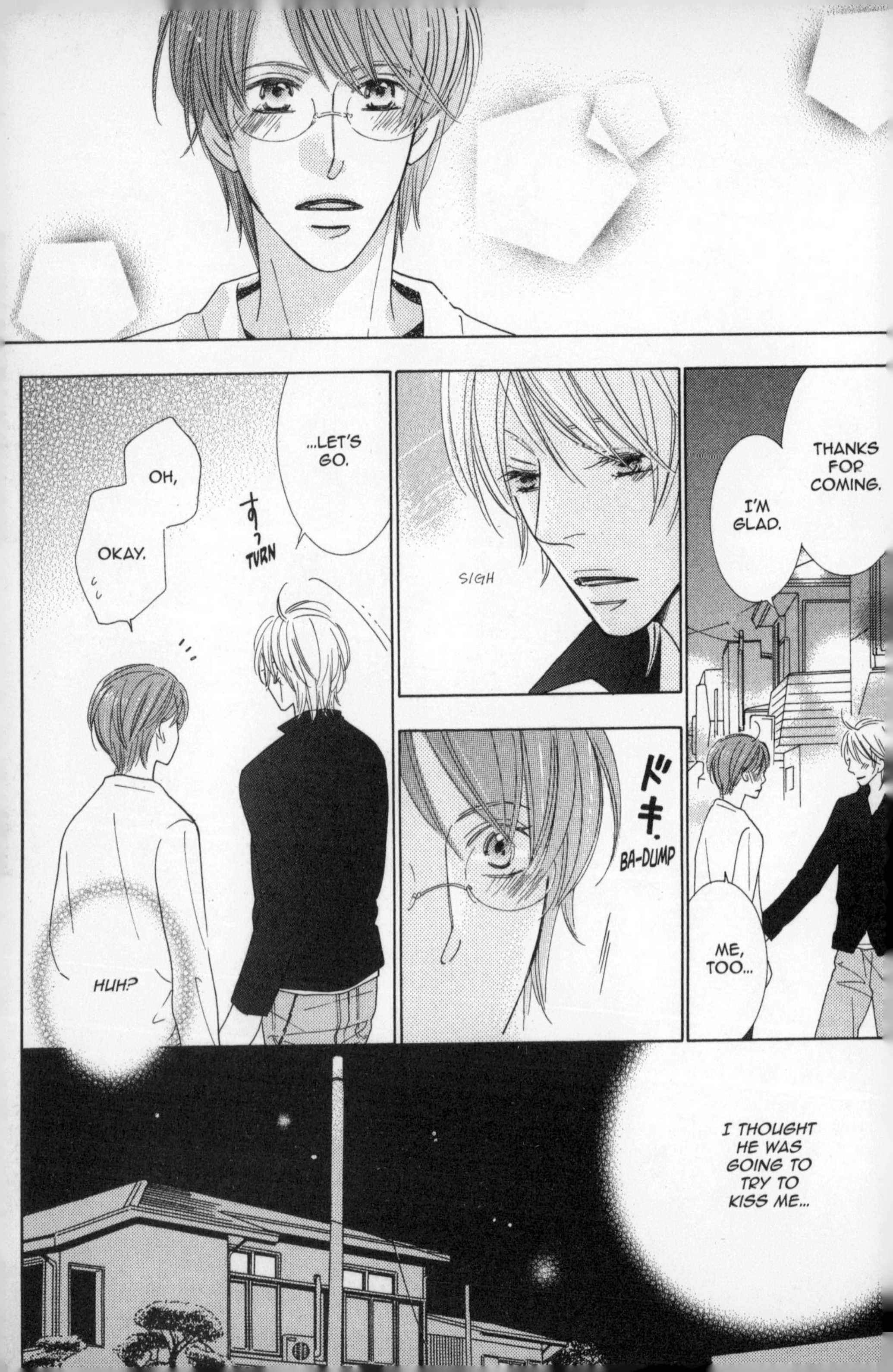
THANKS FOR COMING.
I'M GLAD.
ME, TOO...
SIGH
ドキ
BA-DUMP
...LET'S GO.
すっ
TURN
OH, OKAY.
HUH?
I THOUGHT HE WAS GOING TO TRY TO KISS ME...

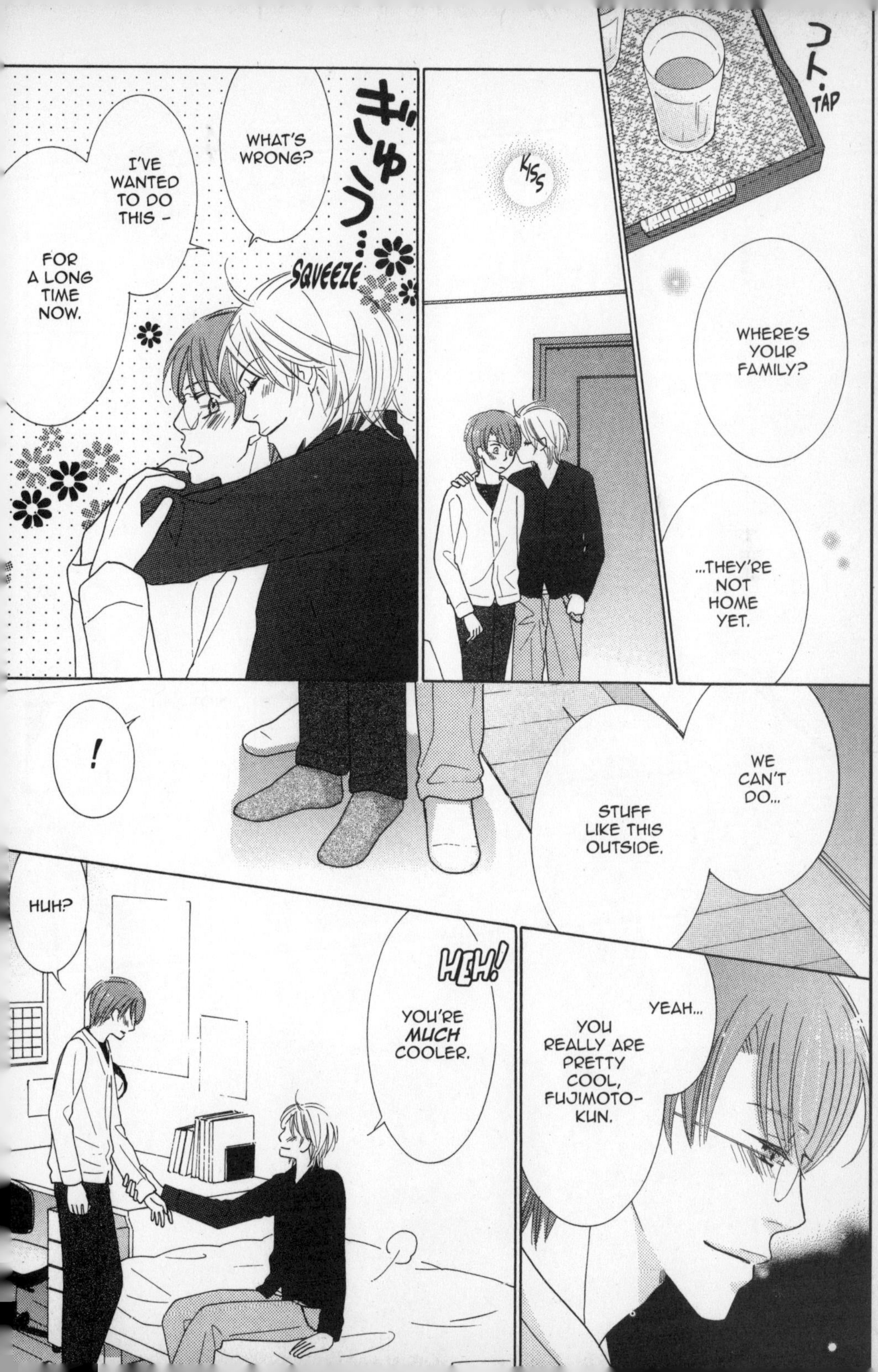
コト・ TAP
WHERE'S YOUR FAMILY?
...THEY'RE NOT HOME YET.
KISS
ぎゅう… SQUEEZE
WHAT'S WRONG?
I'VE WANTED TO DO THIS -
FOR A LONG TIME NOW.
WE CAN'T DO...
STUFF LIKE THIS OUTSIDE.
!
YEAH...
YOU REALLY ARE PRETTY COOL, FUJIMOTO-KUN.
HEH!
YOU'RE MUCH COOLER.
HUH?

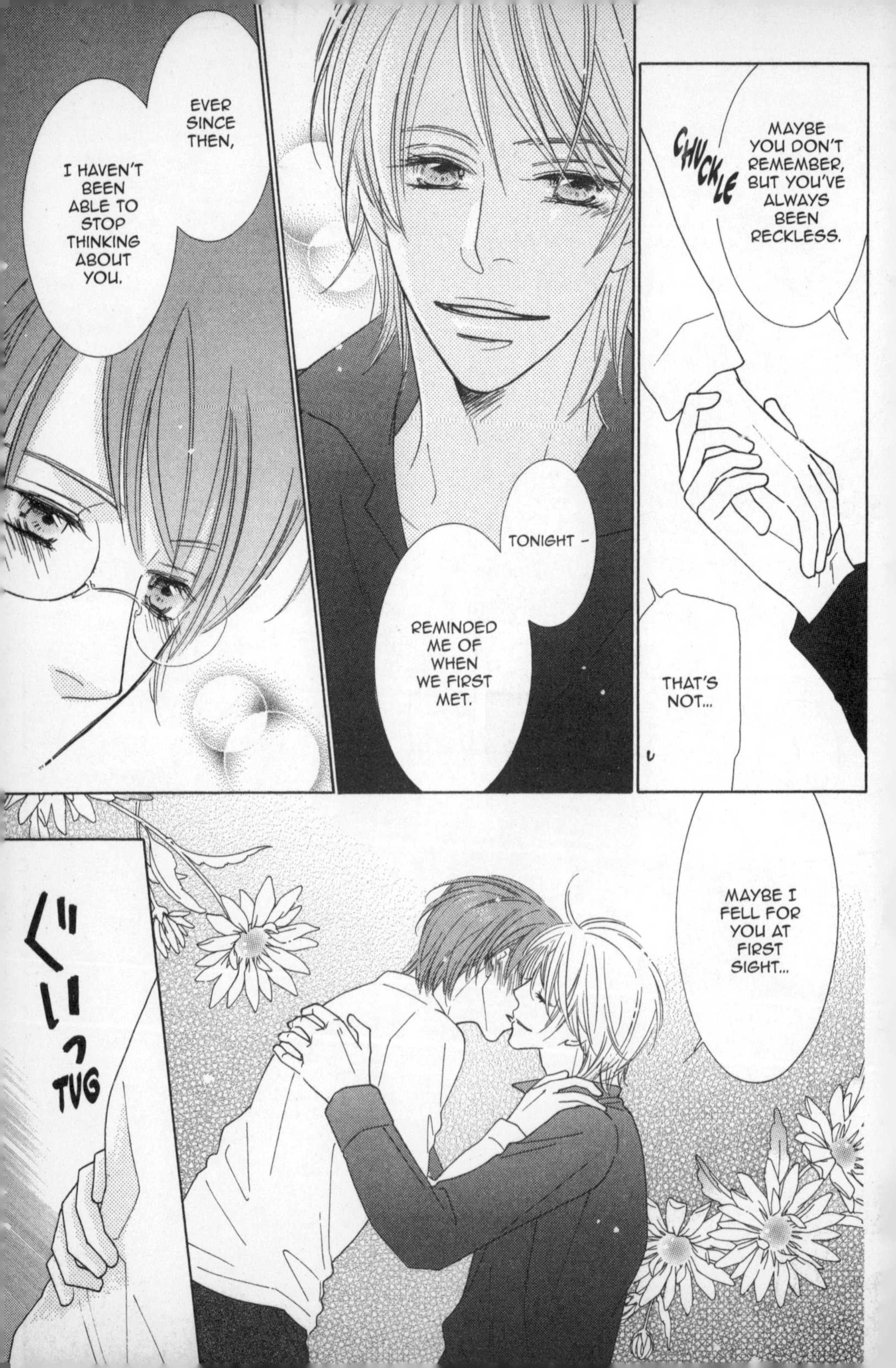
MAYBE YOU DON'T REMEMBER, BUT YOU'VE ALWAYS BEEN RECKLESS.
CHUCKLE
THAT'S NOT...
TONIGHT - REMINDED ME OF WHEN WE FIRST MET.
EVER SINCE THEN, I HAVEN'T BEEN ABLE TO STOP THINKING ABOUT YOU.
MAYBE I FELL FOR YOU AT FIRST SIGHT...
ぐいっ
TUG

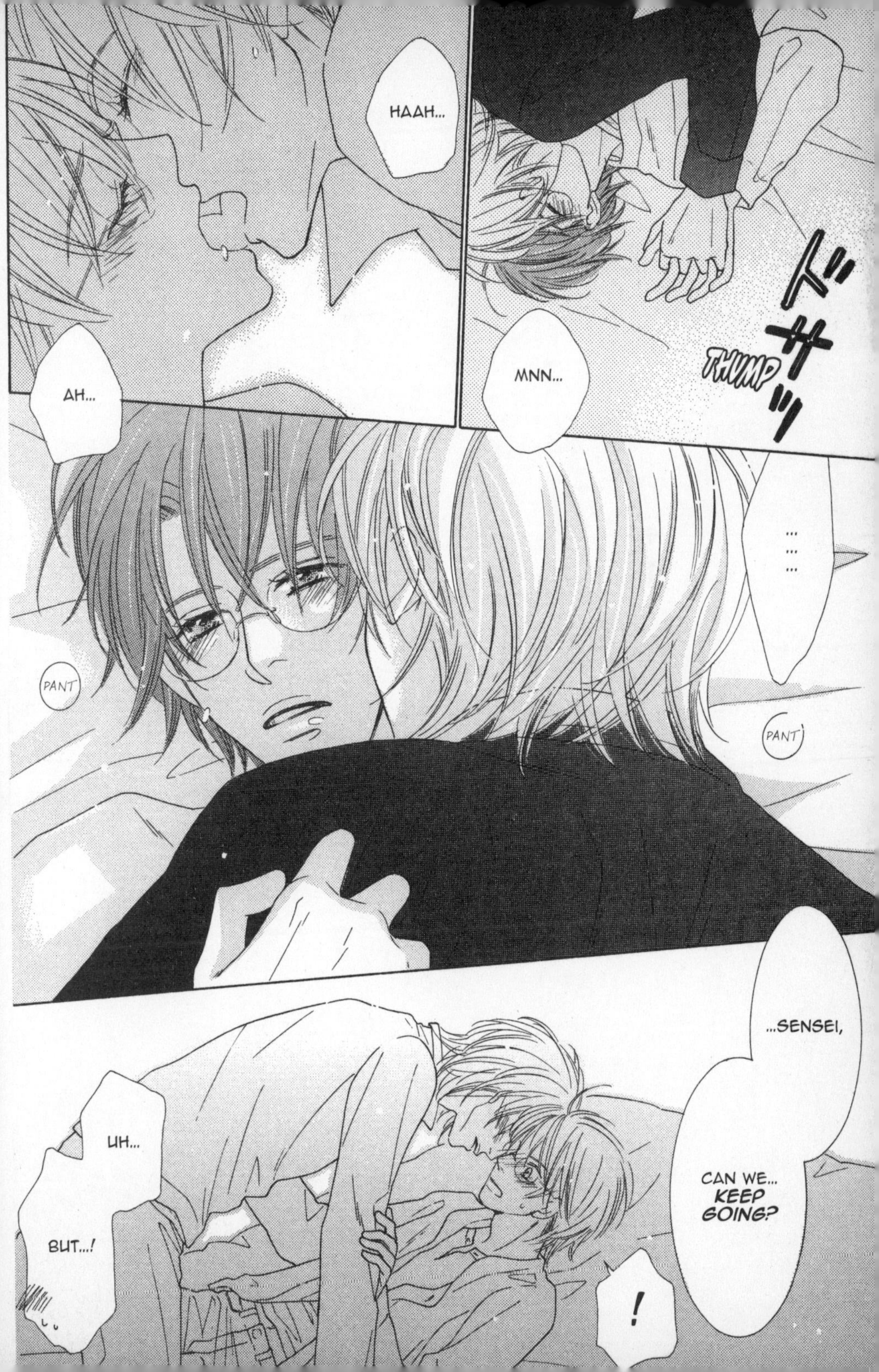

ドサッ
THUMP
MNN...
HAAH...
AH...
...
...
...
PANT
PANT
...SENSEI,
CAN WE... KEEP GOING?
!
UH...
BUT...!

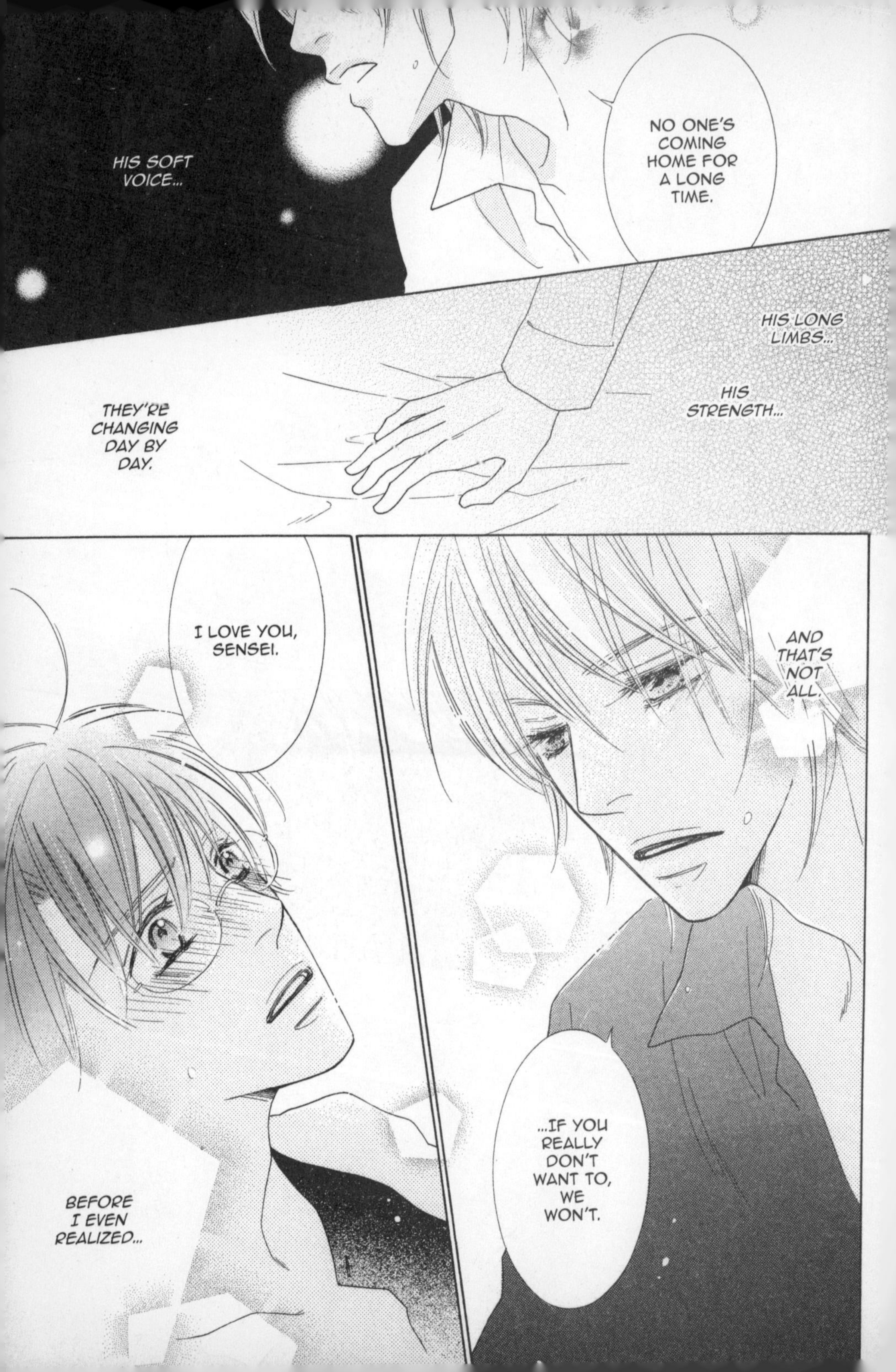
NO ONE'S COMING HOME FOR A LONG TIME.
HIS SOFT VOICE...
HIS LONG LIMBS...
HIS STRENGTH...
THEY'RE CHANGING DAY BY DAY.
AND THAT'S NOT ALL.
...IF YOU REALLY DON'T WANT TO, WE WON'T.
I LOVE YOU, SENSEI.
BEFORE I EVEN REALIZED...

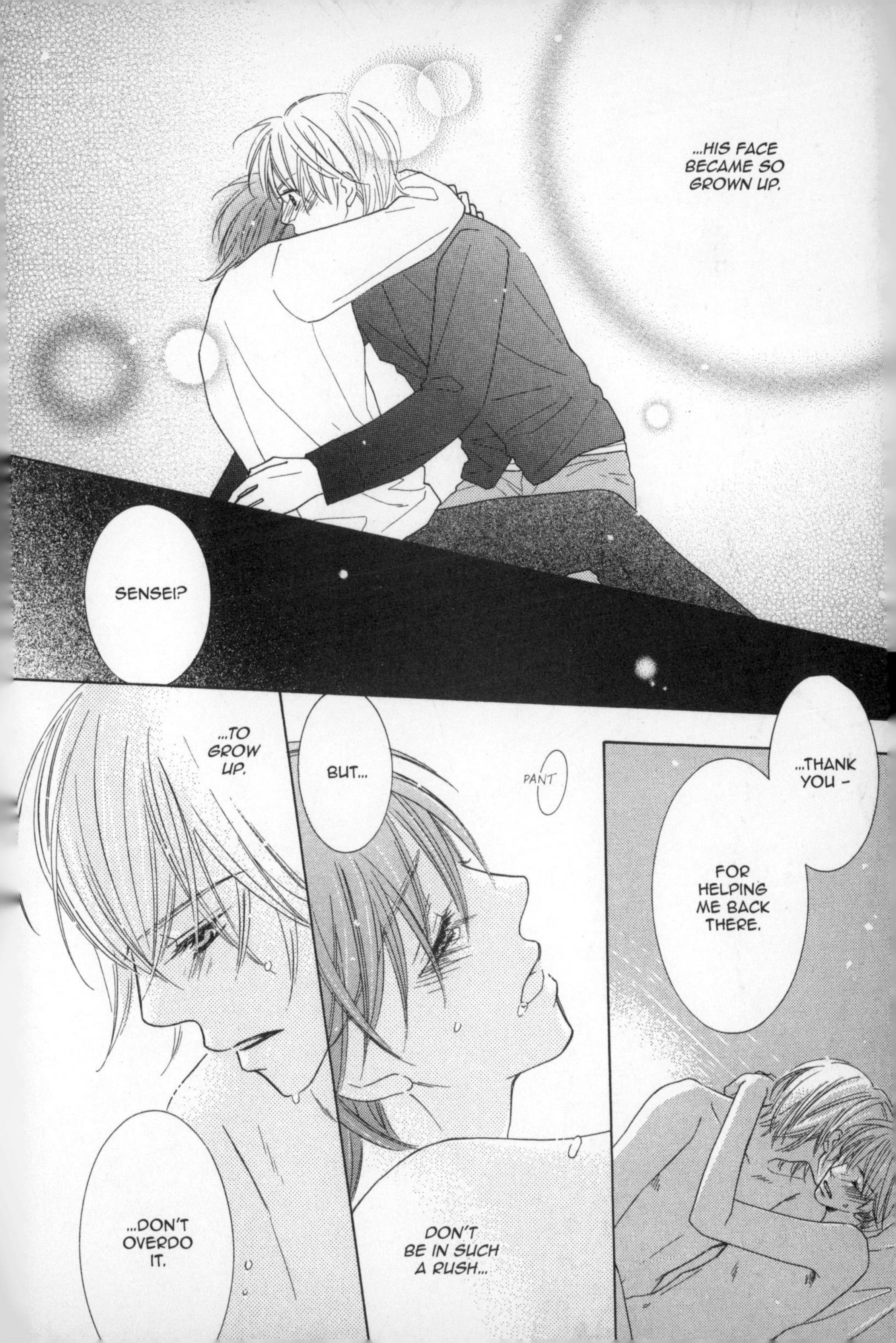
...HIS FACE BECAME SO GROWN UP.
SENSEI?
...THANK YOU -
FOR HELPING ME BACK THERE.
PANT
BUT...
DON'T BE IN SUCH A RUSH...
...TO GROW UP.
...DON'T OVERDO IT.

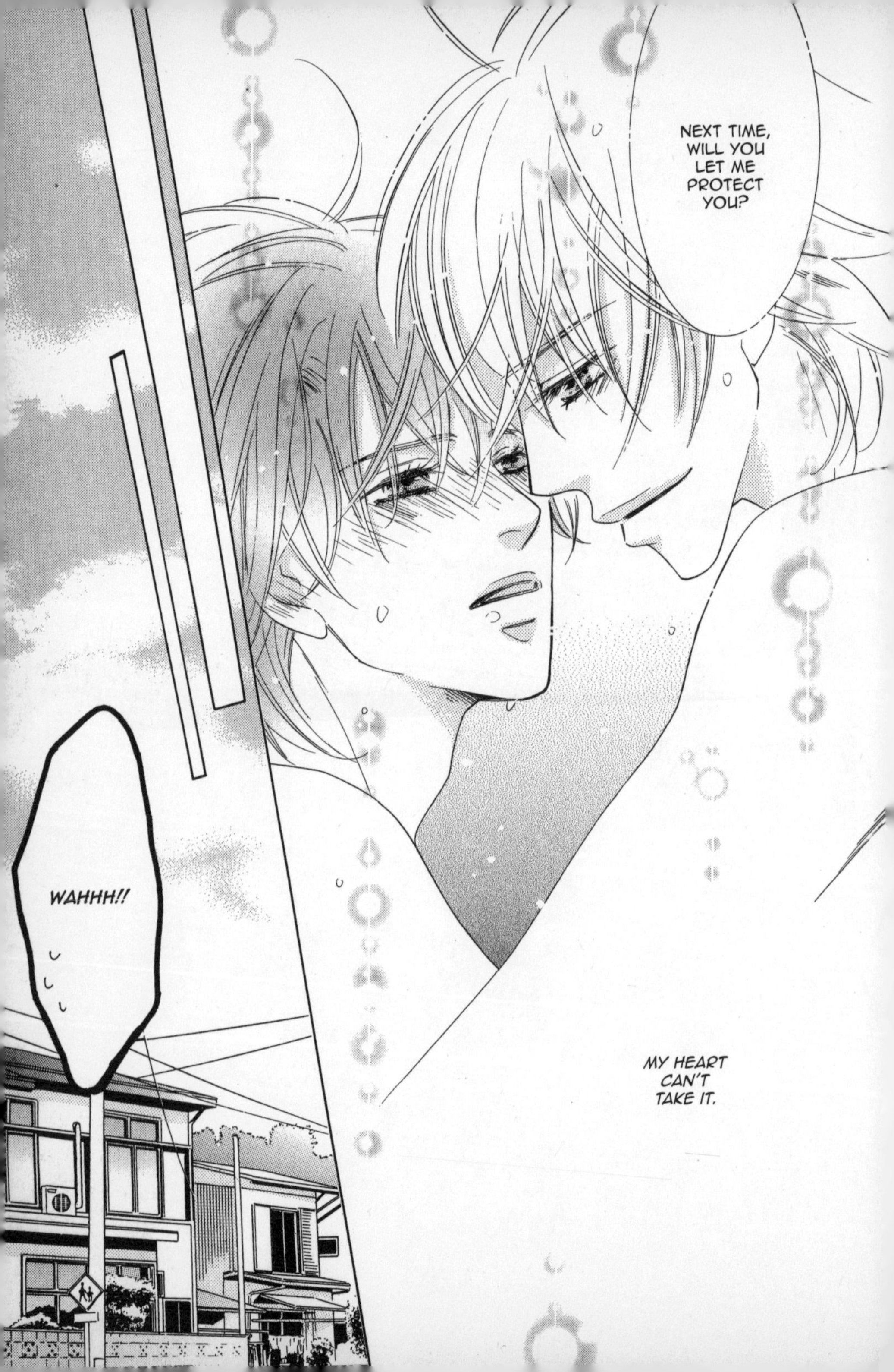
NEXT TIME, WILL YOU LET ME PROTECT YOU?
MY HEART CAN'T TAKE IT.
WAHHH!!

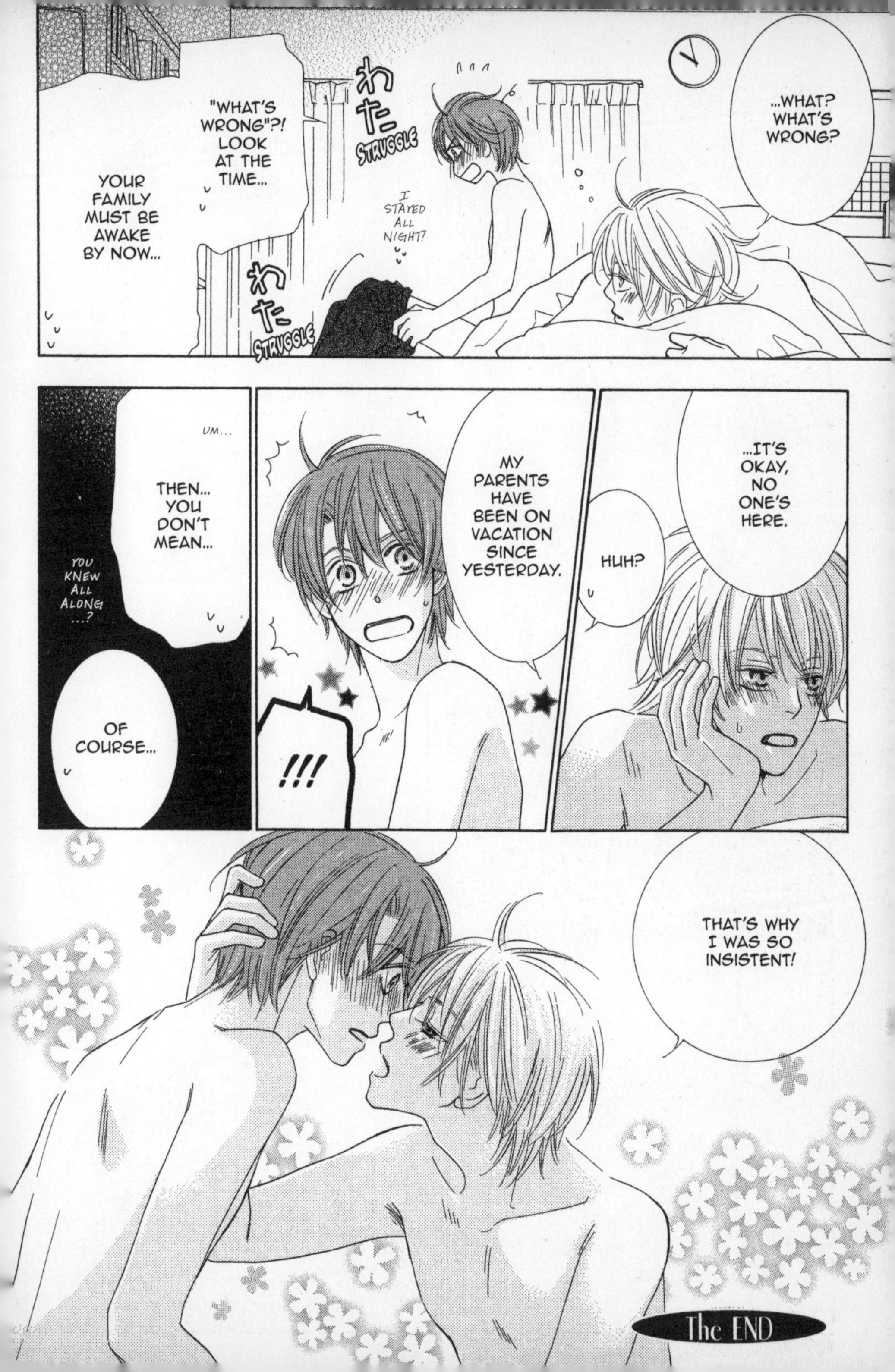
...WHAT? WHAT'S WRONG?
わた STRUGGLE
I STAYED ALL NIGHT!
"WHAT'S WRONG"?! LOOK AT THE TIME...
YOUR FAMILY MUST BE AWAKE BY NOW...
わた STRUGGLE
...IT'S OKAY, NO ONE'S HERE.
HUH?
MY PARENTS HAVE BEEN ON VACATION SINCE YESTERDAY.
!!!
UM...
THEN... YOU DON'T MEAN...
YOU KNEW ALL ALONG ...?
OF COURSE...
THAT'S WHY I WAS SO INSISTENT!
The END

SEQUEL.

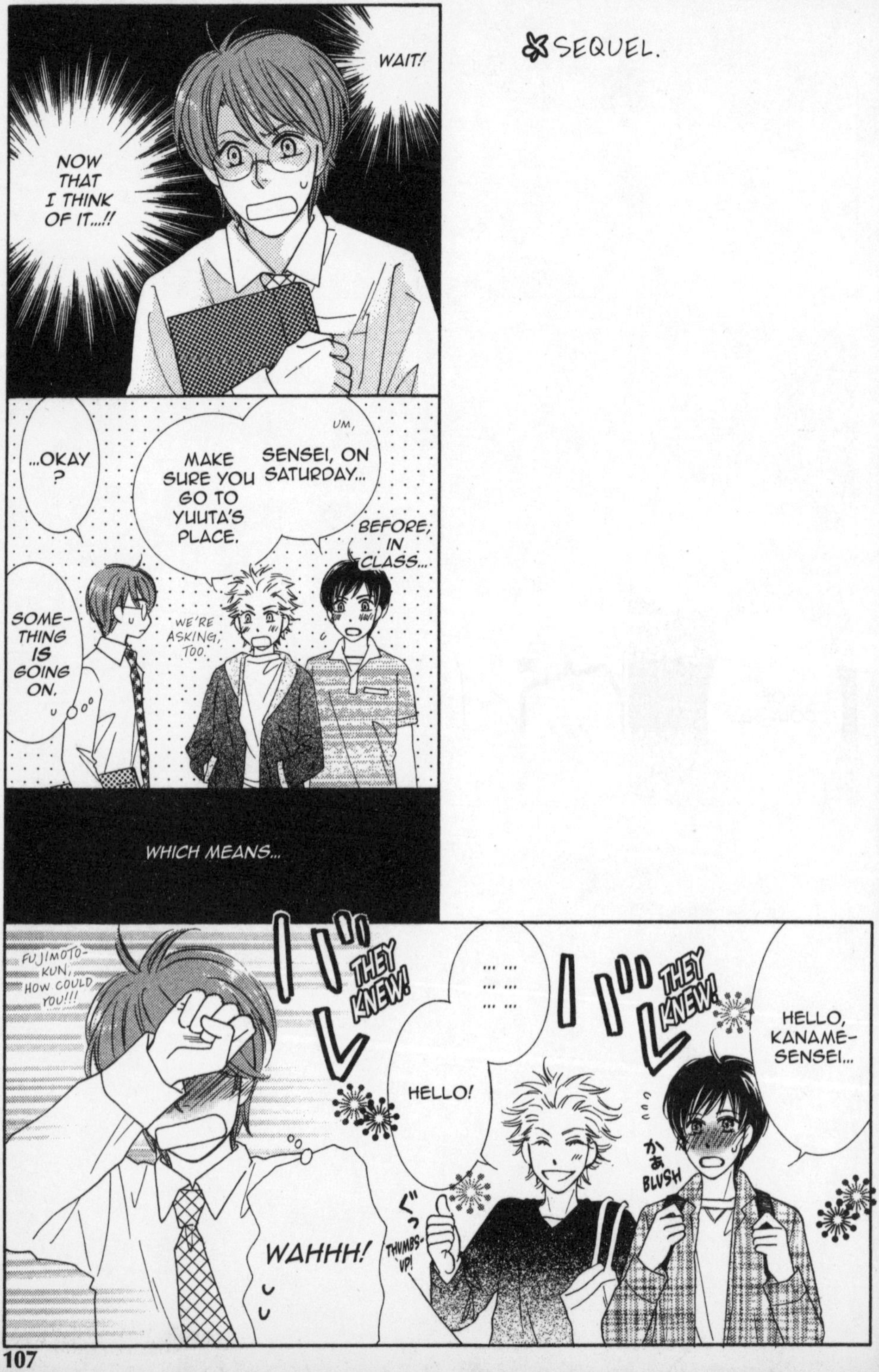
WAIT!
NOW THAT I THINK OF IT...!!
UM, SENSEI, ON SATURDAY...
BEFORE, IN CLASS...
MAKE SURE YOU GO TO YUUTA'S PLACE.
...OKAY?
WE'RE ASKING, TOO.
SOMETHING IS GOING ON.
WHICH MEANS...
HELLO, KANAME-SENSEI...
THEY KNEW!
かぁ
BLUSH
HELLO!
THEY KNEW!
... ...
ぐっ
THUMBS-UP!
WAHHH!
FUJIMOTO-KUN, HOW COULD YOU!!!

Ciao
Ciao
Bambina

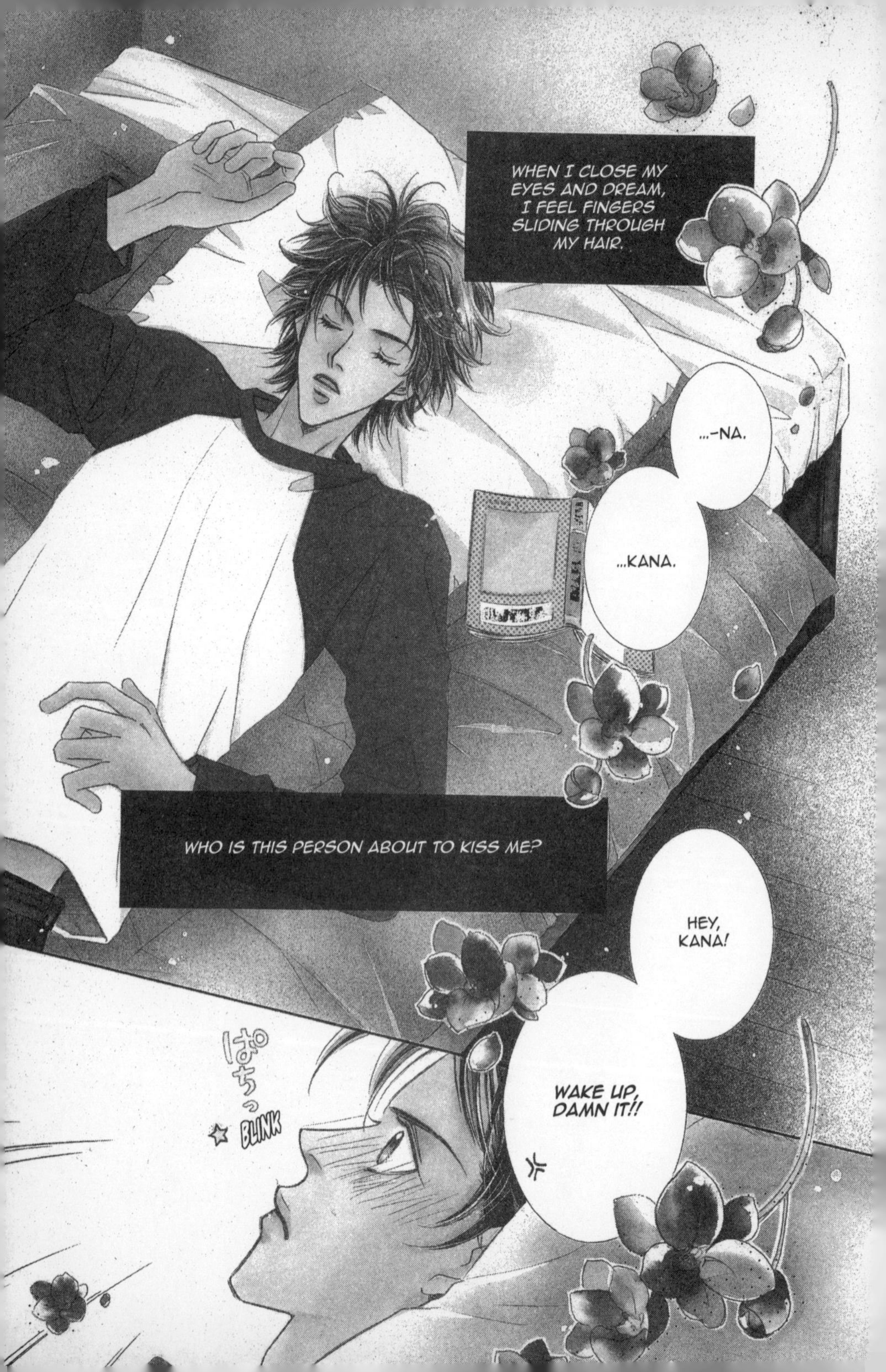

WHEN I CLOSE MY EYES AND DREAM, I FEEL FINGERS SLIDING THROUGH MY HAIR.
...-NA.
...KANA.
WHO IS THIS PERSON ABOUT TO KISS ME?
HEY, KANA!
WAKE UP, DAMN IT!!
ぱちっ
BLINK

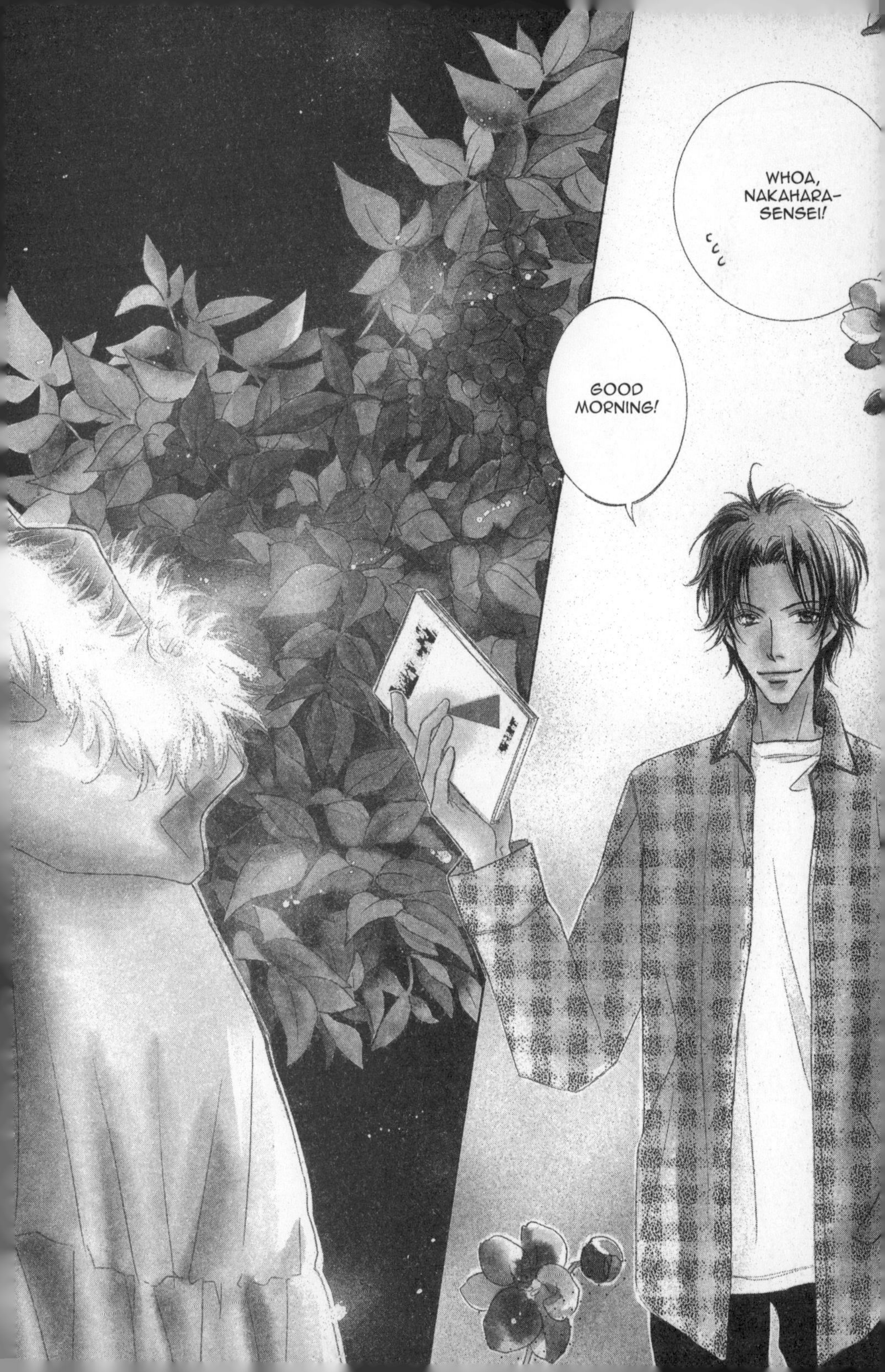
WHOA, NAKAHARA-SENSEI!
GOOD MORNING!

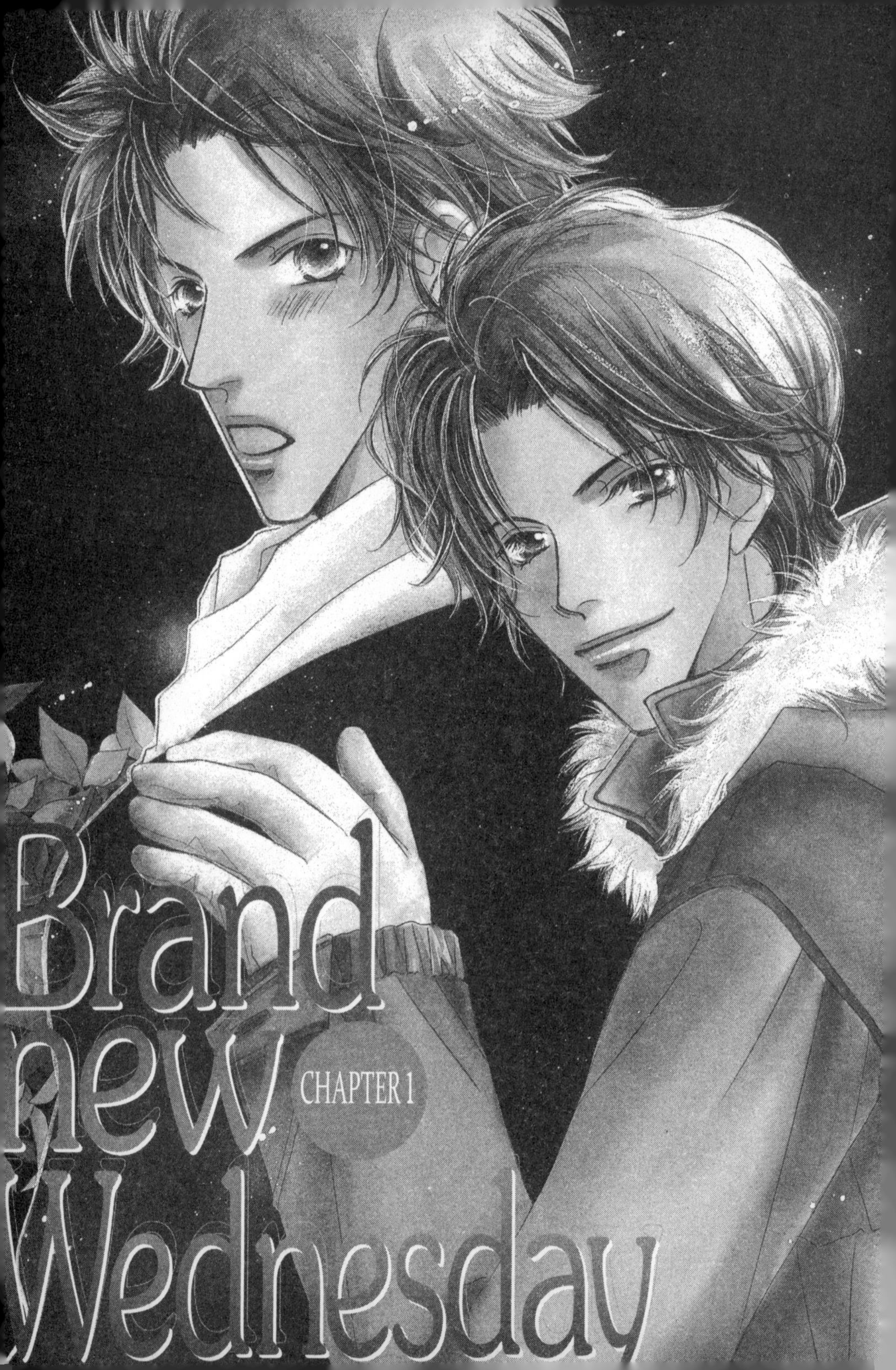
Brand new Wednesday
CHAPTER 1

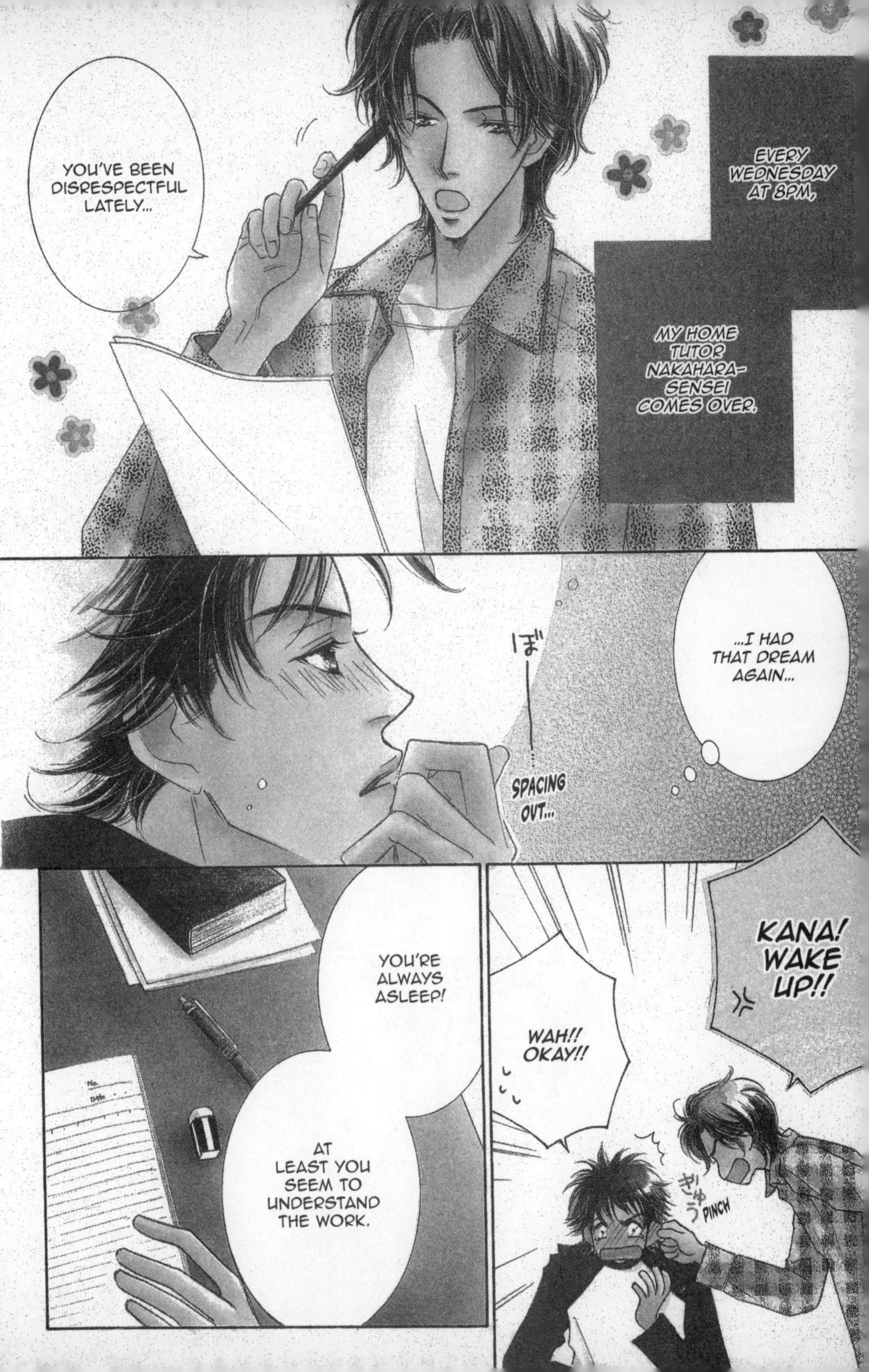
EVERY WEDNESDAY AT 8PM,
MY HOME TUTOR NAKAHARA-SENSEI COMES OVER.
YOU'VE BEEN DISRESPECTFUL LATELY...
...I HAD THAT DREAM AGAIN...
ぼー
SPACING OUT...
KANA! WAKE UP!!
WAH!! OKAY!!
ぎゅう PINCH
YOU'RE ALWAYS ASLEEP!
AT LEAST YOU SEEM TO UNDERSTAND THE WORK.

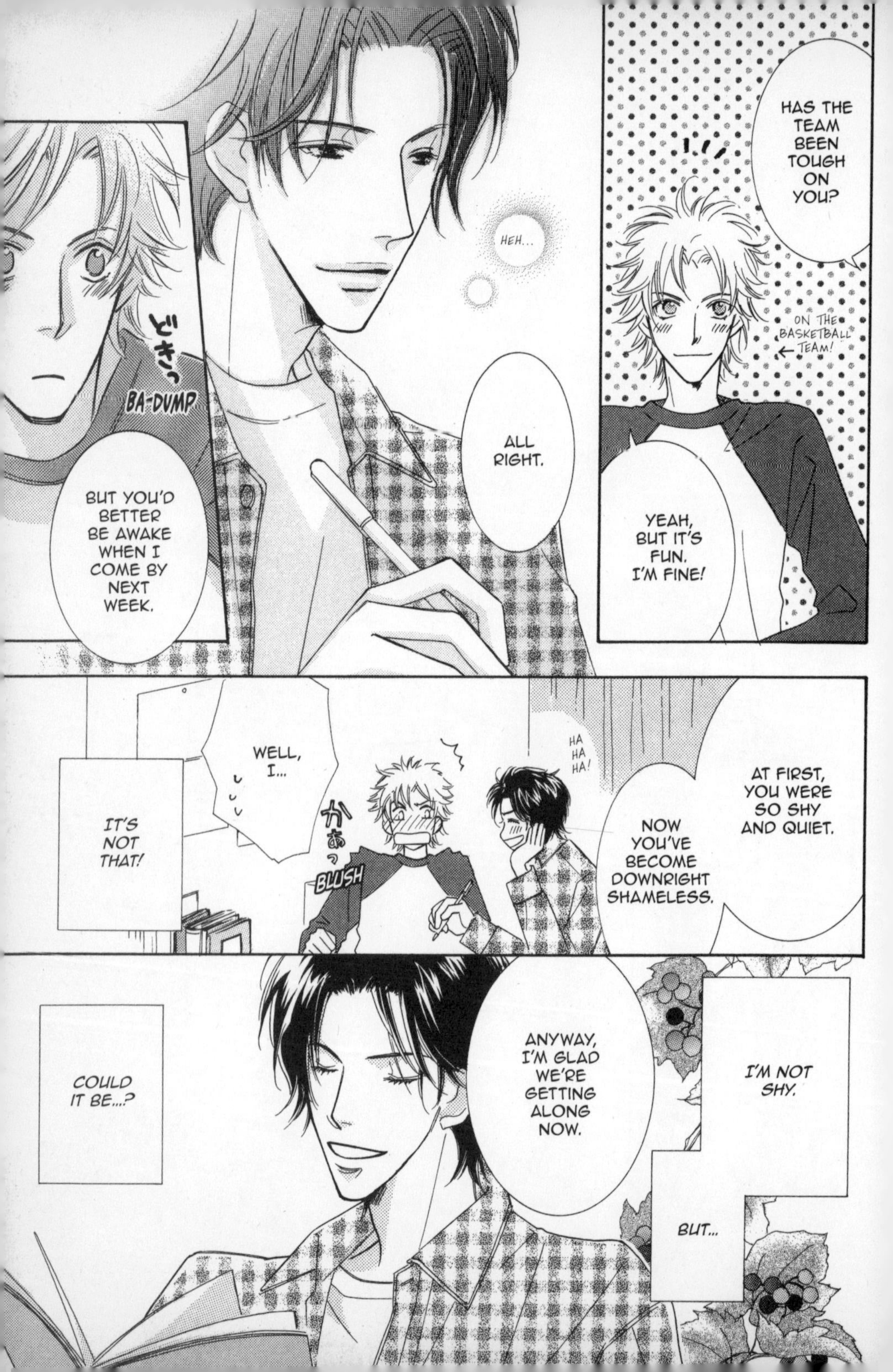
HAS THE TEAM BEEN TOUGH ON YOU?
!!
ON THE BASKETBALL TEAM!
YEAH, BUT IT'S FUN. I'M FINE!
HEH...
ALL RIGHT.
どきっ
BA-DUMP
BUT YOU'D BETTER BE AWAKE WHEN I COME BY NEXT WEEK.
AT FIRST, YOU WERE SO SHY AND QUIET.
NOW YOU'VE BECOME DOWNRIGHT SHAMELESS.
HA HA HA!
かあっ
BLUSH
WELL, I...
IT'S NOT THAT!
I'M NOT SHY.
BUT...
ANYWAY, I'M GLAD WE'RE GETTING ALONG NOW.
COULD IT BE...?

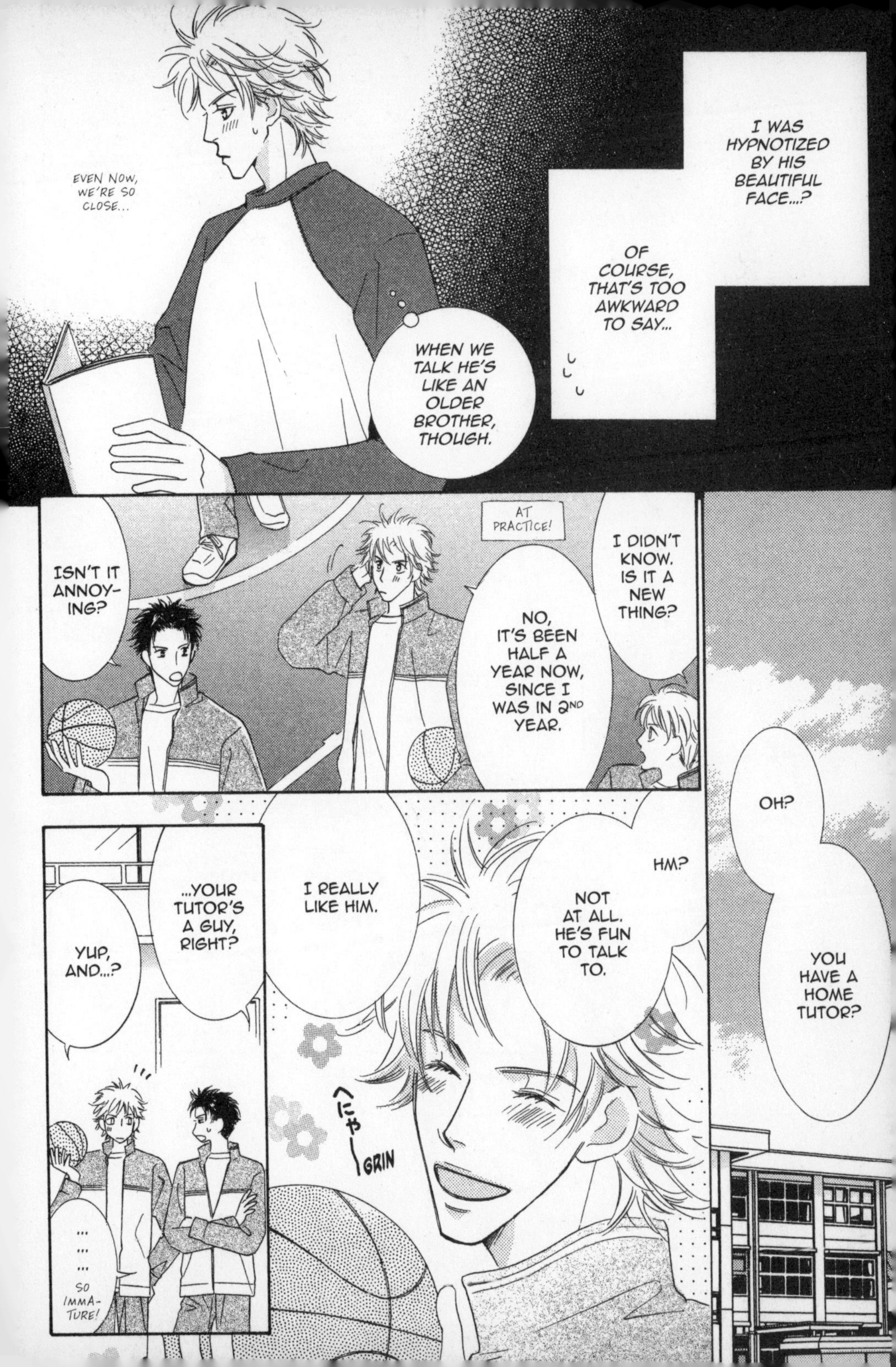
I WAS HYPNOTIZED BY HIS BEAUTIFUL FACE...?
OF COURSE, THAT'S TOO AWKWARD TO SAY...
WHEN WE TALK HE'S LIKE AN OLDER BROTHER, THOUGH.
EVEN NOW, WE'RE SO CLOSE...
OH?
YOU HAVE A HOME TUTOR?
AT PRACTICE!
I DIDN'T KNOW. IS IT A NEW THING?
NO, IT'S BEEN HALF A YEAR NOW, SINCE I WAS IN 2ND YEAR.
ISN'T IT ANNOYING?
HM?
NOT AT ALL. HE'S FUN TO TALK TO.
I REALLY LIKE HIM.
へにゃー GRIN
...YOUR TUTOR'S A GUY, RIGHT?
YUP, AND...?
... ...
SO IMMATURE!

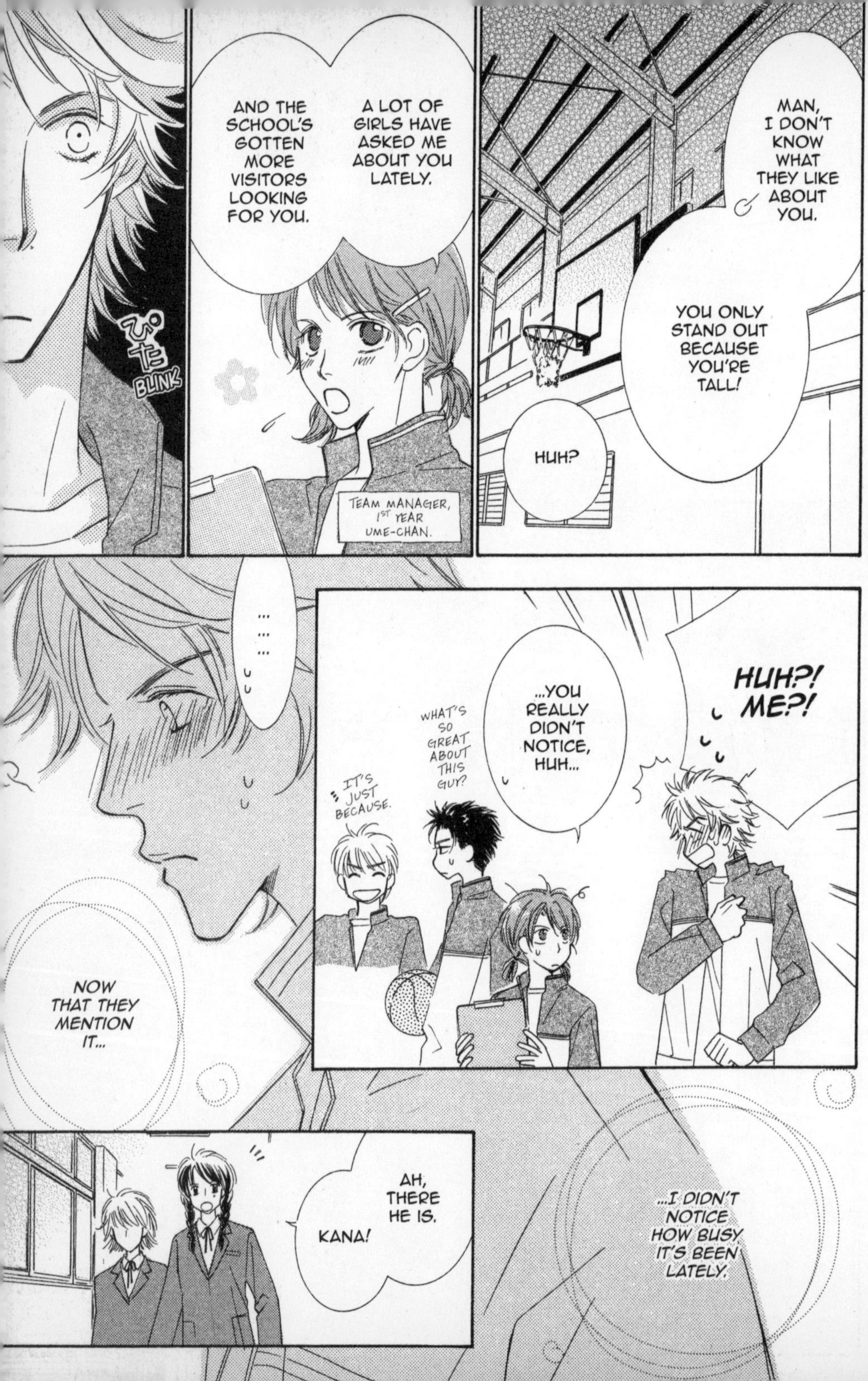
MAN, I DON'T KNOW WHAT THEY LIKE ABOUT YOU.
YOU ONLY STAND OUT BECAUSE YOU'RE TALL!
HUH?
A LOT OF GIRLS HAVE ASKED ME ABOUT YOU LATELY.
AND THE SCHOOL'S GOTTEN MORE VISITORS LOOKING FOR YOU.
TEAM MANAGER, 1ST YEAR UME-CHAN.
ぴた
BLINK
HUH?! ME?!
...YOU REALLY DIDN'T NOTICE, HUH...
WHAT'S SO GREAT ABOUT THIS GUY?
IT'S JUST BECAUSE.
... ...
NOW THAT THEY MENTION IT...
...I DIDN'T NOTICE HOW BUSY IT'S BEEN LATELY.
AH, THERE HE IS.
KANA!

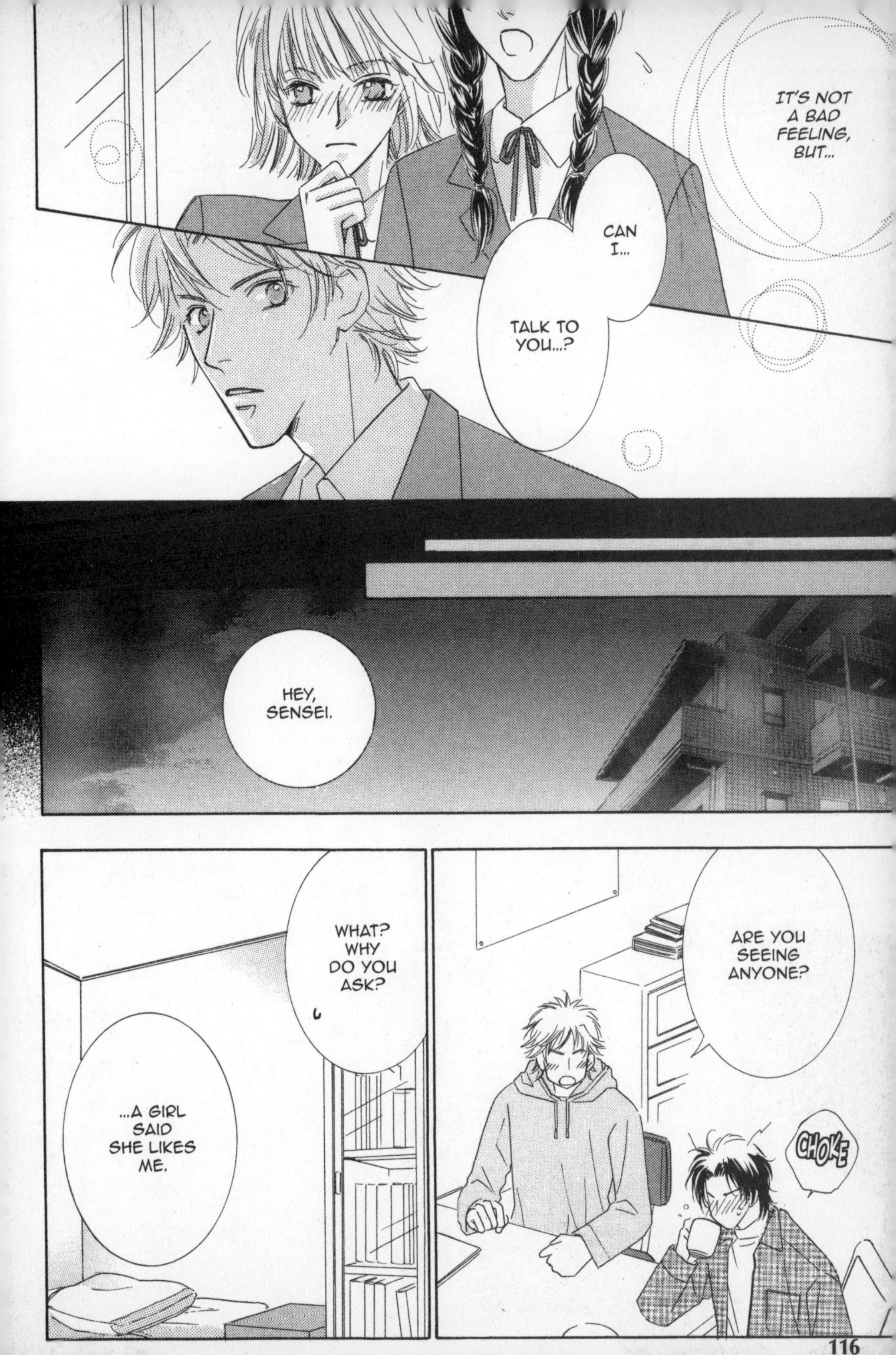
IT'S NOT A BAD FEELING, BUT...
CAN I...
TALK TO YOU...?
HEY, SENSEI.
ARE YOU SEEING ANYONE?
CHOKE
WHAT? WHY DO YOU ASK?
...A GIRL SAID SHE LIKES ME.

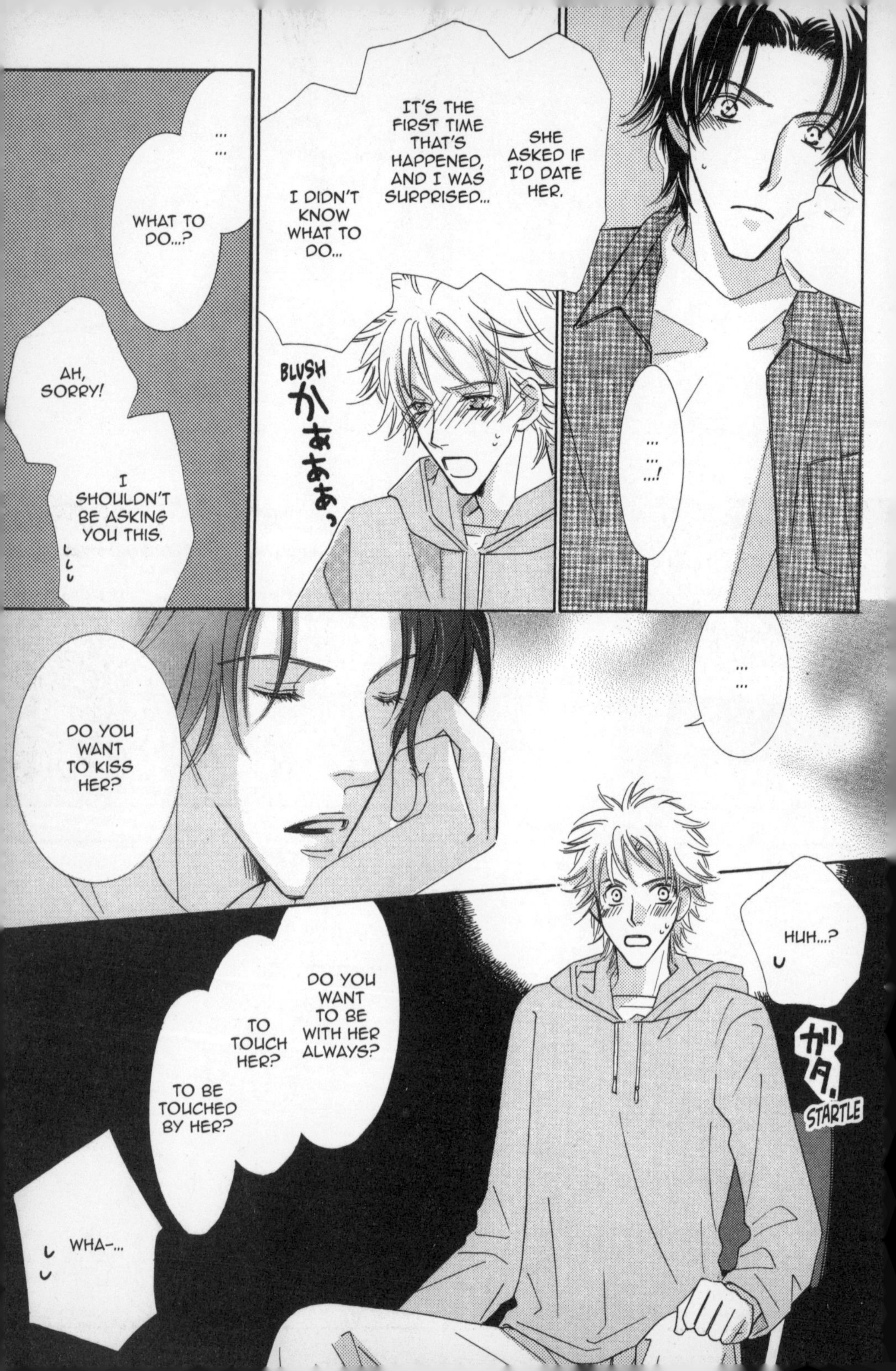
......!
SHE ASKED IF I'D DATE HER.
IT'S THE FIRST TIME THAT'S HAPPENED, AND I WAS SURPRISED...
I DIDN'T KNOW WHAT TO DO...
BLUSH
かあああ
......
WHAT TO DO...?
AH, SORRY!
I SHOULDN'T BE ASKING YOU THIS.
......
DO YOU WANT TO KISS HER?
HUH...?
ガタ
STARTLE
DO YOU WANT TO BE WITH HER ALWAYS?
TO TOUCH HER?
TO BE TOUCHED BY HER?
WHA-...

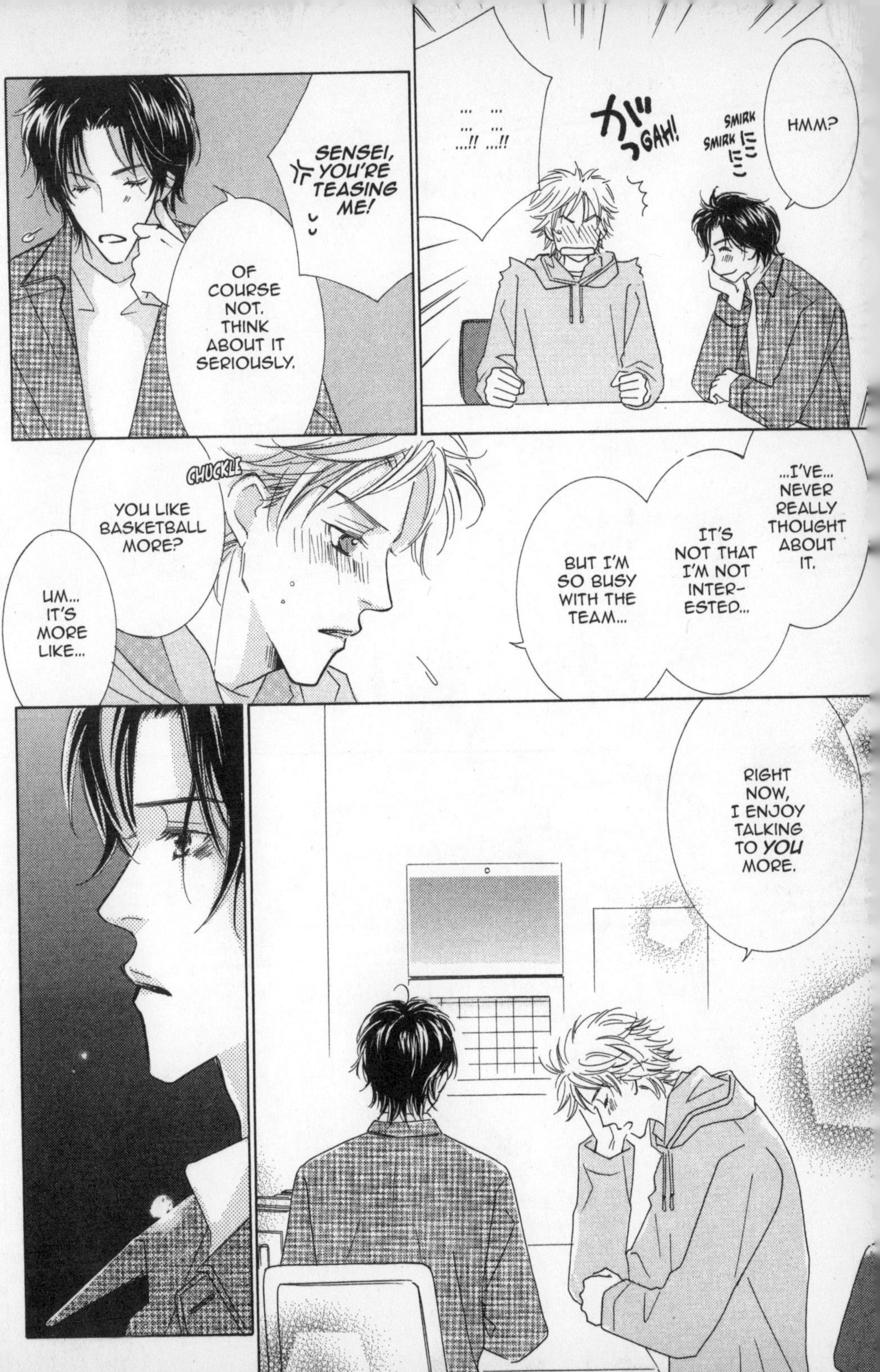
HMM?
SMIRK SMIRK
GAH!
...!! ...!!
SENSEI, YOU'RE TEASING ME!
OF COURSE NOT. THINK ABOUT IT SERIOUSLY.
...I'VE... NEVER REALLY THOUGHT ABOUT IT.
IT'S NOT THAT I'M NOT INTER-ESTED...
BUT I'M SO BUSY WITH THE TEAM...
CHUCKLE
YOU LIKE BASKETBALL MORE?
UM... IT'S MORE LIKE...
RIGHT NOW, I ENJOY TALKING TO *YOU* MORE.

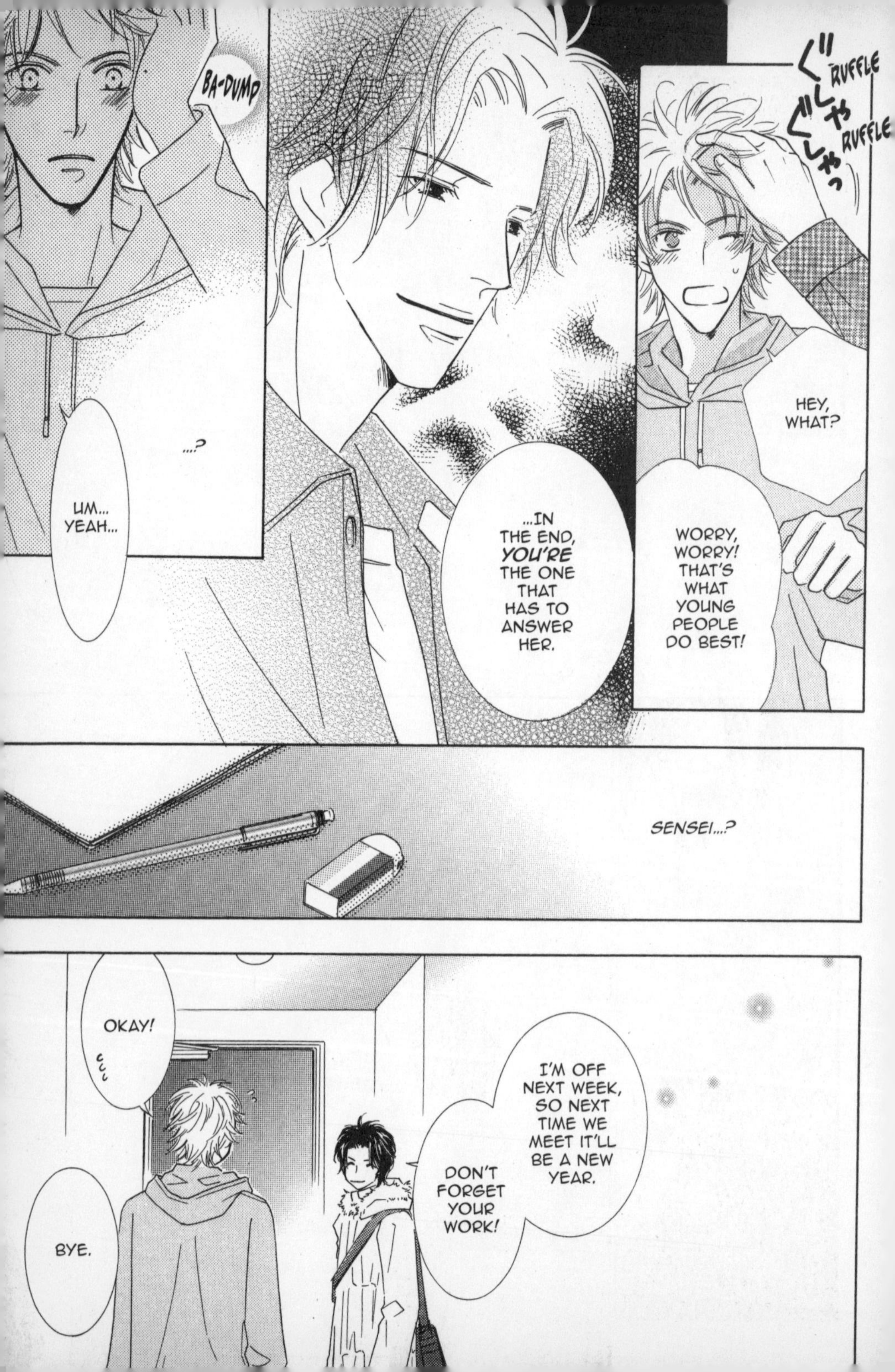
ぐしゃぐしゃっ
RUFFLE
RUFFLE
HEY, WHAT?
WORRY, WORRY! THAT'S WHAT YOUNG PEOPLE DO BEST!
...IN THE END, *YOU'RE* THE ONE THAT HAS TO ANSWER HER.
BA-DUMP
...?
UM... YEAH...
SENSEI...?
I'M OFF NEXT WEEK, SO NEXT TIME WE MEET IT'LL BE A NEW YEAR.
DON'T FORGET YOUR WORK!
OKAY!
BYE.

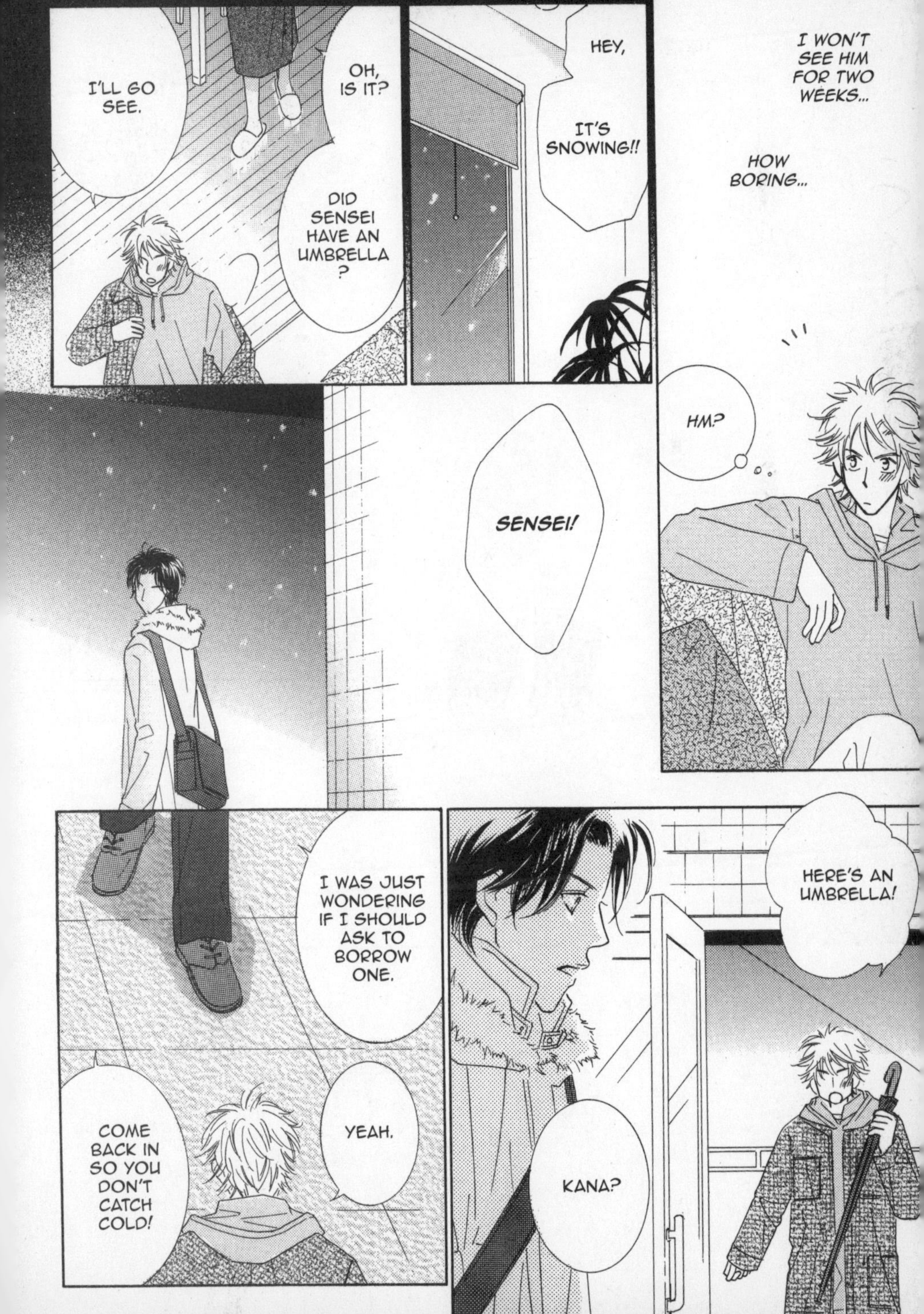
I WON'T SEE HIM FOR TWO WEEKS...
HOW BORING...
HEY,
IT'S SNOWING!!
OH, IS IT?
DID SENSEI HAVE AN UMBRELLA?
I'LL GO SEE.
HM?
SENSEI!
HERE'S AN UMBRELLA!
KANA?
I WAS JUST WONDERING IF I SHOULD ASK TO BORROW ONE.
YEAH.
COME BACK IN SO YOU DON'T CATCH COLD!

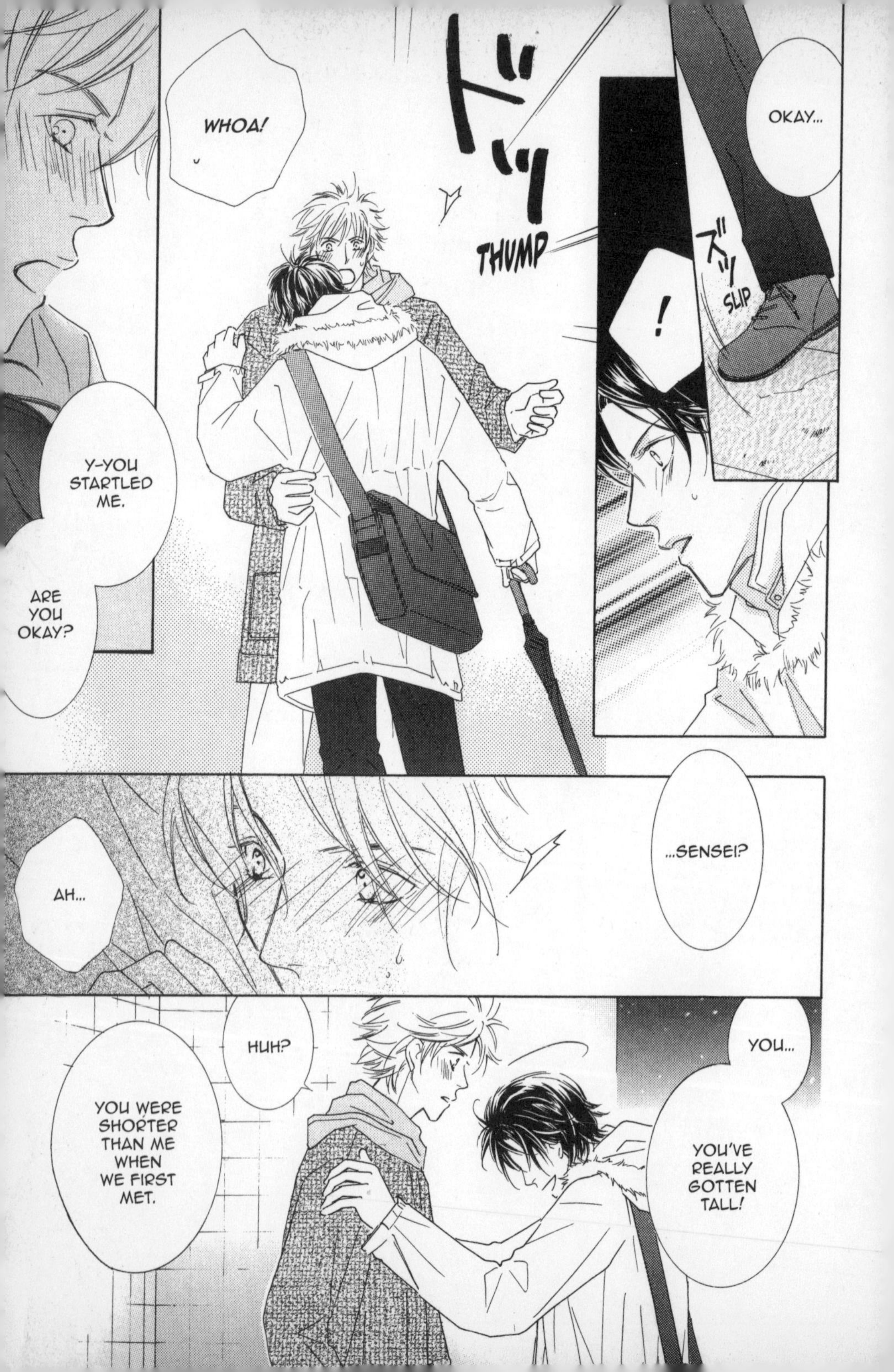
OKAY...
ズッ
SLIP
!
ドッ
THUMP
WHOA!
Y-YOU STARTLED ME.
ARE YOU OKAY?
...SENSEI?
AH...
YOU...
YOU'VE REALLY GOTTEN TALL!
HUH?
YOU WERE SHORTER THAN ME WHEN WE FIRST MET.

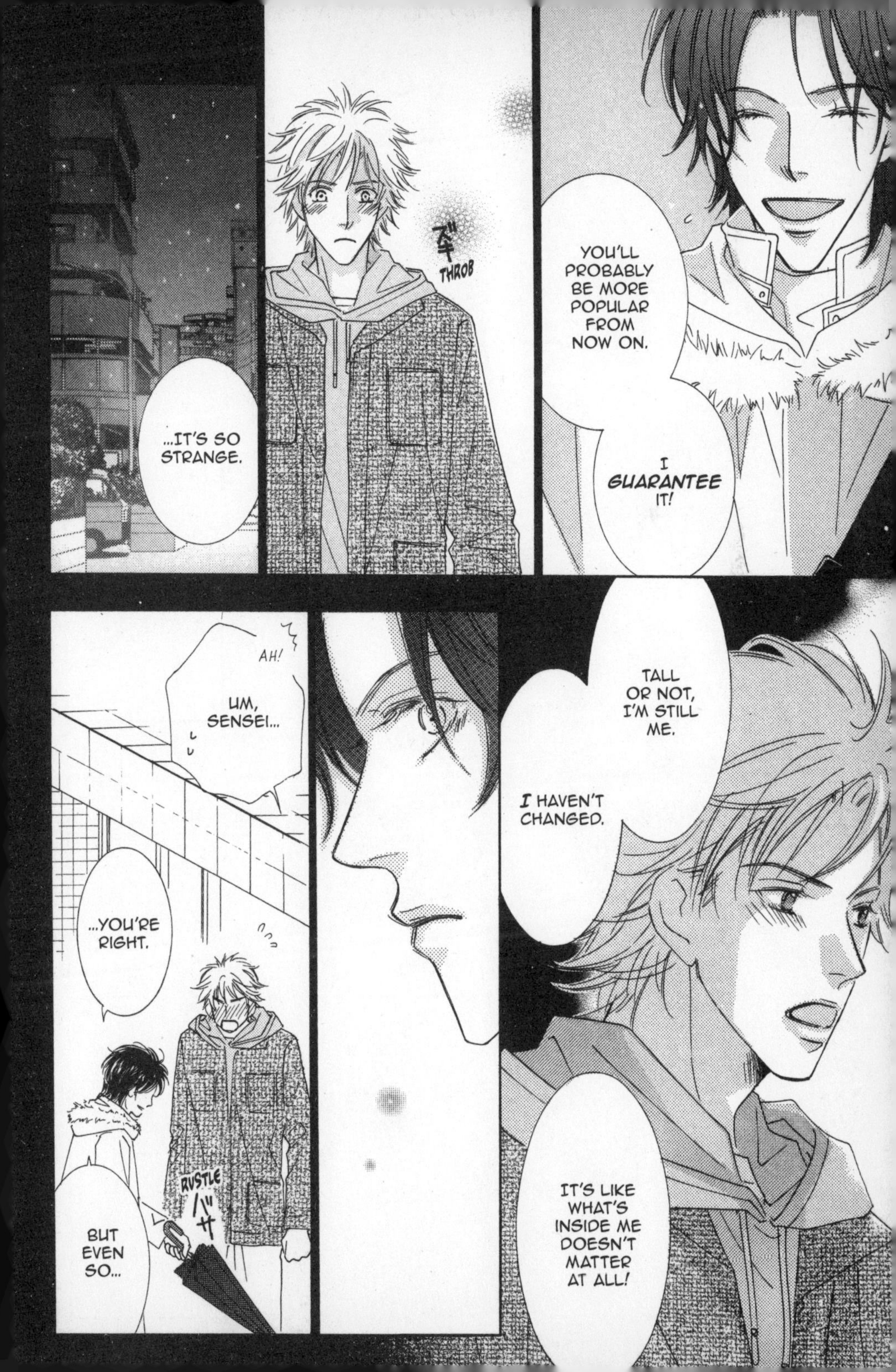
YOU'LL PROBABLY BE MORE POPULAR FROM NOW ON.
I GUARANTEE IT!
ズキ
THROB
...IT'S SO STRANGE.
TALL OR NOT, I'M STILL ME.
I HAVEN'T CHANGED.
IT'S LIKE WHAT'S INSIDE ME DOESN'T MATTER AT ALL!
AH!
UM, SENSEI...
...YOU'RE RIGHT.
RUSTLE
バサ
BUT EVEN SO...

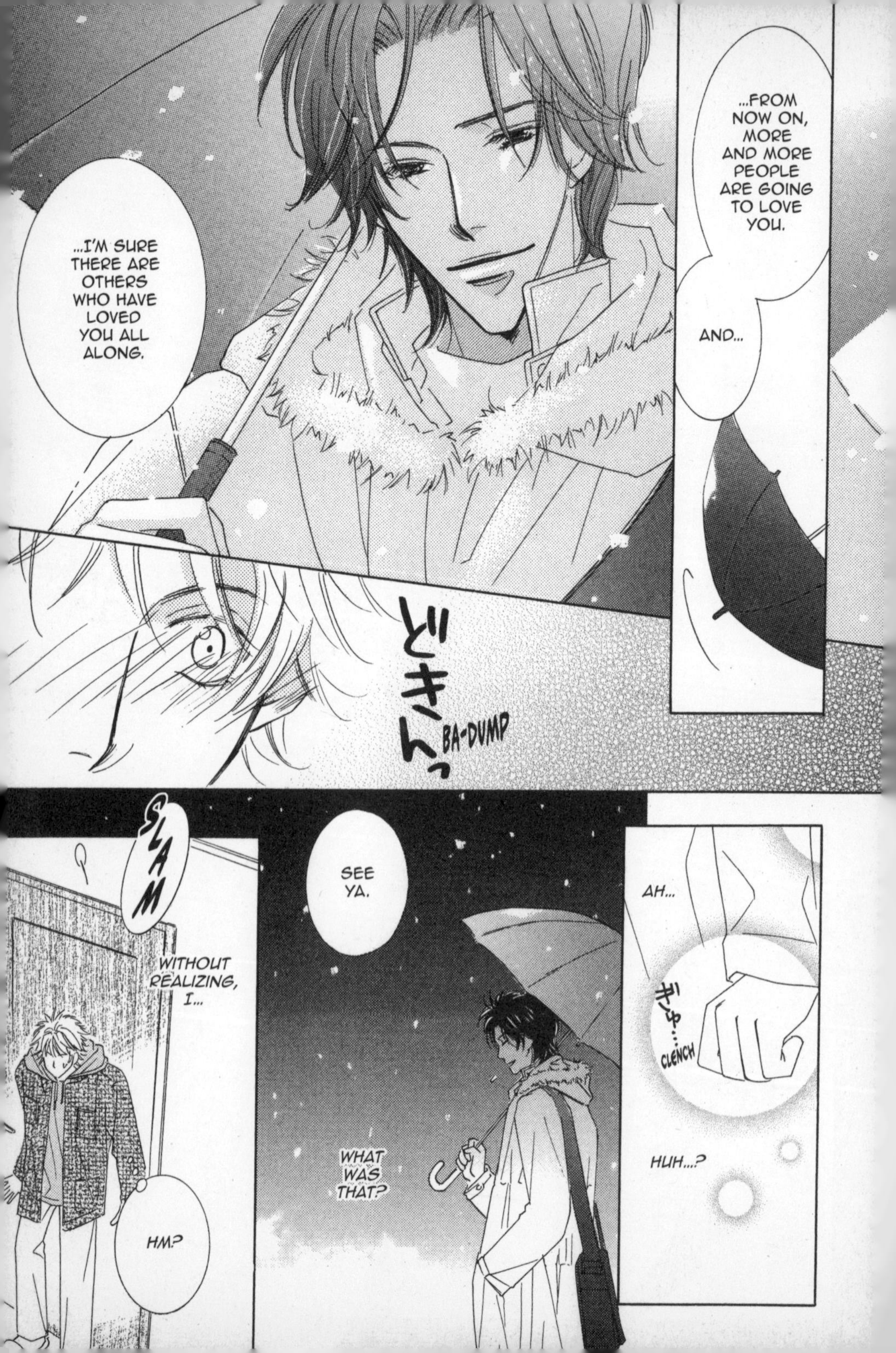
...FROM NOW ON, MORE AND MORE PEOPLE ARE GOING TO LOVE YOU.
AND...
...I'M SURE THERE ARE OTHERS WHO HAVE LOVED YOU ALL ALONG.
どきんっ
BA-DUMP
AH...
ぎゅ...
CLENCH
HUH...?
SEE YA.
WHAT WAS THAT?
SLAM
WITHOUT REALIZING, I...
HM?

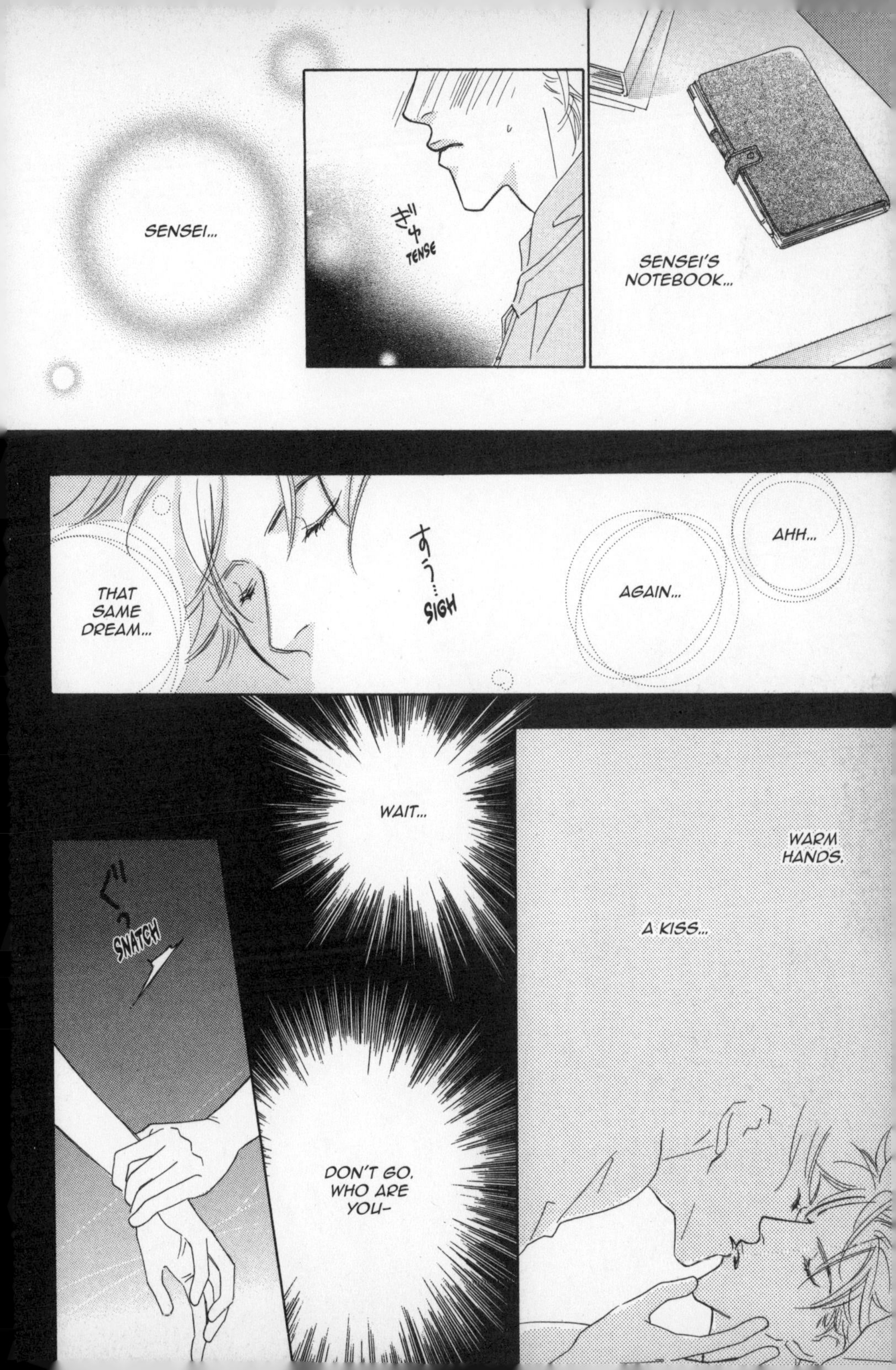

SENSEI'S NOTEBOOK...
ぎゅ
TENSE
SENSEI...
AHH...
AGAIN...
すぅ...
SIGH
THAT SAME DREAM...
WARM HANDS.
A KISS...
WAIT...
ぐっ
SNATCH
DON'T GO. WHO ARE YOU-

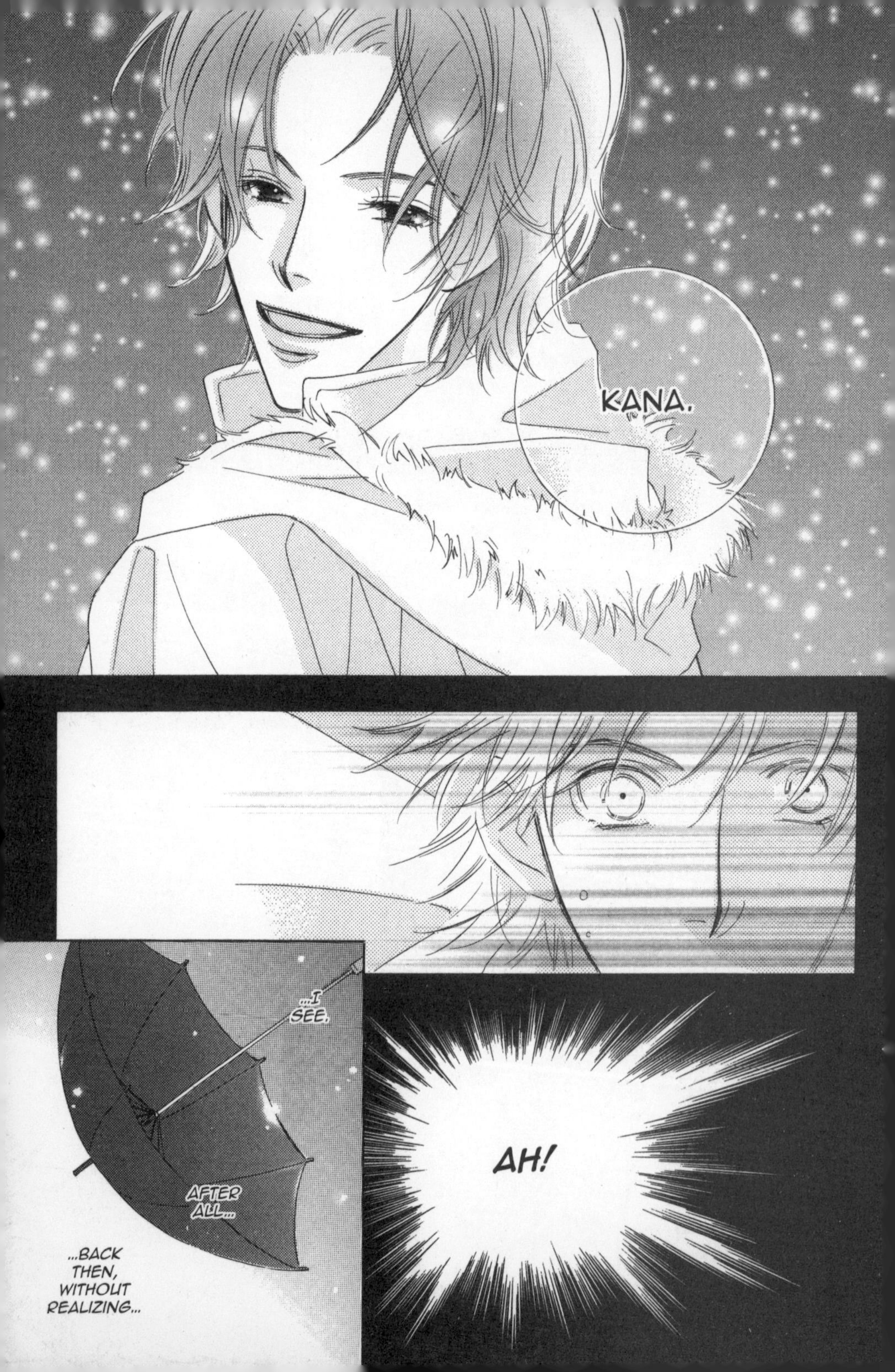
KANA.
AH!
...I SEE.
AFTER ALL...
...BACK THEN, WITHOUT REALIZING...

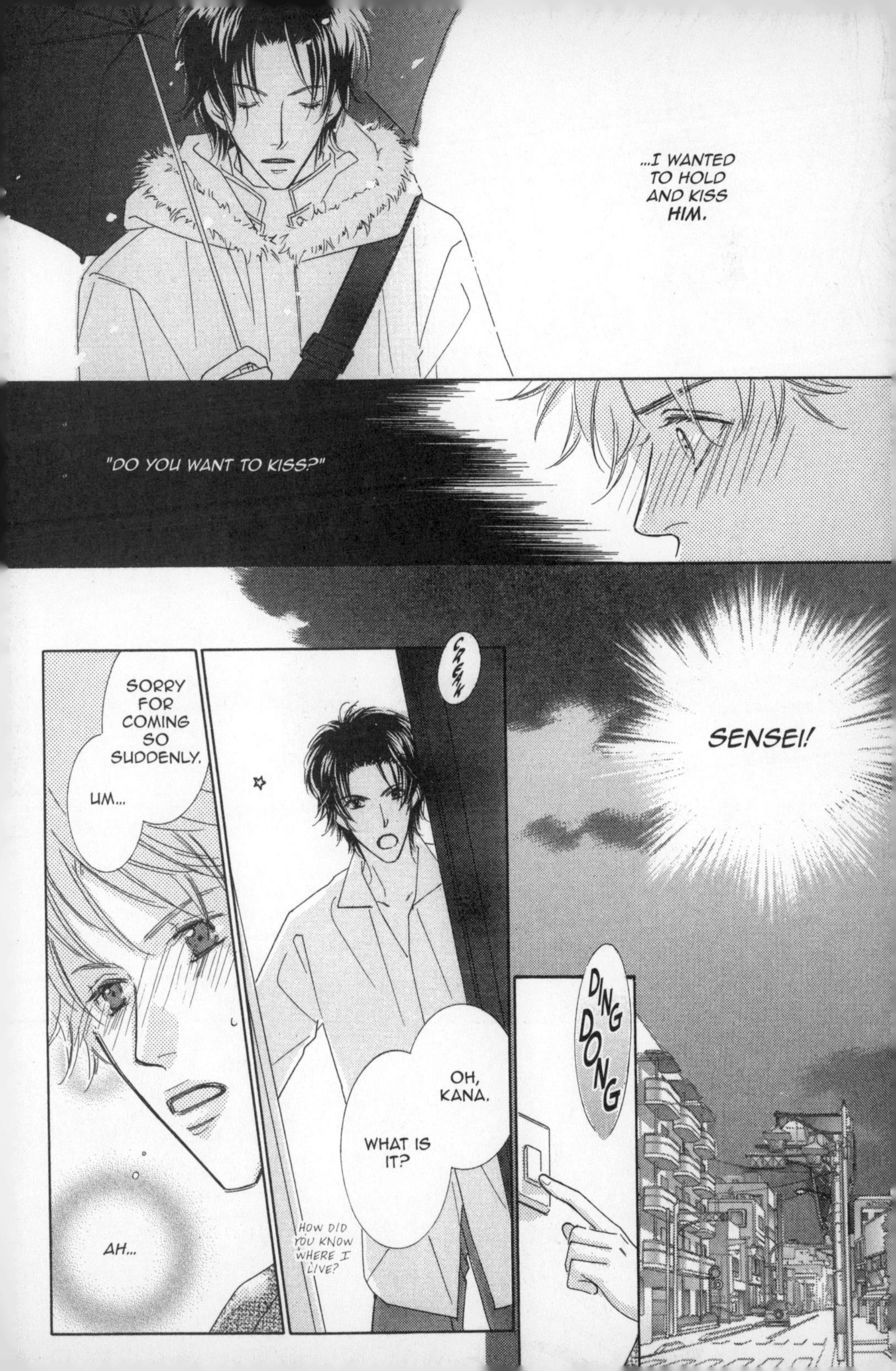

...I WANTED TO HOLD AND KISS HIM.
"DO YOU WANT TO KISS?"
SENSEI!
DING DONG
CREAK
OH, KANA.
WHAT IS IT?
HOW DID YOU KNOW WHERE I LIVE?
SORRY FOR COMING SO SUDDENLY.
UM...
AH...

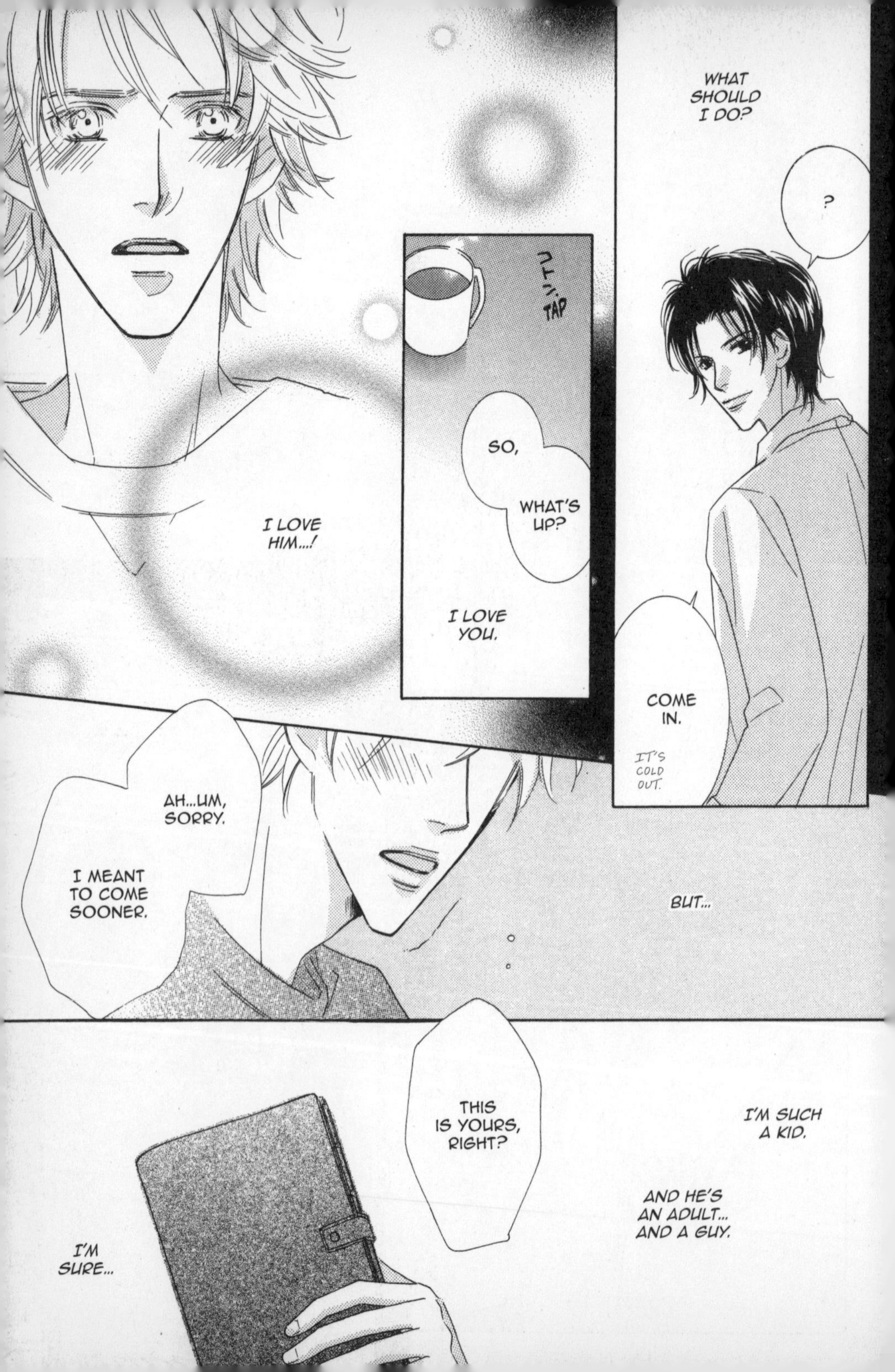

WHAT SHOULD I DO?
?
COME IN.
IT'S COLD OUT.
TAP
SO,
WHAT'S UP?
I LOVE YOU.
I LOVE HIM...!
BUT...
AH...UM, SORRY.
I MEANT TO COME SOONER.
I'M SUCH A KID.
AND HE'S AN ADULT... AND A GUY.
THIS IS YOURS, RIGHT?
I'M SURE...

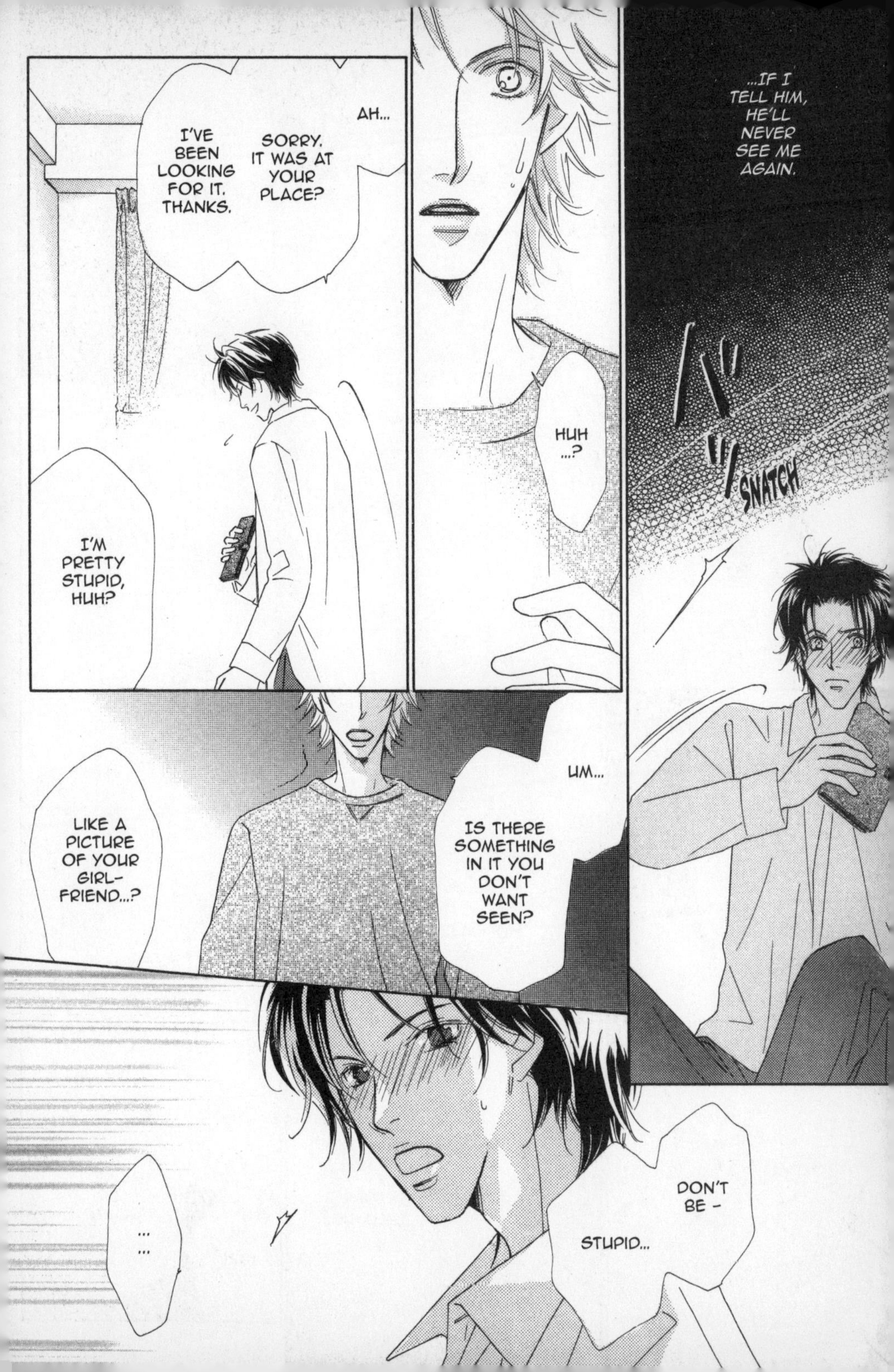
...IF I TELL HIM, HE'LL NEVER SEE ME AGAIN.
SNATCH
HUH ...?
AH...
SORRY. IT WAS AT YOUR PLACE?
I'VE BEEN LOOKING FOR IT. THANKS.
I'M PRETTY STUPID, HUH?
UM...
IS THERE SOMETHING IN IT YOU DON'T WANT SEEN?
LIKE A PICTURE OF YOUR GIRL-FRIEND...?
DON'T BE -
STUPID...
... ...

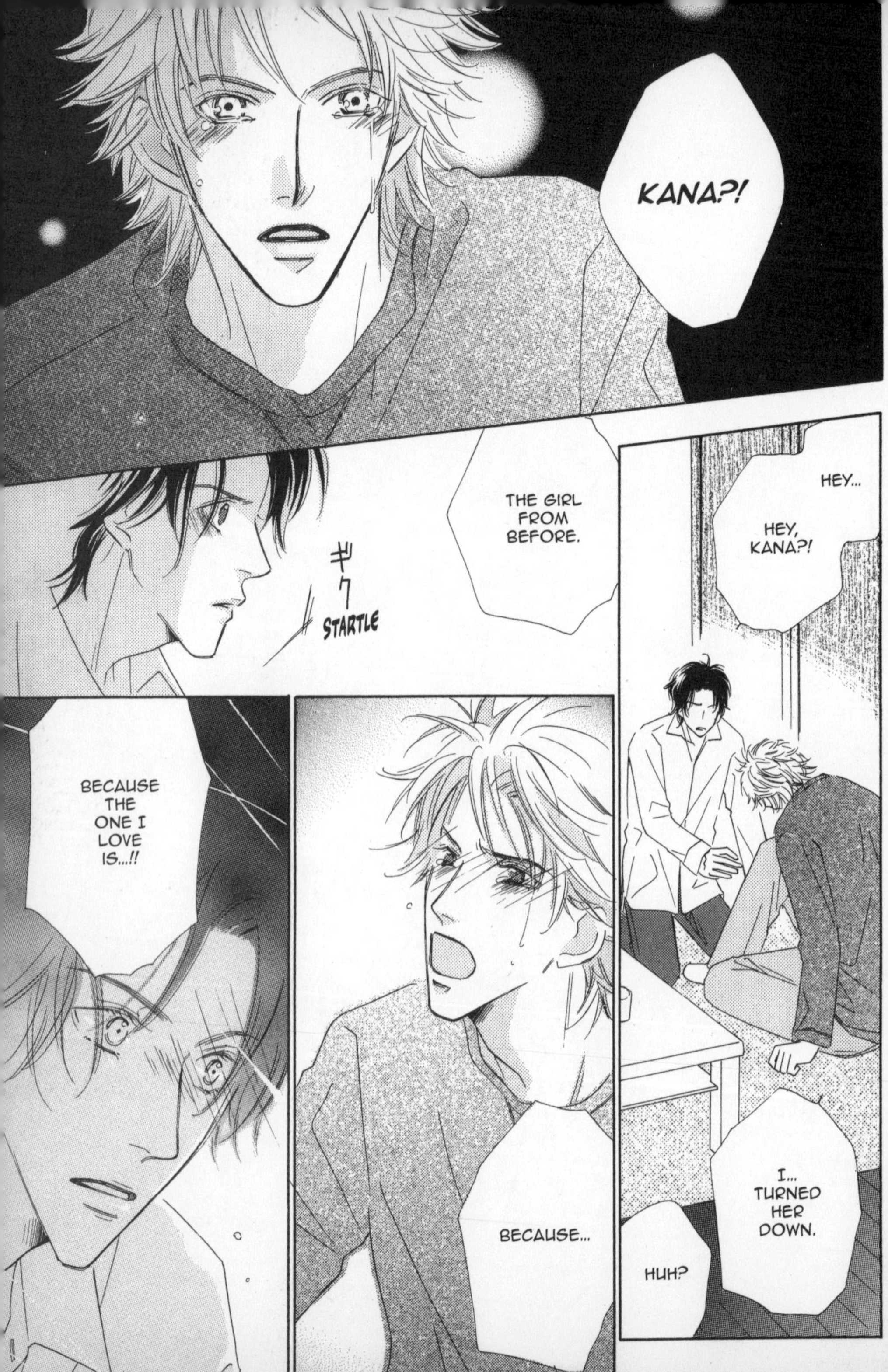

KANA?!
HEY...
HEY, KANA?!
I... TURNED HER DOWN.
HUH?
THE GIRL FROM BEFORE.
ギク
STARTLE
BECAUSE...
BECAUSE THE ONE I LOVE IS...!!

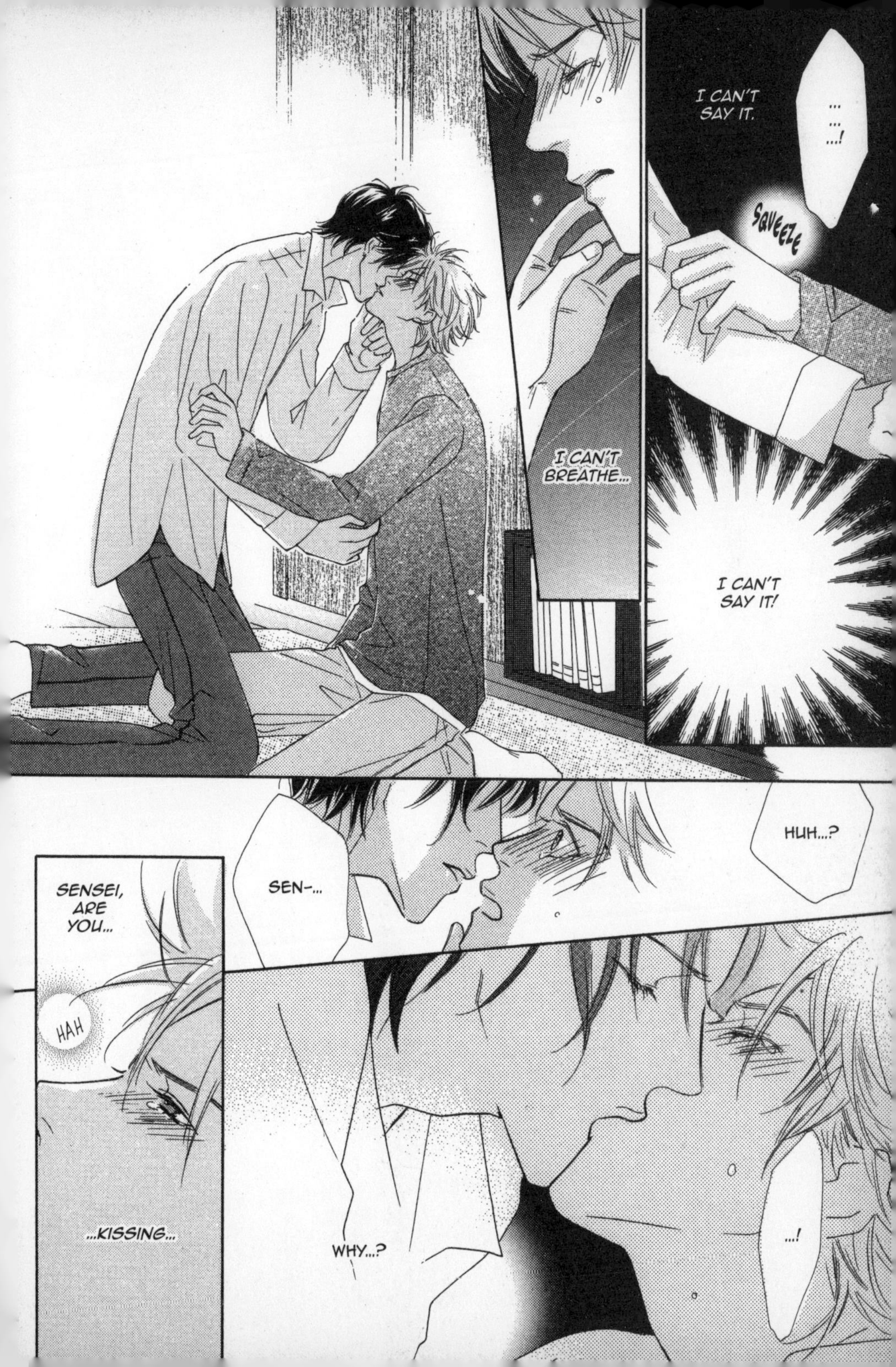
...
...
...!
I CAN'T SAY IT.
SQUEEZE
I CAN'T SAY IT!
I CAN'T BREATHE...
HUH...?
SEN-...
...!
WHY...?
SENSEI, ARE YOU...
HAH
...KISSING...

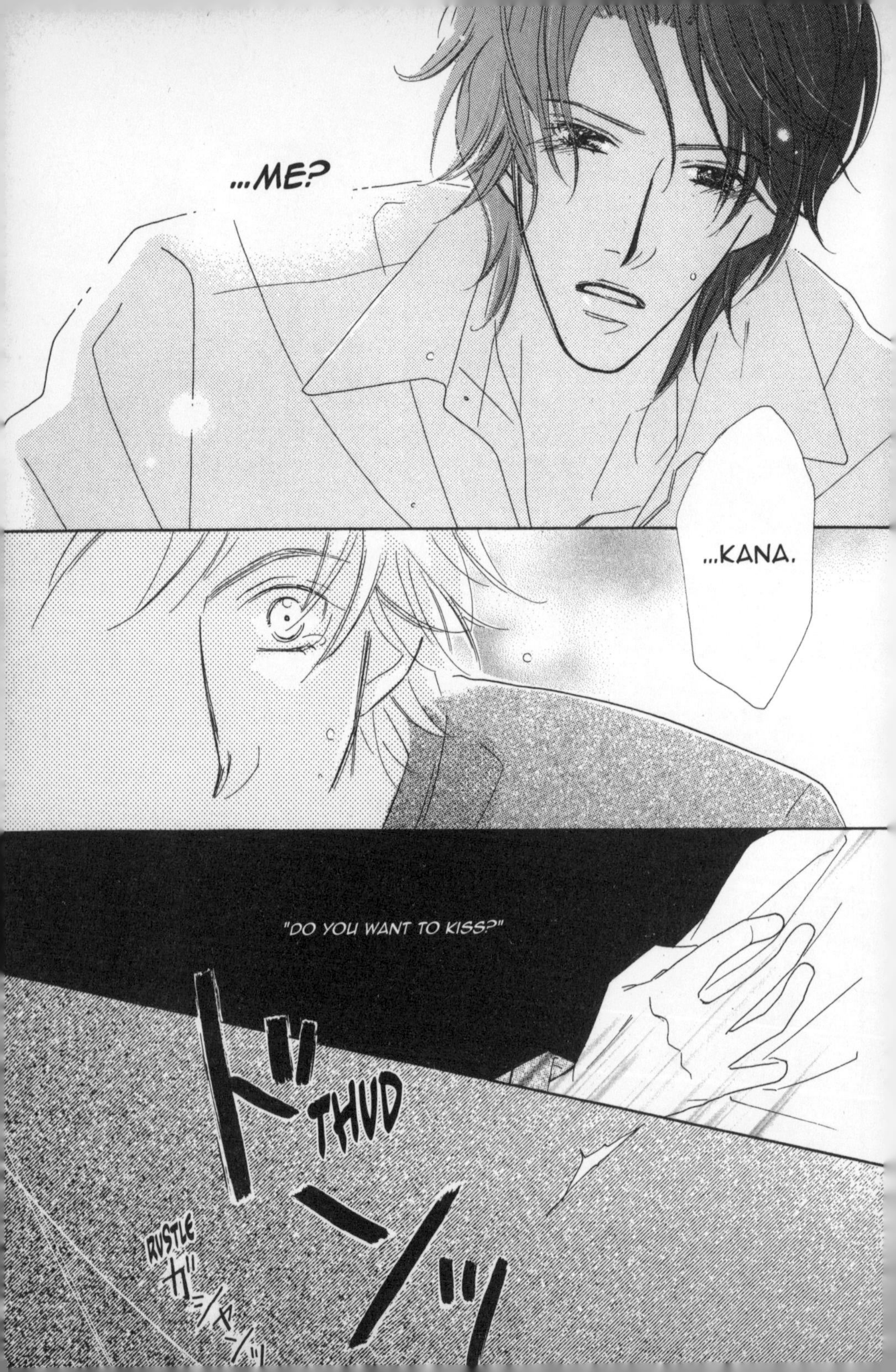
...ME?
...KANA.
"DO YOU WANT TO KISS?"
ドーンッ
THUD
ガシャッ
RUSTLE

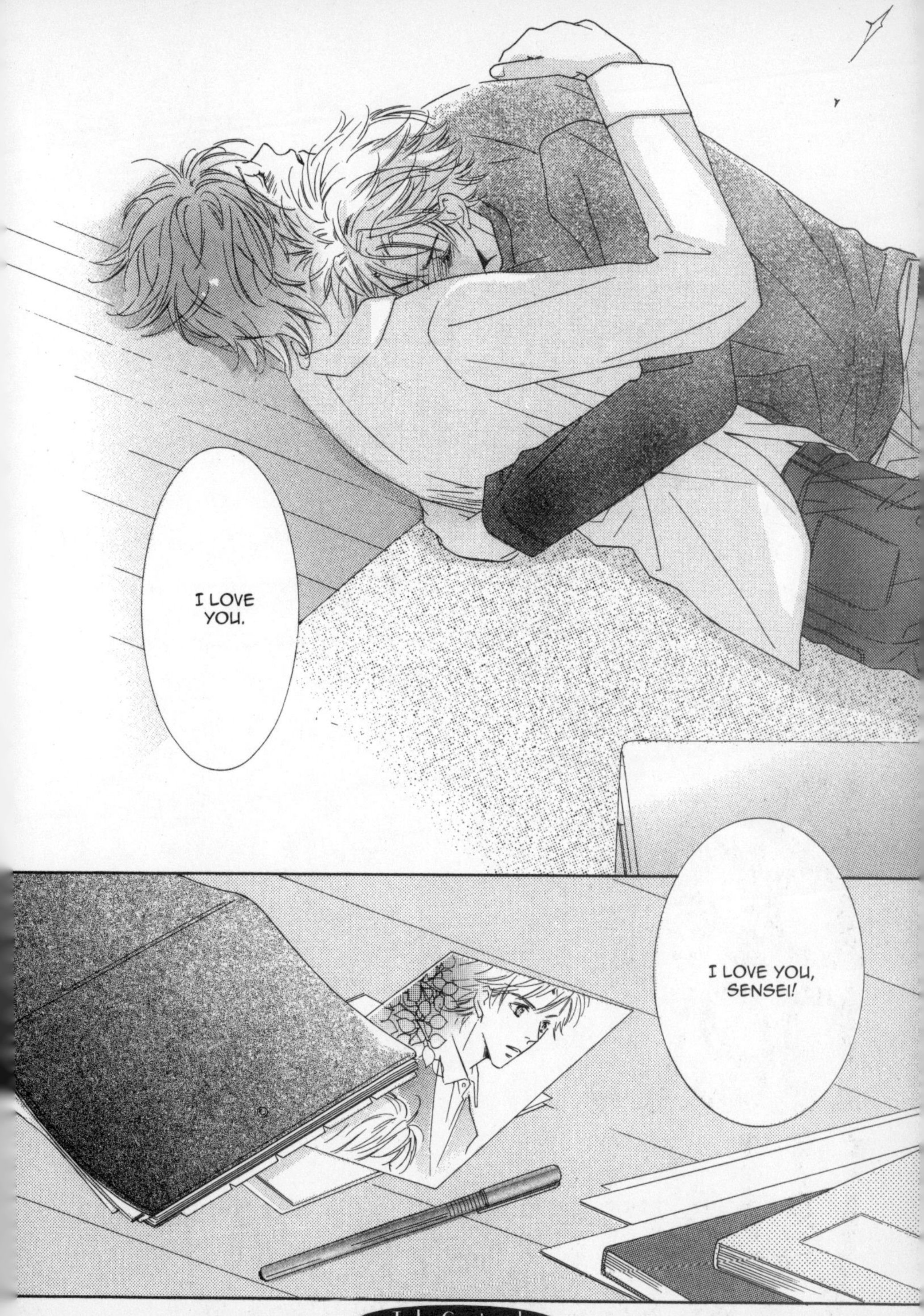
I LOVE YOU.
I LOVE YOU, SENSEI!

To be Continued

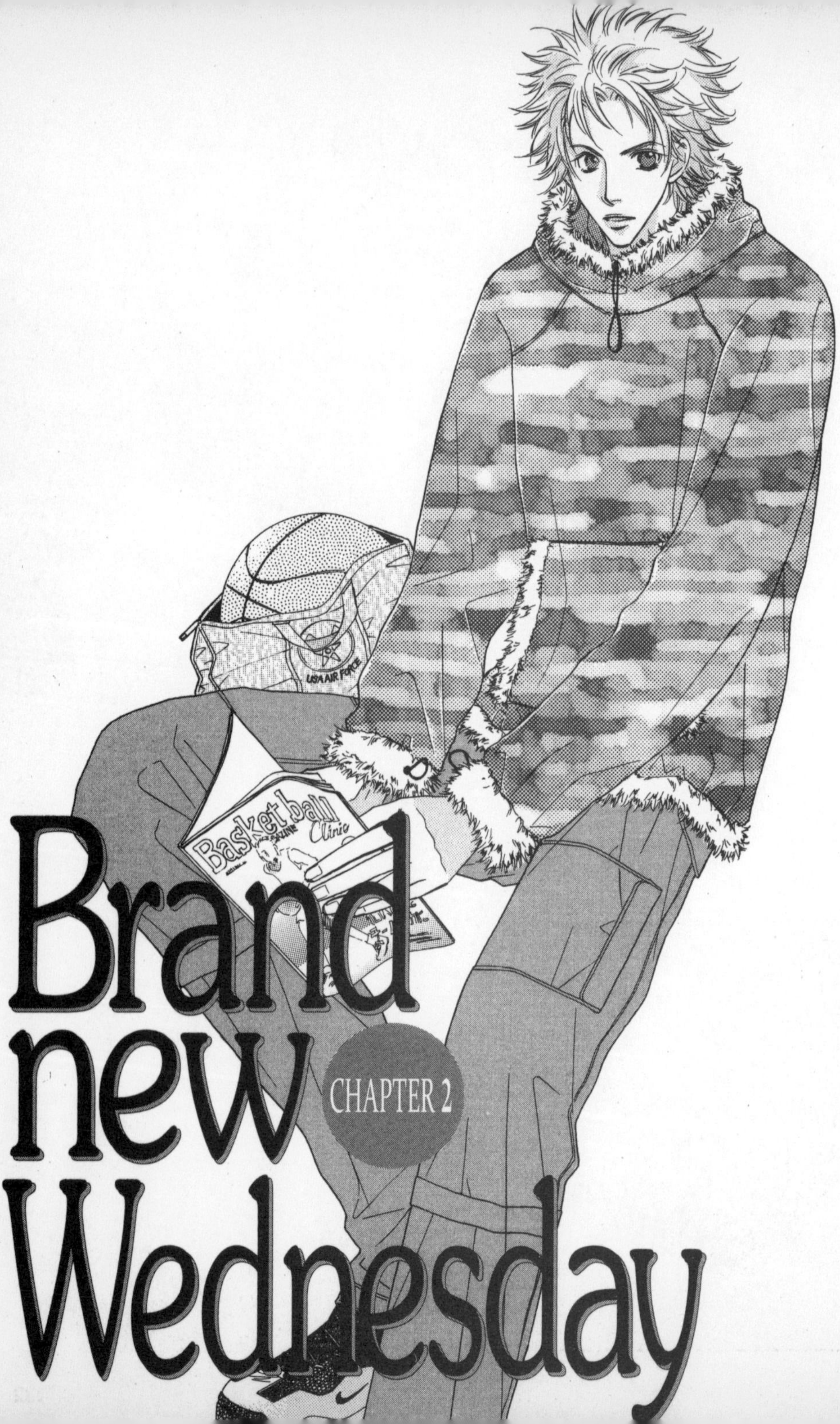
Brand new Wednesday
CHAPTER 2
USA AIR FORCE
Basketball Clinic

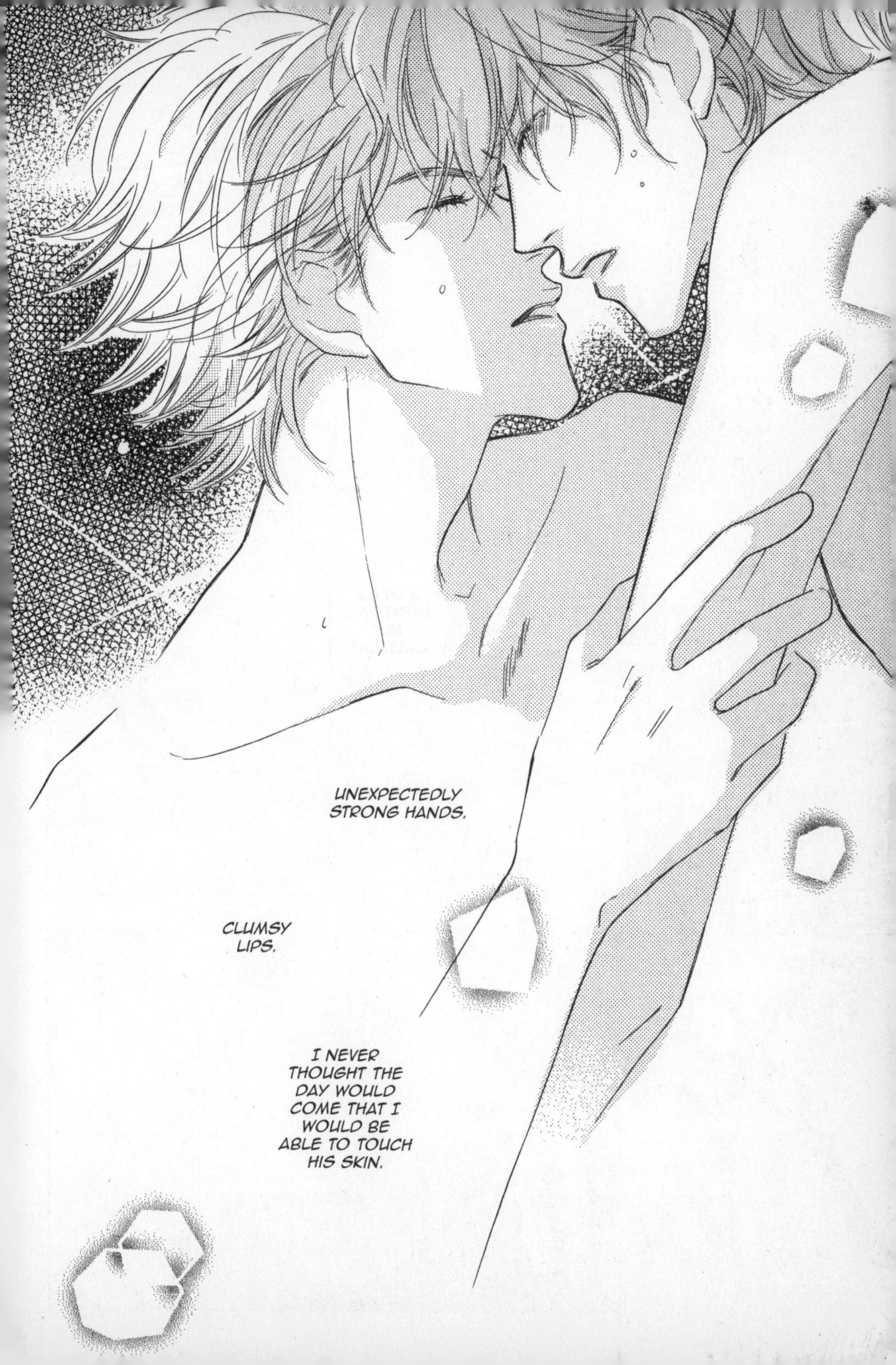
UNEXPECTEDLY STRONG HANDS.
CLUMSY LIPS.
I NEVER THOUGHT THE DAY WOULD COME THAT I WOULD BE ABLE TO TOUCH HIS SKIN.

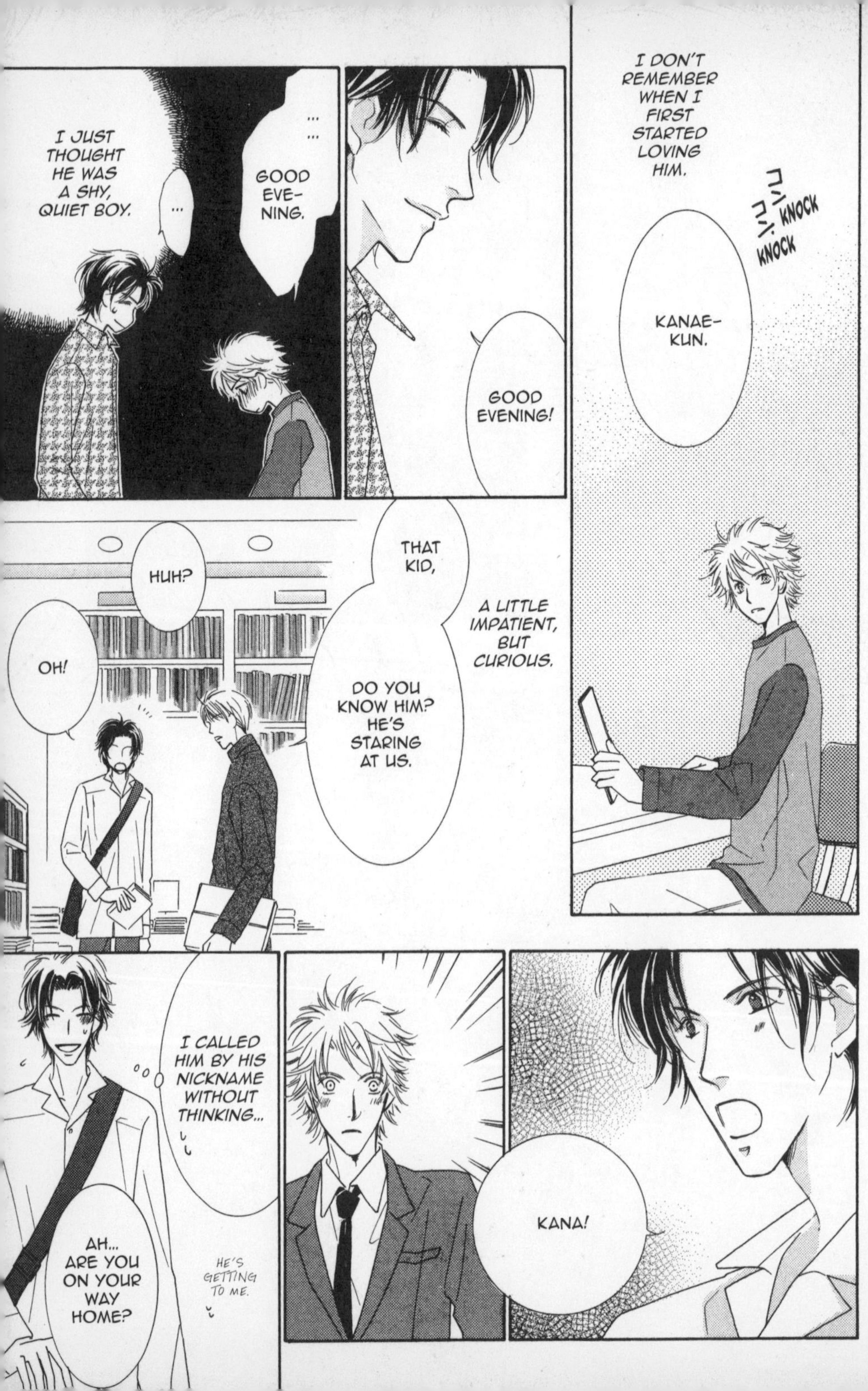
I DON'T REMEMBER WHEN I FIRST STARTED LOVING HIM.
KNOCK KNOCK
KANAE-KUN.
GOOD EVENING!
GOOD EVENING.
... ...
...
I JUST THOUGHT HE WAS A SHY, QUIET BOY.
THAT KID,
A LITTLE IMPATIENT, BUT CURIOUS.
DO YOU KNOW HIM? HE'S STARING AT US.
HUH?
OH!
KANA!
I CALLED HIM BY HIS NICKNAME WITHOUT THINKING...
AH... ARE YOU ON YOUR WAY HOME?
HE'S GETTING TO ME.

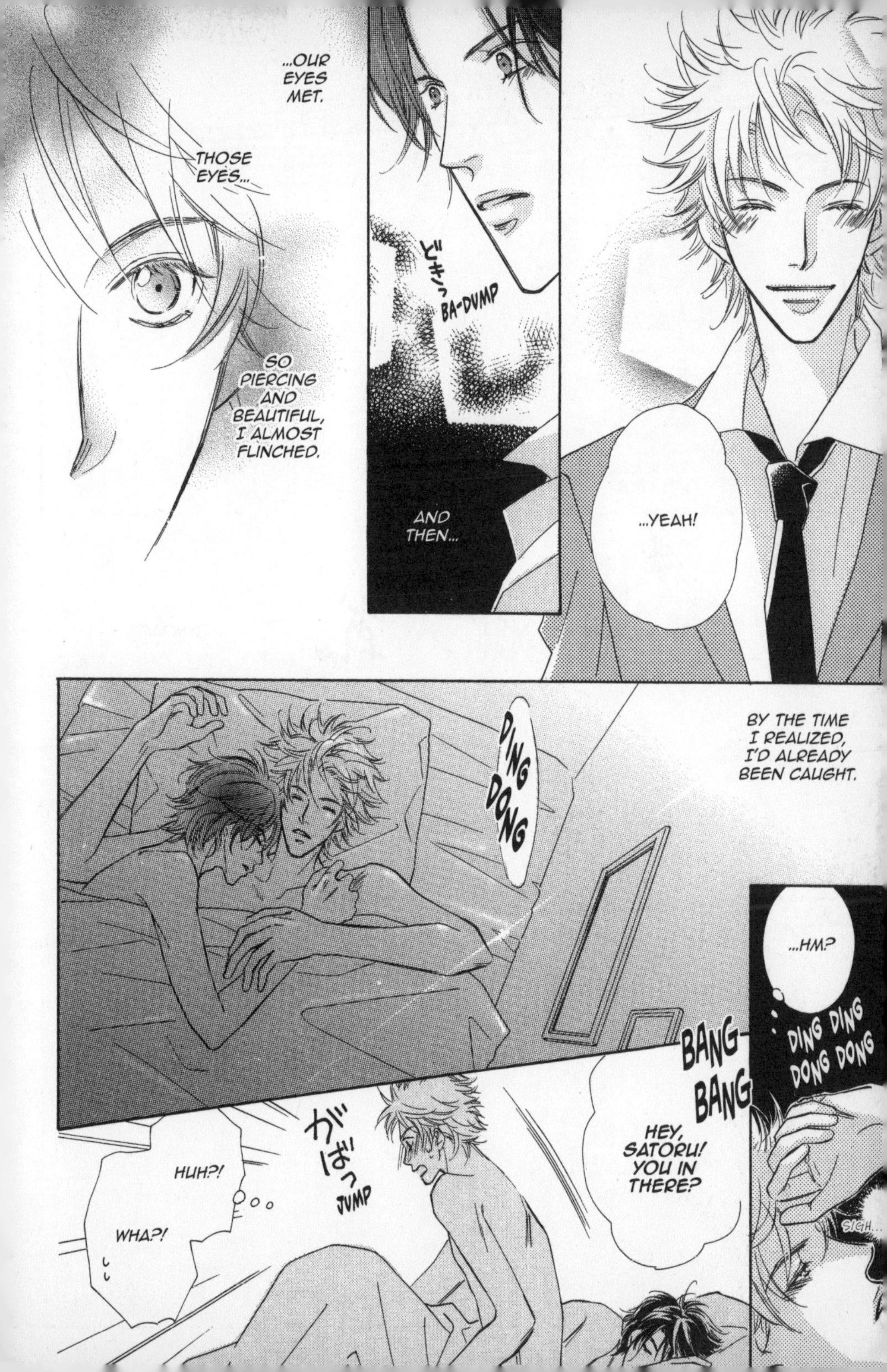
...YEAH!
どきっ
BA-DUMP
AND THEN...
...OUR EYES MET.
THOSE EYES...
SO PIERCING AND BEAUTIFUL, I ALMOST FLINCHED.
BY THE TIME I REALIZED, I'D ALREADY BEEN CAUGHT.
DING DONG
...HM?
DING DING DONG DONG
SIGH...
BANG-BANG
HEY, SATORU! YOU IN THERE?
がばっ
JUMP
HUH?!
WHA?!

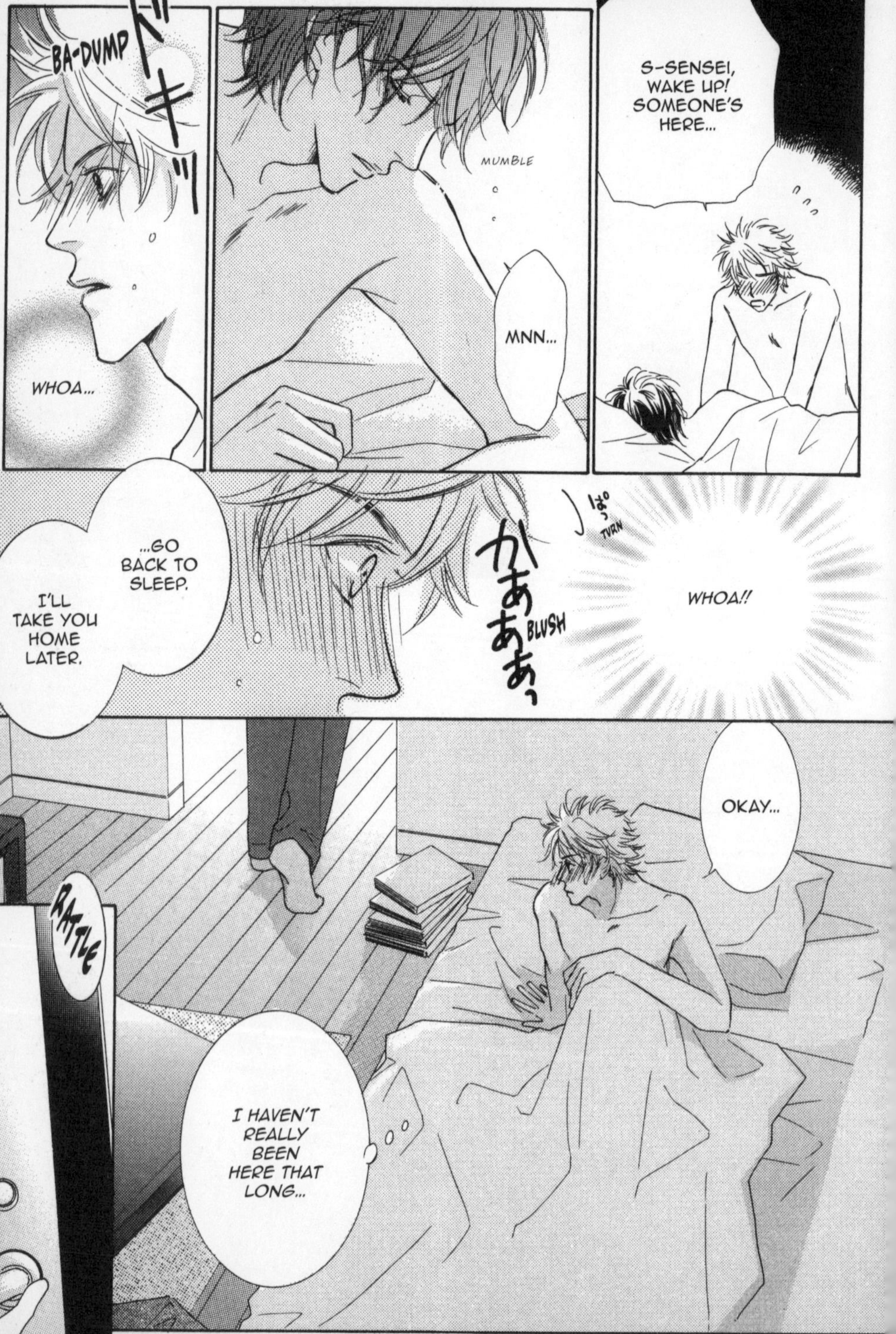
S-SENSEI, WAKE UP! SOMEONE'S HERE...
MUMBLE
MNN...
BA-DUMP
ドキッ
WHOA...
WHOA!!
ぱっ
TURN
かあああっ
BLUSH
...GO BACK TO SLEEP.
I'LL TAKE YOU HOME LATER.
OKAY...
I HAVEN'T REALLY BEEN HERE THAT LONG...
RATTLE

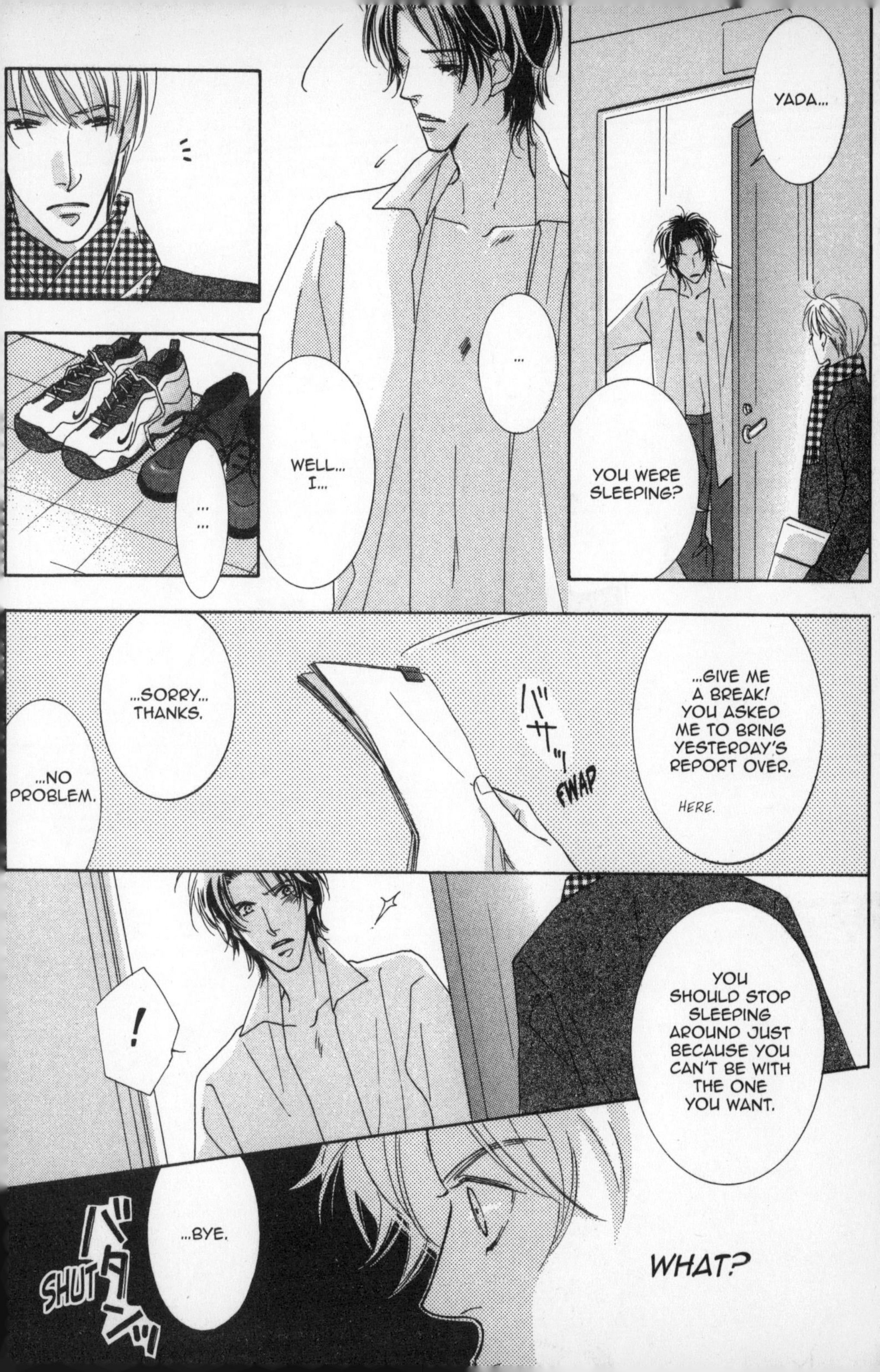
YADA...
YOU WERE SLEEPING?
...
WELL... I...
... ...
...GIVE ME A BREAK! YOU ASKED ME TO BRING YESTERDAY'S REPORT OVER.
HERE.
バサッ
FWAP
...SORRY... THANKS.
...NO PROBLEM.
YOU SHOULD STOP SLEEPING AROUND JUST BECAUSE YOU CAN'T BE WITH THE ONE YOU WANT.
WHAT?
!
...BYE.
バタン
SHUT

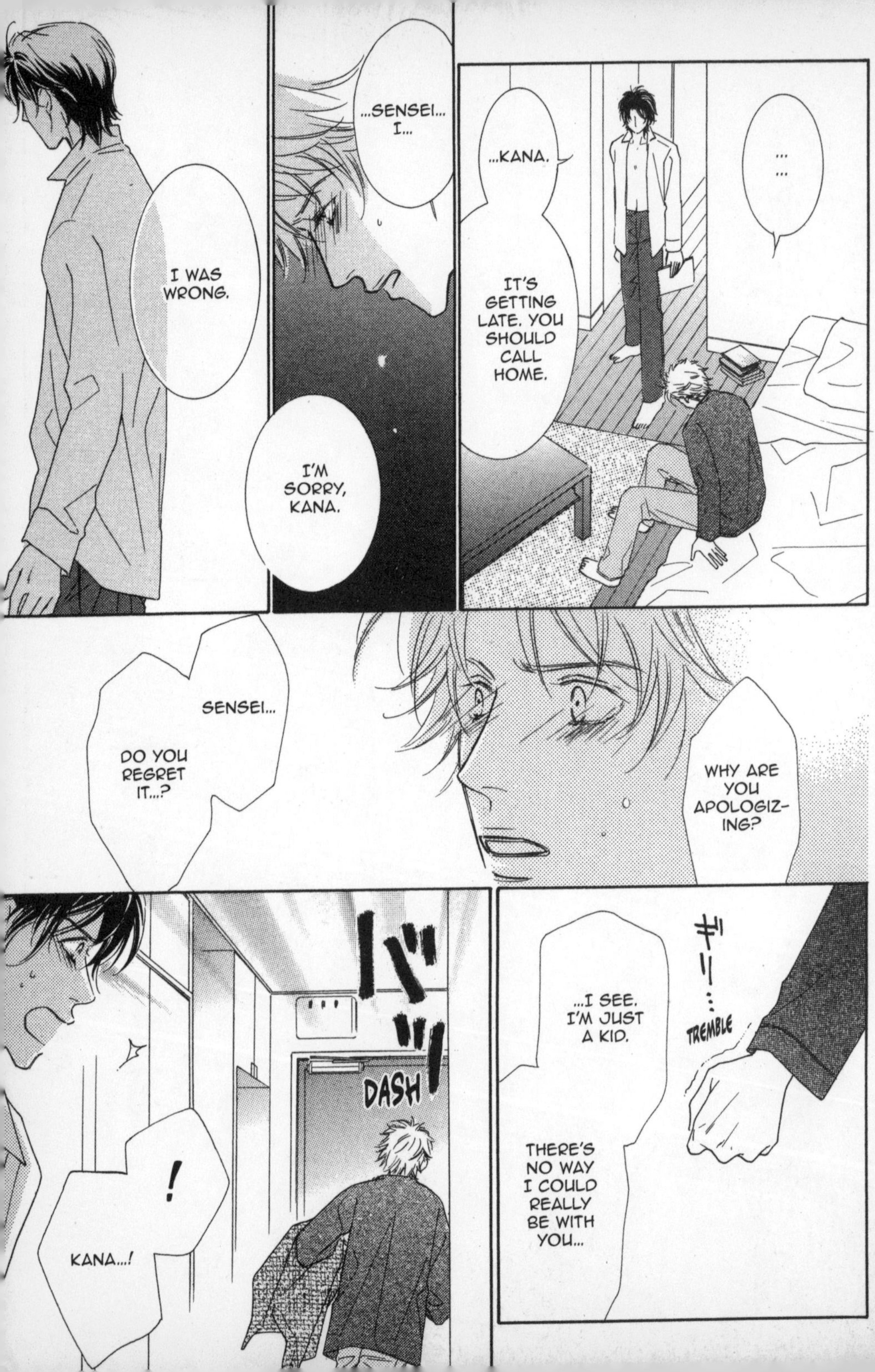
... ...
...KANA.
IT'S GETTING LATE. YOU SHOULD CALL HOME.
...SENSEI... I...
I'M SORRY, KANA.
I WAS WRONG.
WHY ARE YOU APOLOGIZ-ING?
SENSEI... DO YOU REGRET IT...?
ギリ…
TREMBLE
...I SEE. I'M JUST A KID.
THERE'S NO WAY I COULD REALLY BE WITH YOU...
バッ
DASH
!
KANA...!

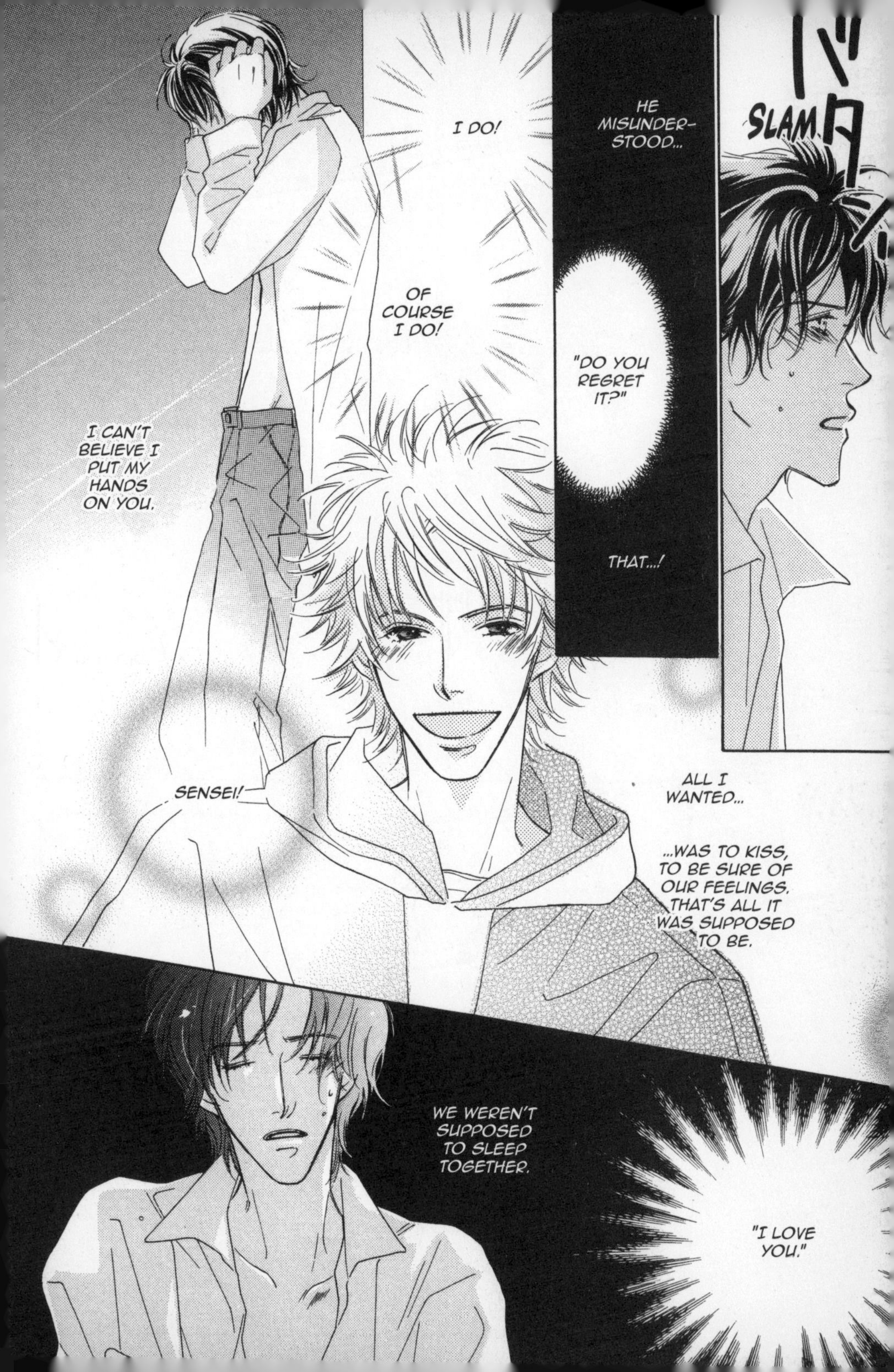

バタ
SLAM
HE MISUNDER-STOOD...
"DO YOU REGRET IT?"
THAT...!
I DO!
OF COURSE I DO!
ALL I WANTED...
...WAS TO KISS, TO BE SURE OF OUR FEELINGS. THAT'S ALL IT WAS SUPPOSED TO BE.
I CAN'T BELIEVE I PUT MY HANDS ON YOU.
SENSEI!
"I LOVE YOU."
WE WEREN'T SUPPOSED TO SLEEP TOGETHER.

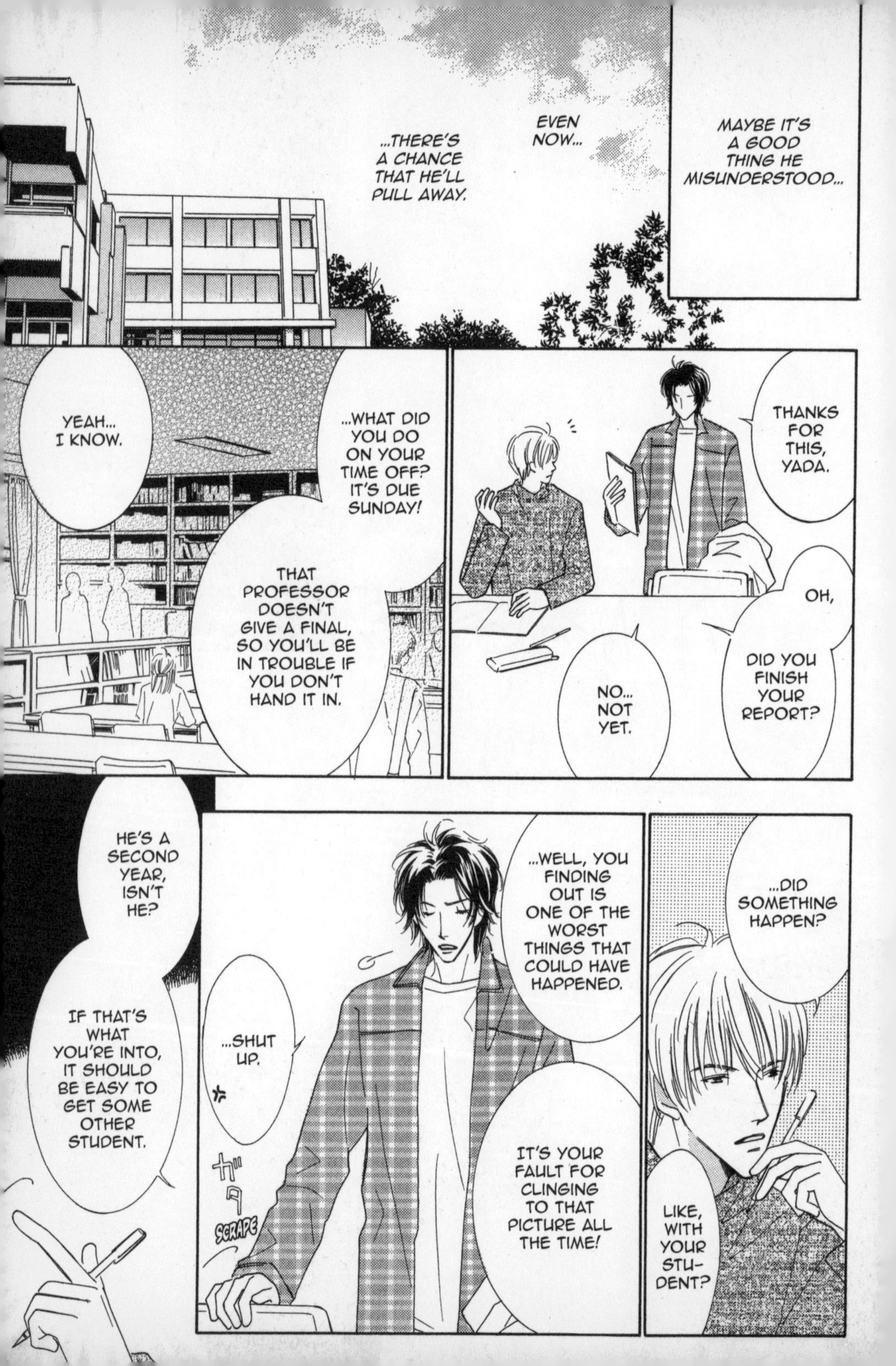
MAYBE IT'S A GOOD THING HE MISUNDERSTOOD...
EVEN NOW...
...THERE'S A CHANCE THAT HE'LL PULL AWAY.
THANKS FOR THIS, YADA.
OH,
DID YOU FINISH YOUR REPORT?
NO... NOT YET.
...WHAT DID YOU DO ON YOUR TIME OFF? IT'S DUE SUNDAY!
YEAH... I KNOW.
THAT PROFESSOR DOESN'T GIVE A FINAL, SO YOU'LL BE IN TROUBLE IF YOU DON'T HAND IT IN.
...DID SOMETHING HAPPEN?
LIKE, WITH YOUR STU-DENT?
...WELL, YOU FINDING OUT IS ONE OF THE WORST THINGS THAT COULD HAVE HAPPENED.
IT'S YOUR FAULT FOR CLINGING TO THAT PICTURE ALL THE TIME!
...SHUT UP.
ガタ
SCRAPE
HE'S A SECOND YEAR, ISN'T HE?
IF THAT'S WHAT YOU'RE INTO, IT SHOULD BE EASY TO GET SOME OTHER STUDENT.

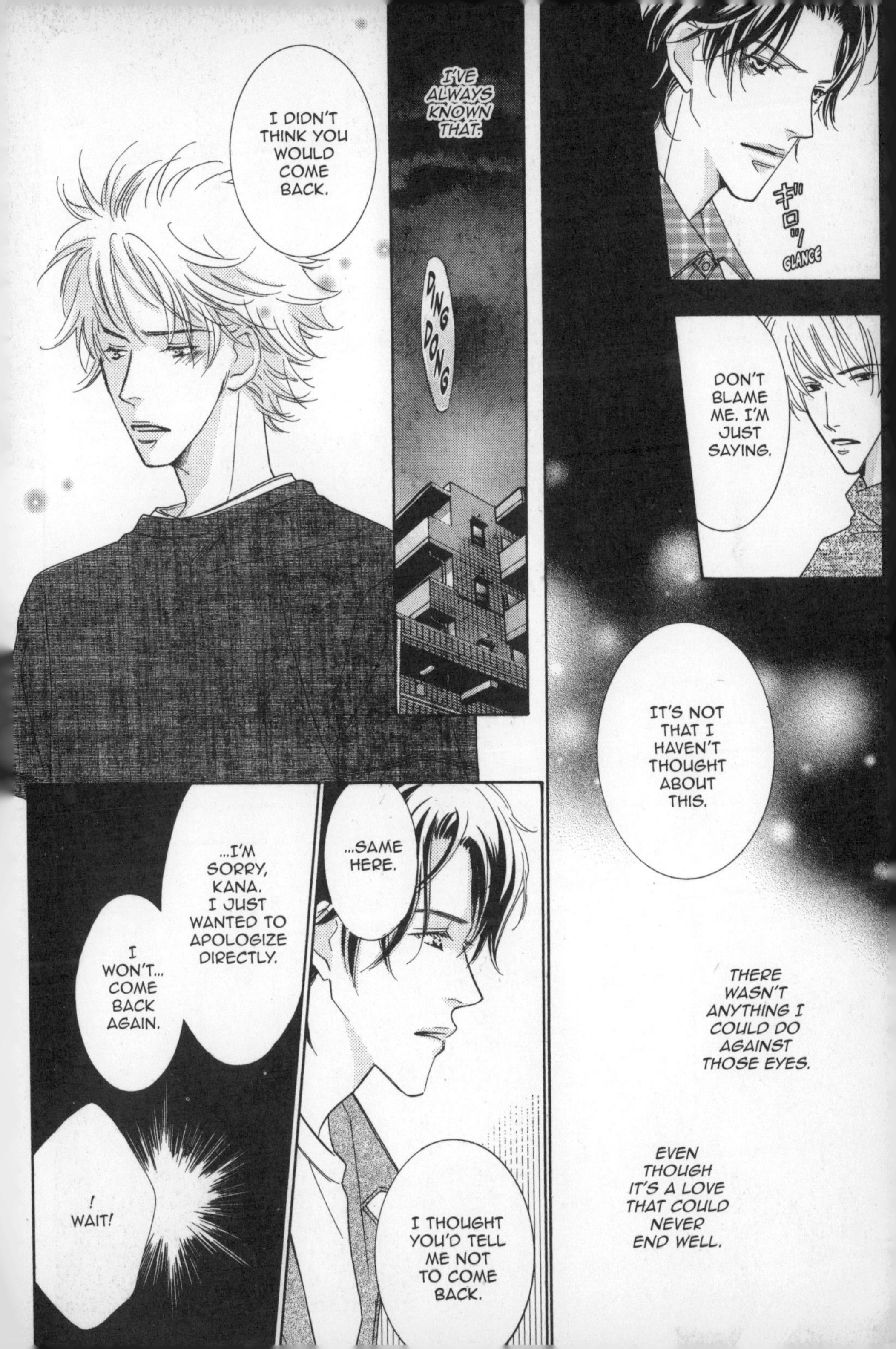
ギロッ
GLANCE
DON'T BLAME ME. I'M JUST SAYING.
IT'S NOT THAT I HAVEN'T THOUGHT ABOUT THIS.
THERE WASN'T ANYTHING I COULD DO AGAINST THOSE EYES.
EVEN THOUGH IT'S A LOVE THAT COULD NEVER END WELL.
I'VE ALWAYS KNOWN THAT.
DING DONG
I DIDN'T THINK YOU WOULD COME BACK.
...SAME HERE.
I THOUGHT YOU'D TELL ME NOT TO COME BACK.
...I'M SORRY, KANA. I JUST WANTED TO APOLOGIZE DIRECTLY.
I WON'T... COME BACK AGAIN.
! WAIT!

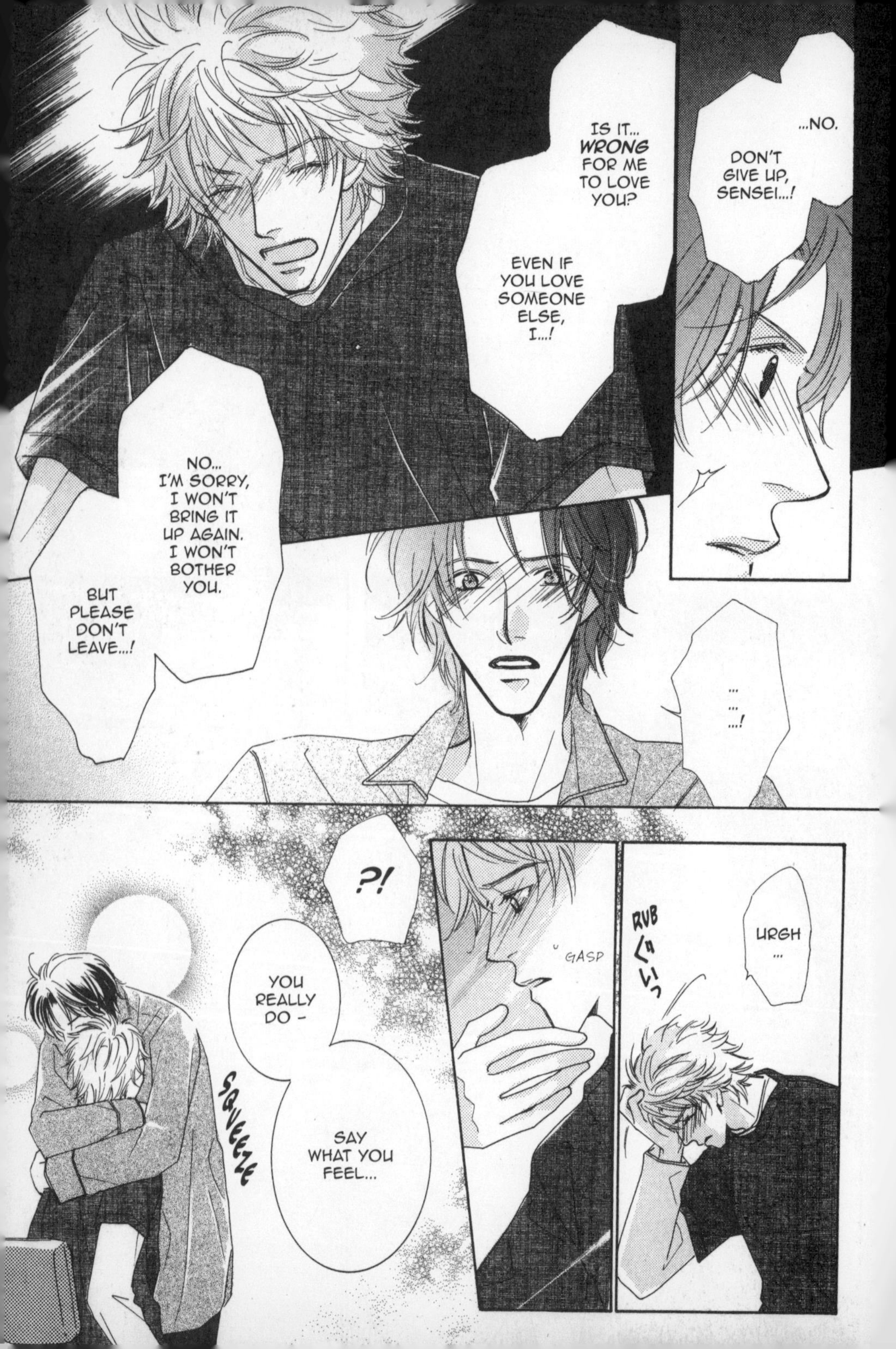
...NO.
DON'T GIVE UP, SENSEI...!
IS IT... WRONG FOR ME TO LOVE YOU?
EVEN IF YOU LOVE SOMEONE ELSE, I...!
NO... I'M SORRY, I WON'T BRING IT UP AGAIN. I WON'T BOTHER YOU.
BUT PLEASE DON'T LEAVE...!
... ...!
URGH ...
RUB
ぐいっ
GASP
?!
YOU REALLY DO -
SAY WHAT YOU FEEL...
SQUEEZE

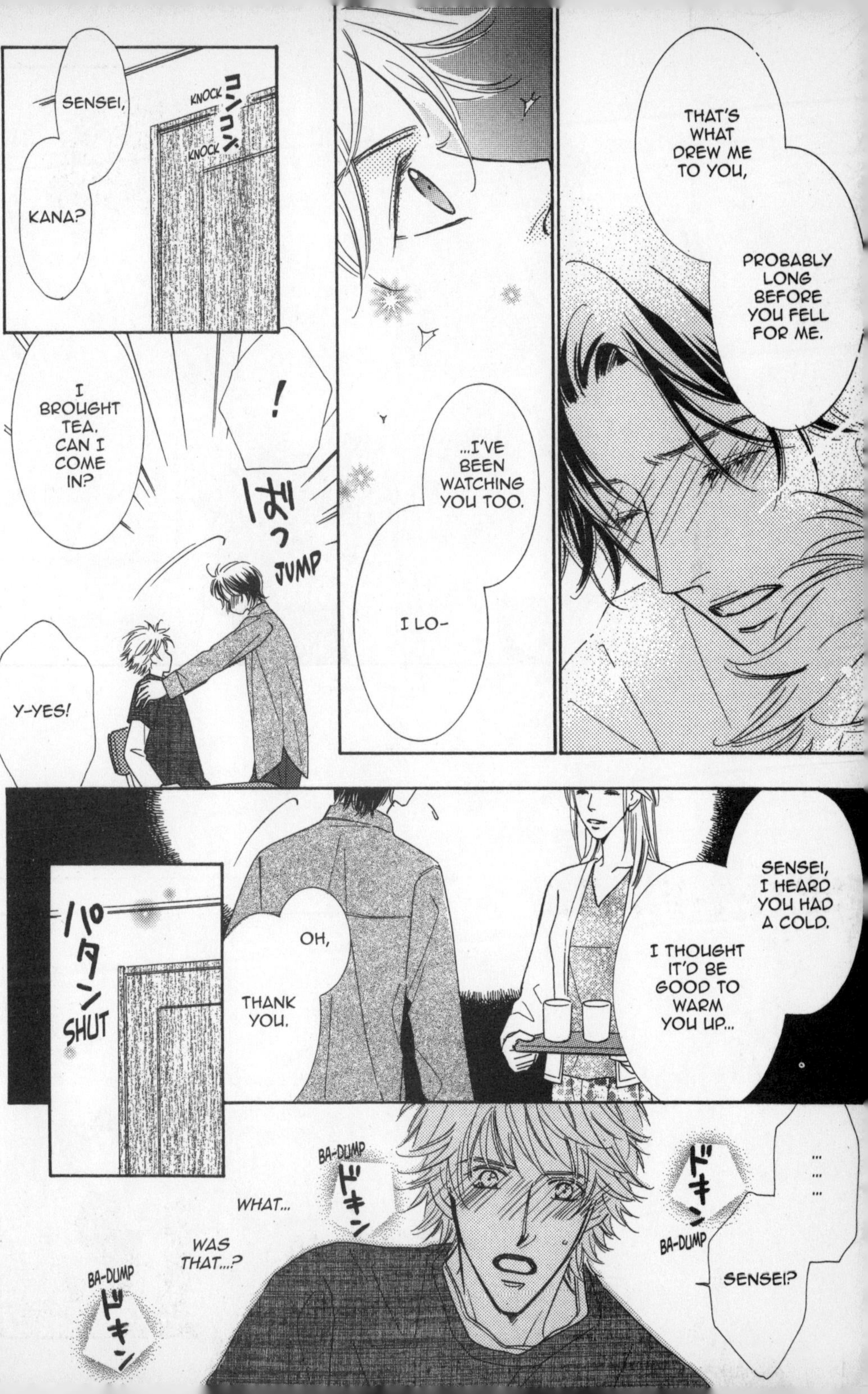
THAT'S WHAT DREW ME TO YOU,
PROBABLY LONG BEFORE YOU FELL FOR ME.
...I'VE BEEN WATCHING YOU TOO.
I LO-
コンコン KNOCK KNOCK
SENSEI,
KANA?
!
ぱっ JUMP
I BROUGHT TEA. CAN I COME IN?
Y-YES!
SENSEI, I HEARD YOU HAD A COLD.
I THOUGHT IT'D BE GOOD TO WARM YOU UP...
OH,
THANK YOU.
パタン SHUT
......
SENSEI?
ドキン BA-DUMP
ドキン BA-DUMP
WHAT...
WAS THAT...?
ドキン BA-DUMP

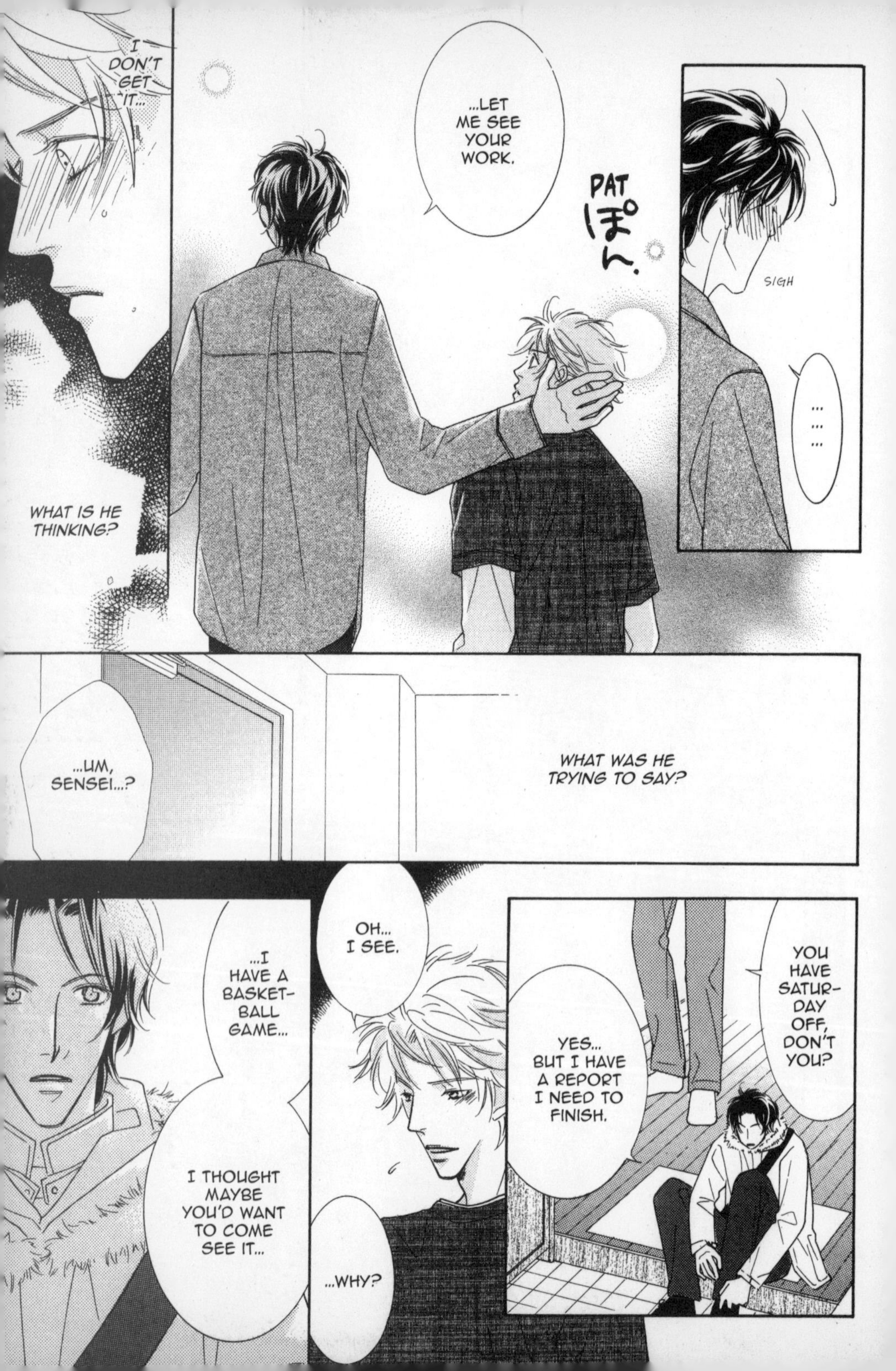

SIGH
...
...
...
...LET ME SEE YOUR WORK.
PAT
ぽん.
I DON'T GET IT...
WHAT IS HE THINKING?
WHAT WAS HE TRYING TO SAY?
...UM, SENSEI...?
YOU HAVE SATURDAY OFF, DON'T YOU?
YES... BUT I HAVE A REPORT I NEED TO FINISH.
OH... I SEE.
...I HAVE A BASKETBALL GAME...
I THOUGHT MAYBE YOU'D WANT TO COME SEE IT...
...WHY?

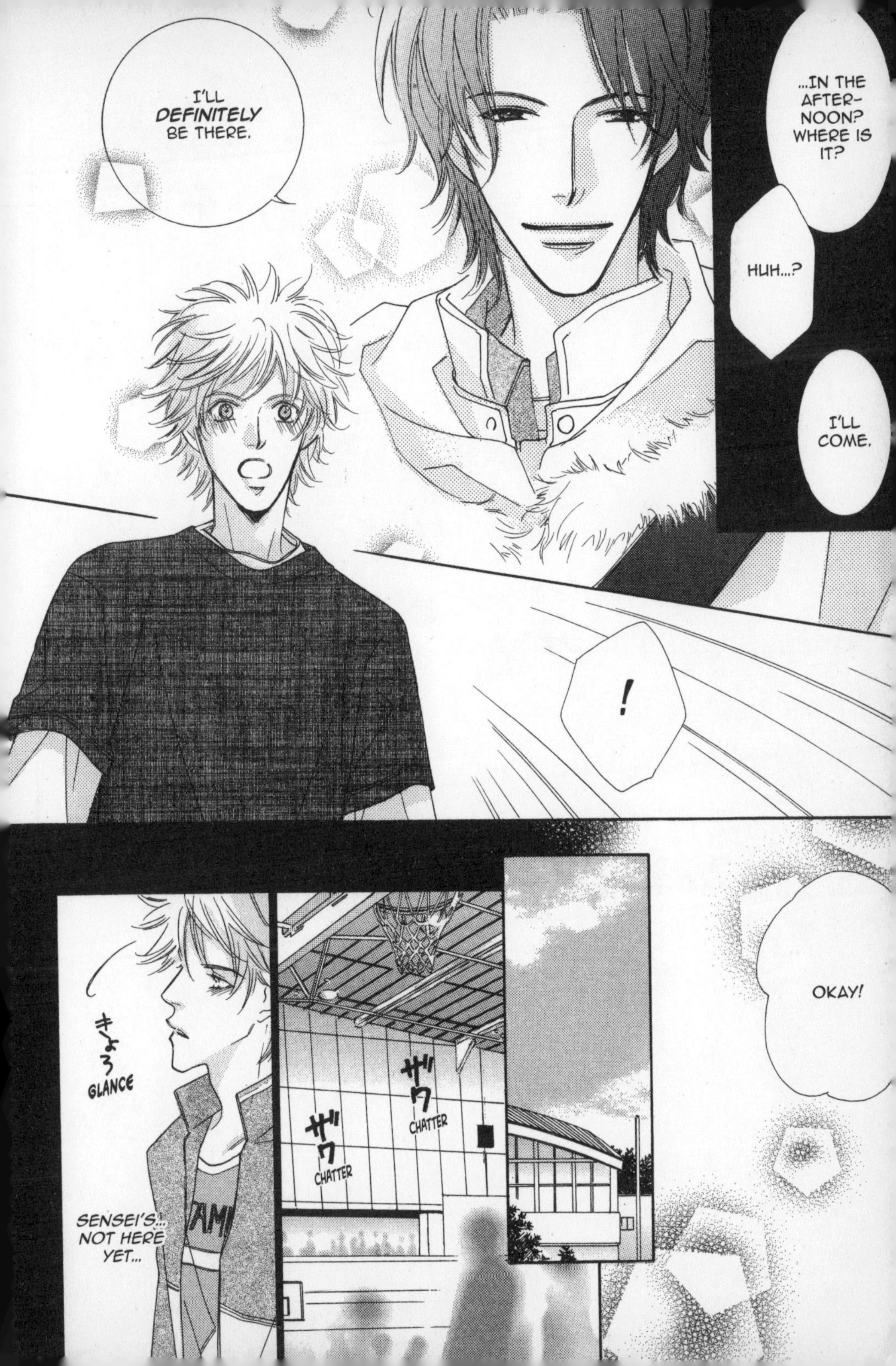

...IN THE AFTER-NOON? WHERE IS IT?
HUH...?
I'LL COME.
I'LL *DEFINITELY* BE THERE.
!
OKAY!
ザワ CHATTER
ザワ CHATTER
きょろ GLANCE
SENSEI'S... NOT HERE YET...

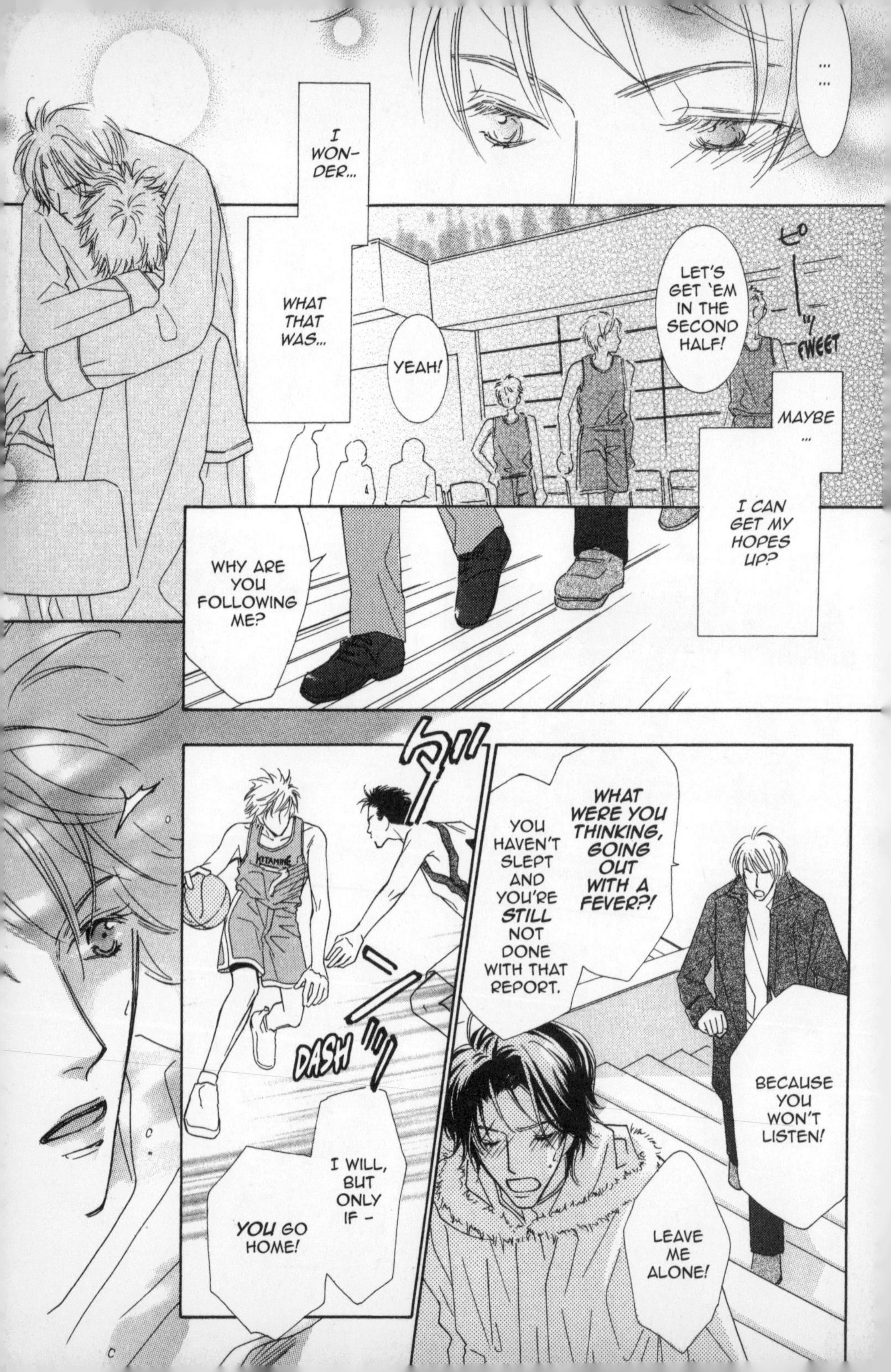

... ...
I WONDER...
WHAT THAT WAS...
LET'S GET 'EM IN THE SECOND HALF!
FWEET
YEAH!
MAYBE ...
I CAN GET MY HOPES UP?
WHY ARE YOU FOLLOWING ME?
WHAT WERE YOU THINKING, GOING OUT WITH A FEVER?!
YOU HAVEN'T SLEPT AND YOU'RE STILL NOT DONE WITH THAT REPORT.
BECAUSE YOU WON'T LISTEN!
LEAVE ME ALONE!
I WILL, BUT ONLY IF –
YOU GO HOME!
DASH

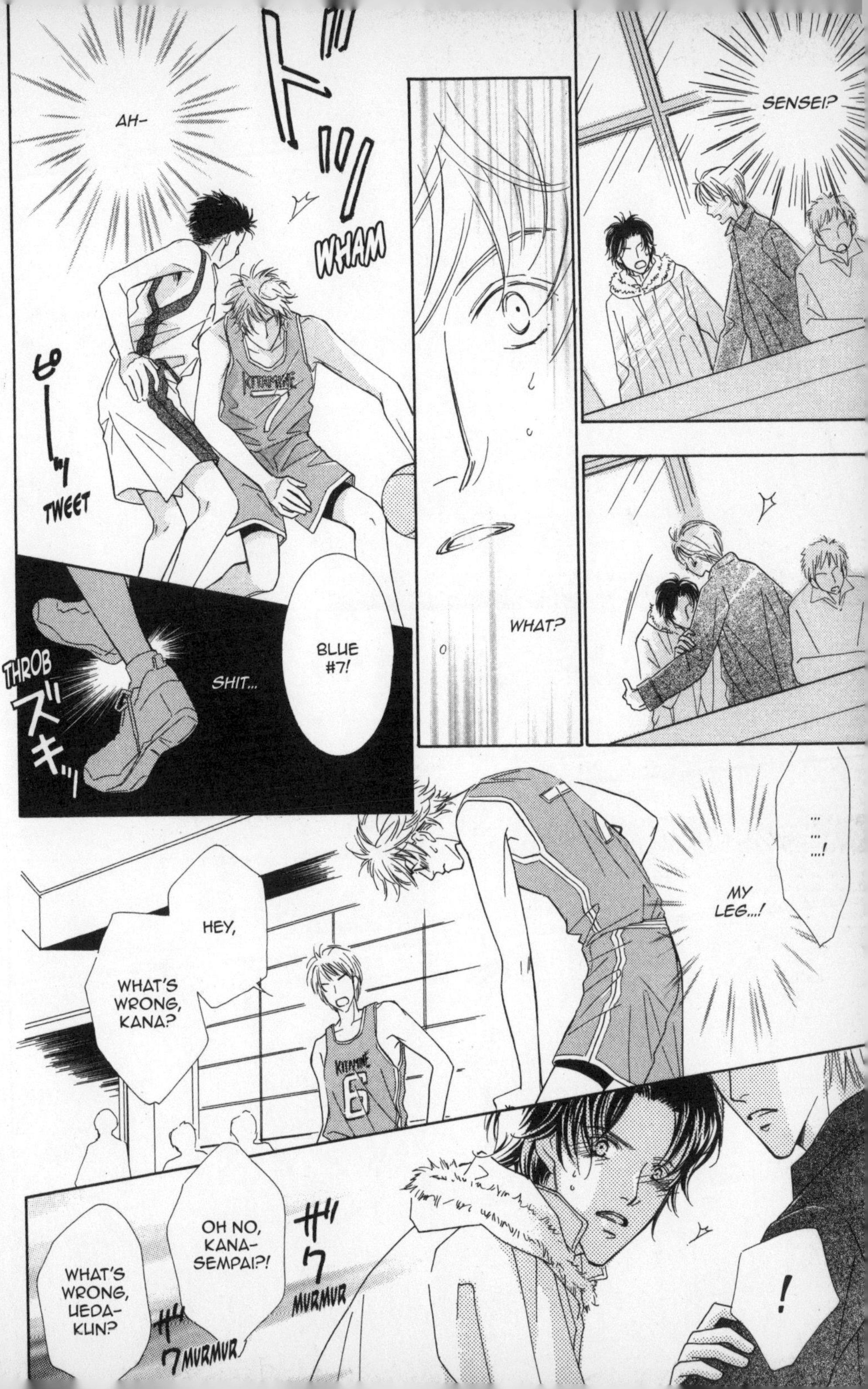
SENSEI?
WHAT?
ドッ
WHAM
AH-
ピーッ
TWEET
BLUE #7!
SHIT...
THROB
ズキッ
...
...
...!
MY LEG...!
HEY,
WHAT'S WRONG, KANA?
!
ザワ
MURMUR
OH NO, KANA-SEMPAI?!
WHAT'S WRONG, UEDA-KUN?
ザワ
MURMUR

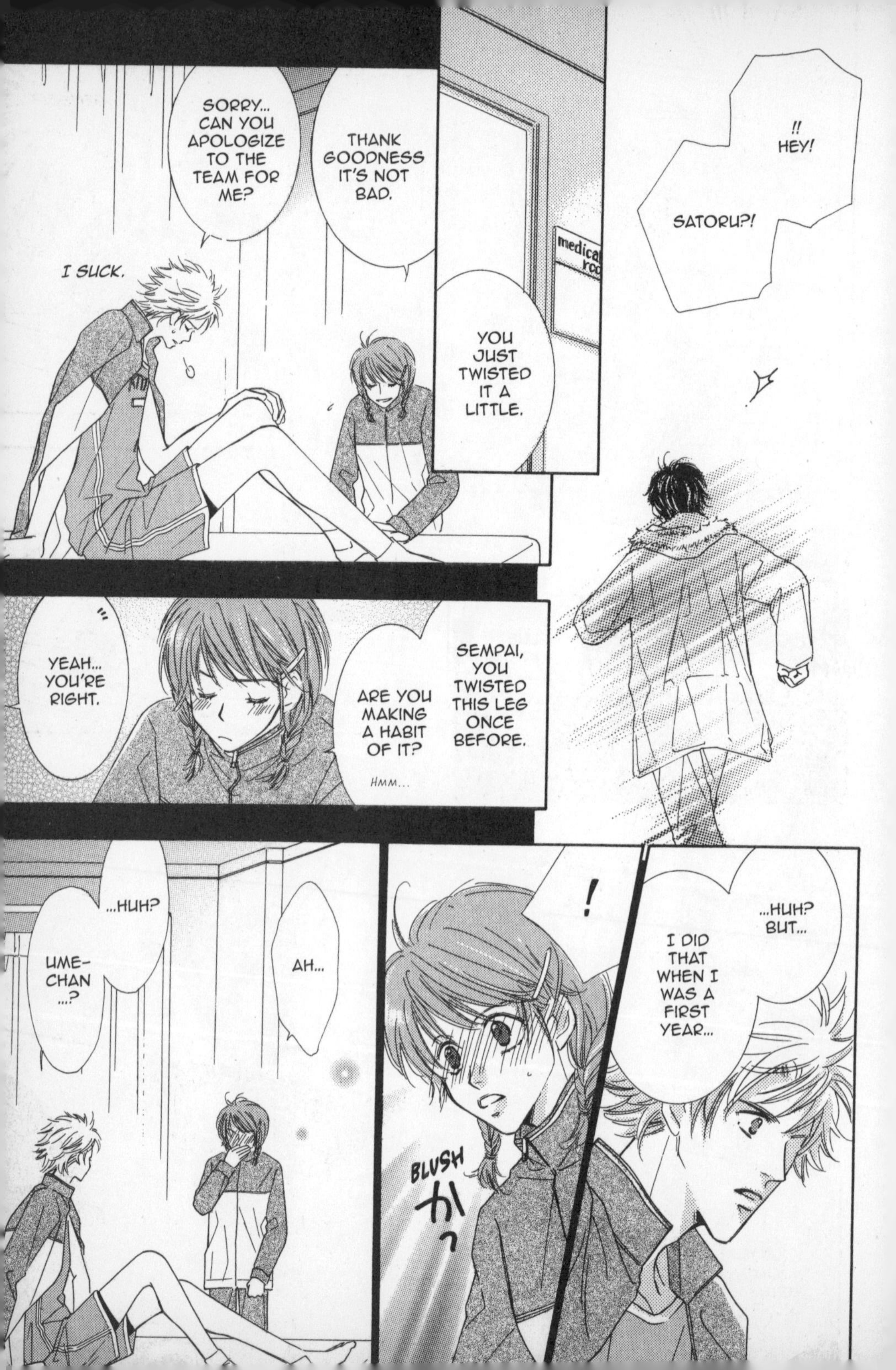

!! HEY!
SATORU?!
YOU JUST TWISTED IT A LITTLE.
THANK GOODNESS IT'S NOT BAD.
SORRY... CAN YOU APOLOGIZE TO THE TEAM FOR ME?
I SUCK.
SEMPAI, YOU TWISTED THIS LEG ONCE BEFORE.
ARE YOU MAKING A HABIT OF IT?
HMM...
YEAH... YOU'RE RIGHT.
...HUH? BUT...
I DID THAT WHEN I WAS A FIRST YEAR...
!
BLUSH
かっ
AH...
...HUH?
UME-CHAN ...?

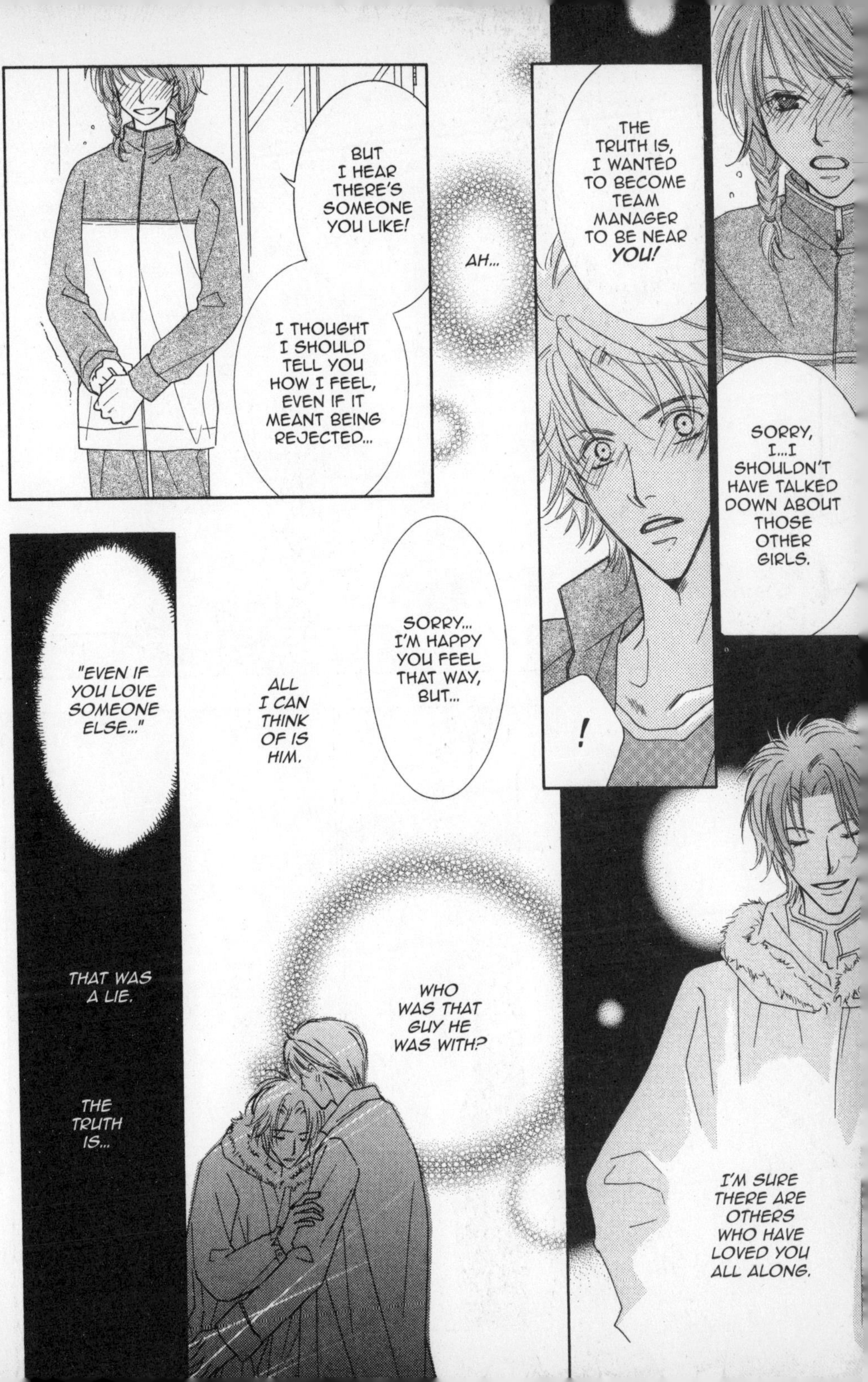
SORRY, I...I SHOULDN'T HAVE TALKED DOWN ABOUT THOSE OTHER GIRLS.
THE TRUTH IS, I WANTED TO BECOME TEAM MANAGER TO BE NEAR *YOU!*
!
AH...
BUT I HEAR THERE'S SOMEONE YOU LIKE!
I THOUGHT I SHOULD TELL YOU HOW I FEEL, EVEN IF IT MEANT BEING REJECTED...
SORRY... I'M HAPPY YOU FEEL THAT WAY, BUT...
ALL I CAN THINK OF IS HIM.
I'M SURE THERE ARE OTHERS WHO HAVE LOVED YOU ALL ALONG.
WHO WAS THAT GUY HE WAS WITH?
"EVEN IF YOU LOVE SOMEONE ELSE..."
THAT WAS A LIE.
THE TRUTH IS...

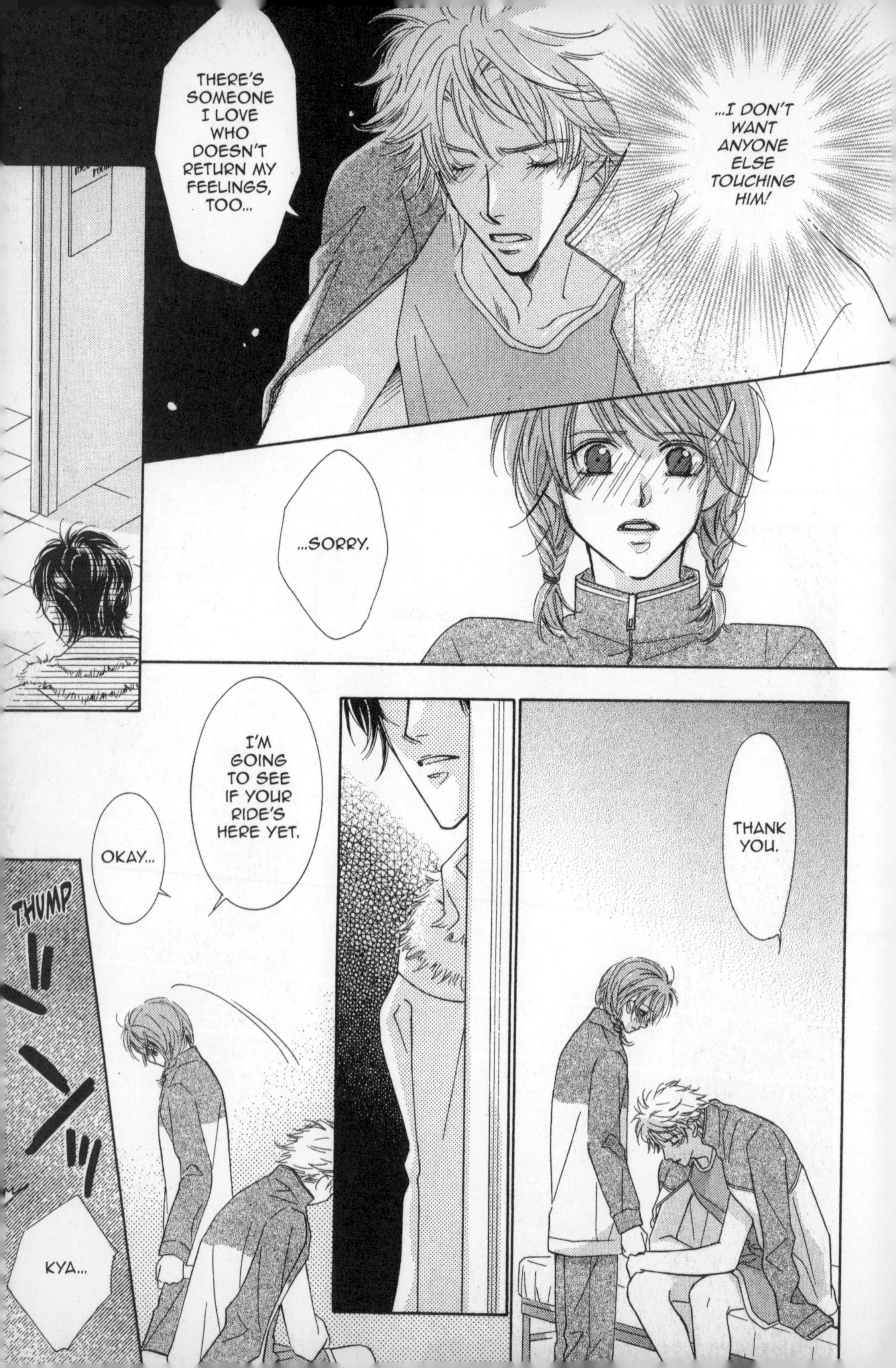

...I DON'T WANT ANYONE ELSE TOUCHING HIM!
THERE'S SOMEONE I LOVE WHO DOESN'T RETURN MY FEELINGS, TOO...
...SORRY.
THANK YOU.
I'M GOING TO SEE IF YOUR RIDE'S HERE YET.
OKAY...
THUMP
KYA...

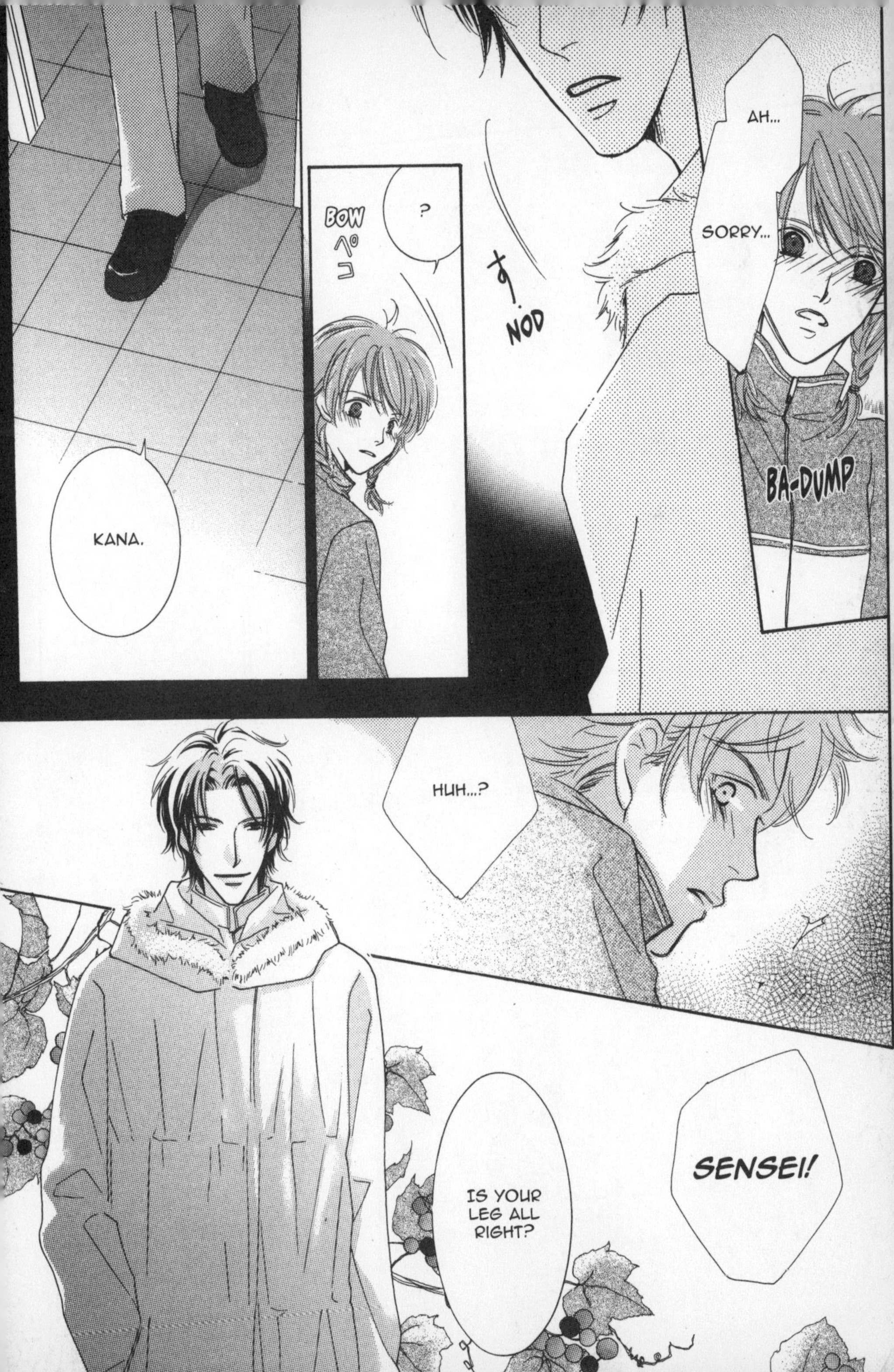

AH...
SORRY...
BA-DUMP
す
NOD
?
BOW
ペコ
KANA.
HUH...?
SENSEI!
IS YOUR LEG ALL RIGHT?

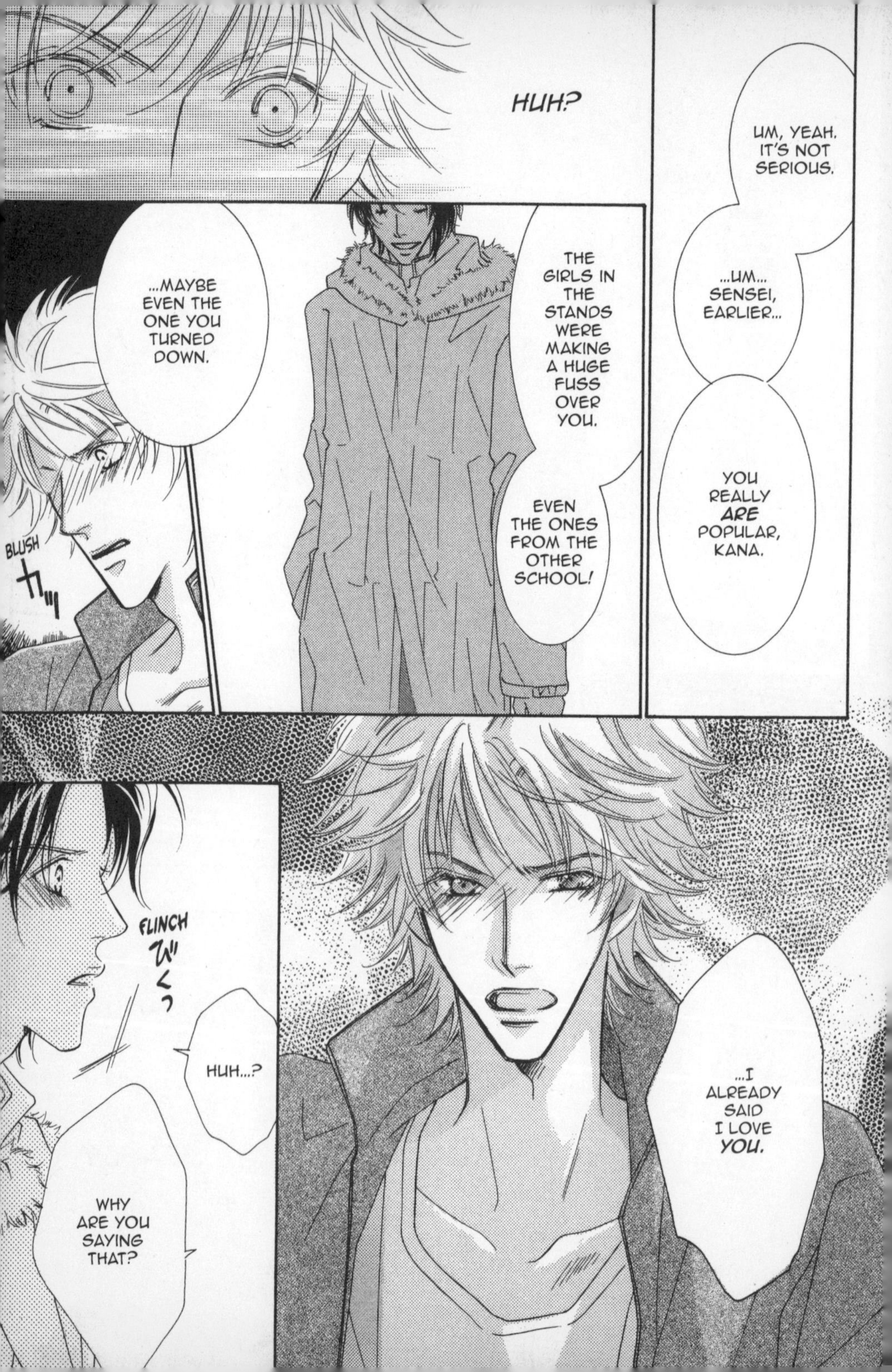
UM, YEAH. IT'S NOT SERIOUS.
...UM... SENSEI, EARLIER...
YOU REALLY **ARE** POPULAR, KANA.
HUH?
THE GIRLS IN THE STANDS WERE MAKING A HUGE FUSS OVER YOU.
EVEN THE ONES FROM THE OTHER SCHOOL!
...MAYBE EVEN THE ONE YOU TURNED DOWN.
BLUSH
...I ALREADY SAID I LOVE ***YOU.***
FLINCH
HUH...?
WHY ARE YOU SAYING THAT?

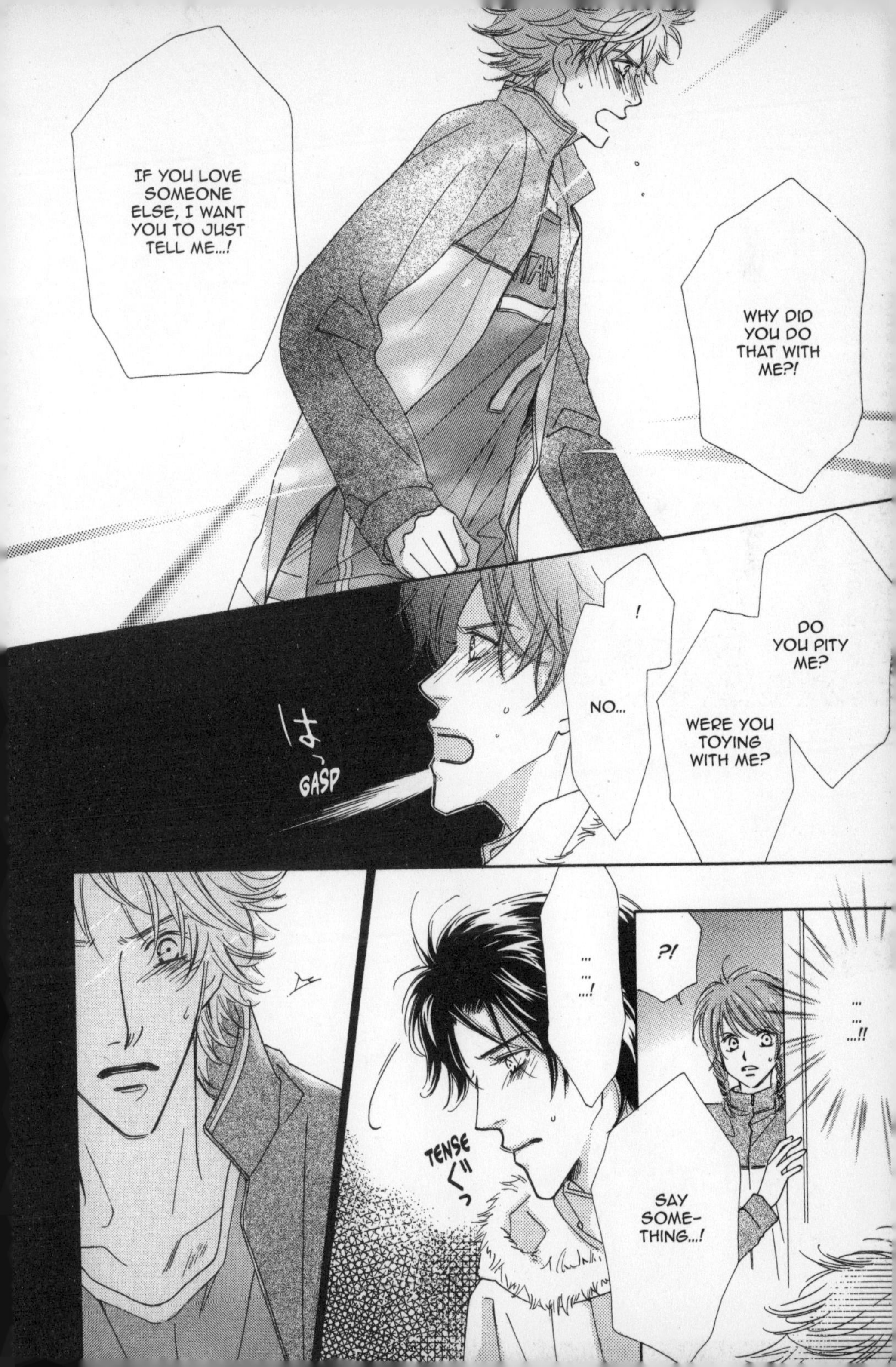
WHY DID YOU DO THAT WITH ME?!
IF YOU LOVE SOMEONE ELSE, I WANT YOU TO JUST TELL ME...!
DO YOU PITY ME?
WERE YOU TOYING WITH ME?
!
NO...
はっ
GASP
...
...
...!!
?!
...
...
...!
SAY SOME-THING...!
TENSE
ぐっ

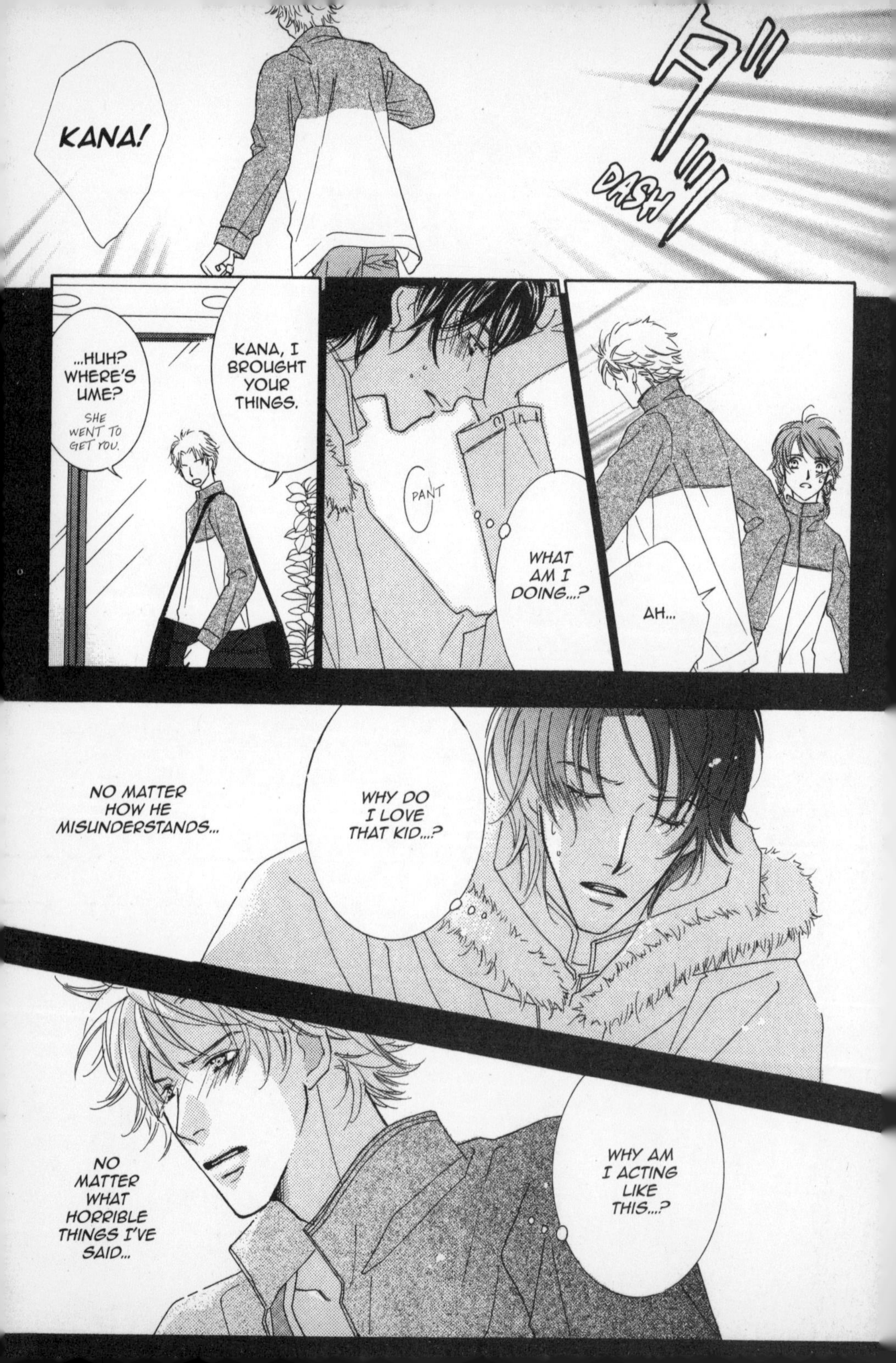
DASH
KANA!
AH...
PANT
WHAT AM I DOING...?
KANA, I BROUGHT YOUR THINGS.
...HUH? WHERE'S UME?
SHE WENT TO GET YOU.
WHY DO I LOVE THAT KID...?
NO MATTER HOW HE MISUNDERSTANDS...
WHY AM I ACTING LIKE THIS...?
NO MATTER WHAT HORRIBLE THINGS I'VE SAID...

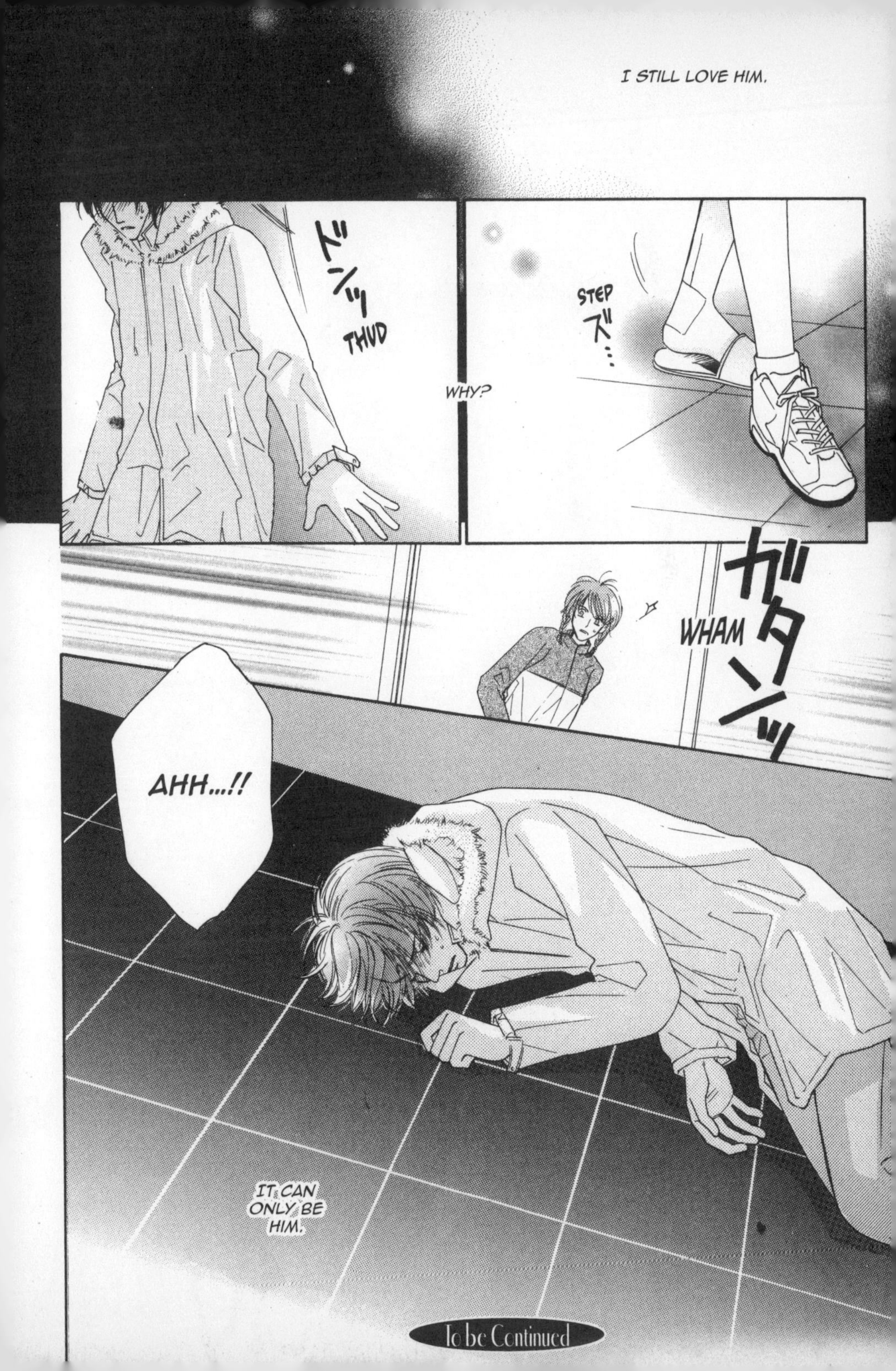
I STILL LOVE HIM.
STEP
ズ…
WHY?
ドンッ
THUD
ガタンッ
WHAM
AHH...!!
IT CAN ONLY BE HIM.
To be Continued

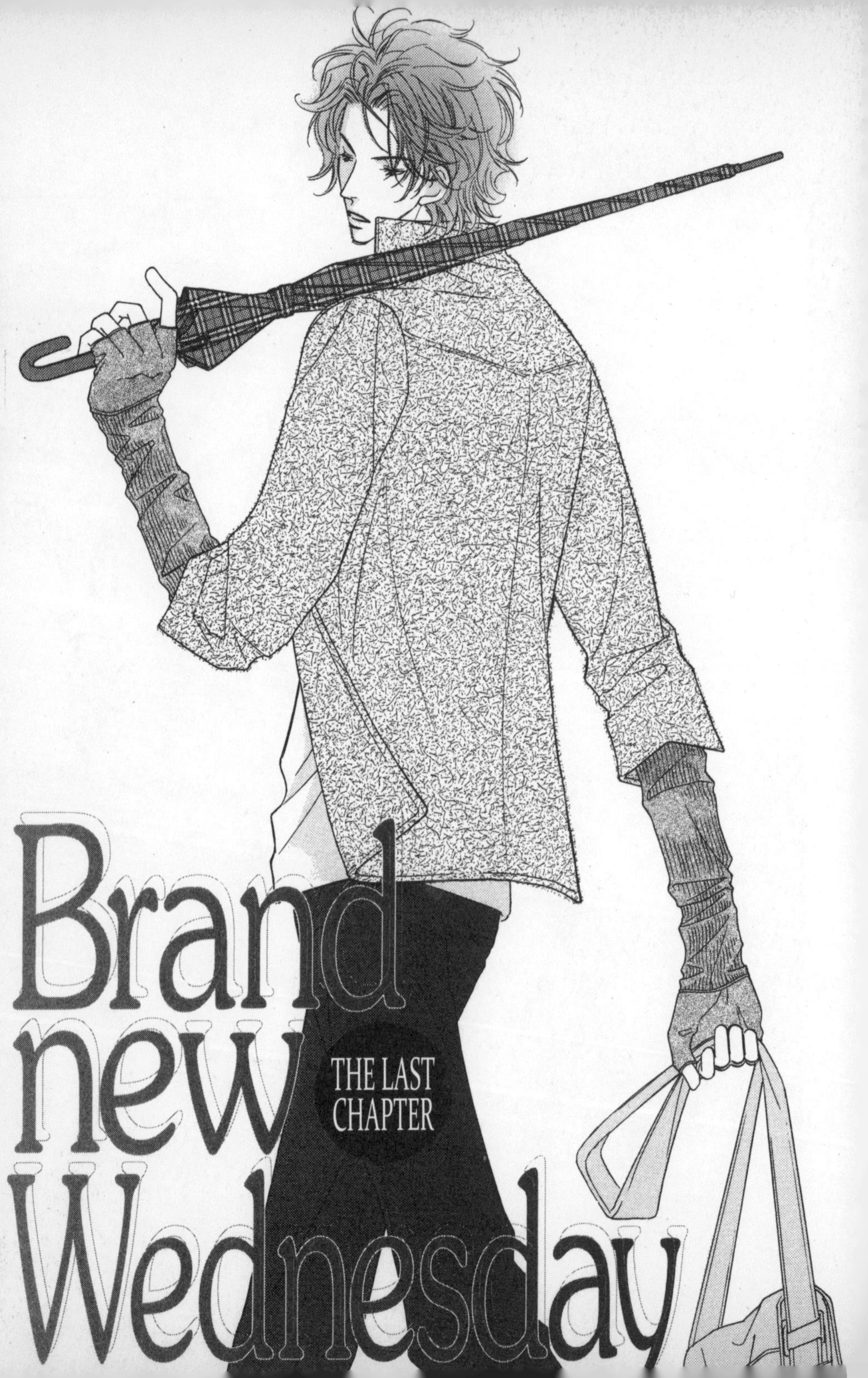
Brand new Wednesday
THE LAST CHAPTER

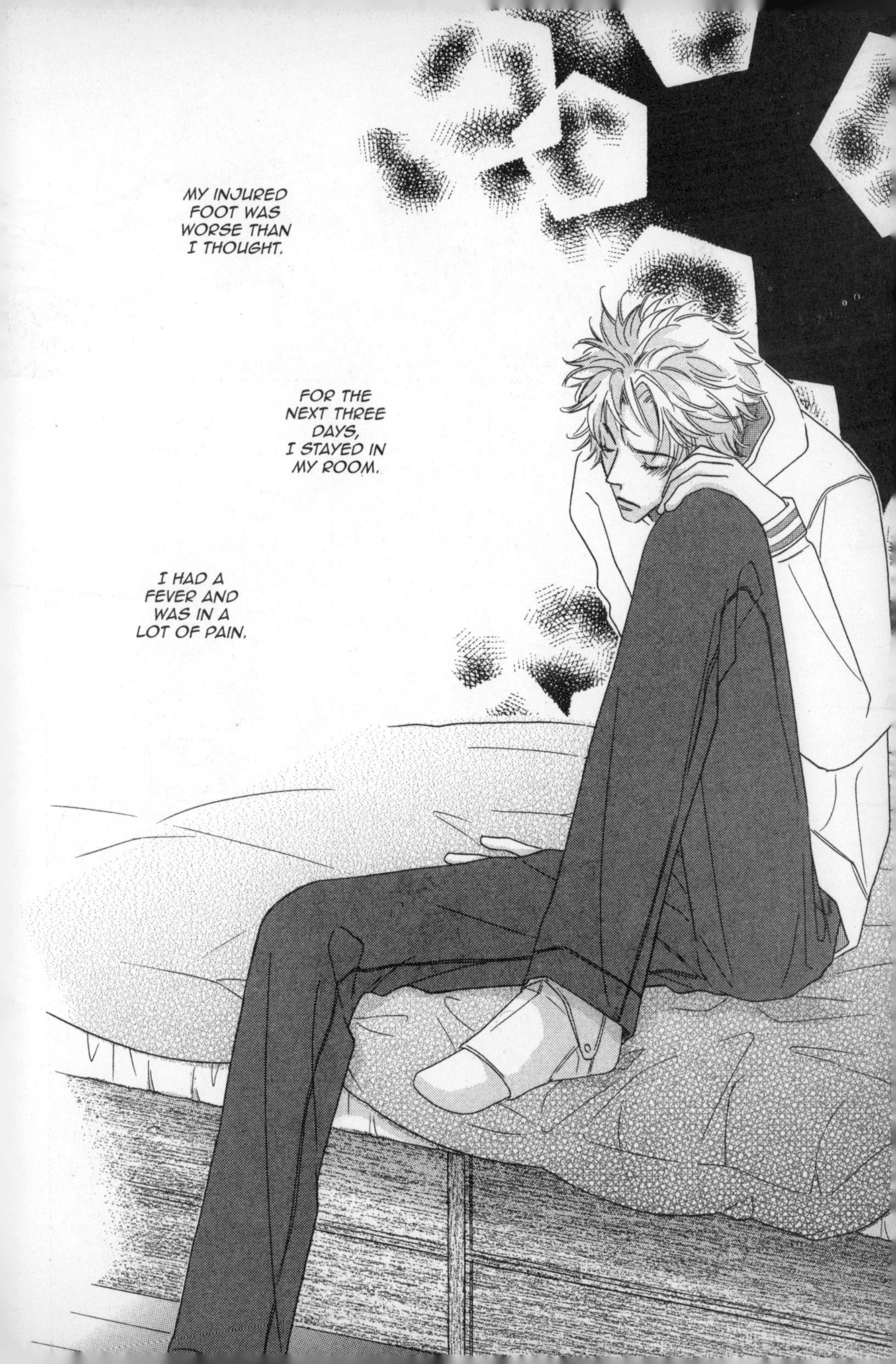
MY INJURED FOOT WAS WORSE THAN I THOUGHT.
FOR THE NEXT THREE DAYS, I STAYED IN MY ROOM.
I HAD A FEVER AND WAS IN A LOT OF PAIN.

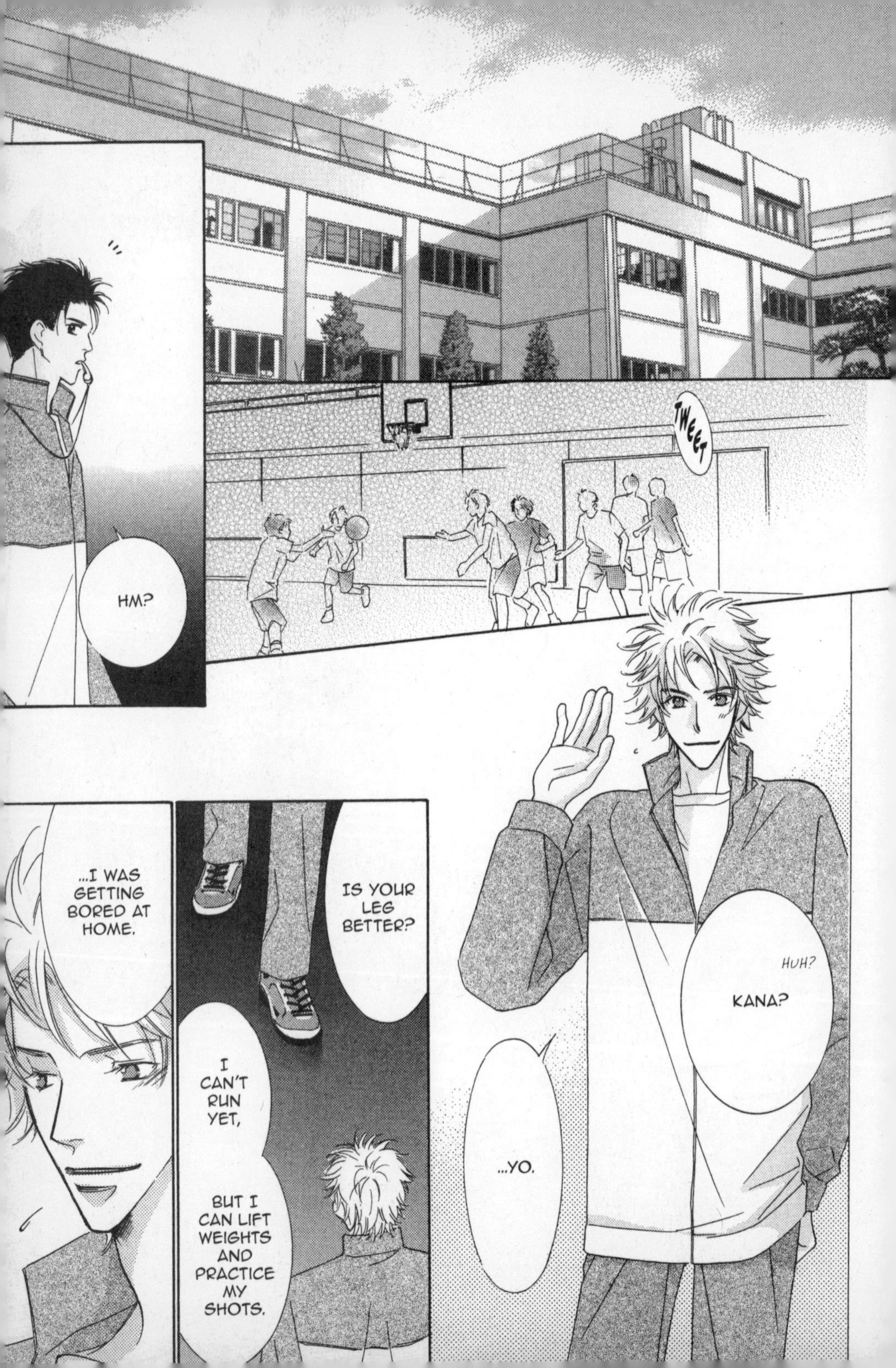
TWEET
HM?
HUH?
KANA?
...YO.
IS YOUR LEG BETTER?
I CAN'T RUN YET,
BUT I CAN LIFT WEIGHTS AND PRACTICE MY SHOTS.
...I WAS GETTING BORED AT HOME.

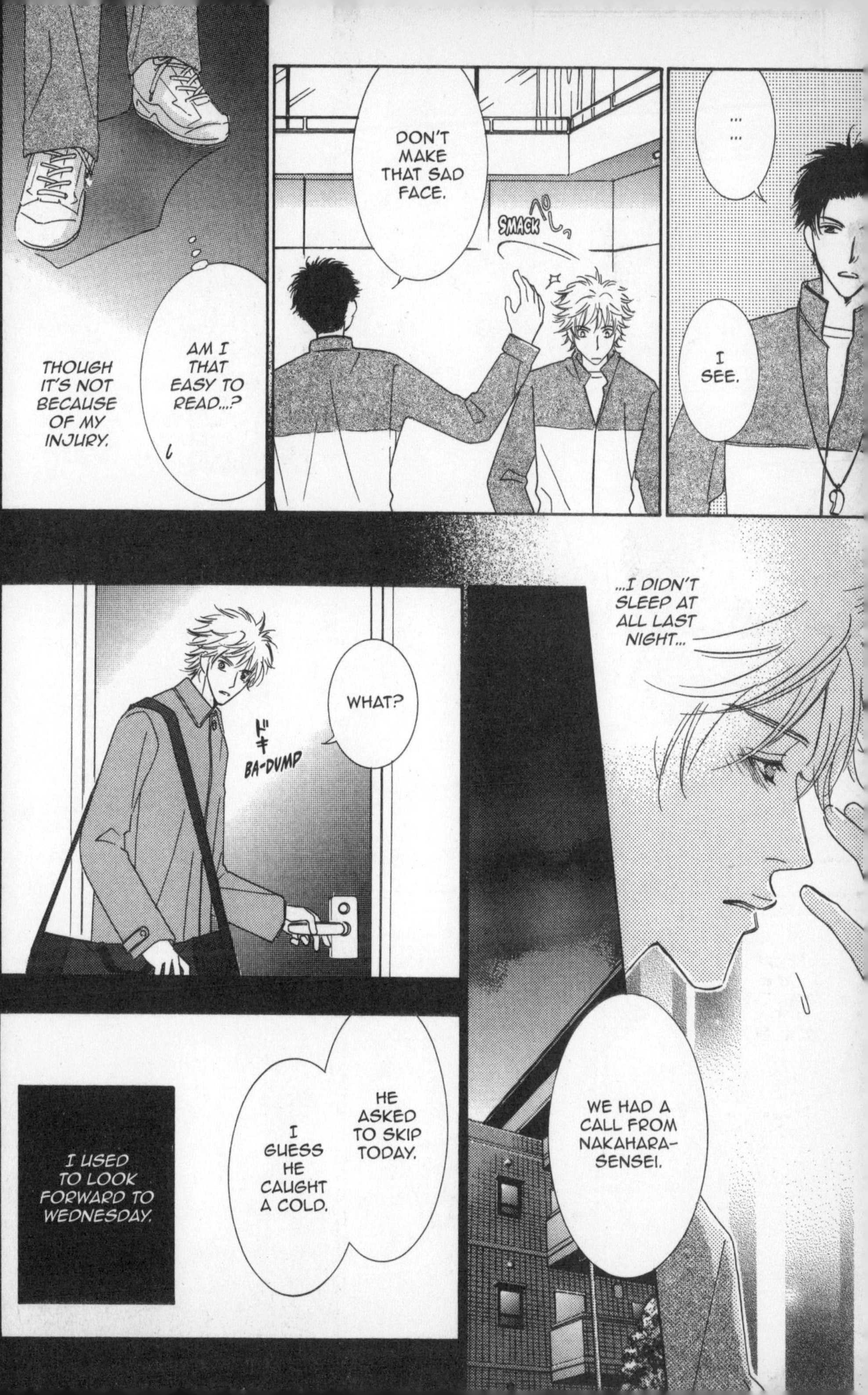
... ...
I SEE.
DON'T MAKE THAT SAD FACE.
SMACK
AM I THAT EASY TO READ...?
THOUGH IT'S NOT BECAUSE OF MY INJURY.
...I DIDN'T SLEEP AT ALL LAST NIGHT...
WE HAD A CALL FROM NAKAHARA-SENSEI.
WHAT?
ドキ
BA-DUMP
HE ASKED TO SKIP TODAY.
I GUESS HE CAUGHT A COLD.
I USED TO LOOK FORWARD TO WEDNESDAY.

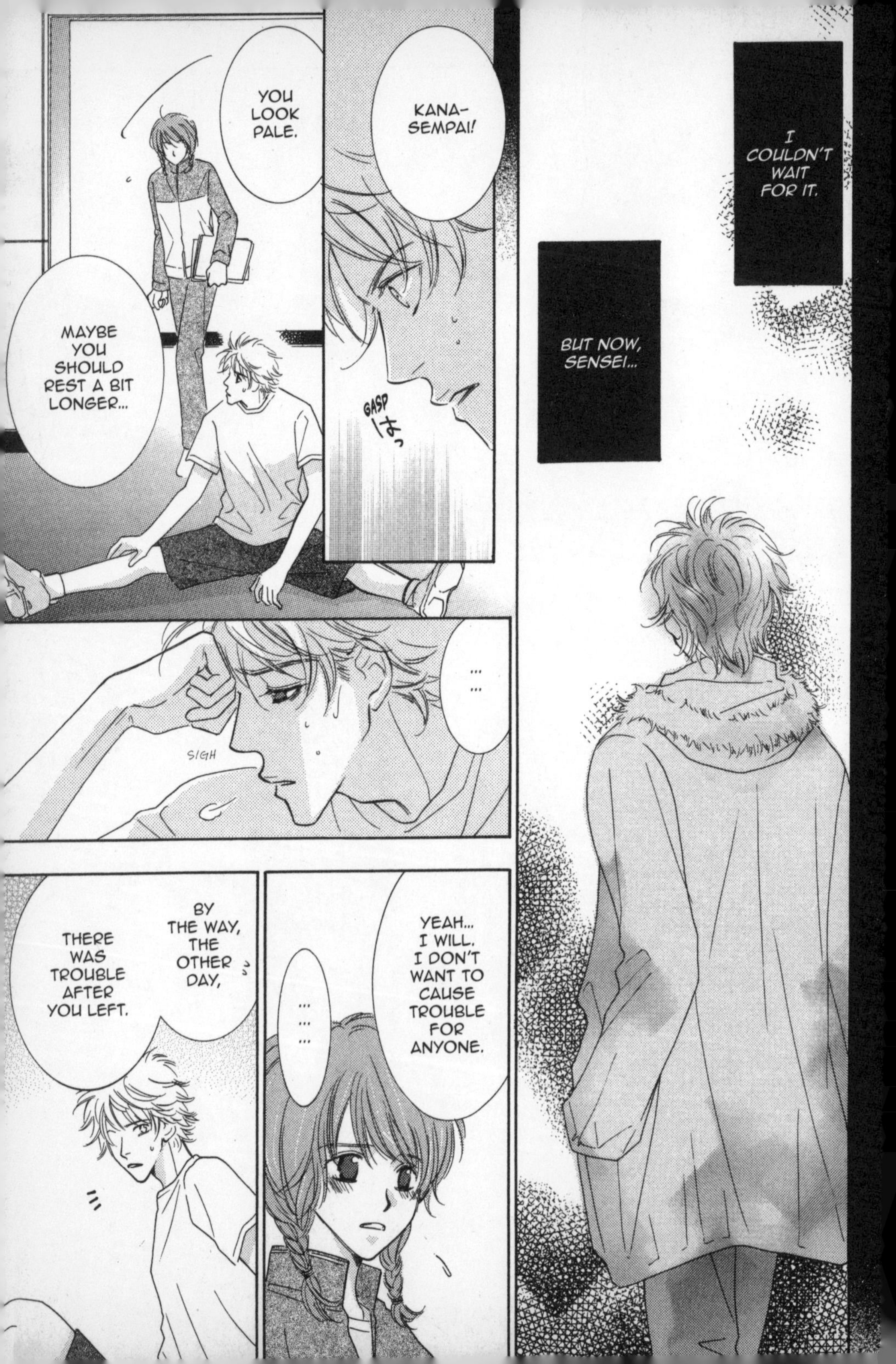
I COULDN'T WAIT FOR IT.
BUT NOW, SENSEI...
KANA-SEMPAI!
GASP
はっ
YOU LOOK PALE.
MAYBE YOU SHOULD REST A BIT LONGER...
... ...
SIGH
YEAH... I WILL. I DON'T WANT TO CAUSE TROUBLE FOR ANYONE.
... ...
BY THE WAY, THE OTHER DAY,
THERE WAS TROUBLE AFTER YOU LEFT.

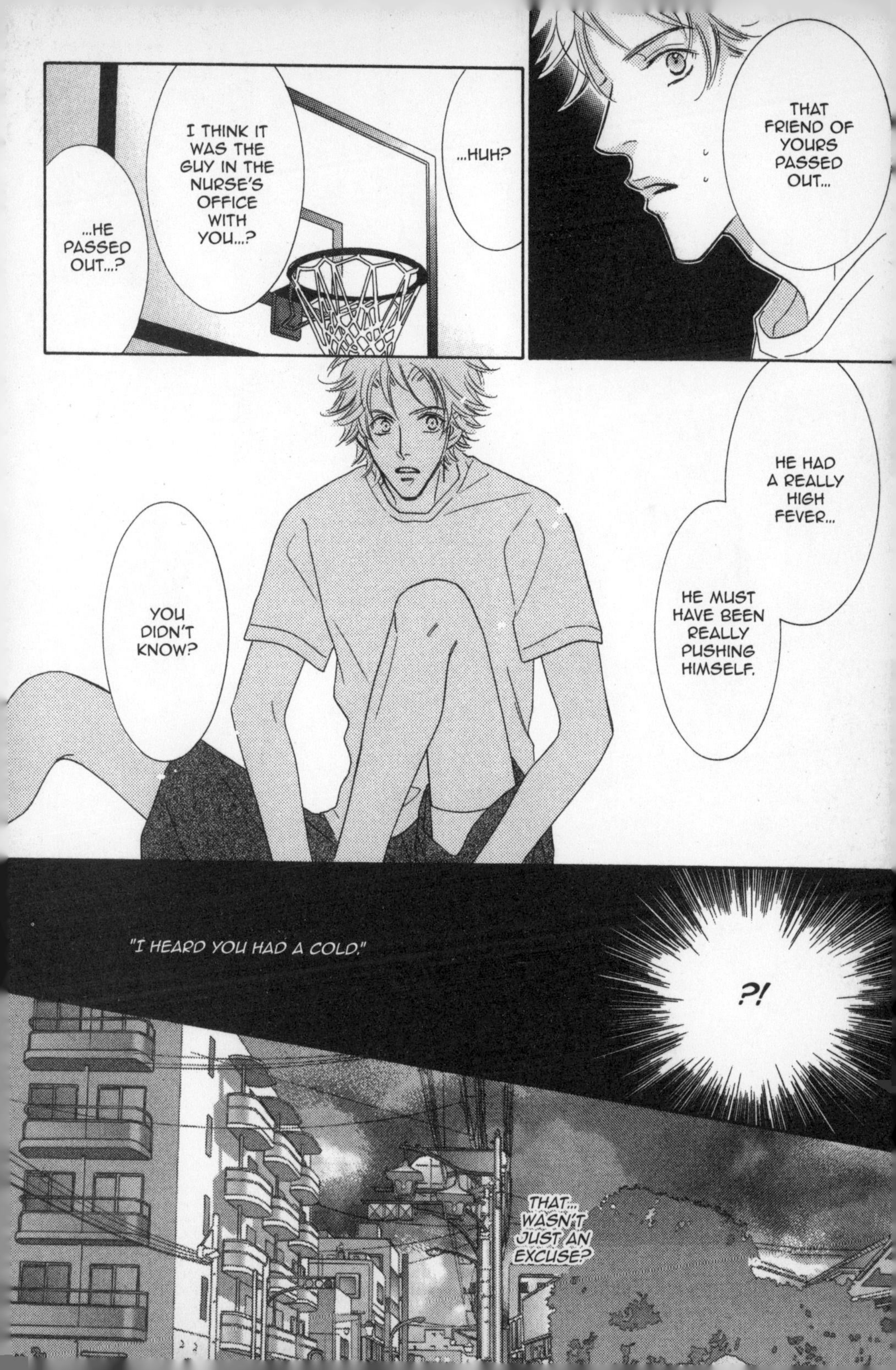
THAT FRIEND OF YOURS PASSED OUT...
...HUH?
I THINK IT WAS THE GUY IN THE NURSE'S OFFICE WITH YOU...?
...HE PASSED OUT...?
HE HAD A REALLY HIGH FEVER...
HE MUST HAVE BEEN REALLY PUSHING HIMSELF.
YOU DIDN'T KNOW?
?!
"I HEARD YOU HAD A COLD."
THAT... WASN'T JUST AN EXCUSE?

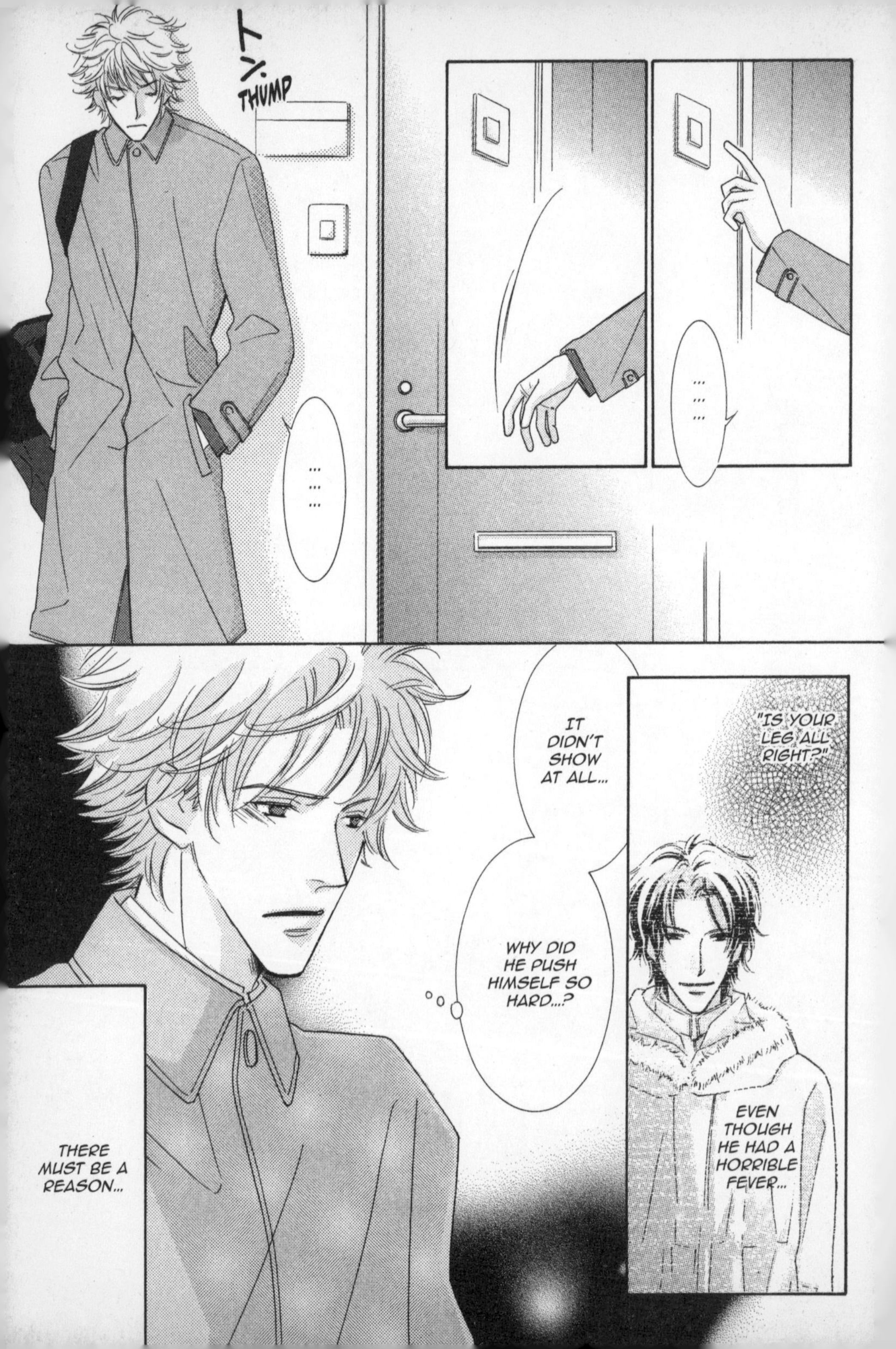

... ...
... ...
トン
THUMP
"IS YOUR LEG ALL RIGHT?"
EVEN THOUGH HE HAD A HORRIBLE FEVER...
IT DIDN'T SHOW AT ALL...
WHY DID HE PUSH HIMSELF SO HARD...?
THERE MUST BE A REASON...

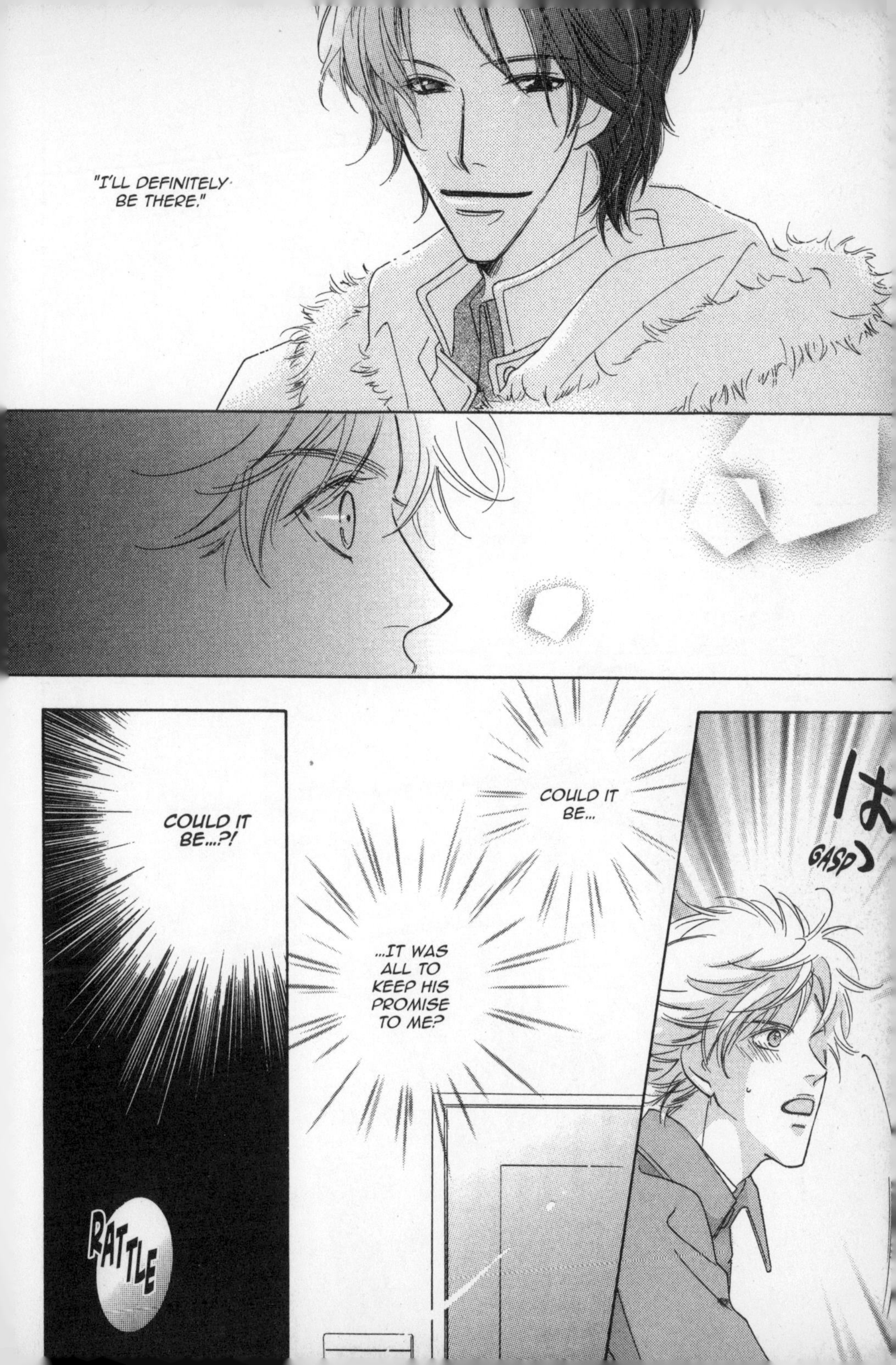
"I'LL DEFINITELY BE THERE."
は
GASP
COULD IT BE...
...IT WAS ALL TO KEEP HIS PROMISE TO ME?
COULD IT BE...?!
RATTLE

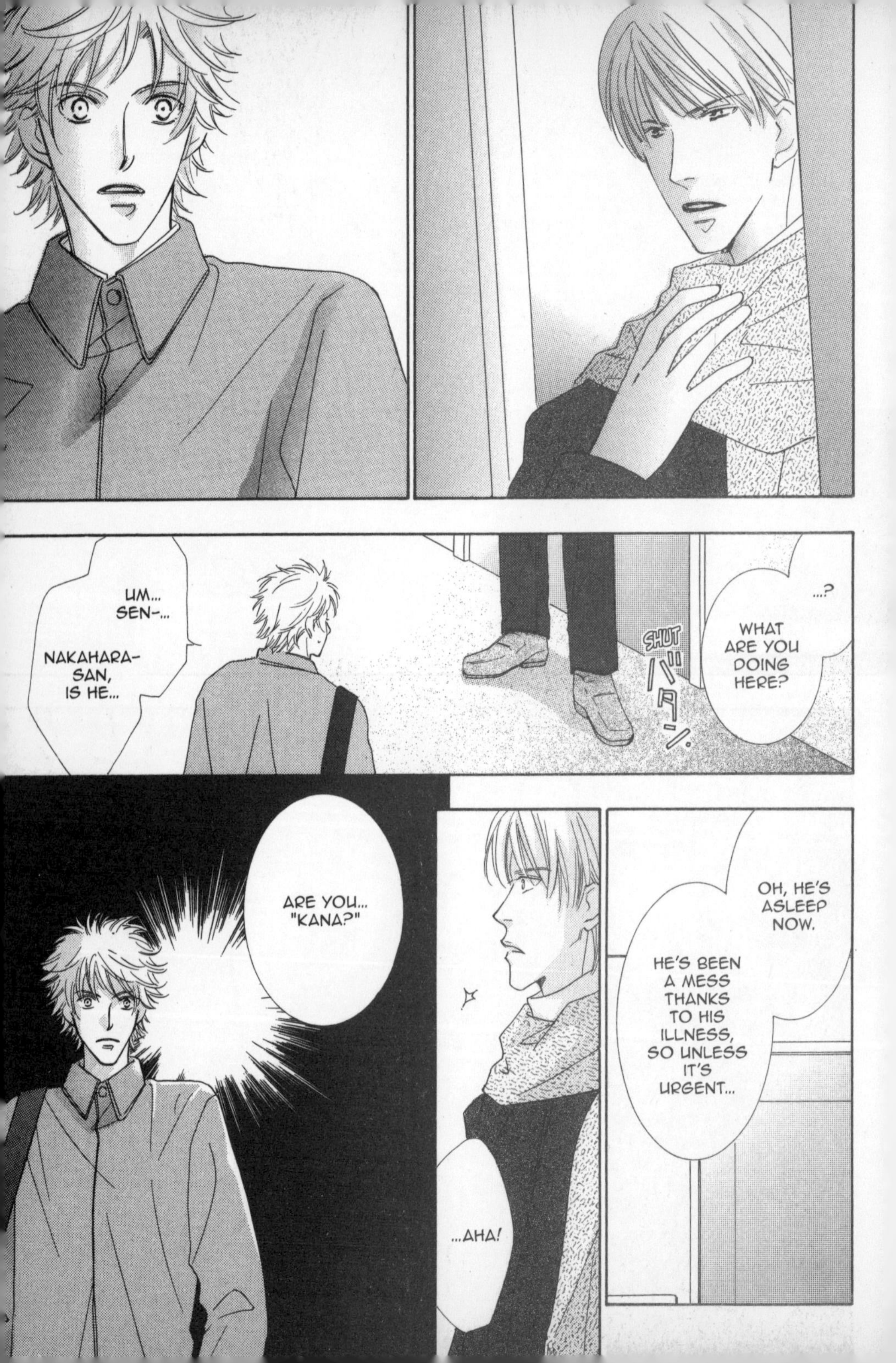
...?
WHAT ARE YOU DOING HERE?
SHUT
バタン
UM... SEN-...
NAKAHARA-SAN, IS HE...
OH, HE'S ASLEEP NOW.
HE'S BEEN A MESS THANKS TO HIS ILLNESS, SO UNLESS IT'S URGENT...
...AHA!
ARE YOU... "KANA?"

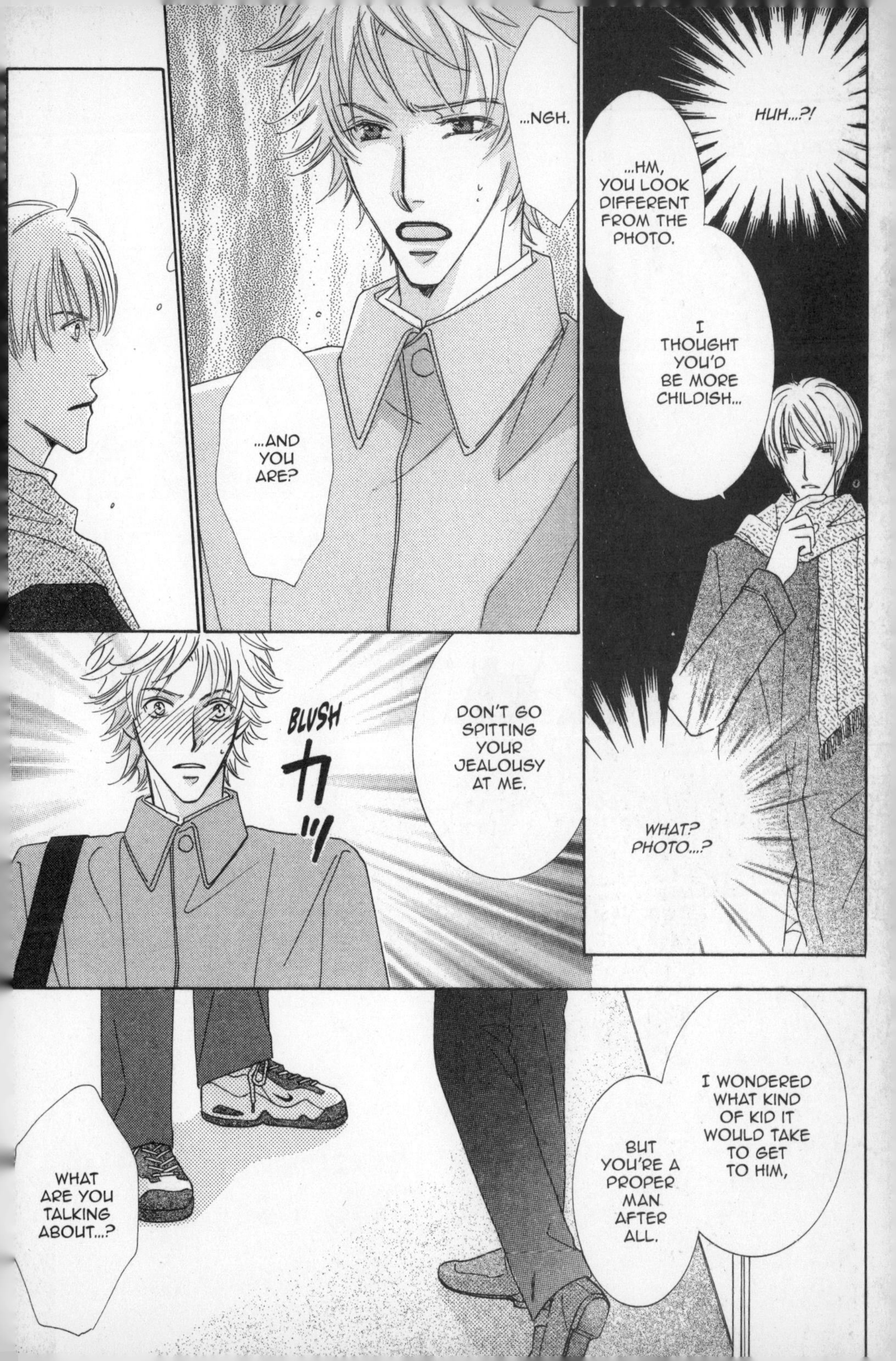
HUH...?!
...HM, YOU LOOK DIFFERENT FROM THE PHOTO.
I THOUGHT YOU'D BE MORE CHILDISH...
WHAT? PHOTO...?
...NGH.
...AND YOU ARE?
DON'T GO SPITTING YOUR JEALOUSY AT ME.
BLUSH
カッ
I WONDERED WHAT KIND OF KID IT WOULD TAKE TO GET TO HIM,
BUT YOU'RE A PROPER MAN AFTER ALL.
WHAT ARE YOU TALKING ABOUT...?

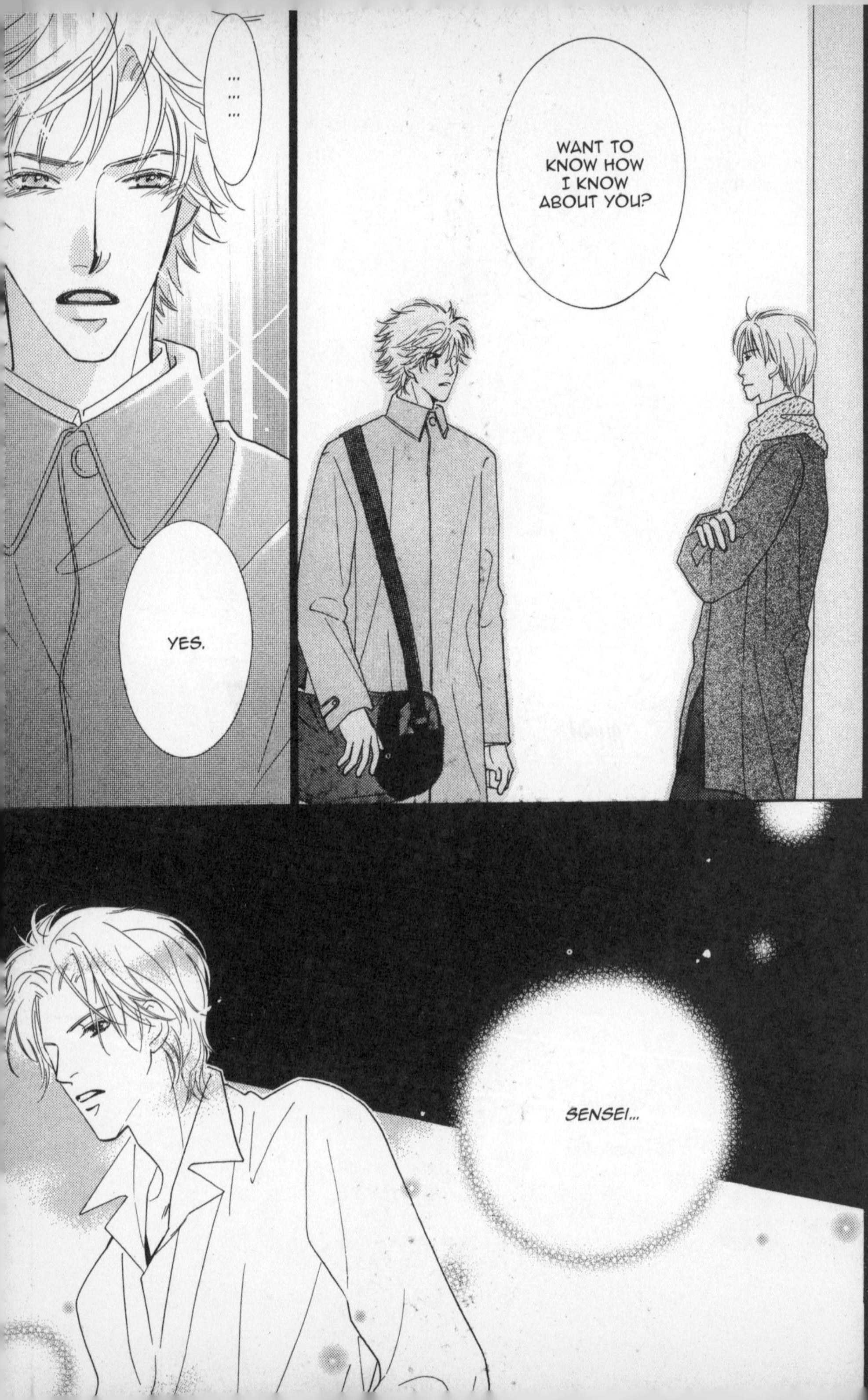
WANT TO KNOW HOW I KNOW ABOUT YOU?
... ...
YES.
SENSEI...

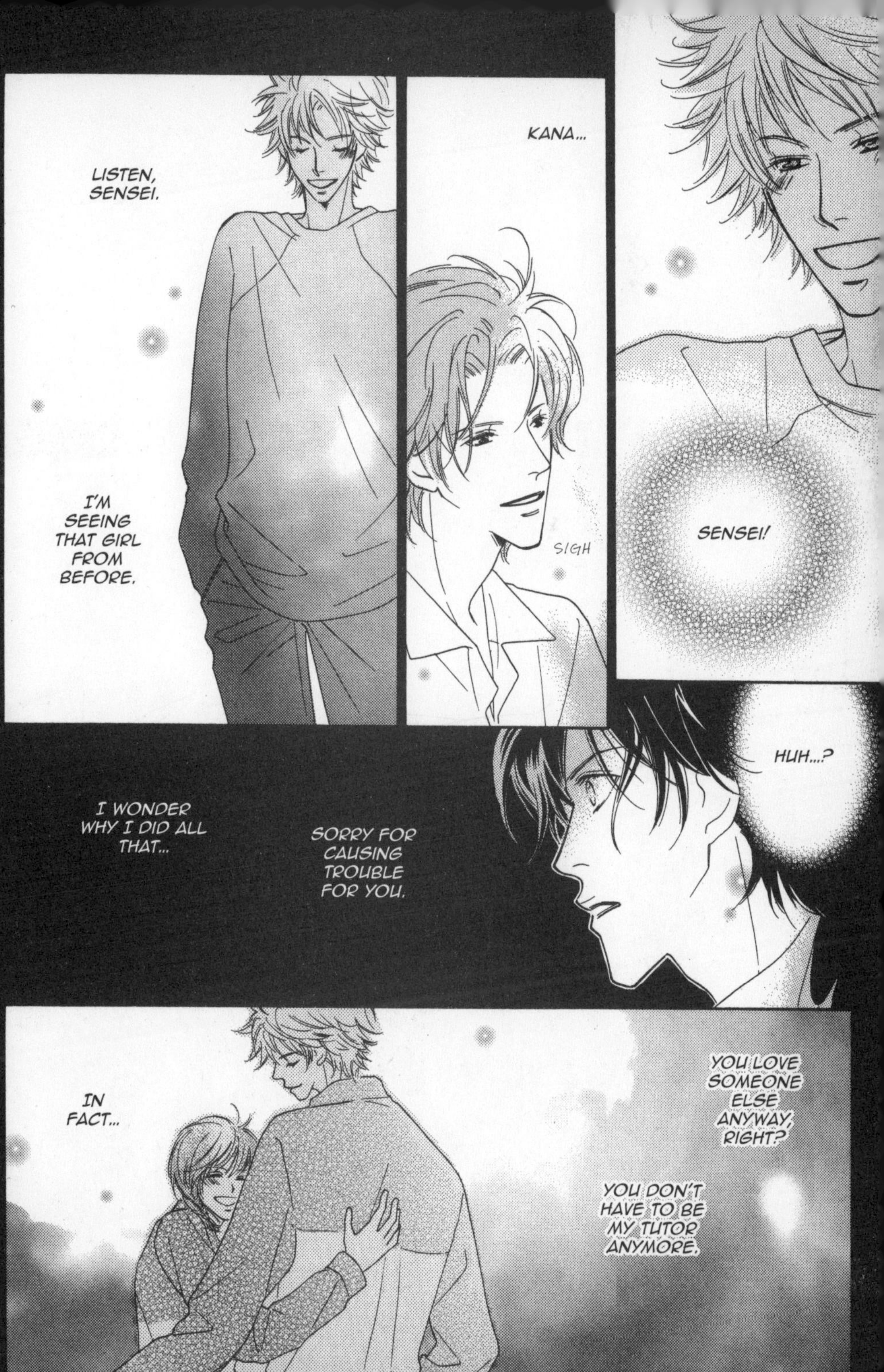
SENSEI!
KANA...
SIGH
LISTEN, SENSEI.
I'M SEEING THAT GIRL FROM BEFORE.
HUH...?
SORRY FOR CAUSING TROUBLE FOR YOU.
I WONDER WHY I DID ALL THAT...
YOU LOVE SOMEONE ELSE ANYWAY, RIGHT?
YOU DON'T HAVE TO BE MY TUTOR ANYMORE.
IN FACT...

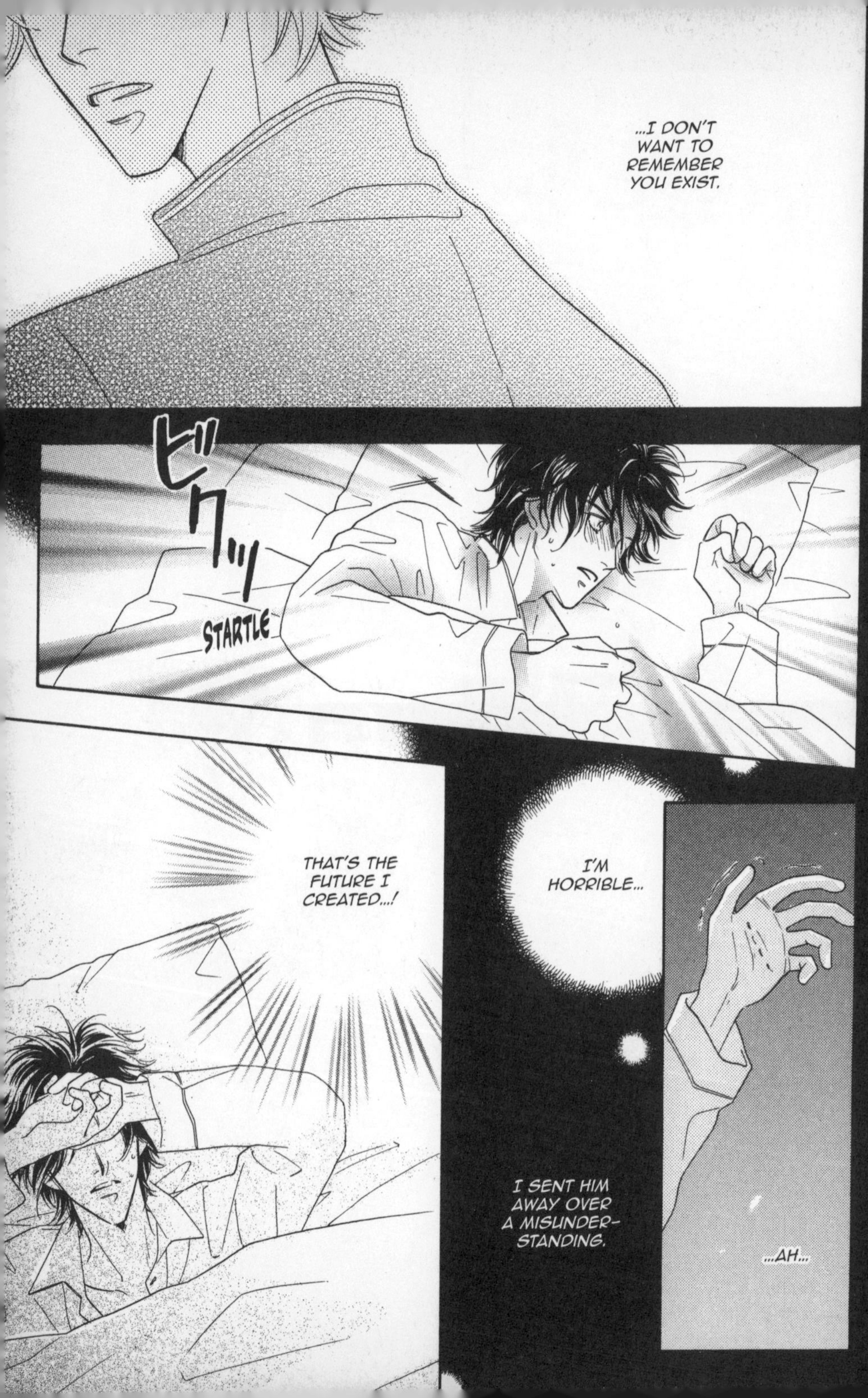
...I DON'T WANT TO REMEMBER YOU EXIST.
ビクッ
STARTLE
I'M HORRIBLE...
I SENT HIM AWAY OVER A MISUNDER-STANDING.
...AH...
THAT'S THE FUTURE I CREATED...!

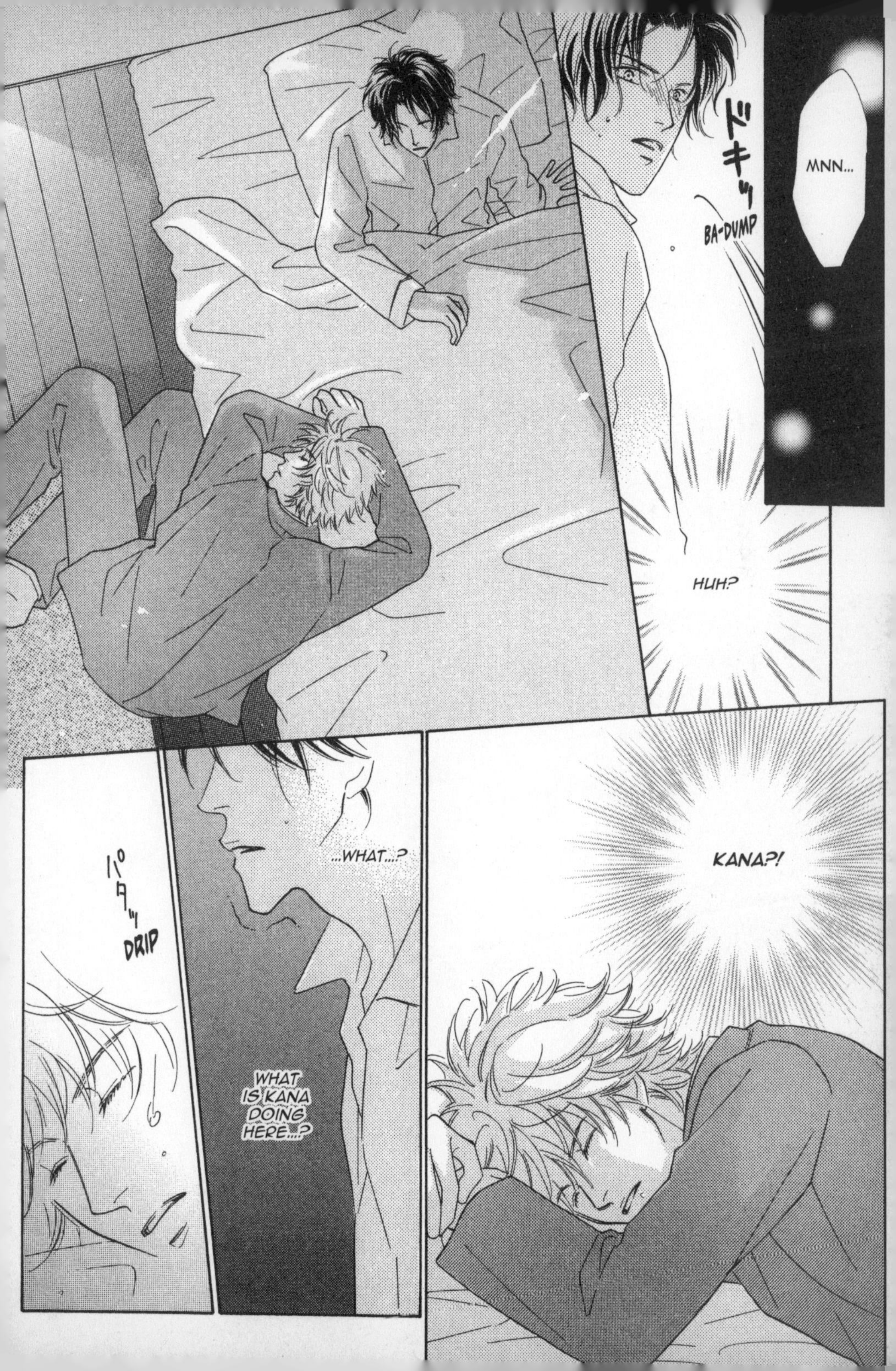
MNN...
ドキッ
BA-DUMP
HUH?
KANA?!
...WHAT...?
WHAT IS KANA DOING HERE...?
パタッ
DRIP

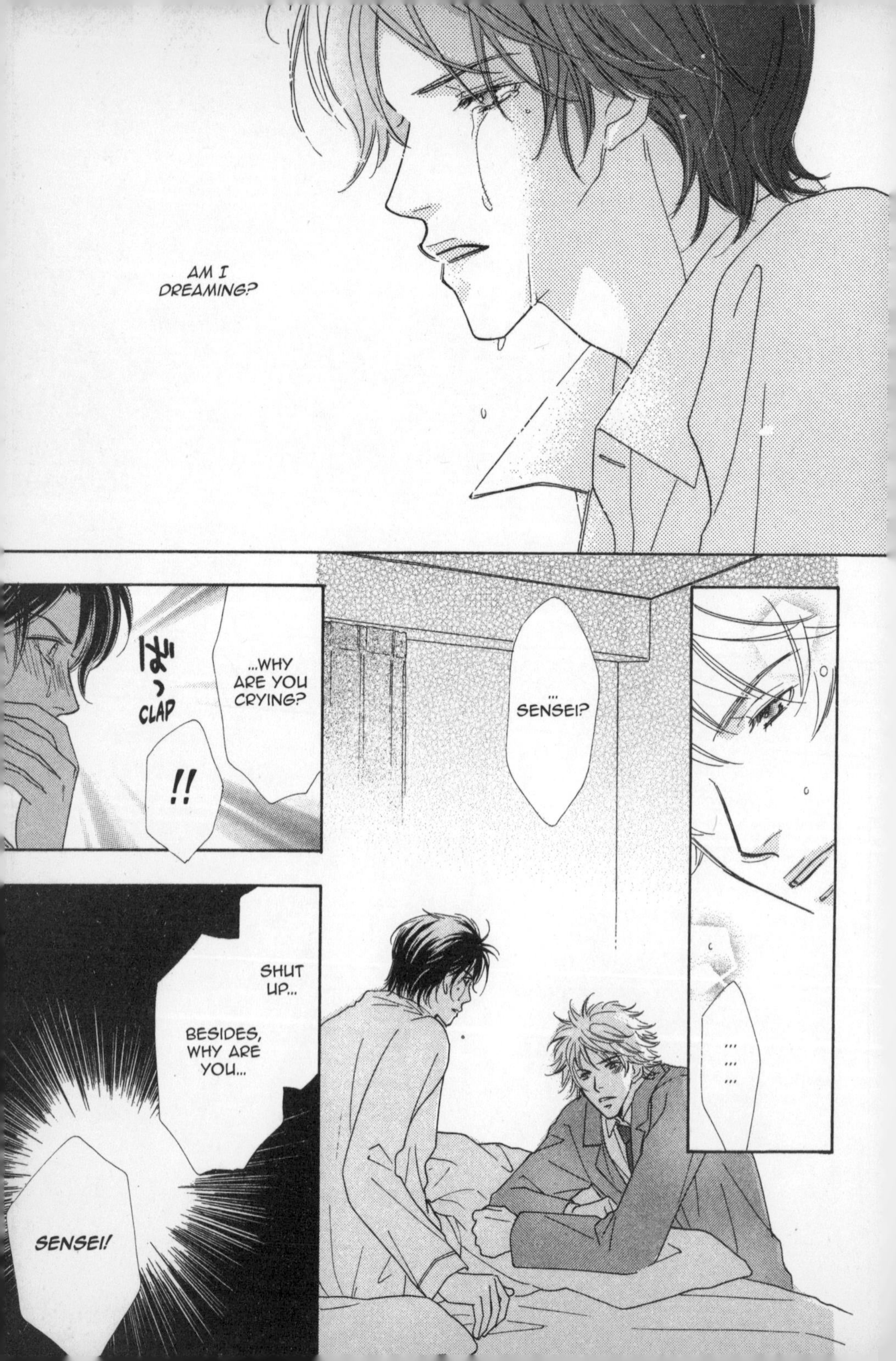
AM I DREAMING?
...
...
...
... SENSEI?
...WHY ARE YOU CRYING?
ぱっ
CLAP
!!
SHUT UP...
BESIDES, WHY ARE YOU...
SENSEI!

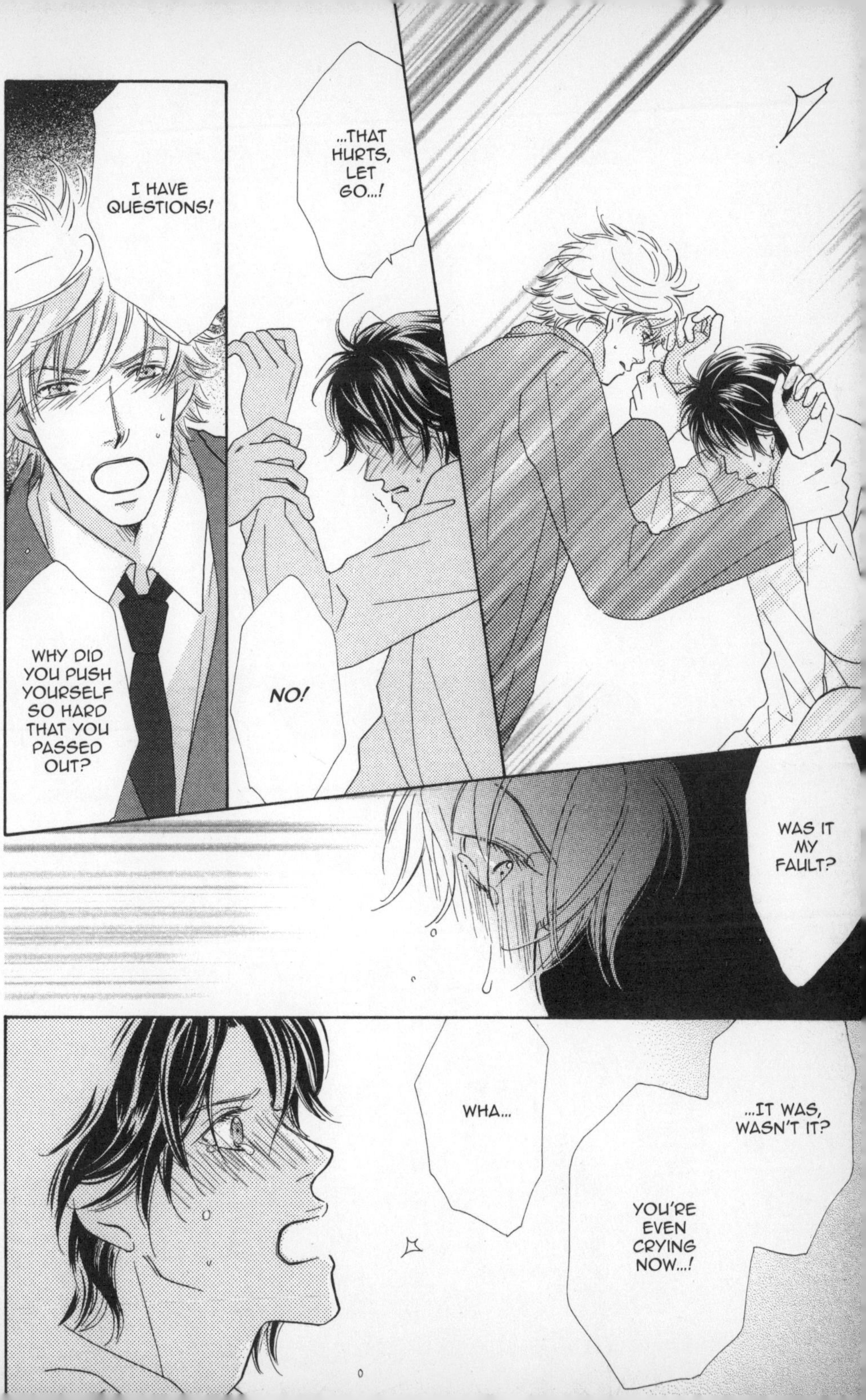
...THAT HURTS, LET GO...!
NO!
I HAVE QUESTIONS!
WHY DID YOU PUSH YOURSELF SO HARD THAT YOU PASSED OUT?
WAS IT MY FAULT?
...IT WAS, WASN'T IT?
YOU'RE EVEN CRYING NOW...!
WHA...

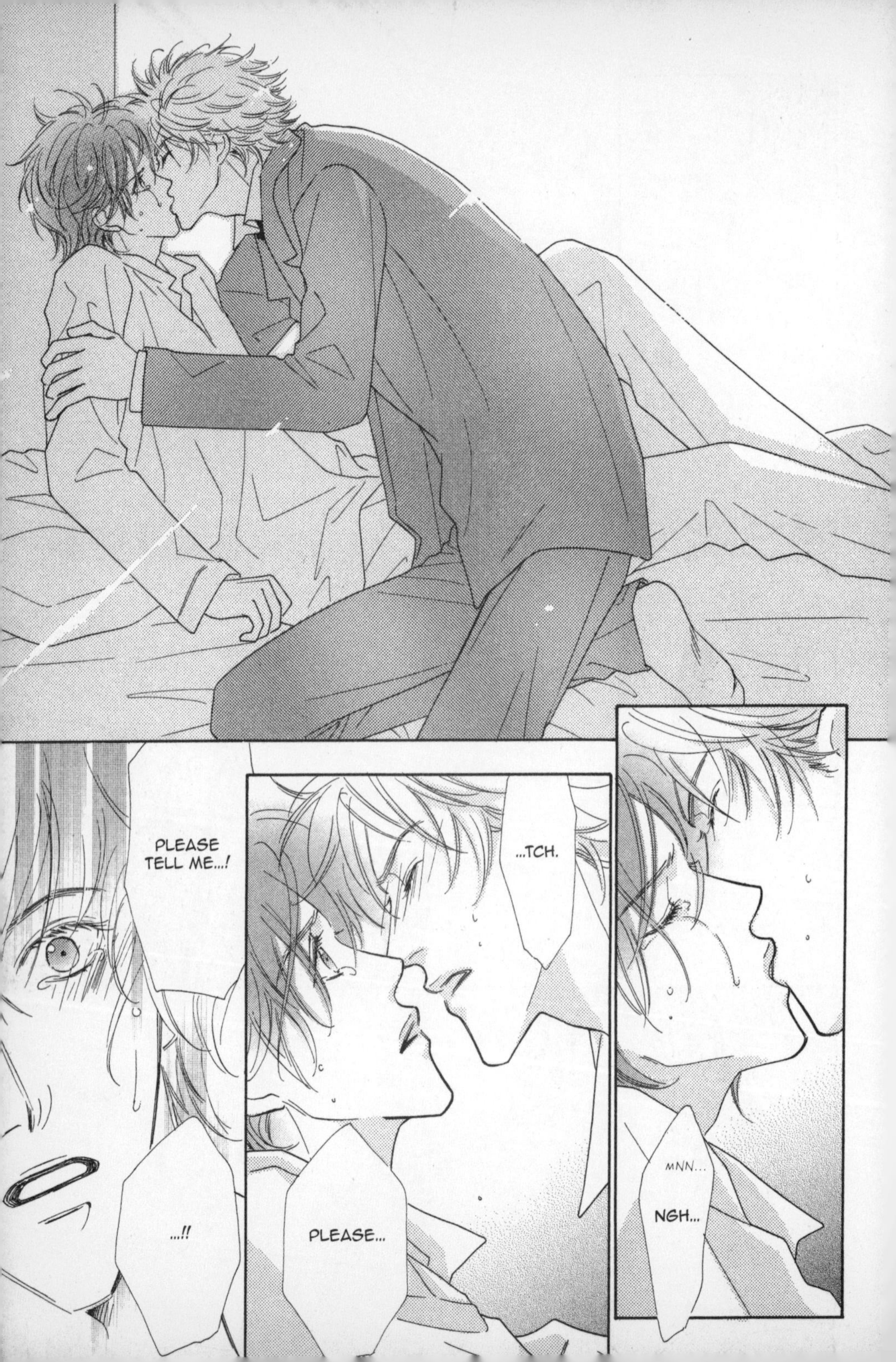
MNN...
NGH...
...TCH.
PLEASE...
PLEASE TELL ME...!
...!!

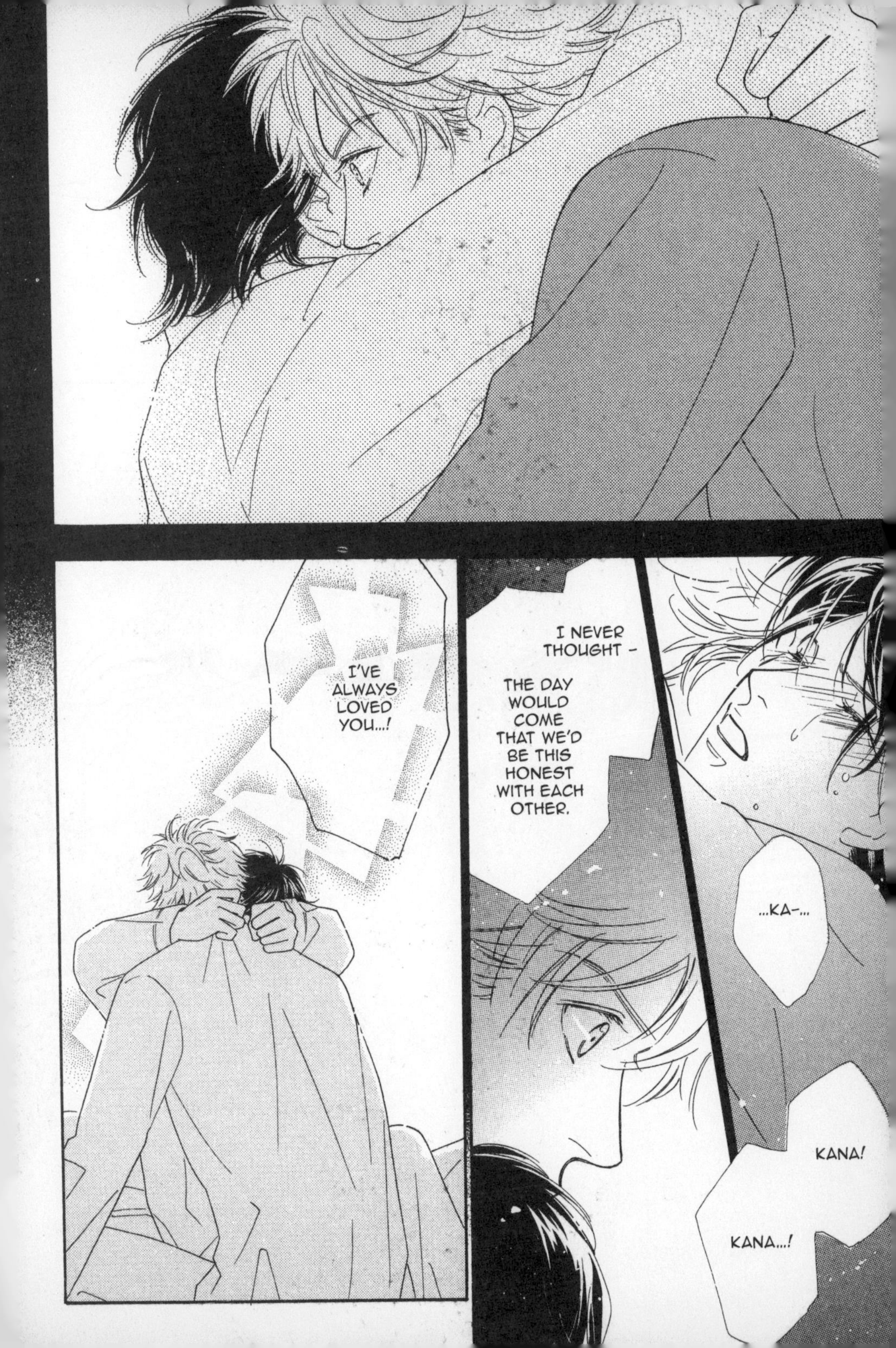
...KA-...
KANA!
KANA...!
I NEVER THOUGHT –
THE DAY WOULD COME THAT WE'D BE THIS HONEST WITH EACH OTHER.
I'VE ALWAYS LOVED YOU...!

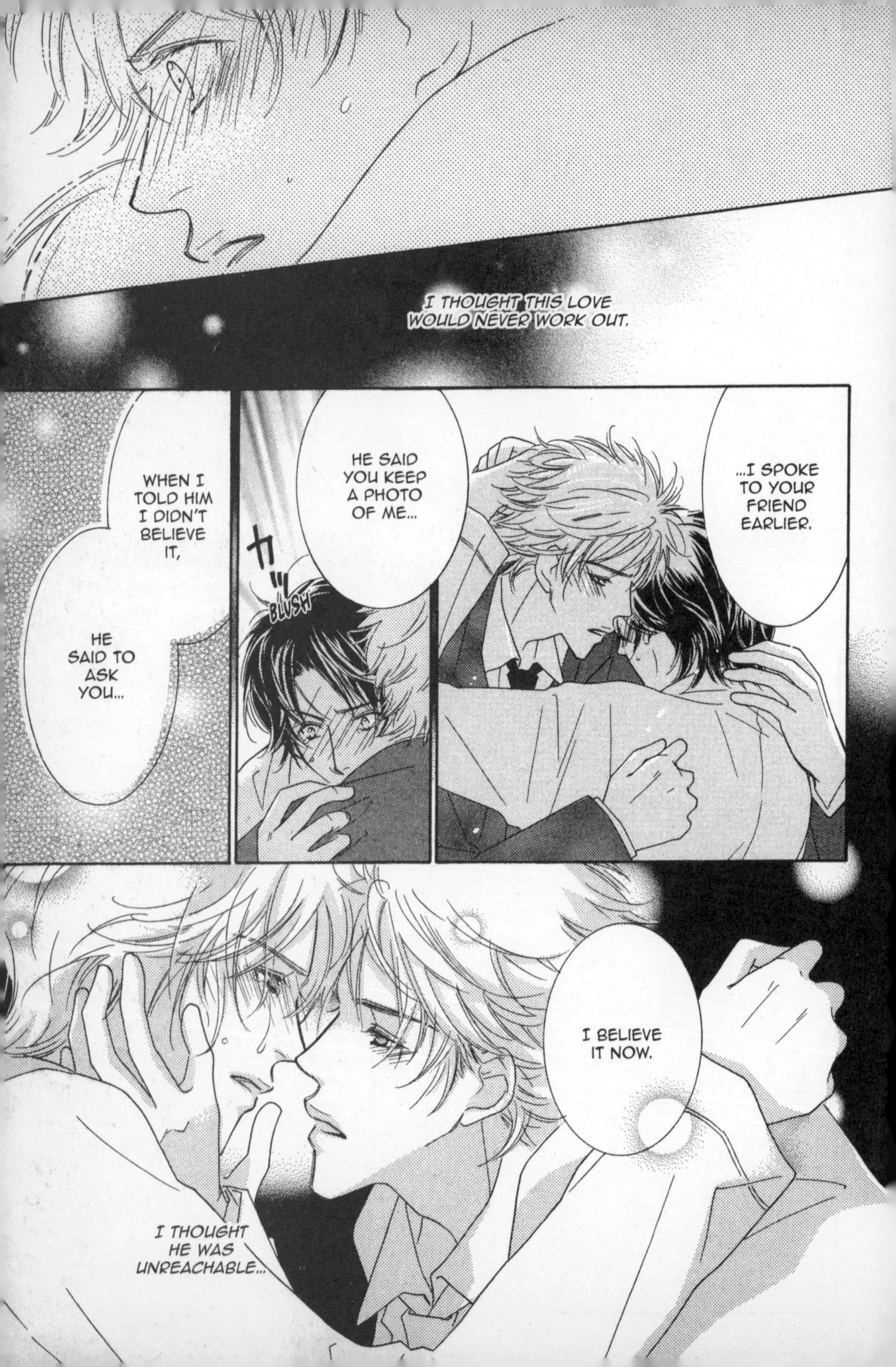
I THOUGHT THIS LOVE WOULD NEVER WORK OUT.
...I SPOKE TO YOUR FRIEND EARLIER.
HE SAID YOU KEEP A PHOTO OF ME...
カッ
BLUSH
WHEN I TOLD HIM I DIDN'T BELIEVE IT,
HE SAID TO ASK YOU...
I BELIEVE IT NOW.
I THOUGHT HE WAS UNREACHABLE...

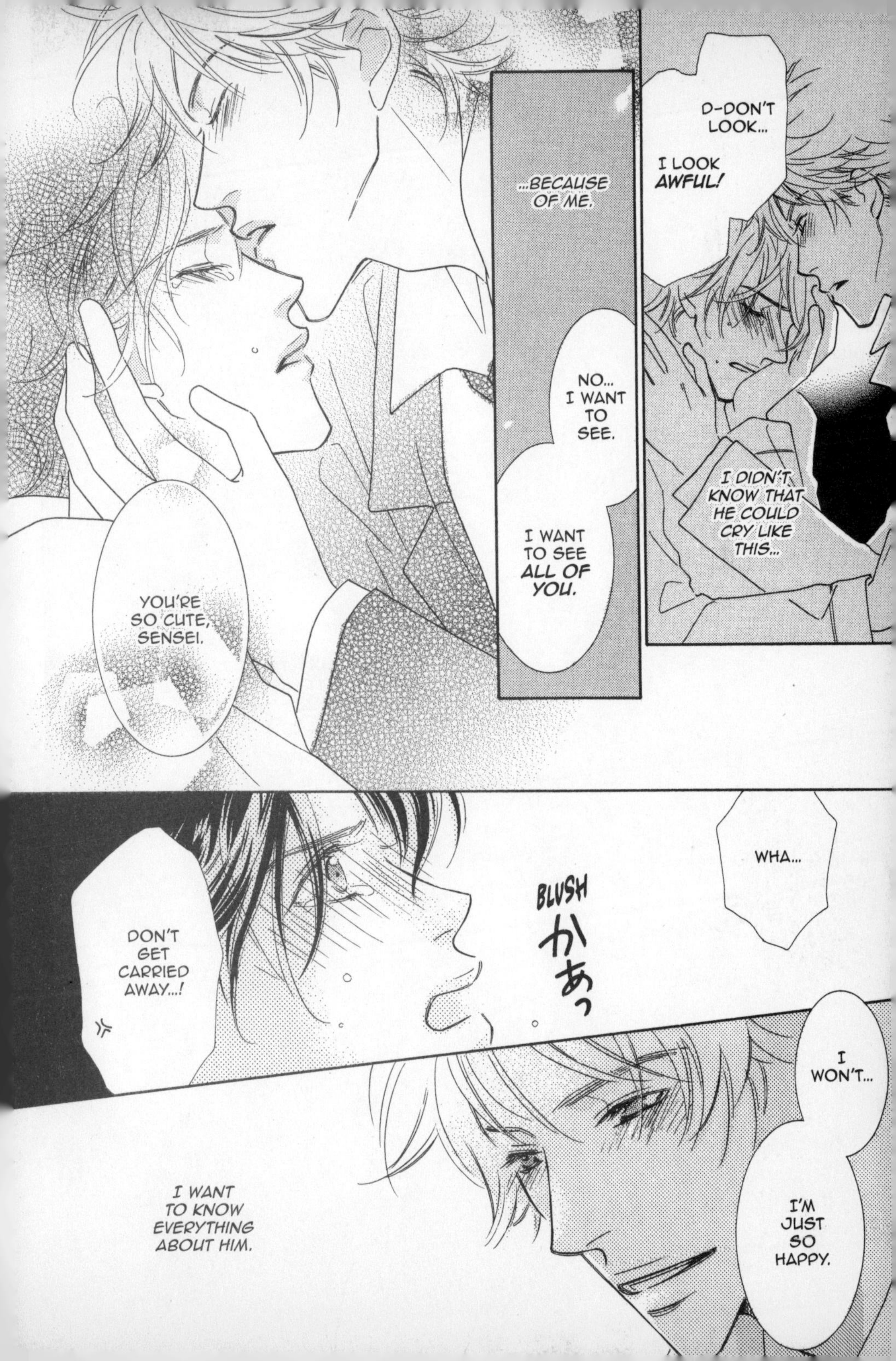
D-DON'T LOOK...
I LOOK AWFUL!
I DIDN'T KNOW THAT HE COULD CRY LIKE THIS...
...BECAUSE OF ME.
NO... I WANT TO SEE.
I WANT TO SEE ALL OF YOU.
YOU'RE SO CUTE, SENSEI.
WHA...
BLUSH
かあっ
DON'T GET CARRIED AWAY...!
I WON'T...
I'M JUST SO HAPPY.
I WANT TO KNOW EVERYTHING ABOUT HIM.

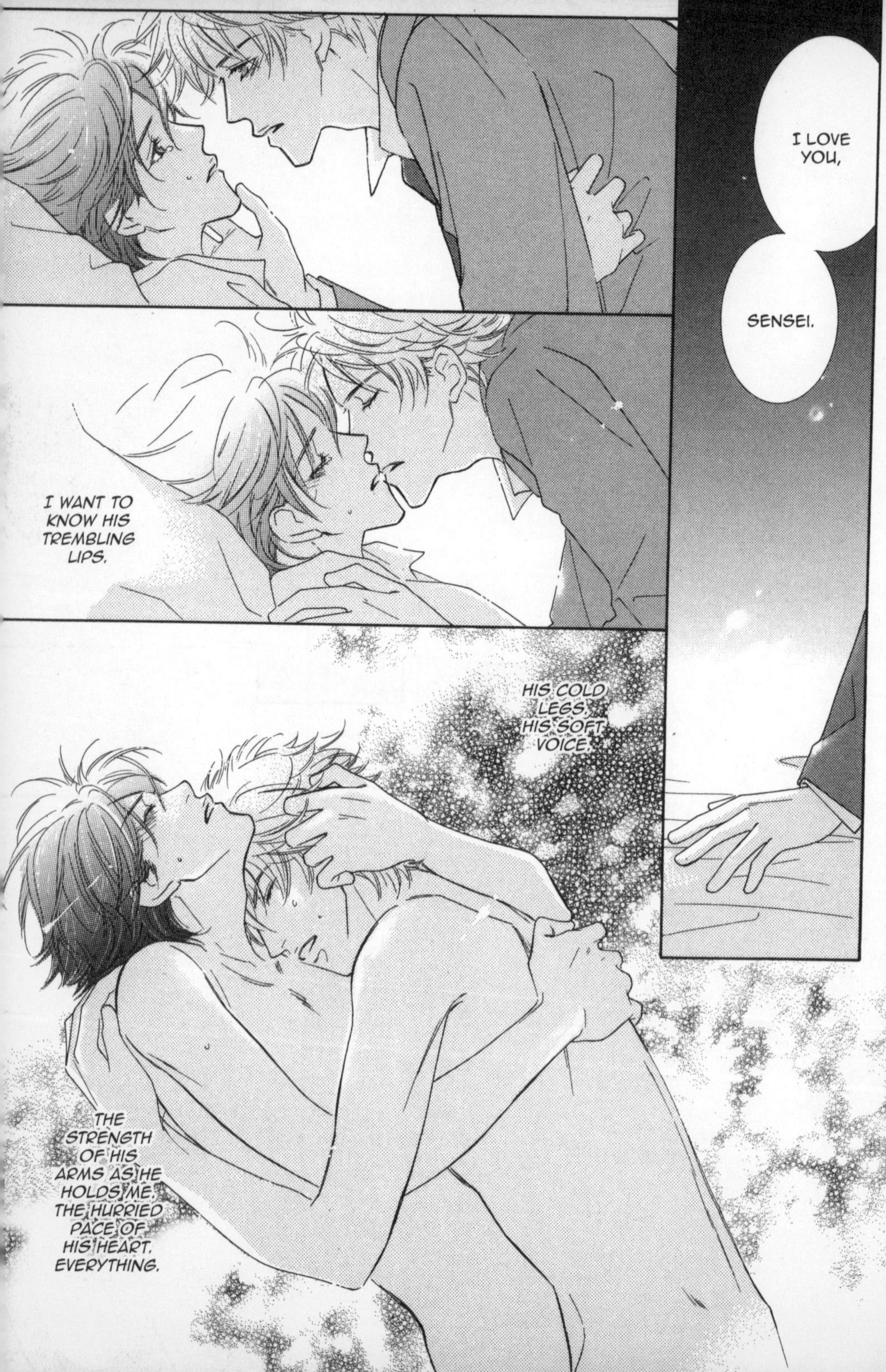
I LOVE YOU,
SENSEI.
I WANT TO KNOW HIS TREMBLING LIPS.
HIS COLD LEGS, HIS SOFT VOICE.
THE STRENGTH OF HIS ARMS AS HE HOLDS ME. THE HURRIED PACE OF HIS HEART. EVERYTHING.

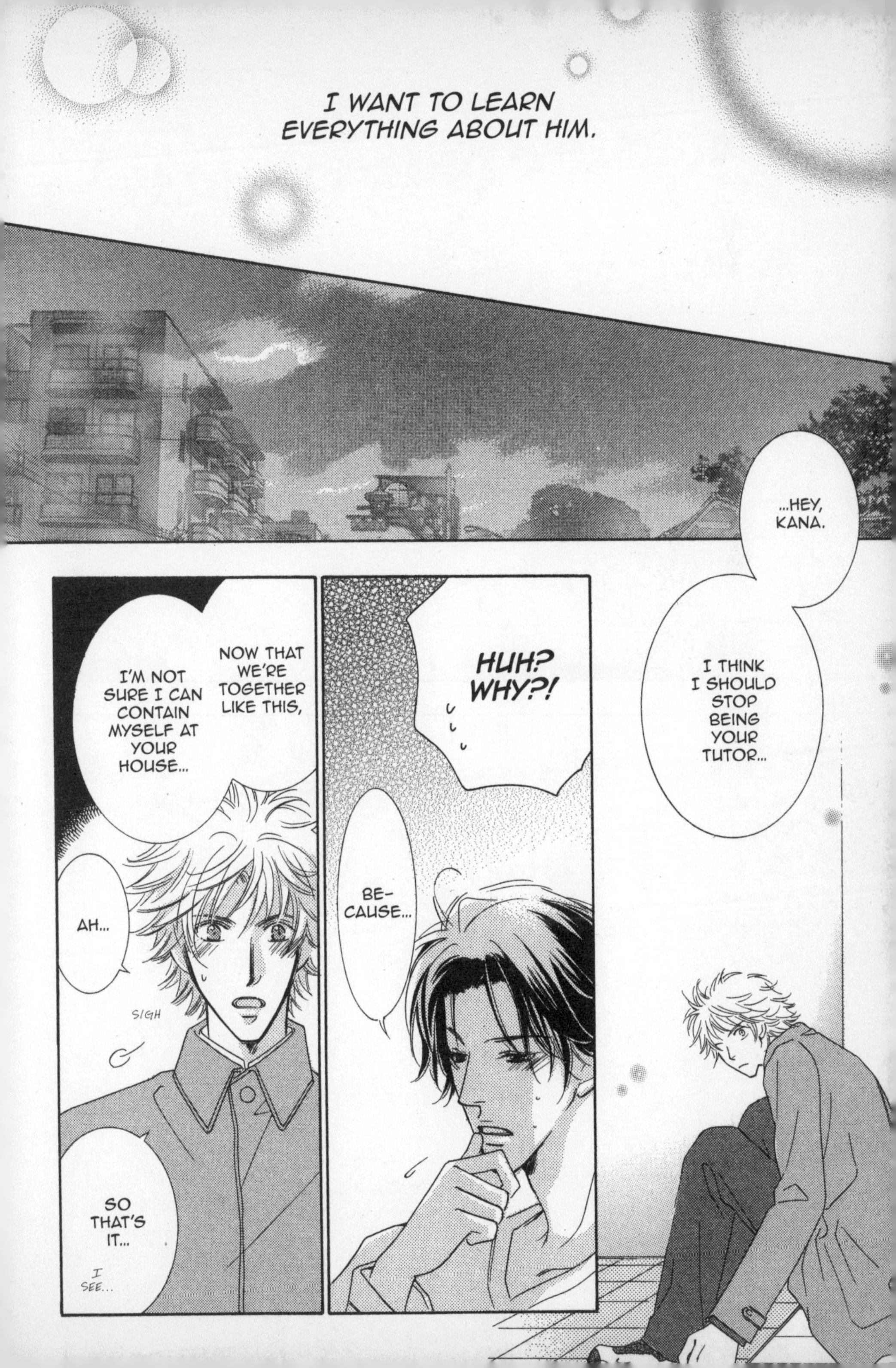
I WANT TO LEARN EVERYTHING ABOUT HIM.
...HEY, KANA.
I THINK I SHOULD STOP BEING YOUR TUTOR...
HUH? WHY?!
BE-CAUSE...
NOW THAT WE'RE TOGETHER LIKE THIS,
I'M NOT SURE I CAN CONTAIN MYSELF AT YOUR HOUSE...
AH...
SIGH
SO THAT'S IT...
I SEE...

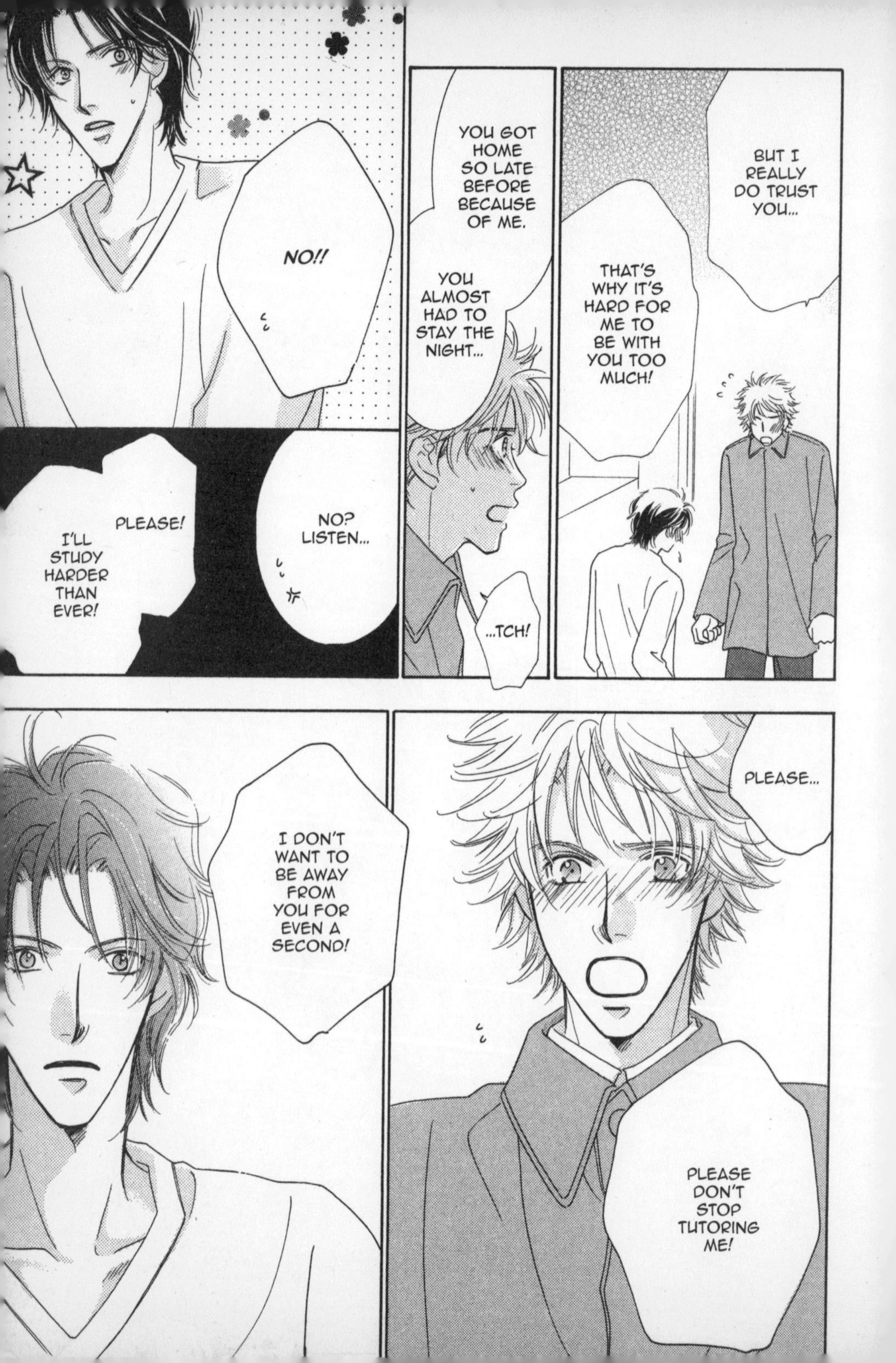
BUT I REALLY DO TRUST YOU...
THAT'S WHY IT'S HARD FOR ME TO BE WITH YOU TOO MUCH!
YOU GOT HOME SO LATE BEFORE BECAUSE OF ME.
YOU ALMOST HAD TO STAY THE NIGHT...
...TCH!
NO!!
NO? LISTEN...
PLEASE!
I'LL STUDY HARDER THAN EVER!
PLEASE...
PLEASE DON'T STOP TUTORING ME!
I DON'T WANT TO BE AWAY FROM YOU FOR EVEN A SECOND!

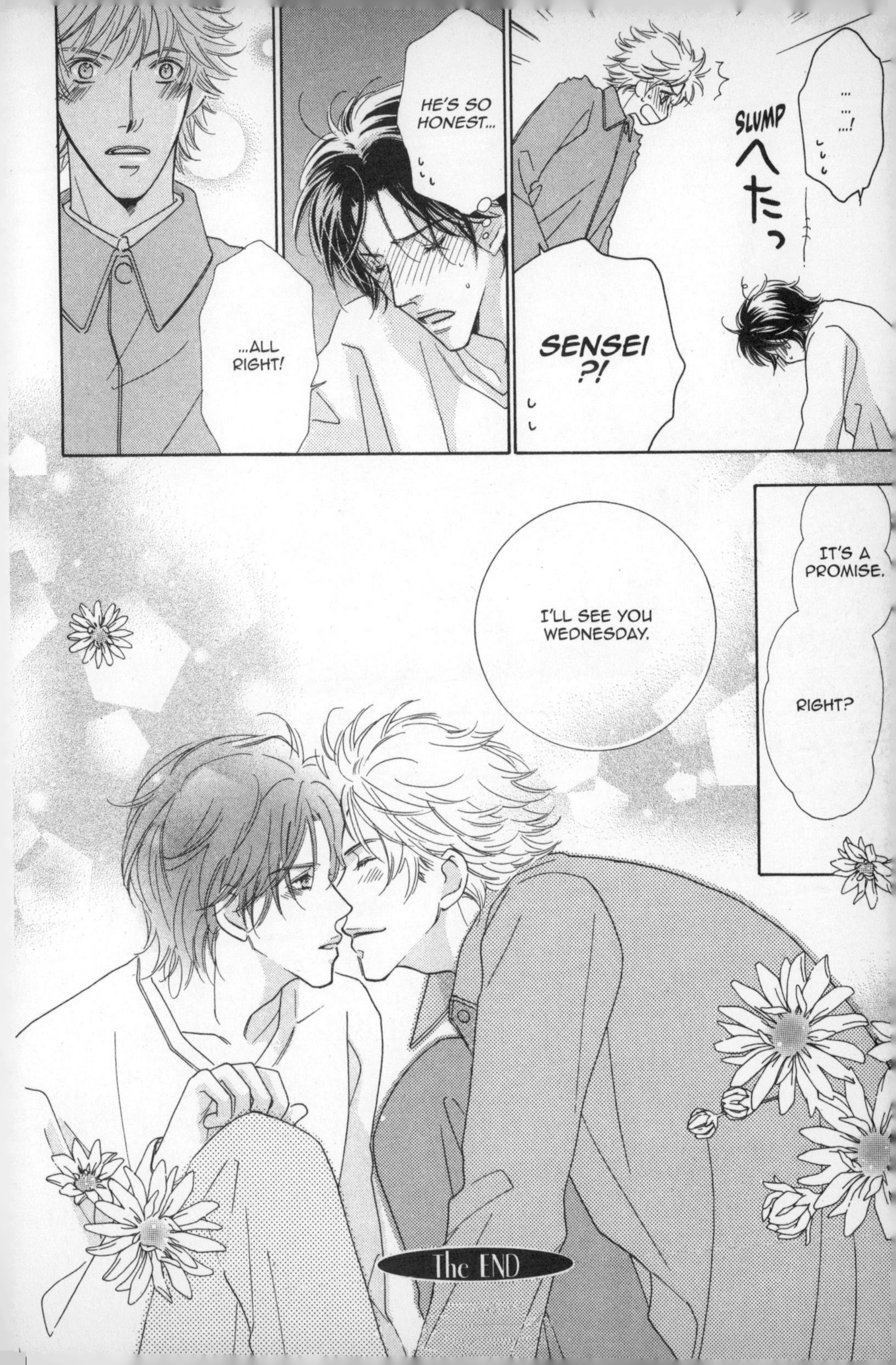
.........!
SLUMP
へたっ
SENSEI?!
HE'S SO HONEST...
...ALL RIGHT!
IT'S A PROMISE.
RIGHT?
I'LL SEE YOU WEDNESDAY.
The END

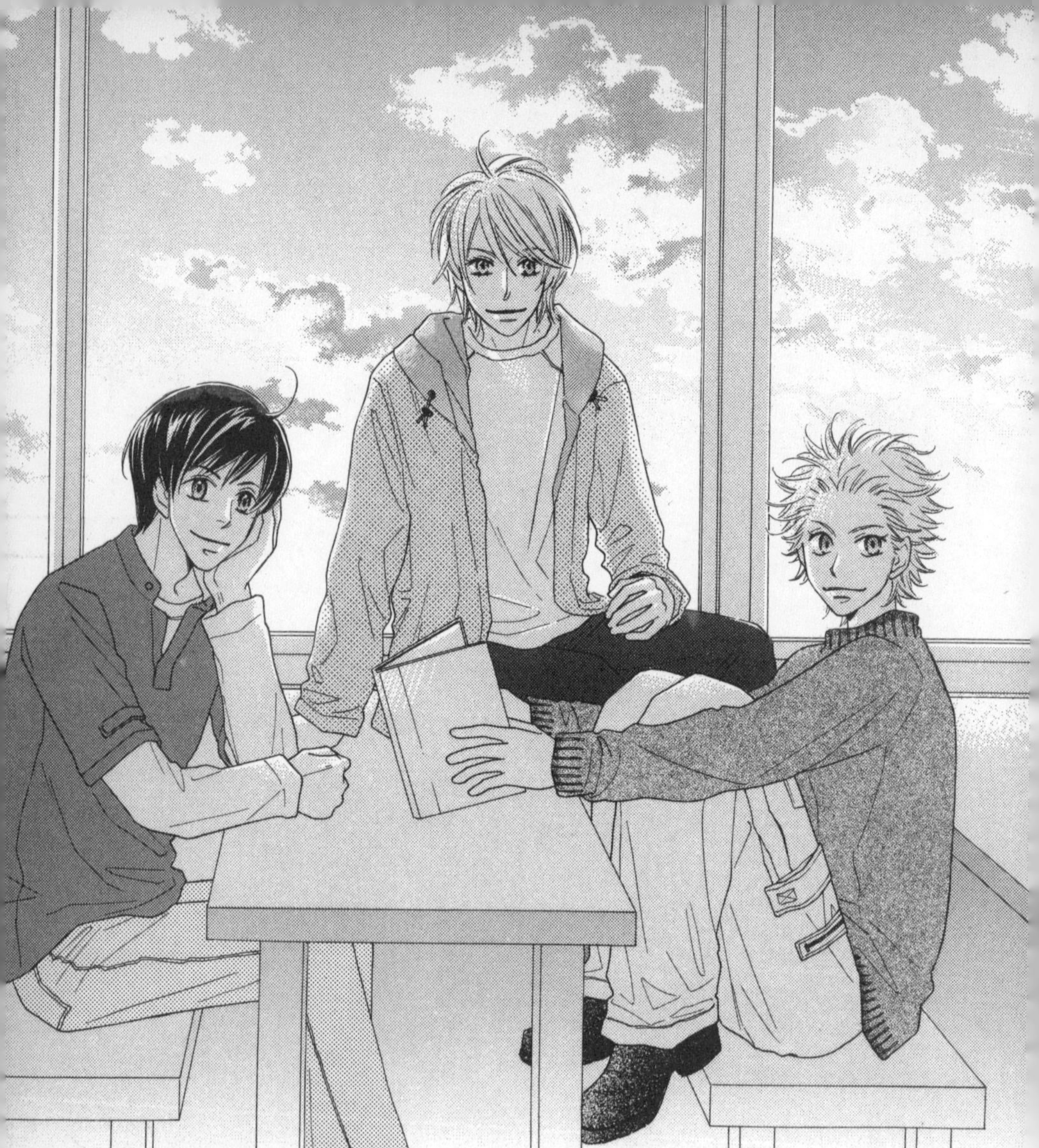

TITLE AFTERTHOUGHTS

- ✿ CIAO CIAO BAMBINO
- HONEY CITRON
- STEADY GOING
- SWING ON OVER
- ✿ Brand new Wednesday

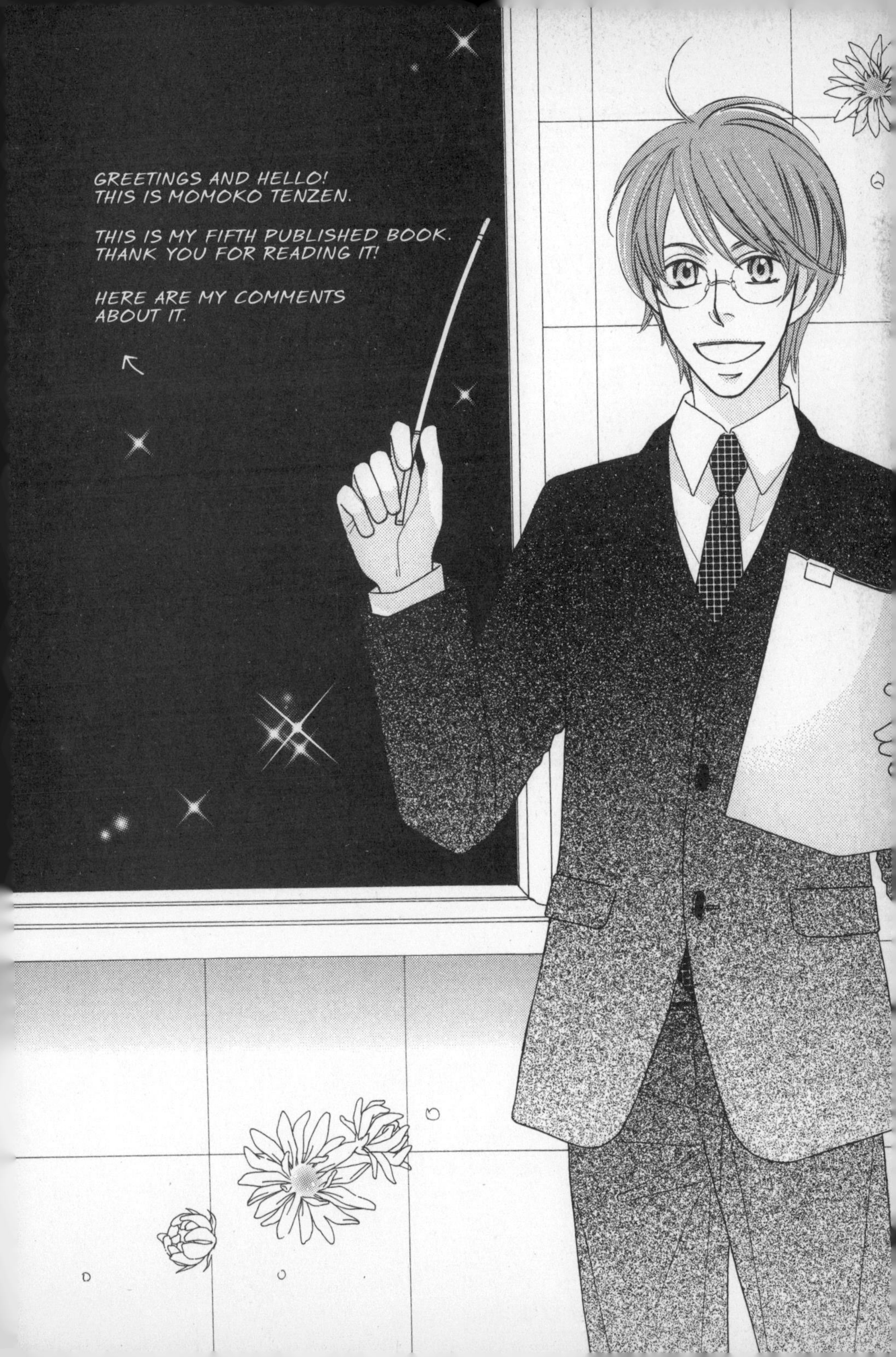
GREETINGS AND HELLO!
THIS IS MOMOKO TENZEN.
THIS IS MY FIFTH PUBLISHED BOOK.
THANK YOU FOR READING IT!
HERE ARE MY COMMENTS
ABOUT IT.

CIAO CIAO BAMBINO (KANAME AND YUUTA)

I LIKE SMALL, CUTE SEME, AND THAT'S HOW THIS STORY CAME ABOUT. YOU COULD SAY HE'S A BISHOJO SEME (WHAT A NICE PHRASE). THE TRUTH IS THAT AFTER THE FIRST STORY I WAS SATISFIED, AND DIDN'T HAVE ANY INTENTION OF CONTINUING... (EVEN WITH AN ENDING LIKE THAT...) I DON'T THINK I WOULD HAVE MADE IT TO "SWING ON OVER" IF NOT FOR MY EDITOR ASKING, "WHAT ABOUT THE REST...?" (I THINK YUUTA WOULD BE REALLY THANKFUL TO MY EDITOR!)

HONEY CITRON (MAKOTO AND KEI)

WHEN I STARTED, THE TWO OF THEM WERE FIRST YEARS IN MIDDLE SCHOOL, BUT ANYWAY... THEY DIDN'T EVEN KISS! THIS IS A BL MANGA AND IT ALL TAKES PLACE BEFORE THE LOVE ACTUALLY HAPPENS (THOUGH THE LOVE SCENES ARE SPARSE IN MY WORK TO BEGIN WITH). BUT IT DIDN'T REALLY NEED ME TO DRAW IT, AND ULTIMATELY I LIKE THESE STORIES WHERE THEY DON'T GO VERY FAR... (I WONDER...) I REMEMBER HOW HAPPY I WAS WHEN THE DRAFT WAS ACCEPTED. I WAS VERY GRATEFUL.

BRAND NEW WEDNESDAY (KANA AND SATORU)

I DREW THIS FOUR YEARS AGO...EEK, HOW SCARY...!! IT'S LIKE I HAVEN'T MADE ANY PROGRESS...ALL I REMEMBER IS THAT I STRUGGLED THROUGH IT. BY THE WAY, "CIAO CIAO" AND "BRAND NEW" ARE BOTH MIDDLE SCHOOL STUDENT X TEACHER...(THE TRUTH IS I'VE ALREADY DONE MIDDLE SCHOOL STUDENT X DOCTOR...) I DIDN'T EVEN REALIZE!!! (HOW SCARY)...I WONDER IF THERE'S SOMETHING IN MY DNA. MAYBE NEXT TIME I'LL CHALLENGE MYSELF WITH TEACHER X STUDENT...

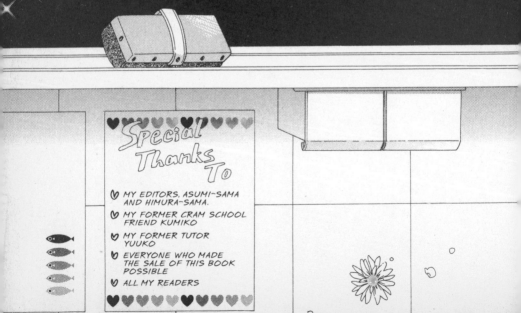

Special Thanks To

♥ MY EDITORS, ASUMI-SAMA AND HIMURA-SAMA.

♥ MY FORMER CRAM SCHOOL FRIEND KUMIKO

♥ MY FORMER TUTOR YUUKO

♥ EVERYONE WHO MADE THE SALE OF THIS BOOK POSSIBLE

♥ ALL MY READERS

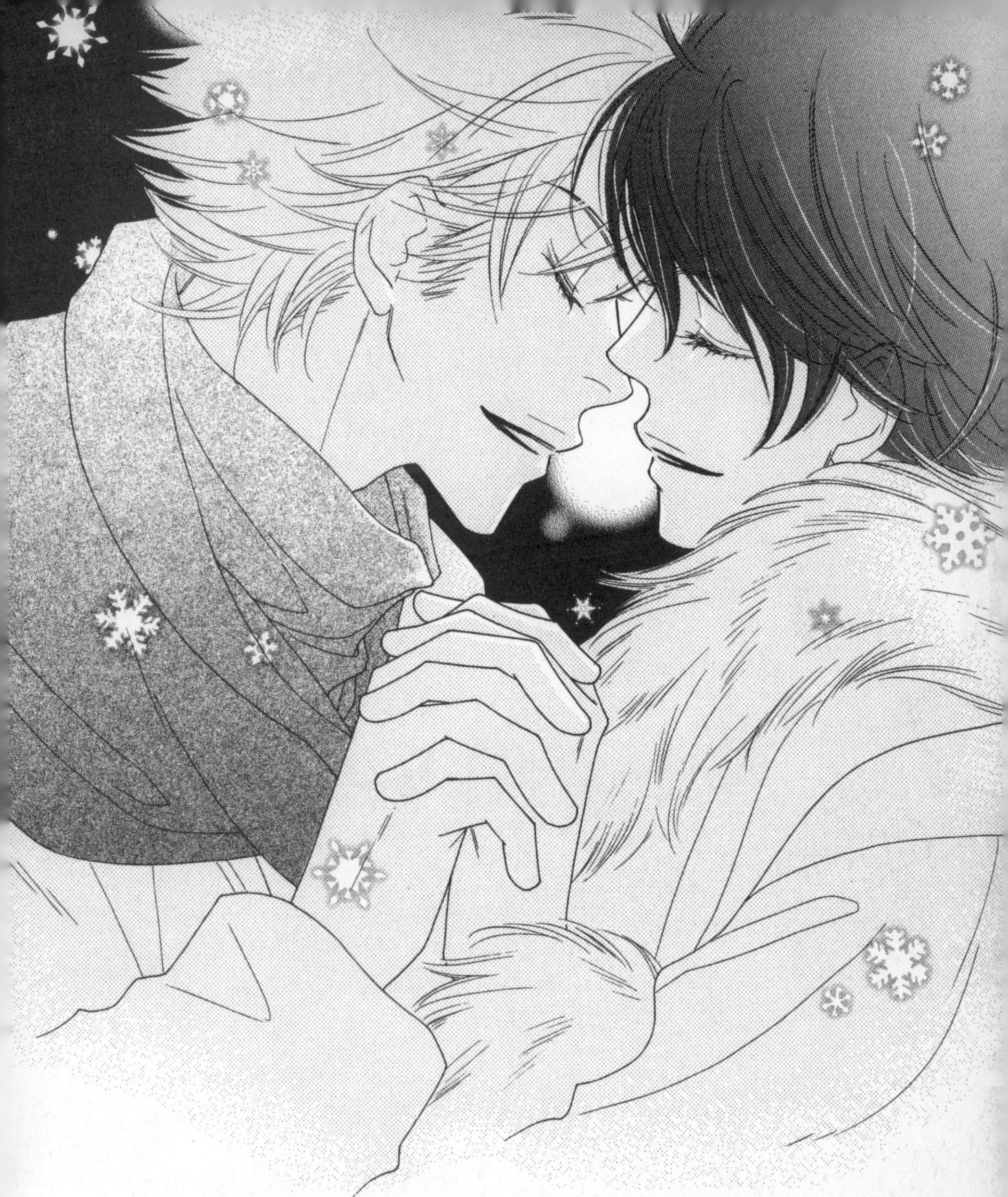

I HOPE YOU ENJOYED IT
MAY WE MEET AGAIN!!

DEC. 2004.
momoko tenzen.

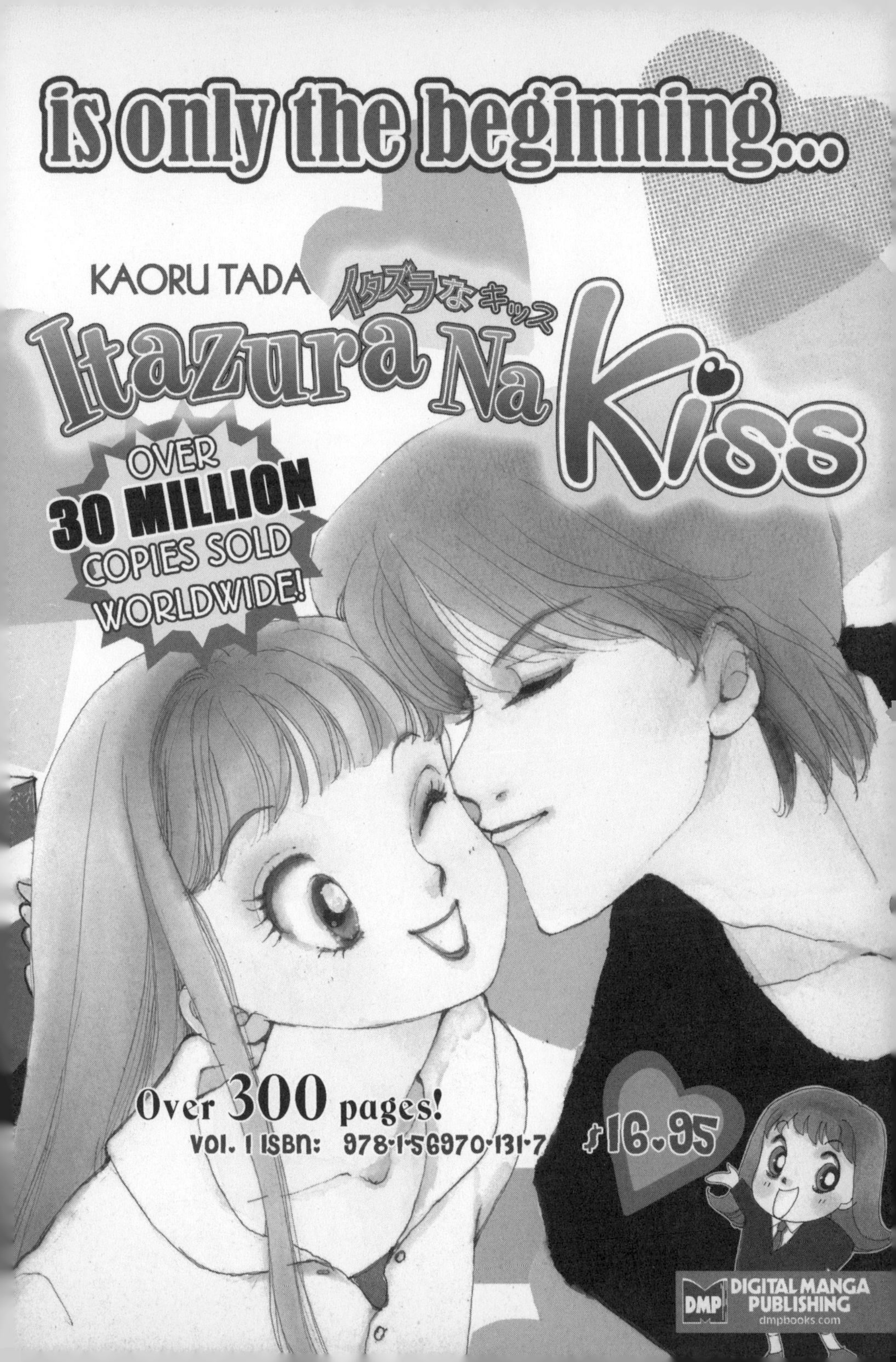

is only the beginning...
KAORU TADA
イタズラなキッス
Itazura Na Kiss
OVER 30 MILLION COPIES SOLD WORLDWIDE!
Over 300 pages!
VOL. 1 ISBN: 978-1-56970-131-7
$16.95
DMP
DIGITAL MANGA PUBLISHING
dmpbooks.com

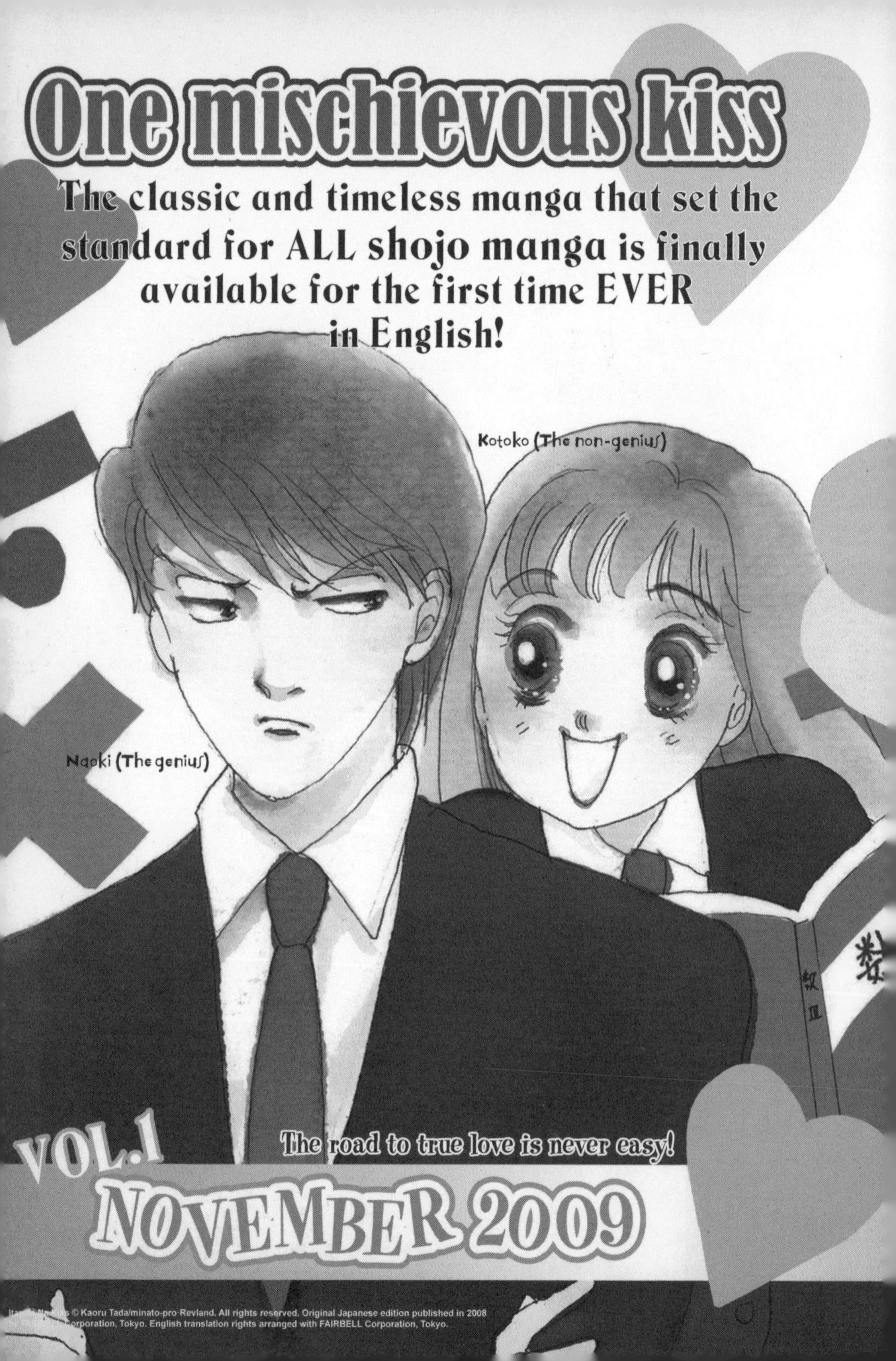

One mischievous kiss
The classic and timeless manga that set the standard for ALL shojo manga is finally available for the first time EVER in English!
Kotoko (The non-genius)
Naoki (The genius)
The road to true love is never easy!
VOL.1
NOVEMBER 2009
© Kaoru Tada/minato-pro·Revland. All rights reserved. Original Japanese edition published in 2008
orporation, Tokyo. English translation rights arranged with FAIRBELL Corporation, Tokyo.

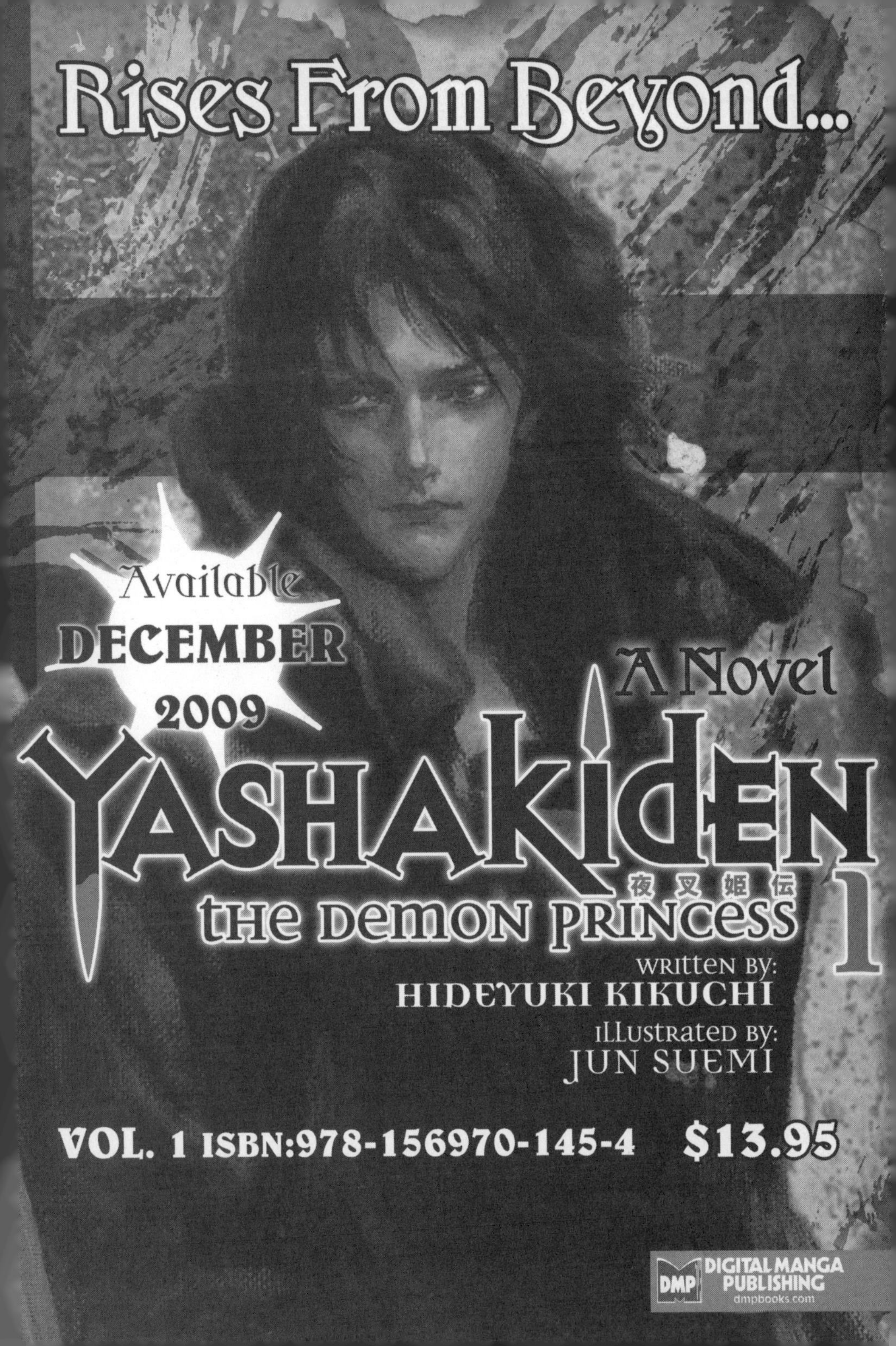
Rises From Beyond...
Available
DECEMBER
2009
A Novel
YASHAKIDEN
夜叉姫伝
THE DEMON PRINCESS
1
WRITTEN BY:
HIDEYUKI KIKUCHI
ILLUSTRATED BY:
JUN SUEMI
VOL. 1 ISBN:978-156970-145-4
$13.95
DMP
DIGITAL MANGA
PUBLISHING
dmpbooks.com

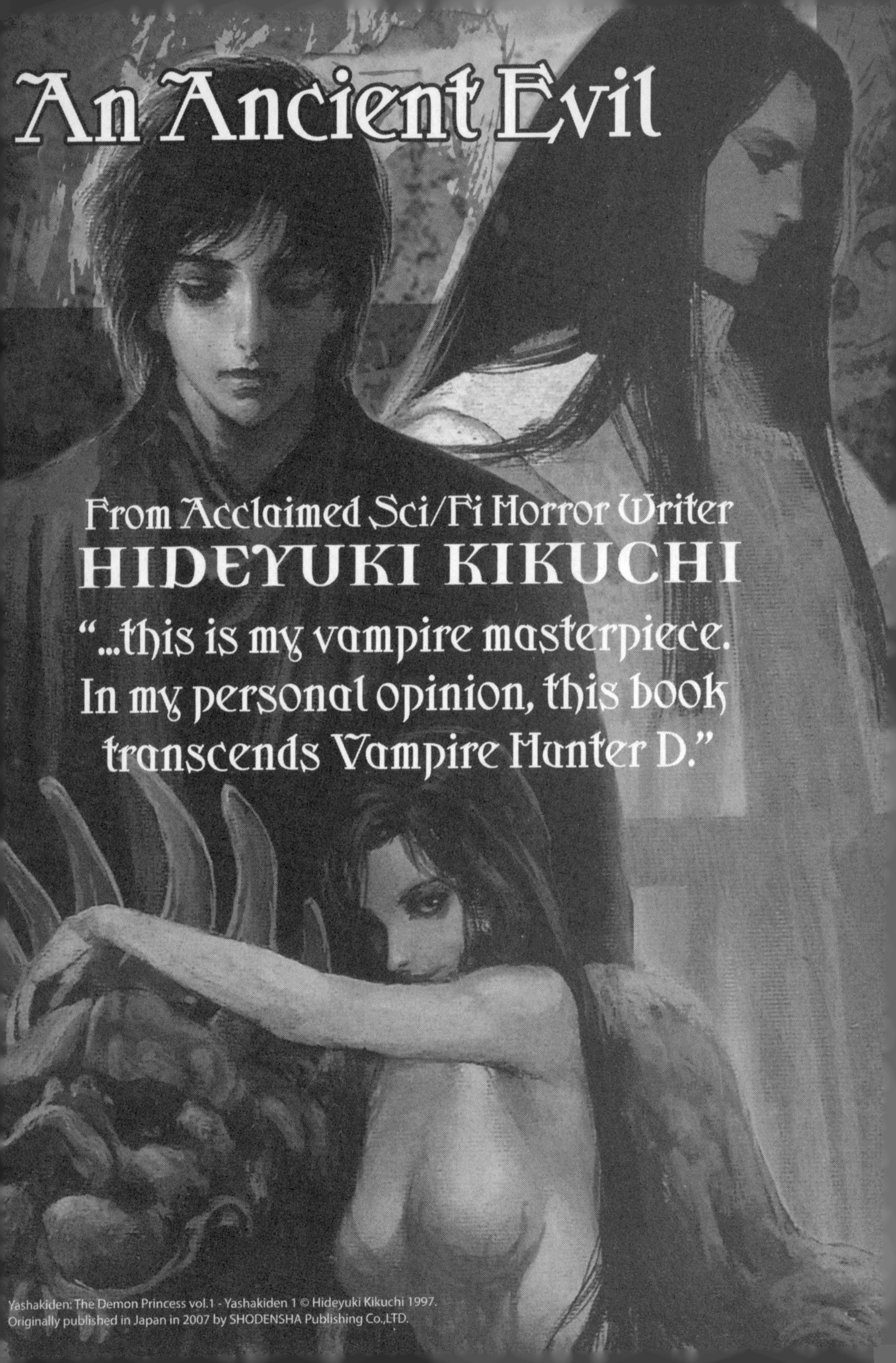
An Ancient Evil
From Acclaimed Sci/Fi Horror Writer
HIDEYUKI KIKUCHI
"...this is my vampire masterpiece. In my personal opinion, this book transcends Vampire Hunter D."

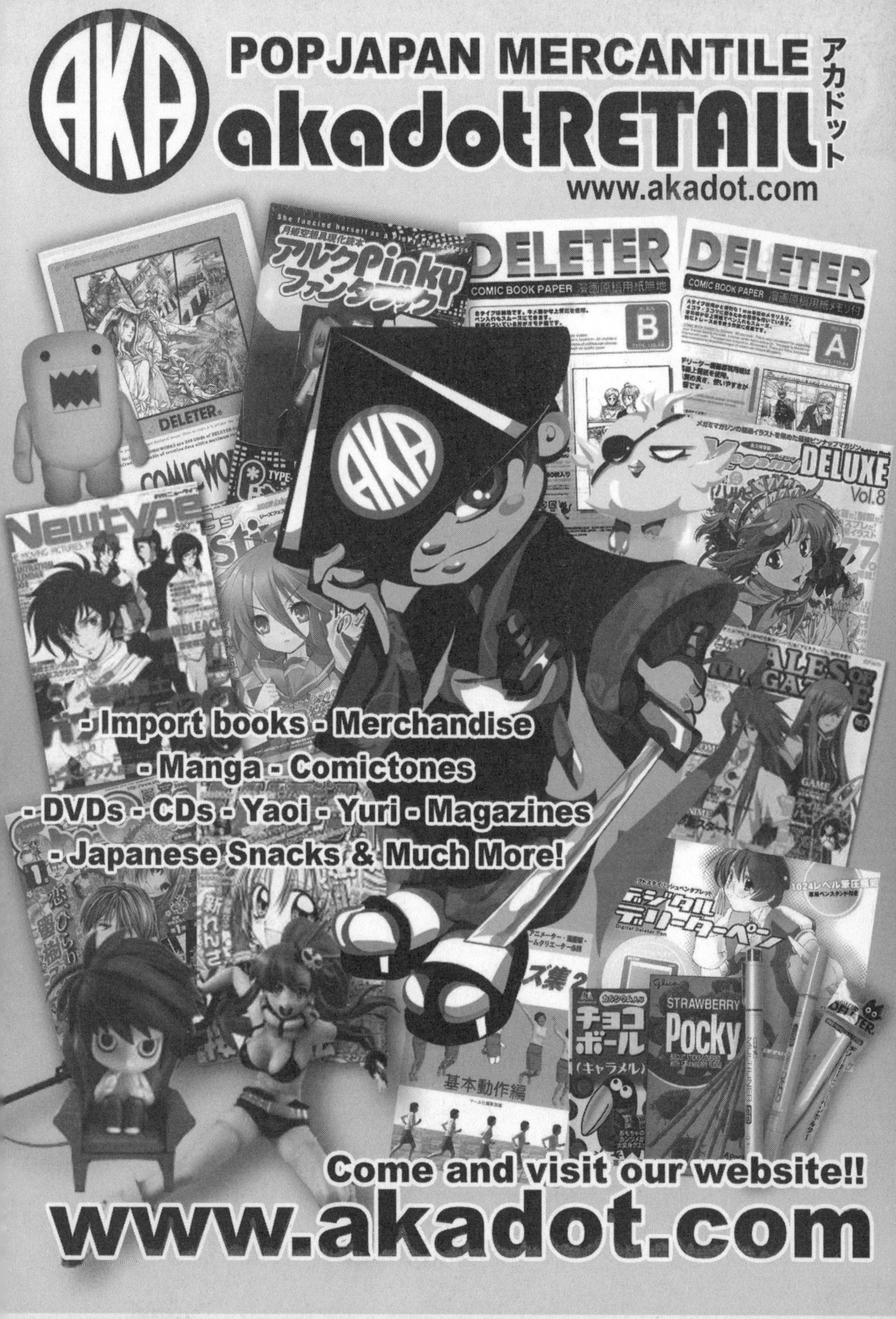
AKA
POPJAPAN MERCANTILE
akadotRETAIL
アカドット
www.akadot.com
- Import books - Merchandise
- Manga - Comictones
- DVDs - CDs - Yaoi - Yuri - Magazines
- Japanese Snacks & Much More!
Come and visit our website!!
www.akadot.com

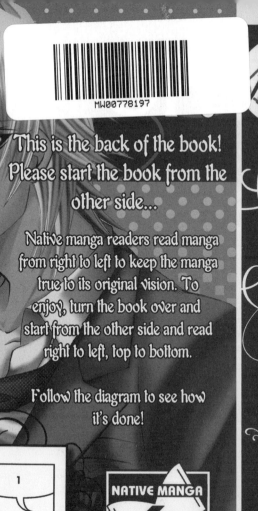

This is the back of the book! Please start the book from the other side...

Native manga readers read manga from right to left to keep the manga true to its original vision. To enjoy, turn the book over and start from the other side and read right to left, top to bottom.

Follow the diagram to see how it's done!

NATIVE MANGA
READ RIGHT TO LEFT

If you see the logo above, you'll know that this book is published in its original native format.

lune

Yaoi ヤオイ Manga